In the Shadow of
Melting Glaciers

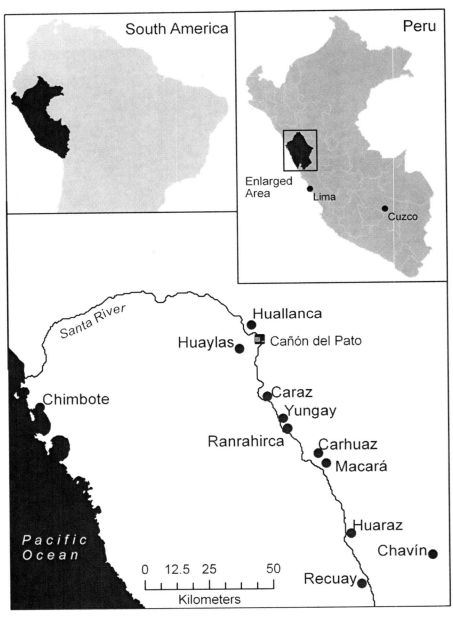

South America

Peru

Enlarged
Area
Lima
Cuzco

Santa River

Huallanca
Huaylas
Cañón del Pato
Chimbote
Caraz
Yungay
Ranrahirca
Carhuaz
Macará
Pacific
Ocean
Huaraz
Chavín
0   12.5   25   50
Kilometers
Recuay

Callejón de Huaylas and Santa River, Ancash, Peru.
Credit: Map by Carol Karsch.

In the Shadow of Melting Glaciers

Climate Change and Andean Society

MARK CAREY

OXFORD
UNIVERSITY PRESS

2010

OXFORD
UNIVERSITY PRESS

Oxford University Press, Inc., publishes works that further
Oxford University's objective of excellence
in research, scholarship, and education.

Oxford   New York
Auckland   Cape Town   Dar es Salaam   Hong Kong   Karachi
Kuala Lumpur   Madrid   Melbourne   Mexico City   Nairobi
New Delhi   Shanghai   Taipei   Toronto

With offices in
Argentina   Austria   Brazil   Chile   Czech Republic   France   Greece
Guatemala   Hungary   Italy   Japan   Poland   Portugal   Singapore
South Korea   Switzerland   Thailand   Turkey   Ukraine   Vietnam

Copyright © 2010 by Oxford University Press, Inc.

Published by Oxford University Press, Inc.
198 Madison Avenue, New York, New York 10016

www.oup.com

Oxford is a registered trademark of Oxford University Press.

Library of Congress Cataloging-in-Publication Data
Carey, Mark (Mark P.)
In the shadow of melting glaciers : climate change and Andean society /
Mark Carey.
    p.   cm.
Includes bibliographical references and index.
ISBN 978-0-19-539606-5; 978-0-19-539607-2 (pbk.)
1. Climatic changes—Peru.   2. Glaciers—Peru.   3. Climatic changes—Social
aspects—Peru.   4. Environmental engineering—Peru.   5. Emergency
management—Peru.   6. Peru—Environmental conditions.   7. Andes Region—
Environmental conditions.   8. Blanca, Cordillera (Peru)—Environmental conditions.
9. Peru—Social conditions.   10. Blanca, Cordillera (Peru)—Social conditions.
I. Title.
QC988.P4C37 2010
551.6985—dc22   2009025809

Printed in the United States of America
on acid-free paper

Acknowledgments

Though I did not realize it at the time, this book was born many years ago when my seemingly disparate interests in Latin American history and glaciers first emerged. David Castle and Daniel Goldrich at the University of Oregon inspired me to pursue a career studying and teaching Latin American history. As a park ranger at Mount Rainier National Park, I walked next to glaciers every day and became profoundly fascinated by these rivers of ice, especially after Carolyn Driedger's superb training in glaciology. These passions for Latin American history and mountain glaciers converged during graduate school, thanks primarily to Chuck Walker, Ben Orlove, and Louis Warren, who all steered me to the Andes, guided my research, and became enduring advocates whom I still rely on regularly. This book never would have come together without Chuck's expert guidance, generosity, jokes, and friendship.

Research and writing were made possible by generous funding from several institutions. The book is based in part upon work supported by the National Science Foundation under Grant No. 0822983. The Social Science Research Council Book Fellowship provided critical support to complete the manuscript, including interaction with other fellows and the skillful editing of Leslie Kriesel. Washington and Lee University provided two Glenn Grants that enabled summer research and writing. The S.V. Ciriacy-Wantrup Postdoctoral Fellowship in the Geography Department at the University of California–Berkeley also allowed time for writing, research, and revisions. The book began as a dissertation, with research and writing supported by: the Mabelle McLeod Lewis Memorial Fund; a History of Science Graduate Fellowship from the American Meteorological Society; an International Dissertation Field Research Fellowship from the Social Science Research Council, with funds provided by the Andrew W. Mellon Foundation; a University of California–Davis Agricultural History Center Dissertation Fellowship; a grant from the University of California Pacific Rim Research Program; and several fellowships from the History Department at the University of California–Davis. Any opinions, findings, and conclusions or recommendations expressed in this book are my own and do not necessarily reflect the views of any of these organizations.

Numerous people in the field and at archives and libraries were essential for research. I owe special debts of gratitude to Alcides Ames, Benjamín Morales, César Portocarrero, Nelson Santillán, and Marco Zapata, all of whom helped me with access to archives and historical data, took me to glaciers and glacial lakes, shared stories, and explained numerous aspects of the Cordillera Blanca and Callejón de Huaylas. Deynes Damaso Salinas Perez, Elizabeth del Pilar Montañez Sanabria, and Niza Tutuy helped enormously with research in Lima. Anibal Mendoza in Huaraz patiently transcribed interviews. I am grateful to Steve Wegner for his detailed knowledge of Huaraz and his generous sharing of difficult-to-find materials. I also thank Mario Aguirre, Christian Alegre Montalvo, Carlos Alva Castro, Jesús Beoutis, Alberto Giesecke, Neydo Hidalgo, Luis Horna, Elmer Montañez, Jorge Ninantay, Florencio Quito, Jorge Recharte, and Juan Sánchez. At Cornell University, David Block helped orient me to Peruvian archival sources and historiography. I thank Elizabeth Teaff at Washington and Lee for quickly fulfilling scores of interlibrary loan requests. I cannot name every one of the dozens of archivists and librarians who generously helped, but I am grateful to others not already mentioned from the Unidad de Glaciología y Recursos Hídricos, Electroperú, Museo de la Electricidad, Archivo del Departamento de Ancash, Archivo General de la Nación, Biblioteca Nacional, and the Instituto Riva Agüero.

Beyond enabling and supporting my research, many people at many other institutions have helped this book come together. Susan Ferber at Oxford University Press has been outstanding to work with, improving the book and moving its production forward quickly. At Washington and Lee University, I am especially grateful to Tyler Dickovick, Jon Eastwood, Molly Michelmore, and Jeff Rahl. At the University of California–Berkeley, my postdoc mentors Nathan Sayre and Nancy Peluso, as well as Mark Healey, Carolyn Merchant, and Michael Watts, provided a stimulating intellectual environment to advance this book and my scholarship more broadly. At the University of California–Davis, I benefited from excellent teachers and mentors, including Arnie Bauer,

Bill Hagen, Tom Holloway, Zoila Mendoza, Ben Orlove, Andrés Reséndez, Alan Taylor, Stefano Varese, Chuck Walker, and Louis Warren. Colleagues from that campus have also supported this project, especially Robert Chester, Kim Davis, Steve Fountain, Willie Hiatt, Alexandra Puerto, Fernando Purcell, Chris Rodriguez, Lia Schraeder, Robbie Weis, and Pablo Whipple. Willie has been particularly helpful, reading most of my work over the years and offering constructive criticism at every stage of the book's evolution. As a graduate student at the University of Montana, I developed a rich foundation in Latin American and environmental history, thanks to the efforts of Pamela Voekel and Dan Flores, as well as Christian McMillen. Others who have either commented directly on parts of the manuscript or contributed to its overall development include Carlos Aburto, Barbara Bode, Jeff Bury, Carlos Contreras, Julie Cruikshank, Greg Cushman, Arnaldo Mera, Anthony Oliver-Smith, José Ragas, Ricardo Ramírez, Lise Sedrez, Lizardo Seiner, Sarah Strauss, Matthias vom Hau, Doris Walter, and Ellen Wiegandt. I thank the anonymous reviewers whose insightful critiques refined and improved the book's arguments.

On technical and scientific details, Kurt Cuffey spent a semester teaching me about glaciers. Georg Kaser has been enormously generous, reading the entire manuscript and providing guidance over the years. Others in his University of Innsbruck Tropical Glaciology Group have helped me, especially Christian Georges, Irmgard Juen, and Thomas Mölg. Bryan Mark has taught me a lot about the Cordillera Blanca and carefully read part of the manuscript. A critical conversation with Guillermo Castro in Lima helped solidify my budding plan to study Peruvian glaciers. Carol Karsch graciously drew the two regional maps, and Esther Hegglin provided the local Huaraz map and photograph. Jennifer Ashworth helped with tables and many other details. Jeff Bury, Paul Illsley, and Nelson Santillán graciously gave permission to publish their photographs.

I also thank those who have supported my more personal journey through this book. It would never have been possible had my parents, Claire and Jack Carey, not instilled in me a curiosity about the world. Regina Aguirre, Fernando Ballón, and Tito Olaza opened their homes and lives to me in Peru—and the payoffs for me extend way beyond these pages. Sandi Palmer's regular visits aided my research and helped keep things going smoothly at home. Retreats with Jason Jannot and Jeff Lydon have helped me navigate the many paths of life, including the book project. My sons, Ryan and Nathan, force me to live every day in the moment, to step back from work and remember that playing soccer, digging in the sand, and eating applesauce are every bit as important as anything else. And last but most, I thank Susan for a decade of inspiration and love. Her influence is everywhere in this book, and she has made the entire process much more enriching and fulfilling.

Contents

Note on Text

To convey concepts to the broadest possible audience, this book occasionally simplifies scientific terminology. It refers, for example, to glacier "retreat" and "melting" instead of the more scientifically accurate but less popularly used "loss of glacier mass."

The text also refers to the 1962 and 1970 glacier catastrophes as "avalanches," though geologists sometimes classify them as "debris flows" or "rock-debris avalanches." For nonspecialists, "avalanche" effectively expresses the sheer violence and speed of these cataclysmic events.

All translations from the original Spanish sources are mine, unless otherwise noted.

The names of people interviewed during research have been omitted or changed to protect their privacy.

ABBREVIATIONS

AGN	Archivo General de la Nación, Lima
BNP	Biblioteca Nacional del Perú, Sala de Investigaciones
CCLCB	Comisión de Control de Lagunas de la Cordillera Blanca (Lakes Commission)
CPS	Corporación Peruana del Santa (Santa Corporation)
CRYRZA	Comisión de Reconstrucción y Rehabilitación de la Zona Afectada
FS	Electroperú "File Service" off site archive
UGRH	Unidad de Glaciología y Recursos Hídricos, Biblioteca, Huaraz

In the Shadow of
Melting Glaciers

— who has the right to manage glaciers?

Introduction

Every day brings more news about the world's melting glaciers and the far-reaching, even catastrophic consequences that vanishing ice will produce. The Greenland ice sheet is sliding away at record-breaking rates. Its disappearance would raise global sea levels by 25 feet and thus submerge many of the world's great cities. Ernest Hemingway's famous "snows of Kilimanjaro" have given way to a darker summit on Africa's most famous mountain, and, in the United States, people think Montana's famous national park should be renamed The Park Formerly Known as Glacier. Ski resorts from Switzerland to British Columbia increasingly rely on artificial snow and even cover glaciers in summer with synthetic white tarps to prevent the melting of valuable ski terrain. Meanwhile, millions of people in and around mountains worldwide face potential water shortages as glaciers disappear. South Americans worry that Lima and La Paz will lose their most critical water sources, Andean glaciers. In fact, a significant portion of the world's population depends upon water released seasonally from mountain glaciers and snow. Natural disasters, water shortages, degraded tourist destinations, and vanishing mountaineering terrain—these are among the ill effects that melting glaciers and global warming increasingly produce around the world. Although some media reports no doubt exaggerate cataclysmic scenarios to prey on people's disaster fears—what the BBC has called "climate porn"—glacier retreat has generated real catastrophes and serious concerns worldwide.[1]

Despite their seemingly remote locations, glaciers have thus advanced to the center of discussions on every continent—about not only science and global warming but also sustainable development, environmental management, watershed protection, recreation, regional and national economies, religion, cultural heritage, and the maintenance of human livelihoods. People around the globe will soon feel the effects, if they have not already, of continued glacier retreat.

Yet, surprisingly, most research on melting glaciers—and research on global warming and climate change more broadly—focuses primarily on scientific processes and the physical environment rather than people.[2] Scientists often study glaciers to predict future climate or to decipher the effects of carbon dioxide and other emissions on climate change.[3] They analyze ice cores and other proxy evidence such as tree rings to understand climate change over hundreds of thousands of years. Researchers then feed data into complex computer-driven mathematical models to project future climate. People are often unaccounted for in this research, or they are included only in broad scenarios that plot polluters against victims of the developed countries' climate-altering emissions. To be sure, science's focus on explanations of the earth's climate system, what drives it, and what it might be like in a hundred years yields vital information. However, the focus on the science of prediction has overlooked the human aspects of climate change, thereby limiting our understanding of how people actually respond to it. For more than a decade, researchers have been investigating the "human dimensions of global change" and, more recently, climate adaptation and the cultural construction of climate science and discourse.[4] But these society-based studies still only account for a tiny fraction of climate research.

After decades of research on climate change and glacier retreat, we know relatively little about how diverse peoples think about climate change: how they respond when a glacier retreats a thousand meters, what they feel when a glacier vanishes, how they grieve when melting ice triggers a catastrophic flood or landslide, what they perceive as the best or perhaps the only acceptable ways to protect their water resources, how their recreational preferences change as temperatures rise and glaciers melt. We know little about why particular sciences and technologies evolve in certain places, how local people influence that evolution over time, how governments make decisions about what to fund (or not), how power imbalances and social relations affect choices about environmental management, and why people continue to inhabit areas vulnerable to climate change and ensuing environmental hazards, even when they know the risks. In short, the science that comprises the vast majority of climate research must be augmented by studying the cultures and societies where climate change occurs.

When it comes down to the actual ways people grapple (or don't) with these environmental changes, culture often matters more than science. People respond to climate change based not only on their scientific knowledge of environmental processes but also on their worldviews and social relations, which are often influenced by power dynamics and economic outcomes.[5] Understanding their reactions to shifting climatic conditions and new natural hazards thus requires knowledge of distinct societies, governments, institutions, economies, science, technologies, and environments that all affect people's behavior. Few researchers have combined the analysis of these diverse issues in a single study, especially for regions outside North America and Western Europe. Fewer still have put local people into the historical analysis of global climate dynamics or glacier retreat.[6] But the world has been warming for nearly a century and a half, and increasingly so in the last few decades. We thus have a record of how societies have been responding to this ongoing change. Historical analysis of climate-society interactions during the last century could help illuminate how climate change affects distinct social groups in complex and far-reaching ways. This research need not offer direct lessons for the future, as if history repeats itself simplistically.[7] But history can provide crucial context for current issues while exposing the types of concerns and challenges that could arise in the future. Just as climatologists use Antarctic ice cores containing 700,000 years of historical data to understand climate today, historians' research on climate-glacier-society interactions over many decades exposes trends that might otherwise be nearly invisible to those lacking a long-term perspective or focusing solely on the physical ice and weather patterns.

The historical effects of climate and glaciers on society have been particularly powerful in the Peruvian Andes, where climate change has caused the world's most catastrophic glacier disasters over the last century.[8] These calamities affected various social groups, including local urban and rural residents, scientists, engineers, water developers, government officials, and tourists. Climate change and the ensuing glacier disasters meant different things to each of these groups. And as the government implemented projects to prevent future glacier catastrophes, some groups arrived in the Andes for the first time or in unprecedented numbers. Each distinct social group then jockeyed for power over both the physical environment and competing interests. Disaster mitigation offered a way to take control of nature and transform the Peruvian Andes into the ideal form that each group conceived. Whereas few outsiders had any interest in or control over the country's glaciated mountains in 1940, locals have since lost power and today comprise just one among many stakeholders in the high Andes—and perhaps the least powerful. Yet no one group consistently won out over the others. At distinct historical moments, each was able to achieve its version of an Andean ideal while thwarting others' agendas. There was a constant negotiation rather than an imposition of power, as studies on the history of science, nation building, and natural disasters often suggest.[9] The history of climate change and glacier control, I contend, is thus a history of power struggles—not just between humans and the physical environment, but among various social groups.

It was the group I refer to as "glacier experts" who generally mediated among these competitors, thus playing a vital role in Andean history. Rather than strictly a social history of local Andean residents living at the edge of retreating glaciers, this book puts scientists and engineers at the center of the story. These experts negotiated with government agencies, companies, community and international groups, and nongovernmental institutions. Engineering projects in response to the changing climate were consequently not just about design and the physical environment. They also involved discussions about economic development, state authority, race relations, class divisions, and cultural values.[10] Studying glacier experts exposes various historical processes and uncovers not just expert views but also those of the various social and political groups trying to influence scientific and engineering projects. Ironically, then, this environmental history of climate and Andean glaciers in one of the most unexamined parts of Peru illuminates central issues in modern power struggles, social relations, state rule, the evolution of science and technology, cultural views of nature, and the consequences of climate change on a global scale.

FIGURE I.I. The Cordillera Blanca's Mount Huascarán towering over the Santa Valley.
Credit: Photo by Paul Illsley.

The Killing Ice of the Andes

Peruvians have suffered the wrath of melting glaciers like no other society on earth. The Cordillera Blanca mountain range in north-central Peru contains more than 600 glaciers, which account for about one quarter of the world's tropical glaciers and half of Peru's glacial ice.[11] These mountains rise up more than 6,000 meters, jutting 3,000 meters above surrounding valleys to make not only a stunning landscape but also a place—as in Scandinavia, Alaska, Iceland, Canada, the Alps, and the Himalayas—where people live in close proximity to glaciers. These Cordillera Blanca glaciers, like most others worldwide, have been retreating since the 400-year Little Ice Age ended in the late nineteenth century. Over time, hundreds of thousands of Peruvians inhabiting mountain slopes and river valleys found themselves living directly beneath crumbling glaciers and the swelling glacial lakes that often formed below them, dammed precariously behind weak moraines (piles of rocks). The number of Cordillera Blanca lakes has risen dramatically from 223 in 1953, the year Peruvians conducted the first lake inventory, to more than 400 today.

As these glacial lakes grew in number and size, they became deadly hazards, just as they have been in the Alps and Himalayas.[12] In the late nineteenth and early twentieth centuries, several Cordillera Blanca lakes ruptured, causing some destruction and a few fatalities. Then, in 1941, a new glacial lake named Palcacocha burst through its natural moraine dam and triggered a flood so catastrophic that it forever transformed Peruvians' views of Andean glacial lakes. As Lake Palcacocha poured out of Cojup Canyon and blasted through downtown Huaraz, the capital city of the Ancash Department (comparable to a U.S. state), it killed an estimated 5,000 people and left a 200-kilometer path of destruction from its glacial source at an elevation above 4,000 meters to the Pacific Ocean.

The 1941 Huaraz disaster was only the first of many that devastated the Cordillera Blanca region during subsequent decades. In 1945, another outburst flood took 500 lives and destroyed the town and ancient ruins at Chavín de Huantar. In 1950, yet another outburst flood demolished the country's highly acclaimed Cañón del Pato hydroelectric station and killed 200 people. A new type of glacier catastrophe pulverized the region in 1962, when a glacier avalanche from Mount Huascarán, Peru's tallest mountain at 6,768 meters, swept through Ranrahirca and killed 4,000 people. Then, in 1970, came the most deadly glacier disaster in world history—another glacier avalanche from Mount Huascarán. Triggered by a massive earthquake, the avalanche killed 15,000 inhabitants and leveled the city of Yungay.[13] In total, nearly 25,000 Peruvians have died in Cordillera Blanca glacier disasters since 1941. During the past century, few other regions in the Western Hemisphere have undergone anything resembling this relentless series of destructive events. Glacier catastrophes, though mostly ignored by historians and policymakers, rank among the most deadly disasters in twentieth-century Peru—a country riddled by earthquakes, volcanoes, El Niño events, and landslides.[14] Though societies in Asia, Europe, North America, and South America increasingly contend with glacier hazards, none have suffered as Peruvians have. Climate change in the Andes has altered life and shaped history for a vast number of people well beyond the Cordillera Blanca.

Since the first major Peruvian glacier disaster in 1941, the local people living around Cordillera Blanca mountains experienced firsthand the cataclysmic consequences of global warming and glacier retreat. They watched floods and avalanches bury their churches, tear down their bridges, demolish their homes, and cover their parks, markets, and boulevards with gray muck 8 meters thick. They were helpless to aid terrified neighbors yelling from second-story windows in mud-surrounded houses. They saw panicked children dart from their homes only to collide with the face of a racing avalanche. They lost friends and family who were sucked beneath churning floods, leaving mourners to search futilely for bodies. They waited through tragic nights and seemingly endless days for emergency aid to arrive. They endured continual disruptions in regional commerce, transportation, and agricultural production. They called the Cordillera Blanca "sick" and "demented" because its glaciers and glacial lakes "betrayed" supposedly fixed divisions between nature and culture, highland and lowland, wild and civilized. Peruvians have paid the ultimate price for melting ice. They paid with their lives, their families, and their communities.

Living beneath melting Cordillera Blanca glaciers, survivors kept waiting, wondering, and hoping—hoping the glaciers would stay attached to the mountain peaks, hoping the engineers would drain the glacial lakes before they burst, and hoping they would not lose yet another town to the catastrophic effects of climate change. Beyond the emergencies, residents have increasingly wondered whether vanishing glaciers will reduce their water supplies for drinking, irrigation, and hydroelectricity. Elsewhere in Peru, religious pilgrims who used to collect sacred glacial ice from Mount Ausangate now leave the ice on the mountain so they do not hasten the glacier's disappearance. Even the pope recently declared Andean glacier retreat a serious humanitarian and religious issue.[15] Meanwhile, mountain guides in the Cordillera Blanca worry that disappearing glaciers will send tourists elsewhere, where snow and ice remain accessible to mountaineers and trekkers who spend tens of millions of dollars annually in the Andes. Even a misplaced threat of glacier disaster, such as in Huaraz in 2003, can devastate a regional economy tied heavily to tourism.[16] In that case, worried tourists canceled Easter holiday plans to visit Huaraz and took their money elsewhere.

But Peruvians never waited idly for a glacier disaster to sweep them away. Locals trekked to the mountains, attended town meetings, and formed community organizations to learn about glacial lakes and understand the risks of melting glaciers. They wrote letters to newspaper editors and held meetings with elected officials and scientists to demand government relief and to insist on the drainage of glacial lakes. They even sent priests to the mountains, appealing to God in their struggle against what they saw as an increasingly hostile environment. Disaster studies have increasingly pointed to the socioeconomic factors that create vulnerable populations: poverty, not nature, creates disasters, most scholars contend.[17] But blaming poverty and racism for vulnerability can overlook the role marginalized populations play in the decision-making processes affecting their livelihoods and community relations and in their vulnerability to environmental hazards. In the Peruvian Andes, populations became vulnerable to climate change and glacier disasters not only because of forces beyond their control, but also because of their own actions and responses.

Scientists, engineers, and government officials helped prevent glacier disasters. They invented new scientific approaches to gain glacier knowledge and pioneered unique engineering practices to drain glacial lakes. Since 1941, these Peruvian experts have drained and dammed 34 dangerous Cordillera Blanca glacial lakes—major engineering projects in a remote part of the Andes. Their extensive disaster prevention programs also account for the longest running research on glacier-climate dynamics in the tropics, monitoring the region's 600 glaciers and the ever-growing number of glacial lakes. In the process, dedicated Peruvian experts like Jorge Broggi, Jaime Fernández Concha, Alcides Ames, Benjamín Morales, Marco Zapata, Marino Zamora, César Portocarrero, and Nelson Santillán have overcome countless obstacles and risked their lives to prevent floods and avalanches. They endured weeks at high-elevation glacial lake labor camps, working in oxygen-deprived air and listening through cold nights as grinding glaciers made haunting sounds overhead. They rigged rubber rafts with makeshift "plows" so they could float on ice-covered glacial lakes and navigate the icebergs without puncturing their boats. They learned to scuba dive in murky waters nearly 4,000 meters above sea level. A few even bivouacked for a night at 6,400 meters as they waited out a blizzard on the edge of a gaping Mount Huascarán crevasse. For nearly seven decades, the Peruvian government has put money into glacier disaster prevention programs, though with the country's long history of coast-sierra divisions and unstable politics, the funding has fluctuated wildly.[18] Experts thus often had to rely on inadequate supplies, outdated instruments, and insufficient financial resources. Undoubtedly, though, they prevented outburst floods and saved lives.

Peruvians have learned a great deal about how to live with glaciers, to manage the melting ice, to understand glacier-climate dynamics, and to engineer the Andes in ways that protect societies. Almost all of their scientific, technical, and engineering innovations were accomplished by Peruvians themselves, with very little input from foreign experts until the last two decades, when international concerns about global warming inspired steadily growing interest in Andean glaciers and climate. Peruvians' achievements offer an excellent example of what historians of science have long referred to as "science on the periphery," or what historian Stuart McCook calls "creole science" because it is hybrid science based on Western traditions that becomes uniquely Latin American.[19] Today, scientists from numerous countries as diverse as Canada and Nepal are learning about these Peruvian innovations to help protect their own societies from melting glaciers.[20]

Melting Ice as Opportunity: Disaster Economics in the Andes

Beyond death and destruction, climate change and melting glaciers also provided opportunities by facilitating modern economic development in the Andes. The 1941 glacial lake outburst flood unleashed a series of historical processes that ultimately led to the commodification of glaciers, the consumption of Andean natural resources and landscapes, and the modernization of Peru. Just days after this flood, for example, scientists sent to determine the disaster's origin diverged from their assigned tasks to note in their technical reports where reservoirs could be constructed to stimulate hydroelectricity generation, irrigation, and other development. Glacier experts later became important advocates for the creation of Huascarán National Park, designed as much for a tourism economy as nature protection. Since the early 1990s, hydroelectricity generators and irrigators have transformed engineering projects designed to prevent glacial lake outburst floods into water-regulating reservoirs. Disaster prevention also allowed for the expansion of roads and trails, the exploitation of natural resources, new opportunities for wage laborers, and greater government control over the Andean environment.

Essentially, the quest to study glaciers and contain glacial lakes encouraged the types of modernization plans and economic development projects that Peruvians—and Latin Americans more generally—had been trying to implement for decades.[21] These transformations might all have occurred around the Cordillera Blanca anyway. The processes had been unfolding elsewhere in Peru, Latin America, and the developing world since the nineteenth century, though they are less well understood in Peru after about 1930.[22] Other factors also explain why developers descended on the Cordillera Blanca: it contains Peru's highest peak to climb, the Santa River has higher year-round water flow than any other river in western Peru, and Huaraz is among the country's—and some say the world's—largest cities in such close proximity to glaciated mountains.[23] Climate change and glacier retreat nonetheless shaped economic development in Ancash after 1941.

The physical environment never acted as a simplistic or deterministic force; rather, glaciers were one among many historical actors.[24] Consequently, the range of economic development projects that exist in the Cordillera Blanca is unmatched in any of Peru's nineteen other glaciated mountain ranges. The lack of development infrastructure in the nearby and equally beautiful Cordillera Huayhuash, for example, clearly shows the discrepancy. Easier access to the Cordillera Blanca and more information about its mountains and resources help explain the divergence, but those factors stemmed partly from the quest to contain glacier hazards. Glacier retreat has been a powerful historical force creating the types of economic, infrastructural, technoscientific, political, social, and even cultural changes that many contemporary policy makers see as the essence of modern Peru. Glacier retreat, in other words, put a price on melting ice. Climate change helped transform mountains, water, and scenery into commodities to consume. And this commodification and consumption of the Cordillera Blanca inspired many other changes. In a strange irony, inhabitants of the Santa valley watched their glaciated peaks become ever more popular and enticing to outsiders while the melting ice caused fatal disasters that obliterated some Callejón de Huaylas communities and continue to threaten others.

Disasters have frequently provided a platform for governments or entrepreneurs to implement political, economic, and social agendas. In Lima after the 1746 earthquake, the Caribbean after several 1980s hurricanes, and Honduras after Hurricane Mitch in 1998, governments and businesses capitalized on the catastrophes to implement new programs in urban planning, social control, tourism, sustainable development, and neoliberal reforms.[25] Some researchers have noted how climate change is creating similar opportunities for neoliberal policies that promote deregulation of the economy, privatization, reduction of government expenditures on social services, guaranteed property rights, and free trade.[26] The United States, Great Britain, and other Western nations, as well as the World Bank and International Monetary Fund, have vigorously advocated for the implementation of neoliberal reforms in countries worldwide since the 1980s. Award-winning author and journalist Naomi Klein links neoliberalism with disaster responses through her concept of the "shock doctrine." She argues that leaders and businesses implemented neoliberal policies when traumatized populations were in shock after catastrophes. Scholars have refined and broadened Klein's provocative notion of "disaster capitalism" to underscore three critical features: the exploitation of disasters to implement policies that empower private, capitalist interests; the promotion of neoliberal agendas in these disaster responses; and the rising influence of private entities in supposedly public responses. Disaster capitalism has played out in a wide range of recent historical events, from Pinochet's dictatorship in Chile to the U.S. war in Iraq and the aftermath of Hurricane Katrina.[27]

Disaster capitalism offers a useful framework for understanding the historical link between glacier disasters and economic development in the Andes. But the connection between disasters and economics runs deeper than Klein's "shock doctrine" and "disaster capitalism" suggest. Glacier disasters jump-started economies long before neoliberalism, and they stimulated state-led as well as private capitalist development. Moreover, the post-catastrophe economic development was not always premeditated. Rather than using Klein's notion of disaster capitalism, then, I offer a concept I will call "disaster economics," which encompasses a broader range of historical forces while maintaining the central relationship between catastrophe and economy. Disaster economics refers to the use of catastrophe to promote and empower a range of economic development interests; this development can follow both disasters and disaster prevention programs and can be private or state-owned, planned or unintentional, neoliberal or otherwise. Disaster economics played out below melting Andean glaciers as a result of both intentional plans and unintended consequences. Various social groups debated its course as persistent fear of real and potential disasters limited some economic opportunities and justified expansion of other development projects.

The Social Geography of Glacier Retreat

The Cordillera Blanca (White Mountains) is Peru's highest and most glaciated mountain range. The range runs 180 kilometers north-south and parallel to the nonglaciated Cordillera Negra (Black Mountains) to the west. The two ranges jut high above the valley between them that Peruvians know as the Callejón de Huaylas. The Santa River, which flows south to north through the bottom of this beautiful valley, has been the region's lifeline for centuries. Seventy percent of Cordillera Blanca glacier meltwater drains into the Santa, which carries more water to the Pacific Ocean than any other river in Peru.[28] At the northernmost point of the Callejón de Huaylas, the Santa River turns west, descends dramatically through the steep-walled canyon known as Cañón del Pato, and then drops several thousand meters before winding through the coastal desert and emptying into the Pacific Ocean just north of the port city of Chimbote. Cañón del Pato has one of the country's important hydroelectric stations. Initial construction began in 1943, but the 1950 Los Cedros glacial lake outburst flood destroyed the station just before completion. It finally opened in 1958 and has continued operation ever since, managed first by the national government and since the late 1990s by U.S.-based Duke Energy. Though non-navigable, the Santa River has nonetheless driven development and attracted people to the valley floor, where they built their communities, infrastructure, markets, and political offices directly in the path of most floods and avalanches. Originally founded by Spaniards during the colonial era, these Callejón de Huaylas urban areas contain a significant portion of the region's population, including the city of Huaraz, which has approximately 100,000 residents today. In total, nearly a half-million people live on slopes and in valleys surrounding the Cordillera Blanca.[29]

To analyze the effects of and responses to climate change in this part of the Andes, it is essential to understand the various social groups who shaped the region's history. Local urban and rural populations, scientists, engineers, water developers, mountaineers, and policy makers perceived and responded to glacier melting differently. Over time, glaciers became natural hazards, natural resources, scientific laboratories, vanishing cultural icons, and markers of social distinction. Disaster mitigation agendas were inextricably bound to these other issues and meanings that transcended natural hazards. Class and race relations often became the most critical factors affecting local views of disaster prevention programs, whereas debates about climate change responses frequently encompassed broader questions about the extent of state intervention in local society and the distribution of rights to access natural resources. These were issues that Peruvians and Latin Americans from Mexico to Argentina have faced more broadly through history.[30] In the Andes, each social group influenced by climate change had something different at stake, and this shaped their responses over time.

Glacier disasters after 1941 brought "glacier experts" to the Cordillera Blanca for the first time. These professional researchers, scientists, and engineers—who were trained in Western science and engineering and often paid by the national government—were distinct from local residents because they came from Lima or were affiliated with state agencies or consultants. Local inhabitants, of course, had their own glacier expertise and knowledge about the Cordillera Blanca. Glacier experts, however, brought different backgrounds and motivations. They were mostly Peruvian, though foreign experts occasionally visited the Cordillera Blanca, such as German scientist-mountaineers in the 1930s, French consultants in the late 1960s, and the international scientists investigating global warming since the 1980s. Peruvian glacier experts often found themselves hemmed in by fluctuating government budgets, political struggles, economic development agendas, and local demands for protection from melting glaciers and glacial lakes. They thus acted as intermediaries among various social groups and interests, as well as between humans and the physical environment. Their views as technoscientific experts shaped Peruvian history, as did the opinions of doctors in Brazil, cartographers in Mexico, and dam builders in Egypt.[31] This analysis of glacier experts uncovers the often overlooked role of science, technology, and technocrats in modern Latin American history.[32] It also offers insight into larger historical debates that experts mediated on such issues as national geographical divisions, state authority, economic development, coastal views of Andean residents, the use of natural resources, conservation, tourism, and environmental management.

The people most affected by Cordillera Blanca glacier disasters have been urban residents living along the Santa River and its tributaries that extend up to the glaciers.[33] Those on the eastern slope, the opposite side of the Cordillera Blanca that drains into the Marañón River, a major tributary of the Amazon, have also experienced glacier disasters, but to a lesser degree than in the Callejón de Huaylas. Vast numbers of urban residents along the Santa River inhabit hazard zones, areas in the direct path of avalanches and outburst floods. Rural communities and homes, in contrast, usually sit far above rivers and streams and thus remain relatively safe from most floods. Over time, then, urban residents have borne the brunt of the death and destruction. They have consequently had the most at stake in the evolution of disaster prevention plans since the 1940s. Surprisingly, urban residents responded to the hazards by advocating a single plan of action: draining Cordillera Blanca glacial lakes. They were not simply passive populations forced into vulnerable places by their poverty or historical marginalization, as disaster scholarship often suggests. Instead, many of these urban inhabitants affected their degree of vulnerability by rejecting plans *within* their communities to protect them. They ignored hazard zoning laws that would have removed them from potential flood paths because they saw glacial lakes as controllable threats that state-funded science and technology could contain. They were often right. But their one-dimensional plan ultimately made them dependent on that science and technology and on the state. Thus, when Duke Energy tried to expand Lake Shallap into a reservoir in 2003, thousands of Huaraz residents took to the street to protest. Even when glacier disasters destroyed their communities, urban residents rebuilt in potential flood and avalanche paths, sometimes with fatal consequences. Their rejection of zoning while demanding lake drainage allowed them to shape the

historical evolution of science, technology, urban planning, and disaster mitigation.[34] But it was at their—and future generations'—own peril.

Rural inhabitants also experienced the consequences of climate change.
Usually referred to as indigenous people, these rural residents and their communities often maintain croplands and pastures that extend far into Cordillera
Blanca canyons, right to the edge of glaciers.[35] Some inhabitants even collect
glacial ice to sell in towns, where vendors make *raspadillas*, the rough equiva-
lent of U.S. snow cones. Many of these rural residents—and often, urban
inhabitants—have long considered glaciers and glacial lakes as enchanted or
capable of acting out against people. Locals generally stayed away from alpine
peaks and lakes, and they usually lived outside hazard zones where floods and
avalanches could pass. Despite their closer proximity to the Cordillera Blanca,
this rural population actually was less affected by glacier disasters than were
the urban residents, and the rural farmers played a smaller role in the politics
of disaster prevention over time. Nevertheless, glacier disasters did destroy
some rural areas, especially through avalanches that did not always follow the
river valleys. More commonly, however, glacier retreat had indirect effects on
the rural population. Rural residents helped scientists and worked on engineering projects. They used new roads and trails constructed to drain glacial lakes
to get to town, and they increasingly encountered tourists, water developers,
national park managers, and government officials following those same routes
into their communities. Over time, these outsiders usurped or at least shared
control over the previously remote Cordillera Blanca. Because of climate change
and decades of glacier retreat, a rural shepherd is far more likely to meet an
engineer or a tourist on the shore of a glacial lake today than he would have
been in 1940, when nobody but locals ventured into Cordillera Blanca canyons.
Future global warming and glacier retreat will likely decrease water supplies
and create new problems for rural farmers who depend on the water from
Cordillera Blanca glaciers. They are already competing with an increasing
number of groups tapping the region's water supplies, as farmers' 2008 contentious takeover of Lake Parón, the region's largest reservoir, illustrated.

Water developers were another group that increasingly moved into the
Cordillera Blanca as glaciers melted. Local farmers and municipalities have
always used glacial runoff for irrigation and drinking. But water developers—that
is, hydroelectricity generators and large-scale coastal irrigators—had barely
tapped the Santa River before the 1940s. State-owned corporations ran the Cañón
del Pato hydroelectric facility from 1943 to 1996, when President Alberto Fujimori
privatized it and Duke Energy subsequently consolidated control. These energy
companies and irrigators now consume vast quantities of glacier meltwater. Over
time, they benefited from ongoing disaster prevention programs initiated in 1941

that furnished hydrological data, built infrastructure, and promoted a discourse about vanishing water towers (melting glaciers) that served water use interests. Water developers benefited from climate change because it helped construct this environmental narrative that expanded their control over a diminishing natural resource.[36] The hydroelectric station's vulnerability to glacier hazards also justified state-funded disaster mitigation projects. Sadly, electricity production was often a more compelling motivation for government disaster prevention programs than were thousands of deaths. Most disaster scholars criticize developers for "capitalizing on catastrophe" or building in unsafe areas such as floodplains or hurricane paths, but the water developers in Ancash played a more varied, sometimes contradictory, role in the disaster equation.[37]

The state was another entity whose activity in the Cordillera Blanca has increased steadily since 1941. The state is hard to pin down as a historical actor because it is always in flux, filled with diverse employees and agencies, and influenced by different people and political movements.[38] In Peru, in particular, the state during the last century has fluctuated between democratically elected governments and military rule. In its varied forms and through its numerous agencies and programs, the Peruvian state helped prevent glacier catastrophes. But leaders also exploited disaster prevention or assistance programs to implement political agendas and to pursue economic development projects, such as hydroelectricity, irrigation, tourism, and road building. Following the 1970 earthquake and avalanche, for example, President Juan Velasco made one of the most blatant attempts to co-opt disaster relief for political goals. He saw the disaster area as a clean slate on which to re-create Peru on his terms.[39] Critics of state rule and nation building point to these and other, more subtle but equally empowering ways that states accumulate control over citizens and space.[40] And while Callejón de Huaylas residents fought bitterly (and successfully) against Velasco, they have also demanded government programs to protect them. Melting glaciers influenced local views of the state as well as state control of the Cordillera Blanca. Yet it was never simply an adversarial relationship, thereby showing the nuances of state-society-environment relations in the modern Andes.[41]

Tourists' relationship with the Cordillera Blanca has also changed dramatically since the 1941 Huaraz glacial lake disaster. Although a few foreigners visited the Cordillera Blanca prior to that time, tourism remained sporadic and limited.[42] After the 1940s, however, mountain tourism expanded steadily. On the one hand, this corresponds with global trends in which the popularity of mountaineering, skiing, adventure travel, and, ecotourism increased markedly after the mid-twentieth century.[43] Wealthy North Americans and Western Europeans doing most of this recreation looked for uncharted, unclimbed, and supposedly untouched places for holidays and sports—places like the Cordillera

Blanca.[44] On the other hand, glacier research, glacial lake engineering, and experts' widespread dissemination of Cordillera Blanca information promoted tourism in the region like nowhere else in the glaciated Andes. Infrastructure constructed for disaster prevention, such as roads, trails, and labor camps, enabled access to rugged canyons and majestic mountains. Glacier experts played active roles promoting tourism. They made up a significant portion of the board of Peru's first mountaineering club. With the creation of Huascarán National Park in 1975, Cordillera Blanca glaciers officially came under the jurisdiction of the government, which promoted conservation as well as mountaineering and tourism. Today, no other glaciated mountain range in Peru—and there are 19 others, crowned by a total of 2,000 glaciers—duplicates the amount of tourist traffic in the Cordillera Blanca. Glacier retreat and the state's responses to it helped spur the historical development of that tourism and recreation.

This book analyzes Peruvian responses to climate change and ensuing glacier catastrophes from 1941 to the present. Chapter 1 examines how the 1941 Huaraz flood brought initial national attention to glacier retreat and glacial lake hazards. Disaster mitigation began right after this Huaraz tragedy, but it progressed haphazardly during the 1940s, without any centralized government institution directing scientific research or glacial lake control. Chapter 2 analyzes how 1940s outburst floods caused both social disasters and physical destruction because they obliterated culturally constructed markers of social distinction that left Huaraz's urban population vulnerable to downward class mobility. Historical divisions that many Peruvians saw between highland and lowland, countryside and city, and nature and civilization shaped the ways in which these local residents saw glacial lake hazards and solutions. After the 1950 outburst flood destroyed the nearly constructed Cañón del Pato hydroelectric facility, President Manuel Odría changed course radically from the unsystematic disaster prevention programs of the previous decade. He created the Control Commission of Cordillera Blanca Lakes (the Lakes Commission), which produced marked scientific and engineering achievements during the 1950s. Chapter 3 explains these accomplishments while demonstrating how coast-focused economic development initiatives rather than humanitarian concerns often motivated government support for the Lakes Commission. Through the subsequent two decades, the state accumulated more control over Andean space, in part with local support because residents wanted the government to prevent floods. Chapter 4 focuses explicitly on disaster economics triggered by Lakes Commission projects, uncovering ways in which glacial lake flood prevention programs provided a springboard for hydroelectricity, road building, tourism, and labor practices.

A new type of glacier disaster pummeled the Callejón de Huaylas in 1962 and 1970: glacier avalanches instead of glacial lake outburst floods. Because these avalanches were unpredictable and uncontrollable, the government tried more forcefully than it had during previous decades to implement hazard zoning. Chapter 5 focuses on local residents' successful resistance to those zoning plans. It shows how glacier and glacial lake science became contested knowledge that various social groups sought to control in pursuit of their own agendas, whether for or against hazard zoning laws. Ironically, locals opposed zoning to keep the state out of their communities. But by inhabiting hazard zones they ultimately became even more dependent on the government because they needed state programs to monitor glaciers and drain glacial lakes above their still vulnerable communities. Chapter 6 analyzes various discourses about shrinking glaciers that emerged after the 1960s, when the state hydroelectric company—first the Santa Corporation and then Electroperú—took over disaster prevention programs and began conducting its own glacier research. By the 1980s and early 1990s, the economic emphasis of these evolving environmental narratives had helped turn retreating glaciers into vanishing water towers, which enabled company control over Andean water. Yet glacier hazards persisted as global temperatures rose and ice kept melting in the 1990s and early twenty-first century. At the same time, neoliberal reforms led to the 1997 disintegration of the government's glaciology office—the first break in continuous Cordillera Blanca glacier and glacial lake monitoring since 1951. Chapter 7 analyzes the effects of this neoliberal privatization that made Duke Energy a major but highly contested stakeholder in the management of the Santa River and its tributaries in the Cordillera Blanca. It also examines continued threats from climate change, such as at Lake Palcacocha above Huaraz where everyone from local residents to the U.S. space agency NASA have been involved. Fortunately for the region's vulnerable populations, the Peruvian government reopened a new government division to manage the country's glaciers in 2001. Marco Zapata has since managed this Glaciology and Hydrological Resources Unit valiantly but with a minuscule budget and few resources. Meanwhile, glaciers continue to retreat, new hazards keep emerging, and water sources dwindle.

I

Melted Ice Destroys
a City: Huaraz, 1941

In December 1941, residents of Huaraz did not realize that a
retreating glacier tongue above the city was about to cause death and
destruction. Lake Palcacocha, also known as Lake Cojup because it
lies at the head of the Cojup Canyon, had grown considerably during
previous years, as the glacier where it formed shrank by nearly a
half kilometer. When the glacier retreated, a new lake formed in the
bathtub-like basin that had been filled with ice and surrounded by
glacial moraines, piles of rocks and sand that glaciers carry down
mountains and then deposit either alongside the glacier (lateral
moraines) or at the glacier terminus (terminal moraines). As a
glacier at the head of the Cojup Canyon advanced during cooler
periods of the Little Ice Age, it carved a trench into the valley floor
with a terminal moraine at its lowest point and lateral moraines
along the two edges of the advancing ice. When the Little Ice Age
ended, the glacier retreated from its terminal moraine, leaving
glacial Lake Palcacocha in the newly created basin between the
moraine and the glacier tongue. Similar processes occurred
throughout the Cordillera Blanca and in other mountain ranges
worldwide.[1] By 1941, Lake Palcacocha had grown to a half kilometer
long, a quarter kilometer wide, and 50 meters deep—with 14 million
cubic meters of water, or more than 3.5 billion gallons. Climate
change and glacier retreat had spawned this large lake that filled its
entire basin to the brim of its weak moraine dam.

Just before dawn on December 13, 1941, glacial ice crashed into Lake Palcacocha and generated large waves that washed over and immediately destroyed the moraine dam. Most of the lake poured out the ever-expanding hole within minutes. Water mixed with mud, rocks, and glacial ice to plow down the valley with the consistency of wet cement. It moved slowly (probably 30 to 40 kilometers per hour) compared to an avalanche, but with a force almost beyond comprehension. A few kilometers below Palcacocha, the liquefied mass poured into another lake called Jircacocha. Lake Jircacocha withstood the violent intrusion only for a moment before quickly filling, spilling over, and then rupturing its dam, unleashing the combined contents of Lakes Palcacocha and Jircacocha toward Huaraz.[2] Within minutes, thousands were dead, and a third of the city was obliterated.

In the aftermath of the Huaraz glacial lake disaster, Peruvians scrambled not only to survive and rebuild but also to determine what was happening, to rationalize and explain their losses, and to learn how to cope with the new era of threatening glacier retreat. Experts began arriving in Huaraz within days of the 1941 flood and worked through subsequent years and decades to solve the outburst flood conundrum and implement plans to avoid future glacier disasters. Local residents had to deal with an influx of state agencies that came to manage disaster relief and oversee hazard mitigation programs. These outsiders had different views of the problem, and each offered distinct solutions. What's more, no one saw the catastrophe simply in its physical form: the Huaraz tragedy and subsequent glacier disasters were as much social, economic, political, and even cultural disasters as they were "natural" disasters.

Peruvian government leaders and scientists—both groups historically centered in Lima—had previously possessed little knowledge about the Cordillera Blanca, especially regarding the effects of global climate change on its glaciers and the vulnerability of Ancash populations. Ever since Spaniards founded Lima there was a divide between the coastal European capital and the Inca capital of Cusco in the mountains. By the twentieth century, the division had, in many Peruvians' minds, become geographical, political, social, and even racial. This georacial fissure was primarily imagined and characterized by contradictory elements.[3] On the one hand, elite *Limeños* (Lima residents) historically regarded the mountains (sierra) as backwater indigenous territory. On the other hand, they always sought to control the sierra and its people, while also relying on Andean laborers to extract highland natural resources and labor for coastal profit. These tensions influenced disaster responses during the 1940s.

Melting glaciers thus unleashed a host of historical processes that were sometimes only tangentially related to glaciers, climate, science, or disasters. Disaster prevention science and engineering responded to these various forces,

FIGURE I.I. Depiction of outburst flood devastating Huaraz.
Credit: Image from *Noticias é Informaciones*, Huaraz, 10 January 1942.

rather than being purely objective. Various local residents, glacier experts, and government officials shaped the evolution of glacier science, glacial lake engineering, and disaster mitigation agendas through the 1940s and after. Social relations, economics, and regional and national politics all influenced disaster prevention programs.[4] Ultimately, responses to the 1941 Huaraz disaster transformed global climate change and Andean glacier retreat into a national problem in which the state became responsible for preventing disasters. Just as the 1941 flood made urban residents in Huaraz intimately aware of the previously unrecognized melting glaciers hanging over their city, the glacial lake disaster made Peruvians in Lima and elsewhere significantly more aware of the Andean mountains—both their peril and their possibilities.

Disaster in Huaraz

Huaraz, located 20 kilometers and 1,000 vertical meters below Lake Palcacocha, has a long history as the principal city in this region of Peru. Founded in its present location by Spaniards in the sixteenth century, the city takes its name from the pre-Hispanic indigenous people, the Waras, who had previously settled the area. Huaraz became the regional center and by 1693, its population had grown to 6,500, consisting of 4,000 Indians and 2,500 Spaniards and mestizos.[5] During the colonial era, Huaraz and other Callejón de Huaylas towns transformed from predominantly indigenous in the sixteenth century to mostly Spanish and mestizo by 1800. The urban residents generally worked as government bureaucrats, artisans, farmers, and merchants.[6] As the Ancash Department capital city, Huaraz served as a government center for the entire region. It was larger and had more concentrated political and religious power than Caraz,

Lake Palcacocha

Lake Cuchillacocha

Lake Tullpacocha

Llaca Valley

Lake Llaca

Cojup Valley

Lake Churup

Quilcayhuanca Valley

Lake Shallap

Shallap Valley

Lake Rajucolta

HUARAZ

Quilcay River

nta River

N

0   5   10 Km

MAP 1.1. Huaraz and nearby canyons with glacial lakes.

Credit: Map and photograph by Esther Hegglin. Adapted from Hegglin and Huggel, "An Integrated Assessment of Vulnerability."

Yungay, Carhuaz, and other smaller towns within the Callejón de Huaylas. Huaraz also had several of the region's oldest Catholic churches, and the bishop was stationed in the city. Festivals and other religious ceremonies brought people from surrounding regions to Huaraz regularly. Residents in 1940 defined four segments of the population: *indios* (Quechua-speaking indigenous farmers); *cholos* (urbanized, educated, or wealthier indigenous people); *mestizos* (bilingual mixed population of Spanish-indigenous descent); and *criollos* (Spanish-speaking, usually urban, upper-class residents).[7] These categories had blurred boundaries, even though contemporary residents, especially the upper and middle classes, tried hard to demarcate these racial and class groups.

In the late nineteenth and early twentieth centuries, Huaraz underwent a period of urban growth and modernization, expanding into a new district, Centenario, north of the city that quickly emerged as one of the wealthiest neighborhoods. Over subsequent decades, Centenario and Huaraz in general became more modernized and linked to the outside world through telegraph lines, telephones, radios, and roads, especially after President Leguía's controversial but expansive road-building campaigns of the 1920s. With the new development, Huaraz increasingly offered its citizens a range of services and cultural opportunities. A public library opened in 1887, and in 1935 the prefect, Colonel Pedro José Carrión, updated it and built the Municipal Library. Huaraz had a movie theater as early as 1909, a lawn tennis club, an electric plant at Patay, and the brand-new Tourist Hotel, which was poised to open in late 1941. It was part of a national network of tourist hotels that the government had been building since 1937 in cities with impressive archaeological ruins or stunning scenery, such as Arequipa, Cusco, Ayacucho, Huancayo, Tumbes, Tingo María, and Huaraz.[8] For many Huaraz residents, construction of the Tourist Hotel proved that their city was modern and worthy of showcasing to other Peruvians and foreigners. By 1941, then, Huaraz was the administrative, commercial, transportation, and Catholic religious hub for most of Ancash. And to many of its residents, the Centenario district exemplified the city's progress and modernity. Huaraz remained quite connected to the countryside, too. The city borders gave way to fields and pastures, and even after the 1940s many urban residents' homes had corrals for animals, spaces for grain storage, and plots for growing food. Additionally, farmers increasingly migrated to Huaraz or regularly brought their goods and crops to sell at the urban market. In 1940, the Huaraz province had approximately 70,000 inhabitants, of whom 23,700 were classified white or mestizo and 44,549 as Indians. The city itself had 11,054 residents.[9] The blurry boundaries between urban and rural, mestizo and indigenous, and rich and poor became ever more porous in twentieth-century Huaraz. The outburst flood would erode those social divisions even further.

By 6:45 A.M. on December 13, 1941, residents of Huaraz, at least those who had risen from their beds, were just beginning their Saturday morning routines. Many had gone to church or the market, others to work as tailors, carpenters, shoemakers, farmhands, artisans, doctors, and lawyers. Well before 7 A.M., streets like the bustling Fitzcarrald Avenue in Centenario and the beautiful eucalyptus-lined Raimondi Alameda began filling with local residents and rural farmers arriving in Huaraz to sell the milk from their cows, the chairs they had crafted, or the alfalfa they had grown. Reynaldo Coral Miranda, a young student, awoke early and went to study in peace at his parents' shop in Centenario. He was there doing homework when he heard the guttural roar of the approaching flood. Eusebio Yanac, a nearby tailor, stepped from his shop to the street and decided the distant cloud was just smoke from a fire. So he went back inside to keep working.[10] Another student, Juan Manuel Ramírez, had plans to study with friends that morning on the banks of the Quilcay River. The Quilcay, which flows through downtown Huaraz and the Centenario district, begins its course above the city, at the confluence of three rivers that come from three Cordillera Blanca canyons: Shallap, Quilcayhuanca, and Cojup. When Ramírez awoke that morning, however, he felt a strange and ominous premonition. He decided not to go with his friends after all. His premonition saved his life.[11]

Farther up the Quilcay, the flood from Palcacocha descended violently, accumulating more debris as it stormed out of the Cordillera Blanca's Cojup Canyon toward Huaraz. Rural villagers in such communities as Pitec and Unchus witnessed the passing flood but could do nothing except hope, pray, and watch. One Unchus resident, only nine years old at the time, still remembers the tremendous cloud above the flood's path. As the cloud enveloped the village, his family could barely breathe. Fortunately, the flood passed beneath their community. The stench, he recalls vividly, was like dynamite. He could smell it even before the flood arrived, and afterward it clung to the barren flood path for a week.[12] Though most of these rural communities were, like Unchus, high up the riverbank and out of harm's way, some houses close to the river succumbed to the glacial lake disaster. An indigenous woodcutter named Alberto Minaya was on a hillside overlooking his village when he saw the flood approaching. He fell to his knees and pleaded, "My God, save my family!" Moments later, his wife darted from their home with their four children, but the flood overtook them and ripped the baby out of his son's arms. Miraculously, the older three children and his wife escaped from the edge of the flood by grabbing a tree branch. More miraculously, they managed to find the baby farther downstream, alive.[13] Few others in the path of the flood would be so lucky.

When the outburst flood roared into Huaraz just before 7 A.M., it plowed through the city with relentless force. Appearing as a 15-meter-high wall of

FIGURE I.2. Flood Path along the Quilcay River through Huaraz, 1943. The Santa
River flows right to left at bottom.
Credit: Photo by Peruvian Servicio Aerofotográfico Nacional.

debris (some say as high as 30 meters), the flood consisted of water, mud, ice,
trees, houses, livestock, and human bodies. Before the flood wall was visible,
people yelled out thinking it was an earthquake, a volcano, or even a Japanese
air attack, since Pearl Harbor had been bombed just six days before.[14] Panicked
people ran in every direction, not knowing how to save themselves. Some ran
back inside their homes, thinking that was safest. Others sprinted uphill. Many

cried for missing family members—a son, a wife, a husband, a grandmother. Some looked to the city's most modern structure, the Tourist Hotel in Centenario, to save them. Residents flocked to the building, but the floodwaters continued relentlessly. The refugees kept climbing to rise above the water—to the second floor, to the third, then onto the roof, where they screamed for help. But the great new hotel could not withstand the force. The roof floated momentarily like a raft before the floodwater sucked its terrorized passengers under the muck. Not even a trace of the city's newest, most modern representation of national status and prestige remained in Centenario.[15] The flood spread half a kilometer across the city, washing away nearly everything in its path. Fitzcarrald Avenue, the Raimondi Alameda, the National Women's School, the bullfighting ring, the lawn tennis club, the Colegio Nacional de La Libertad, and several "chalets" where doctors and business families lived in downtown Huaraz all vanished. The flood even damaged the Huaraz jail, ripping a hole in the prison wall through which the inmates quickly escaped—at least those who lived. When thirteen of them returned to the prison later that day, authorities promptly released them for their valiant conscience. Others, not surprisingly, just vanished.[16]

An estimated 5,000 people perished in Huaraz that morning, and one-third of the city was obliterated. Most of the destruction occurred in Centenario, what many Huaraz survivors and government officials in Lima called the part of the city where "the best" of the population lived.[17]

The outburst flood, however, did not end there. It gushed down the Santa River, ripping out bridges, sections of highway, eucalyptus groves, and homes. On that same morning, geologists Alberto Giesecke from Lima and Luke Lowther from Canada were in the Santa River's narrow Cañón del Pato, about 100 kilometers downstream from Huaraz. The two had been conducting geological studies for Swedish investor and industrialist Axel Wenner-Gren. Peruvian officials and developers invited Wenner-Gren to visit Chimbote and Huallanca to consider financing what later became the mission of the Peruvian Santa Corporation: to construct a hydroelectric facility at Cañón del Pato that would provide energy for industrial steel plants in Chimbote. Wenner-Gren agreed to invest 100 million soles in the project, and by November 1941 he had contracted Giesecke and Lowther to investigate a possible construction site. But in the wake of the Pearl Harbor attack and the U.S. declaration of war against the Axis powers, the U.S. government put Wenner-Gren on a blacklist and froze his assets in banks outside Sweden because of his investments in Germany and his alleged financial support for the Nazis.

On the morning of December 13, 1941, Giesecke had just learned he was out of a job. He and Lowther decided to spend one last day at Cañón del Pato before returning to Lima. At about 9 A.M., they heard a noise like "stampeding elephants" and saw an immense cloud billowing above the Santa River upstream from them. They quickly realized it was an outburst flood. But they were wedged in the canyon between near-vertical rock cliff walls that rise hundreds of meters. As Giesecke recalls: "We achieved the impossible—to climb the wall of the right bank to about 20 meters above the water level where we reached a ledge from where we watched the debris filled with trees and wood, construction materials, dead animals, cadavers, equipment and goods pass by."[18] The flood continued on to destroy the Chimbote-Huallanca railway line, tunnels, bridges, and other infrastructure along the Santa River.[19] One of the world's most deadly and devastating glacial lake outburst floods in history finally ended its 220-kilometer journey when it emptied into the Pacific Ocean. No other outburst flood in Peruvian history—and perhaps no other glacial lake outburst flood anywhere—killed as many people as the 1941 Huaraz disaster.

The "Sick" City and a National Catastrophe

Survivors in Huaraz struggled with grief and anxiety following the catastrophe. Under the headline "Huaraz Is Sick," a front-page story in the local newspaper reported a month after the disaster that "people meet each other but there is nothing else to talk about except the tragedy."[20] Despair and uncertainty hung over the city, infecting everyone. Five hundred bodies taken to the hospital had overflowed it. But most bodies were never recovered. The day after the flood, ten trucks filled with food and basic supplies arrived from Lima; then five more arrived with medicine, equipment, nurses, and doctors. But distribution was difficult because of destroyed bridges and the wide swath of the vacant disaster plain. The prefect, bishop, mayor, and many others tried to organize and calm the population. Many survivors fled toward Recuay farther up the Santa River, hoping the higher ground would provide safety in the event of another flood. Chaos and sadness, death and destruction overtook Huaraz.

News of the catastrophe spread quickly through Peru and to the outside world. Despite preoccupation with World War II, people sent support and sympathy for the victims. "Every community in the country has received news of the Huaraz catastrophe with profound sorrow," wrote Lima's El Comercio on December 16, 1941. On Christmas Eve, El Eco in Iquitos sent condolences to the people of Huaraz living amid "debris and ruins" and thanked the U.S. Red Cross for its help in the aftermath. Peru's Radio Nacional announced five days after the disaster that, with the destruction of Huaraz and the beautiful Centenario neighborhood, the entire country suffered and the whole hemisphere joined together in solidarity. The live radio program praised President Manuel Prado for visiting Huaraz "with dynamism and strong character" the day after the disaster. His presence in the region, the radio announcement concluded, "has initiated new optimism" to overcome the pain and suffering among Huaraz survivors. In the days and weeks after the outburst flood, Huaraz received an array of condolences, donations, and aid to help overcome the hardship and begin rebuilding.[21]

President Prado's visit not only represented a new level of compassion for highland communities by a Peruvian president but also inspired hope and good feelings amid the wave of despondency that blanketed Huaraz. Within hours of the flood, Prado cancelled other engagements and began planning for the trip. He left at dawn the day after the disaster, heading north from Lima with his daughter, Rosa, who was a nurse; the minister of development, Carlos Moreyra y Paz Soldán; and several other high-level government and military officials. Their caravan had traveled only a short distance when an earthquake caused a major landslide near Chancay, covering the highway and making travel impossible on this sole route to Huaraz. Determined to get there, Prado summoned two airplanes from the Las Palmas Air Force Base in Lima to transport his team over the landslide. As he awaited the planes at the Ancón air base, the president even considered flying his delegation in some small training airplanes instead. Finally, though, the Condor and Grumann planes arrived from Lima and flew Prado's delegation to Paramonga near Pativilca, on the Lima-Ancash border. The minister of development and his top roads superintendent stayed behind to repair the damaged highway for Prado's return. New obstacles greeted the president in Paramonga. When his delegation landed, they needed to borrow cars—and find gasoline—to take them to Huaraz. Prado's caravan finally arrived in the devastated zone after dark, where they met crowds of traumatized people, overwhelmed officials, the overflowing hospital, and overworked priests, including Huaraz Bishop Monsignor Valdivia.

A newspaper article later told the story of Prado's visit to Huaraz, reporting almost exclusively on how "it seemed as if the elements had conspired against President Prado to delay his trip."[22] In fact, numerous Lima publications—from newspapers to official government documents—focused on the obstacles he overcame just to get to Huaraz, as if his mere arrival was all that mattered. These narratives, while accurate about the lack of efficient transportation, demonstrate the literal and figurative gulf many Peruvians saw between the coast and the highlands. Leaving Lima for Huaraz meant overcoming nature—an earthquake, a landslide, the elevation, the bad weather—to visit a place destroyed by nature, by the raw power of Andean glaciers, lakes, and rivers. So much emphasis on how Prado got to Huaraz, rather than on what he actually did there, shows that his presidential visit was a gesture out of the ordinary. It also demonstrates how melting glaciers, the glacial lake outburst flood, and the catastrophe in Huaraz helped connect Lima with highland Peru in new ways—symbolically, politically, and discursively.

President Prado stood with his daughter on a boulder in the barren zone of flooded Huaraz and proclaimed not only his support for the grieving families but also his financial commitment to rebuilding the city. Back in Lima, on December 31, 1941, he passed a bill that allocated 5 million soles to support survivors and rebuild. Prado's pledge to reconstruct Huaraz and resolve the glacial lake problem came during a period of increasing state devotion to public works projects in highland Peru. This change had begun under President Leguía in the 1920s. Leguía's massive increase in the number of state bureaucrats, his support for road building and public works projects, and his quest to expand infrastructure, irrigation, and industry nationally set a precedent for using state expenditures for previously ignored projects.[23] President Prado established another trend: state support for disaster victims. He had provided aid for Peruvians after the May 24, 1940, earthquake that affected Lima and many other cities. His support for people in crisis made the people believe it was the state's obligation to help citizens in the aftermath of disaster.[24] Not surprisingly, Huaraz residents called on the president to help. At church services, funerals, social gatherings, town meetings, and even in the national congress during December 1941, residents of Ancash demanded aid for their fellow citizens and their beloved city, and they were joined by numerous groups, dignitaries, and officials throughout Peru. Prado listened, but in the end much of the 5 million soles never arrived in Huaraz, going instead toward the coast and reconstruction of the Chimbote-Huallanca railway. Another important part of Prado's disaster aid focused on preventing additional glacial lake catastrophes in Huaraz. But first, scientists and engineers needed to determine what had caused the disaster in the first place.

Peruvian Science in the High Andes

While Huaraz residents struggled to make sense of the catastrophe, scientists and engineers poured into the Cordillera Blanca to analyze both glacial lake outburst floods and future lake threats. Most scientists in Peru and elsewhere had just begun to understand twentieth-century global climate change and its effects on glaciers. Guy Stewart Callendar had proposed his theory about the effects of carbon dioxide on climate in 1938, but few accepted it until decades later.[25] In 1939, François Matthes coined the term "Little Ice Age" to define a cooler period when glaciers advanced, up to about 1850, at which point glacial recession began

worldwide.[26] In the 1930s, scholars were only just discovering that retreating glaciers could produce outburst floods; previously, they had attributed such floods
primarily to advancing glaciers, since they had occurred countless times and with
deadly consequences in Europe during the Little Ice Age.[27] Some floods from
melting glaciers had occurred in Peru's Cordillera Blanca in the 1930s, but with
the exception of an Austrian scientist, Hans Kinzl, no one studied them systematically or predicted future glacial lake catastrophes until after the 1941 Huaraz disaster.[28] Overall, prior to the 1940s, most of the world's scientists investigating
climate-glacier dynamics studied Ice Ages, focusing on explanations for the
advance and retreat of continental ice sheets thousands of years earlier. Many
scientists before 1950 even regarded climatological theories about the contemporary era with disdain.[29] That began to change after the disaster in Huaraz.

Alberto Giesecke and Luke Lowther were among the first experts to examine
Lake Palcacocha in December 1941. After barely surviving the flood, the two scientists climbed down from their narrow Cañón del Pato ledge and followed the
path of devastation back upstream along the Santa River. Surveying the flood
damage over the 110-kilometer walk to Huaraz, they finally arrived in the devastated city. The Ancash prefect, Lorenzo Sousa Iglesias, greeted the professional
geologists enthusiastically and immediately sent them to investigate the source of
the flood. On their four-day expedition to Cojup Canyon and Lake Palcacocha—as
well as Lakes Tullparaju and Cuchillacocha in the nearby Quilcayhuanca Canyon—
they weathered a vicious snowstorm and survived landslides that crashed down
from steep canyon walls. Giesecke and Lowther returned to Huaraz and reported
directly to the prefect. He organized a town meeting so anxious residents could
hear firsthand about the status of these glacial lakes. Speaking into a loudspeaker,
Giesecke told residents that the lakes did not pose imminent danger. Lake
Tullparaju, however, was sufficiently large (one kilometer by a half kilometer) and
had a sufficiently high volume of water that, if the right conditions arose, it could
someday produce a catastrophic flood. The geologists also explained that Lake
Cuchillacocha could become dangerous in the future. Giesecke and Lowther made
three recommendations: first, that Huaraz residents educate themselves and stay
informed about glacial lake threats; second, that authorities establish a "permanent surveillance system" at the glacial lakes that was "reliable and well-organized";
and, third, that the government take aerial photographs of Cordillera Blanca glacial lakes above every Callejón de Huaylas town to evaluate the potential for other
outburst floods.[30] Huaraz residents did try to stay informed during subsequent
years, especially in the aftermath of each new disaster or false alarm. But it was not
until 1948 that the National Aerial Photography Service (SAN) began taking photographs of Cordillera Blanca glacial lakes, and not until the 1950s did the surveillance system emerge—and then only temporarily.

In the meantime, other scientists and government officials began conducting additional studies. The Huaraz City Council contracted a private engineering firm in mid-1942. When Moisés Rajavinschi finished that study, he submitted the results to Huaraz Mayor Ernesto Salazar, who then sent the report on to both the Ancash prefect and President Prado.[31] Local, regional, and national levels of government had all become involved with the new glacier threats. Rajavinschi recommended draining some of the remaining water in Lake Palcacocha and partly draining the recently formed and expanding Lake Tullparaju in the Quilcayhuanca Canyon. By mid-1942, workers were digging trenches from these lakes to remove water and minimize future flood potential.[32]

Prefect Sousa Iglesias also ordered a glacial lake study from the preeminent geologist Jorge Broggi. One of the founding members of the Geological Society of Peru in 1924, Broggi was a leading expert on Andean glaciers and a logical choice to research the stability of Cordillera Blanca glacial lakes. But his investigations did not go smoothly, and in July 1942 Sousa Iglesias complained in a letter to President Prado that Broggi had proved disappointing: a day after arriving in Huaraz, he was planning to go back to Lima because of "the lack of roads and other indispensable resources" that his research team needed. Sousa Iglesias argued that Broggi was abandoning his responsibilities while panicked Huaraz residents waited to learn more about the status of their glacial lakes.[33] Broggi did submit what he called a "preliminary report" on the lakes and outburst flood threats. But he also complained about these "frigid and inhospitable parts," the absence even of hiking trails, the need to transport equipment by horseback, and the lack of housing, especially heated facilities, at the glacial lakes.[34] "This was not supposed to be a mountaineering expedition," Broggi quipped in a letter to the national government's director of the Water and Irrigation Division, Luís Chavez Badani, to explain why he had only partly completed his study.[35]

In the end, Broggi recommended the formation of a systematic, organized, and well-funded team of researchers in applied geology to conduct more studies and take the necessary precautions to protect communities beneath the Cordillera Blanca's melting glaciers. He suggested that this team from Lima go to Huaraz and train for one month to achieve adequate physical condition for work at high-elevation Cordillera Blanca glacial lakes. To be sure, doing field research above 4,000 meters is not easy, especially for someone just arrived from his home at sea level. Yet Broggi's complaints also demonstrate the figurative gulf between Lima and the Cordillera Blanca. Knowledge was difficult to acquire in the remote, high-elevation, uninhabited Cordillera Blanca canyons. But what did Broggi expect? He knew from his own extensive research that Peruvian glaciers did not exist below 4,000 meters. His disdain for Huaraz and the alpine environment thus comes as a surprise to those familiar with his respected research, especially because by 1943, well ahead of most of the world's scientists, he was making claims about how contemporary climate change created glacier hazards.[36]

Other engineers and scientists managed to carry out several studies at Cordillera Blanca glacial lakes in 1942 and subsequent years. In general, their research focused on three areas: explanations of outburst floods, especially the one that destroyed Huaraz; the degree of danger that glacial lakes posed; and the process and extent of glacier retreat, especially as it related to glacial lake formation. Experts studying the Cordillera Blanca became some of the first in the world to understand the interconnected dynamics of climate change, glacier retreat, glacial lake formation, and outburst floods. Most of the studies focused on the lakes above Huaraz, but later analyses of other floods allowed comparisons that demonstrated how rock and ice that falls into glacial lakes caused weak moraine dams to rupture.[37] More glacial lake moraine dam failures would occur before experts understood the precise mechanics. But in the 1940s, these scientists and engineers offered a perspective on glacial lake outburst floods that most today still consider accurate and relevant as glacial lake threats continually emerge on various continents. Peruvian experts played a key role in the initial development of the science to understand what is today a growing problem in glaciated mountain ranges worldwide.

The combined analysis of these three research areas allowed scientists to recognize that the Huaraz flood was part of a pattern rather than an isolated event. In the late 1930s, Kinzl realized that a relatively small 1938 Cordillera Blanca outburst flood was just one in a series of inundations in the region.[38] The earliest record of glacier-related disasters in the Callejón de Huaylas dates to January 6, 1725, when an often-mentioned but rarely documented glacier-related disaster supposedly obliterated the Callejón de Huaylas town of Ancash. Glacial lake outburst floods became more common after the late nineteenth century. An 1869 outburst flood had killed eleven people in the Callejón de Huaylas town of Monterrey. Then, in 1883, Lake Rajucolta (Tambillo) burst its moraine dam and inundated the valley below, destroying schools, houses, cemeteries, and families in the village of Macashca. Between March 1932 and April 1941, three lakes in the Cordillera Blanca (Solteracocha, Artesa, and Magistral) and one in the nearby Cordillera Huayhuash (Suerococha) burst their dams and caused damaging outburst floods that destroyed bridges, roads, trails, agriculture, irrigation canals, and livestock.[39] But these received little attention beyond the specific locales.

After the Huaraz disaster, however, scientists began to recognize that these floods followed a protracted period of climate change and ensuing glacier retreat. Building both on the numerous Peruvian studies after the 1941 Huaraz flood and on Kinzl's 1930s Cordillera Blanca studies, Jorge Broggi drew innovative conclusions about the effects of climate change on glacier retreat, lake

FIGURE I.3. Lake Solteracocha with glacier plunging into water, 1936.
Credit: Photo courtesy of Hans Kinzl Archive, Institute of Geography, University of
Innsbruck, Austria.

formation, and outburst floods in the period after 1850.[40] Though Broggi never used the phrase "Little Ice Age," he described how glaciers had expanded then. Little Ice Age glacier advances in the Andes remain little studied even today, but elsewhere in the world they affected societies in diverse ways—for example, by triggering catastrophic outburst floods in Switzerland, destroying homes and crops in France, and affecting indigenous migration patterns in Alaska and Canada's Northwest Territories.[41] Perhaps the 1725 Ancash disaster was an Andean counterpart to the climate-caused Little Ice Age glacier disasters in Europe. What was clear to Broggi about the Cordillera Blanca and the Andes more generally was that glacier retreat had begun in the late 1800s and generally continued through the twentieth century, with a brief period of glacier growth in the 1920s.[42] This generalized glacier retreat has been and continues as a worldwide phenomenon, though with exceptions because of local climate anomalies and differences in glacier dynamics that sometimes create unique circumstances.[43] Broggi, Kinzl, and others thus concluded by the early 1940s that Cordillera Blanca glacier retreat created the conditions for glacial lake formation: lakes formed behind terminal moraines and kept expanding as glaciers kept retreating. Rockfalls or snow and ice avalanches into these lakes could trigger outburst floods, just as they had above Huaraz in 1941. The experts nonetheless knew little about where these glacial lakes existed in the Cordillera Blanca, how many there were, which ones were most likely to produce deadly outburst floods, or when these outburst floods would occur.

The gathering of this 1940s geological, glaciological, and hydrological data—and its publication in Peruvian journals and newspapers—gave both Limeños and foreigners far more knowledge about the Andes than they had before the disaster. Engineers, scientists, government officials, and the public learned about Cordillera Blanca glaciers and glacial lake hazards as well as about the regional population and water resources for coastal development projects. Scholars have shown elsewhere how the collection of environmental data can help states rule more effectively over remote regions and peoples. Surveyors in Mexico and engineers in Egypt, for example, helped postcolonial states acquire more power, while engineers' river exploration in the United States served hydroelectric development.[44] These experts' observations, descriptive language, and quantification of rivers ushered in a new cultural relationship with physical environments. When engineers quantified water flows, meaningful local knowledge gave way to statistics that best served hydroelectricity interests. Advances in glacier science and glacial lake hazard investigations during the 1940s, then, should be contextualized within these larger historical trends that included the commodification and standardization of water resources as well as disaster prevention programs.

The Social Construction of Glacier Science

To pinpoint precise glacial lake threats and learn about specific glacier and glacial lake conditions during the 1940s, experts often relied on or were influenced by local residents. In one case immediately following the Huaraz disaster, "a commission of Indians" reported a potentially dangerous lake above the town of Carhuaz and demanded studies to investigate it.[45] Residents and authorities in Caraz were even more outspoken in their requests for research at Lake Parón, the largest Cordillera Blanca lake. In early January 1942, an "extraordinary" number of people gathered for a public meeting in which they discussed the threat of an outburst flood as well as measures they could take to prevent catastrophe. Following the town meeting, the subprefect sent a telegram to Lima conveying the "persistent fear and anxiety in this city." In light of what he reported as an "imminent threat" of an outburst flood from Lake Parón, the subprefect demanded that the government send a professional geologist to examine the lake.[46] Authorities in Caraz continued their requests for lake research throughout 1942 until Subprefect Francisco Malaspina finally persuaded Lima officials to act. Antonio Grüter, an engineer from Lima, arrived in Caraz in early November and promptly set out on the difficult journey to Lake Parón. He was accompanied by the subprefect himself, many Caraz residents, and three dozen men to carry equipment. The geologist assigned to Grüter's team never showed up, however. Lamenting the absence of this critical geological study, Grüter nonetheless reported that Parón's natural dam seemed stable. But he suggested that an outburst flood could occur if a large avalanche or rockfall crashed into the lake. He thus called for additional studies, including geological analysis, and a minimum of three or four annual inspections to monitor its stability.[47] For the moment, Parón remained stable, though in 1951 its natural dam would be tested dramatically. In the meantime, scientists and engineers continued studying Parón. It was usually wealthy Caraz residents and authorities who demanded the research, thereby influencing where and when science was conducted.[48] Throughout the 1940s, Peruvian experts studied the lakes above Huaraz, Caraz, Chavín, and Cañón del Pato.

Political pressure often influenced where Cordillera Blanca disaster prevention studies occurred. Most lake studies and all but one lake drainage project during the 1940s occurred above Huaraz. The other lake engineering project took place at Lake Jankarurish, which was above a sparsely inhabited but potentially lucrative area for hydroelectricity, Cañón del Pato. In Huaraz, a second outburst flood would have likely caused little death and destruction because the 1941 disaster had already obliterated a large swath of the city near the Quilcay and Santa Rivers. But Huaraz was the wealthiest, most powerful city in Ancash. Demands from its population often went directly to the prefect, the highest government authority in the department. Caraz also received preferential treatment from the national government, in part because of Lake Parón's immense size but also because the repeated requests for studies came from the subprefect and wealthy residents. Carhuaz, on the other hand, did not receive such quick responses from Lima. In early 1942, local indigenous residents demanded that the government investigate Lake Quechka.[49] When bad weather hindered engineers' access to the lake, the government abandoned the study and did not, to my knowledge, visit the lake for several years. Chavín also received only scant attention, even after the catastrophic flood in 1945. State officials sent almost no scientific delegations to assess the possibility of more glacial lake outburst floods above Chavín. In fact, the Chavín flood triggered new research and projects primarily in Huaraz, where a nervous population put increasing pressure on the national government. A hierarchy existed during the 1940s by which power and politics affected where scientists and engineers studied glacial lakes.

Local residents also shaped disaster mitigation science and engineering by providing data about geomorphology, glacier behavior, lake histories, and outburst floods. In 1945, Eulogio Rímac and Eudasio Cruz from the rural communities of Hato and Chichucancha helped scientists understand what had caused an outburst flood at Chavín de Huantar. The two farmers had been tending their cattle at the base of Mount Huantsán when they saw a large "avalanche of snow and rocks" fall into Lake Ayhuinyaraju. That lake quickly overflowed its moraine dam, then poured into Lake Carhuacocha, which also eroded its dam and morphed into the infamous Chavín flood. This eyewitness account helped scientists confirm their hypotheses that rock and ice avalanches provided the immediate catalysts for glacial lake outburst floods.[50] In a 1948 study at the far north end of the Cordillera Blanca, Luis Ghiglino also relied on some rural farmers for lake data. Ghiglino did not have time to visit all the glacial lakes he hoped to analyze, so he interviewed farmers and shepherds about Lake Yurac-Kocha. Reporting that the lake was roughly a kilometer long, they also told him that it had a moraine dam, that its water drained through subterranean seepage through the moraine (a dangerous condition because it weakens dams—and levees), and that the glacier tongue was in direct contact with the lake water. Farther north on the same research trip, Ghiglino asked residents of the Alpamayo hamlet deep in the Cordillera Blanca for information about Lake Jankarurish, at the head of the Los Cedros Canyon. At the time, Jankarurish was a half-kilometer long and 400 meters wide. But locals reported that it had been only a puddle 20 years earlier, indicating to Ghiglino just how rapidly a glacial lake could form and grow to dangerous dimensions. Inspired in part by this evidence, Ghiglino persuaded the Peruvian government to begin draining the rapidly expanding and potentially unstable Lake Jankarurish, a project that ultimately proved to be too little too late.[51]

Ghiglino was more direct than most in divulging the ways local knowledge informed his research. But he was also studying the region during a time period—the 1940s and early 1950s—when experts from Lima arrived in the Cordillera Blanca with little understanding of its topography, its environmental history, or its glacier and glacial lake hazards and had to rely on local information and guidance. Over time, scientists' dependence on locals would wane as they became more familiar with the Cordillera Blanca terrain, turned to aerial surveillance, and sent more engineers to gather data. But in the 1940s, local residents partially influenced glacial lake studies and projects, though the details of their personal interactions with glacier experts remain difficult to find in the historical record. On the one hand, shepherds' information about glacial lake conditions did not radically alter the specific development of glacier science or glacial lake engineering. They enabled some studies, but the experts likely could have found the hazardous lakes anyway with more time. On the other hand, politics influenced the course of 1940s disaster prevention because the most powerful urban centers received the most attention. Decisions in Lima about where to send glacier experts and how much money to allocate—or whether to supply personnel and funds at all—stemmed in part from which groups made the most convincing claims to policymakers. The wealthiest, most educated, most politically connected groups had the best opportunities to influence high-level authorities.

Just as residents shaped scientific knowledge, experts brought outside influences that shaped their science and initiated the disaster economics that unfolded through subsequent decades. Jorge Broggi saw the Cordillera Blanca through the lens of economic development and natural resource use. In his technical reports and correspondence about glacial lakes above Huaraz—ostensibly about environmental hazards and people's safety—Broggi devoted considerable attention to potential water use. For him, the Cordillera Blanca represented both an unstable mountain range of hazardous glacial lakes and a great economic opportunity. He cringed at the thought of draining dangerous lakes because he believed the national government should exploit the region's abundant hydrological resources, what he considered the greatest source of water on the entire western slope of the Andes. He thought engineers could simultaneously control glacial lakes to prevent outburst floods and convert the lakes into reservoirs to regulate Santa River water flow. Then developers would be able both to construct a hydroelectric facility at Cañón del Pato and to irrigate the coast. With much foresight, Broggi worried that ongoing glacier retreat would eventually reduce water flow in the Santa River. His proposed reservoirs for what he saw as an underutilized river would thus serve both short- and long-term interests in electricity and irrigation.[52] Other Peruvian glacier experts echoed Broggi's pro-water-use agenda in their analysis of lake hazards. Luis Ghiglino suggested that "Nature has offered us one of the greatest natural reservoirs, which we must conserve for future profit," and David Torres Vargas argued that Cordillera Blanca glaciers and glacial lakes would have "practical importance for the national economy."[53] Broggi's technical reports also recommended other types of economic development, such as mountaineering and alpine tourism.[54]

These scientists' sentiments about Cordillera Blanca water and tourist potential repeated those of their peers in Lima, who had for centuries been trying to tap the Andes for coastal profit. By the late nineteenth century, Latin American leaders and engineers increasingly worked with foreign enterprises to extract natural resources, agriculture, livestock, and labor from the most remote locations, such as the pampas of Argentina, the Atlantic Forest of Brazil, and the Putumayo region of the northwest Amazon. In twentieth-century Peru, interest in Andean goods and resources continued. Lima-based scientists and engineers took an increasingly active role in the process, working through such organizations as the Cuerpo de Ingenieros de Minas and the Sociedad Geográfica de Lima. They sought to mine precious metals, boost irrigation and hydroelectricity generation, construct infrastructure, improve agriculture and ranching, build industries, and expand tourism.[55] The Geographical Society of Lima, founded in 1888, had long influenced the Limeño elite's attitude toward the Andes. The society offered a scientific rationale for the racialized division of Peru into coast versus highlands. Furthermore, its members—like other geographers and similar institutions throughout Latin America—had from the outset linked geographical research to nation building, economic development, and the demarcation of international boundaries between countries.[56] Luis Gamio exemplified this thinking in the early 1940s. He offered an inventory of potential Ancash economic contributions, noting everything from ranching and mining in Bolognesi to medicinal hot springs in Chancos to a detailed tourist itinerary including driving times and scenic points. He saw the landscape, the water, the glaciers, the lakes, the eucalyptus trees, town plazas, precious metals, and every other possible resource as an economic opportunity for the nation, not just for Ancash.[57] Neither Gamio nor Broggi nor any of the glacier experts conducted science in isolation from the broader political and economic contexts that had shaped Peruvian science and engineering since the nineteenth century.

This larger historical context for Limeño scientists' and engineers' utilitarian, development-oriented views of Cordillera Blanca glacial lakes demonstrates how nonscientific influences shaped expert science during the 1940s. In 1943, Jorge Broggi remarked that the outburst flood in Huaraz was a tragedy "not just because it caused immense damage to the inhabitants' property and lives, but also because it diminished water reserves that sustain or could sustain the country's agricultural industry: that of the Coast."[58] His view affected the course of scientific research on glaciers and engineering projects at glacial lakes. As much as it focused on hazards, it also examined the economic potential of glaciers and glacial lakes. Huaraz newspapers and many residents with enough education to write editorials supported this water use and related hydroelectric and irrigation projects. These societal forces affecting science and disaster prevention were thus not drawn along rigid local versus national, expert versus Indian, or coast versus highland demarcations that more traditional views of Peruvian history might suggest.

Disaster Engineering and the Failed Retaining Walls

During the early 1940s, the national government developed three strategies to protect the population from Cordillera Blanca hazards: drain glacial lakes, prohibit urban reconstruction in the floodplain, and build retaining walls in Huaraz to contain the Quilcay River. Engineers immediately initiated several projects to partly drain unstable glacial lakes, mostly above Huaraz. Scientific studies had pointed to potential dangers from glacier retreat and subsequent glacial lake formation. Experts—and many local residents vulnerable to floods—believed the best way to avoid an outburst flood was by eliminating the water to begin with. Consequently, in the first months of 1942, Ministry of Development engineers working with the Civil Guard and rural laborers began draining Lakes Palcacocha, Cuchillacocha, and Tullparaju. The projects progressed slowly because of the remoteness of the work sites, difficult working conditions, freezing weather and snow, lack of previous knowledge about how to drain glacial lakes, and, according to some engineers, an unreliable labor force.

Despite complaints about slow progress and transient workers, the government-funded drainage projects continued. After nearly two years of work at Lake Palcacocha, engineers had lowered the lake level by nearly 4 meters, removing almost a half-million cubic meters of water, or 130 million gallons. At Lake Cuchillacocha, engineers had by late 1943 removed 1.5 million cubic meters of water. Victor Oppenheim, a geologist from Latvia who was studying Andean glaciation in the mid-1940s, recommended that they remove another

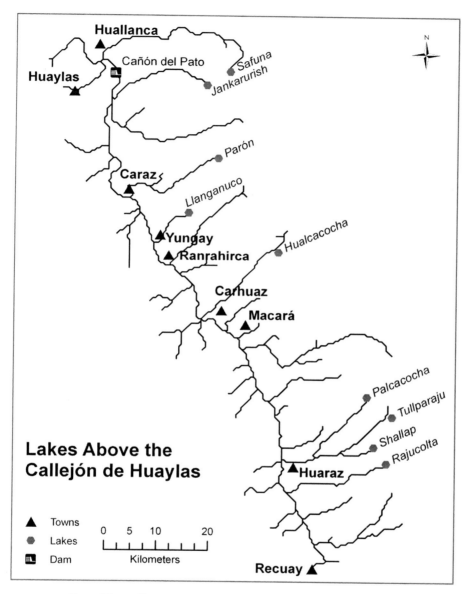

MAP 1.2. Santa River tributaries and referenced glacial lakes.
Credit: Map by Carol Karsch.

1.5 million cubic meters to make the lake safer. By 1950, the Ministry of Development and Public Works had partly drained Lakes Palcacocha, Cuchillacocha, and Llaca and was in the process of draining Lake Jankarurish. Experts still did not know how many Cordillera Blanca lakes existed, which

ones were most dangerous, or even if their actions sufficiently protected inhabitants. They thus advocated additional disaster prevention plans from the outset, such as constricting water flow in the Quilcay River and preventing people
from rebuilding Huaraz in the floodplain.[59]

Jorge Broggi became a particularly strong advocate for new zoning measures along the Quilcay. Lamenting what he called the "geological myopia" of
current residents and the Spaniards who had founded Huaraz (and other
Callejón de Huaylas towns), he explained that residents should not rebuild
where the flood had passed. He noted that pre-Columbian indigenous groups,
aware of flood dangers, had chosen to live higher above the valley floor, out of
harm's way. In the aftermath of the 1941 tragedy, he suggested that the city and
national governments create building codes to stipulate that reconstruction be
done up hillsides and out of danger rather than horizontally across the valley
floor.[60] Authorities agreed and by 1942 had declared the *cono aluviónico*, the
1941 flood path, off-limits for future construction.

But hazard zoning ultimately failed, as it has elsewhere in Peru and internationally, reflecting the tendency of populations worldwide to inhabit dangerous areas.[61] Most in Huaraz favored reconstruction directly inside the floodplain,
rejecting the calls of some to build only public parks and playing fields (rather
than homes and businesses) in the 1941 flood path.[62] Residents lamented lost
buildings and thoroughfares, such as the eucalyptus-lined Raimondi Alameda,
and they demanded that government officials re-create the city in its former
location.[63] Some emphasized the importance of the destroyed section because it
had previously been the heart of the city and an important area for habitation.[64]
One resident commented that construction there was a positive step toward
"achieving the existence of order and urban harmony in the structures of the
outburst flood zone."[65] Others demanded the reconstruction of a market, a
cathedral, a Tourist Hotel, the Raimondi Alameda, and a forum for cultural
activities, as well as the restoration of running water, electricity, sewer systems,
and paved streets.[66] Another resident argued that the only way to overcome the
"anxiety, discouragement, and fear" that reigned in Huaraz after 1941 was by
"encouraging progressive initiatives for the locality" that involved rebuilding the
destroyed neighborhoods. Without these symbols of progress and modernity,
Huaraz "would be shamed," according to the city's educated, property-owning,
and non-indigenous populations.[67]

Besides attempting hazard zoning, authorities and engineers also tried to
construct retaining walls in Huaraz that would channel potential floodwaters
flowing down the Quilcay River. Through the second half of 1943, engineers
and construction workers built large walls lining the Quilcay. The objective was
to direct water through the city without allowing it to escape and destroy urban

structures. Although a few people were in favor of these retaining walls, most Huaraz residents opposed them as being too costly, an ugly intrusion in the city, or a diversion of funds away from reconstruction.[68] One person, for example, exclaimed that the reconstruction of other buildings was more important, including the bridge over the river, public buildings, and an electric plant. This view seemed not to recognize that new bridges and buildings would be pointless in the event of another outburst flood.[69] Others agreed, though, that money spent on retaining walls would be much better spent on rebuilding the city.[70] Many also pointed to shoddy retaining wall construction, complaining that the cement used for the walls was too diluted with water to withstand a major flood. It turned out that they were right. One evening in late 1943, when workers draining Lake Cuchillacocha above Huaraz released some lake water, the river surge in Huaraz destroyed the retaining walls—and generated significant panic among the population.[71] But national government determination to build the retaining walls persisted. In July 1945, President Prado reported to the Peruvian Congress that he was still allocating money for the construction of defensive levees on both sides of the Quilcay River.[72] Ultimately, the residents won: retaining walls do not line the river today. Local opposition to both floodplain zoning and retaining walls occurred during a period of widespread concern about glacial lake hazards. Locals were thus not ignorant of the risks. Rather, they were unwilling or unable to alter their community and believed instead that environmental control (lake drainage) could protect them. They put the onus on the national government to prevent additional disasters by engineering the Andes.

Huaraz residents' current vulnerability to potential floods stems from their historical decisions to inhabit the hazard zone—decisions that would create significant anxiety and tension in subsequent decades. People in the 1940s and 1950s broke the law to inhabit vulnerable locations. At the same time, they demanded that the government drain and dam unstable glacial lakes. During and after the 1940s, Ancash residents did not develop evacuation plans or implement hazard zoning that could have provided long-term security against glacial lake outburst floods. Consequently, when engineers did not drain lakes fast enough or completely enough, and when Huaraz was not rebuilt quickly in its precise former location, local residents complained that the national government had failed to deliver its promised aid and had thus abandoned them. To a degree, they were right: the promised money did not all arrive, much of it being spent on coastal projects instead of in Huaraz. Glacial lakes above Huaraz, Caraz, Carhuaz, and many other towns still contained vast amounts of water dammed precariously behind unstable moraines. The government response was slow and unsystematic compared to what Prado promised. Despite the president's post-disaster visit,

Lima's traditional neglect of highland populations continued with lethargic disaster aid, relief, reconstruction, and mitigation.

Yet the national government worked much more diligently and effectively than it had following the previous series of glacial lake outburst floods in the 1930s and before. In the process, state scientists and engineers learned significantly more about the Cordillera Blanca, Andean glaciers, mountain water supplies, and economic potential. Many educated, property-owning urban residents demanded a particular type of government response aimed primarily at draining lakes and rebuilding a destroyed city in a hazard zone. They saw hazard zoning and retaining walls as obstacles to "effective" disaster prevention and signs of government neglect, even though these two strategies were well-intentioned plans to protect the population. Whereas most disaster scholars argue that vulnerability stems from poverty, racism, and other forces that push marginalized populations onto marginal lands or into substandard housing, this Huaraz case shows that vulnerable populations are not just passive victims of historical processes beyond their control. Rather, to rebuild their lives, they rebuilt in the floodplain.

Responses to the Huaraz disaster reveal several ways in which disaster prevention science and engineering evolved not simply as objective strategies to prevent climate catastrophes but through social and historical processes. Whether demonstrating how botany and botanical gardens served European empires that collected plants for food, medicine, and commerce or how health and sanitation campaigns in eighteenth-century Latin America enabled elite control over vagrants and the poor, historians have exposed the social, political, economic, and cultural forces affecting the evolution of science and technology.[73] After the 1940s Cordillera Blanca catastrophes, disaster prevention science and engineering were also influenced by social factors. Certain cities like Huaraz, Caraz, and Huallanca received more attention, not based on the number of vulnerable people but on regional politics and the hierarchy of "most important" cities. Local residents also influenced how disaster mitigation evolved by providing information or guiding glacier experts into the Cordillera Blanca. Urban residents rejected hazard zoning and retaining walls, and their rejection led to a more technoscientific approach to disaster mitigation. Scientists and engineers also brought their utilitarian views of Andean resources into disaster prevention campaigns. A dialogue thus emerged among various local populations, scientists, engineers, and national government officials—all in response to shrinking glaciers and expanding glacial lakes. To better comprehend local views and especially why Huaraz survivors chose to defy hazard zoning and rebuild in vulnerable locations, it is necessary to understand social issues that led many to construe glacial lake outburst floods as social disasters rather than environmental hazards.

2

Georacial Disorder
beneath Enchanted Lakes

The 1941 Huaraz inundation was much more than a flood. It was an environmental disaster that also created social, cultural, political, and spiritual disasters. For some residents, such outburst floods ruptured the balance among the human, spiritual, and physical worlds. Enchanted lakes lashed out as a result of human transgressions against different dimensions of these interconnected worlds. For the people most affected, the urban Huaraz population, the disaster not only leveled physical structures but also toppled symbols of social standing, wealth, status, and even the culturally constructed racial categories that supposedly distinguished Indians, mestizos, and creoles (*criollos*, whites). Of course, such sharp divisions were never so clear in reality; people in the Andes had intermixed since Pizarro arrived in 1532. By the 1940s, people's daily movements between town and country, the annual laborer migrations between highlands and coast, the ongoing process of twentieth-century urban migration, and the general fluidity among social groups, classes, and racial categories meant that the neat labels many Peruvians sought to impose were actually fictitious.[1] Nevertheless, class divisions did exist, and urban residents generally comprised the region's wealthier classes.[2] Their socioeconomic standing, however, hinged on the maintenance of clearly demarcated boundaries between nature and humans, country and city, highland and lowland, and Indian and mestizo. The 1941 glacial lake outburst flood shattered those boundaries.

Social disaster unleashed by post-catastrophe upheaval has occurred else-where, too. Elite Limeños panicked after the 1746 earthquake-tsunami, when lower-class residents roamed through the city, crossing social spaces that had previously been geographically and architecturally divided to segregate upper-class residents.[3] In New Orleans during the 1850s, mosquitoes—and the yel-low fever they transmitted—flew through the city without regard for supposed distinctions between poor and wealthy, littoral and land, or public and private spaces.[4] And in Huaraz after the 1970 earthquake, many urban survivors viewed the rural residents descending to the destroyed city to collect aid as invaders who moved unjustly into the urban space that the higher-class urban population had previously controlled.[5] This historical intersection of social and physical disaster demonstrates the unnatural nature of disasters and the ways in which nature and culture blur together.[6] Seeing climate change and glacial lake disasters in the Andes as the combination of societal and environmental forces—rather than just the physical processes of climatic warming and glacier retreat—helps explain why Huaraz residents rejected hazard zoning and chose to rebuild the destroyed city in the potential path of another flood. It also explains why Huaraz urban inhabitants turned to the state, science, and tech-nology to protect them from both climatic and social disasters.[7]

Making Sense of a Deadly Lake

In the aftermath of the Huaraz disaster, grieving survivors and other residents sought to understand why Lake Palcacocha had punished them. In the pre-dominantly Catholic society, many saw the flood as God's wrath for their sins. Others identified less moralistic explanations, such as increased rainfall that made the lake overflow or a recent heat wave that had melted the glacial ice and filled Lake Palcacocha to the brim. Still others subscribed to a worldview that saw the disasters as originating in enchanted lakes. These various accounts illustrate ways of understanding Andean hydrology and environmental pro-cesses that are entirely different from the explanation which scientists and engineers offered in their technical reports or at local town meetings.

Many distinct Peruvian societies from the pre-Columbian era to the pres-ent have viewed Andean waterways as enchanted or spiritually significant.[8] For the Inca, water embodied spiritual, political, social, and agricultural forces. Human death produced water, which allowed irrigation and food production—and thus human life. Lakes, especially Lake Titicaca on the Peru-Bolivia border, were sources of this water, but water ultimately originated in the Pacific Ocean and reached the highlands through underground canals, a belief held during the Inca Empire and retained by many still today. Subterranean water canals run throughout the Andes, according to these understandings, and lakes or springs provide access. The conquest of new land often meant the acquisition of new water sources. Lakes, then, have been sites of vast spiritual, hydrological, economic, and political power. They connected life with death, people with gods, ocean with highlands, soil fertility with agricultural yields, and behavior with health.[9] Residents have also long believed that lakes possess curative powers as well. Many lakes in the far north, such as Lakes Negra and Shimbe, continue to attract Peruvians, who bathe in the waters to restore their health or rebalance their internal equilibrium.[10]

Yet some lakes were "wild" or what Callejón de Huaylas residents refer to as "enchanted lakes," which could act out against individuals or local societies.[11] Transgressions against the gods, failure to give the proper offering to a healing lake, or sometimes even just approaching a wild lake can cause it to lash out by creating hailstorms and generating lightning, freezing someone bathing in lake water, or, in the worst cases, producing outburst floods.[12] A local woman divulged that Lake Awkish Qoca "wants to spill over.... It can burst out without warning."[13] A rural resident of Vicos explained that lakes communicated with one another, sometimes arguing and threatening to produce storms or send down a small flood.[14] For centuries, people have seen lakes as both life-giving and life-taking, as productive sources of water and power but fearful forces to treat properly according to local beliefs and rituals. As a result, many people throughout Peru continue to perform rituals to tame Andean lakes, to act in certain ways when near specific lakes, or to just stay away from them altogether.

Such beliefs about enchanted lakes provided one explanation for the 1941 Huaraz glacial lake outburst flood. A *campesino* was tending his livestock near Lake Palcacocha at the head of the Cojup Canyon when he heard a tremendous sound of giant rocks crashing down from the mountaintop. Startled, the *campesino* was trying to locate the source of the sound when he saw a "small but extremely muscular man with burning hair and bright red skin, armed with a broad, glistening machete" emerging from the lake. This "monster" danced wildly for two hours, throwing rocks and boulders and eventually transforming the lake into a churning mixture of foaming waves. Mounting a giant black horse, the monster then galloped out of the lake, bringing the turbulent water down the valley behind him and "sweeping away everything it found in its path." When the monster was about to bring the floodwaters through Huaraz, "an immaculately dressed boy appeared on Pumakayán Hill and, with a gesture with his right arm, deflected the flood's course." The monster continued its destructive path down the Santa River, defeating an Inca in a "colossal battle"

FIGURE 2.1. Glacial ice collector carrying ice to town, 1930s.
Credit: Photo courtesy of Hans Kinzl Archive, Institute of Geography, University of
Innsbruck, Austria.

on the way through the Callejón de Huaylas.[15] The great Ancash compiler of
local histories, Marcos Yauri Montero, does not divulge who told him the story,
though he mentions that he compiled oral histories from rural Quechua speakers, bilingual urban residents, and educated Spanish speakers, suggesting that

the legends and stories appealed to residents of different races and classes. The flood explanation is interesting for its blend of folk beliefs and scientific accuracies. On the one hand, the story depicts an avalanche into the lake, which created waves that eventually broke out of the lake bed. This view largely corresponds with scientists' assessment of the outburst flood's origin. On the other hand, the legend describes a monster that emerged from within the lake and led the onslaught down the valley. This more closely resembles the view of enchanted lakes.

Other stories, oral histories, and beliefs at the time—and still today—portray the region's lakes as enchanted. A beautiful girl, for example, was said to have once emerged from Lake Rajucolta just south of Huaraz to entice a young shepherd into the lake, where he saw a "marvelous palace," gold, and many other beautiful things. The story describes Rajucolta as a blood-colored lake with floating icebergs. Interestingly, the lake has for a long time been in direct contact with the glacial ice that feeds it and periodically produces icebergs. For the young shepherd in the story, the lake became a curse: after being lured beneath the surface, the boy became enchanted himself, much to the dismay of his parents.[16] In another story, a young girl tending her family's sheep was once drawn to Lake Churup by the sudden appearance of cooking utensils, beautiful jewelry, gold, and silver on the shore. As she came to see these marvelous objects, she also took a drink from the lake to quench her thirst. But when she looked back away from the lake to see her sister, she turned to stone.[17] A mid-1940s story about Lake Purhuay, on the eastern slope of the Cordillera Blanca near the town of Huari, describes another enchanted lake that attracted a woodcutter searching for medicine to cure his sick son. Lake spirits helped until the woodcutter betrayed a promise, at which point the lake captured him underwater, never to escape.[18]

Local residents have historically performed rituals to "tame" wild lakes and glaciers. For many, these acts of appeasing or controlling mountain spirits were part of maintaining reciprocal relations with Cordillera Blanca water and ice. Sometimes people put flowers in lakes, especially the *rima rima* flower, as an offering. They also placed crosses at lakes to utilize the power of God to prevent the lake spirits from harming or enticing humans. Likewise, people had to tame what they called *chúkaro*, a Quechua term meaning "raw nature."[19] Raw nature consisted of those areas where nature remained wild, and it could commit violent acts against people, such as avalanches or outburst floods. The hands of humans, then, could help pacify nature so long as this was done according to proper local customs instead of through force or blind transgressions. One way that people historically contained lakes that remained *chúkaro* was by throwing salt in the water. At Lake Huarancayoccocha, for example, the

Salt - taming elements

nearby hacienda owner used to throw salt in the water while a priest said prayers from the shore.[20] Some residents also took large quantities of salt onto glaciers, where they dumped it into crevasses and performed a ritual to protect themselves from dangerous spirits.[21] Flowers were an offering, but salt was a taming element because supernatural beings sought to avoid it. As one legend about Lake Parón explained from the perspective of a spirit in the lake, "Here, everyone is immortal because we do not eat salt."[22]

These stories about enchanted Cordillera Blanca lakes often conveyed a similar message: stay away from the lake.[23] A reckless person who got too close risked being swallowed. The victim usually found a richly adorned and beautiful underwater world. But when the person left that lake world, he or she almost inevitably failed to keep the secret or became overly greedy about acquiring more riches. The enchanted lake would punish the offender, turning the person to stone, taking him or her permanently to the other world, or otherwise ending earthly life as the victim knew it. Most who knew the stories kept a safe distance from alpine lakes and glaciers. Their reluctance to approach lakes may also have helped preserve clean water sources by keeping people and livestock away from the shores. Overall, these stories about Cordillera Blanca lakes and the 1941 Huaraz outburst flood uncover a discursive construction of the Andean environment and its processes. Although many outsiders today might relate more to a Western scientific analysis that explains how global climate change caused glacier retreat, lake formation, and subsequent collapse of the moraine dam, the local explanations give meaning to the people's world for themselves. These popular views represent unique ways of knowing and explaining environmental change, while also illuminating both culture and hydrological processes.[24]

Stories and metaphors to explain the 1941 Huaraz disaster were not confined to the rural populations or people without formal education. A few weeks after the December 13, 1941, outburst flood, the Huaraz newspaper *Noticias é Informaciones* printed a fictional explanation for the catastrophe, an allegory written by a well-educated resident from a prominent Huaraz family. Julia Barrionuevo began her tale by saying, "The inexplicable tragedy of the 13th, like everything unexplainable, has an explanation." She then recounted how her family's indigenous dairymaid came down from the mountains to tell her why the flood destroyed Huaraz:

> After many days, the dairymaid returned to us. She came as she always did, burdened by the years, burdened with rags, burdened with firewood, burdened with milk.... Only we, she said, know the motive behind this horrible disaster. Not long ago, and I don't know

why, the spirit of the canyon became offended and so ascended up to the mountain peaks, where its sad grieving reverberated through the valley, on the plateaus, and among the peaks. Saddened clouds then began to weep, and the anxious mountains let blocks of ice fall into the enchanted lakes. This infinite sadness was absorbed into the pure water of Lakes Acosha-cocha [Palcacocha] and Jirca-cocha, which also sobbed and increased their volume of water. And then, this creation of the mountains, creation of the lakes, astonished the valley; the infinite anguish turned into terrible rage and transformed into a band of warriors that marched out of the valley. We Indians saw this horrible marching... The band persisted in indescribable confusion: the enraged water tumbling violently, the mud and sand sweeping into every crevice, inundating everything; the boulders that momentarily blocked its path only heightened the rage of the vengeful band. And with them and after them, the immense blocks of granite annihilated and crushed everything: trees, farms, gardens, avenues, streets, chalets, houses; children, women, the elderly, men. And so you have seen how the bitter teardrops of the mountains and the lakes have left the place they inundated: as sand, rock, gravel. A terrible punishment, an unnamable punishment. And the dairymaid, burdened by the years, burdened with rags, and free of the firewood and milk, returned again to her peaks.[25]

Barrionuevo's fictional story reveals the various types of explanations that emerged following the flood. Though the specifics of the fable must be treated carefully as historical evidence, the way this educated woman from Huaraz presented the story is itself significant. Barrionuevo's explanation is reminiscent of the era's *indigenismo* movement, a late-nineteenth and twentieth-century political-intellectual movement in Peru, Mexico, and elsewhere in Latin America. *Indigenista* views varied widely among countries, within each country, and among the various schools of thought. Generally, the movement was characterized by many contradictions. Indigenistas advocated for indigenous rights but were usually educated mestizos from urban areas. They claimed to celebrate and value Indians, but they usually only praised ancient Indians such as the Inca and Aztecs while portraying contemporary indigenous populations as inferior. They lamented Indians' poor treatment but offered no ways for Indians to overcome the traditional socioeconomic hierarchy. They spoke of equality but often remained racist, condescending, and paternalistic toward the group they identified as Indian. Despite its condescending paternalism, indigenismo did open discussion about Indians' position in Latin American societies.[26]

Barrionuevo's allegory fits with Peruvian indigenista literature and with the views held by some of the movement's most famous writers, such as Luis Valcárcel, who saw Indians as inherently rural, Andean, and close to nature and thought they had been exploited by contemporary labor and sociopolitical relations.[27] Her analysis of the dairymaid, the indigenous witnesses, the mountains, the animated natural world, and the reduction of the city to gravel all point to broader indigenista issues: race relations, views of nature and geography, and the social construction of identity in the twentieth-century Andes. According to the story, a wild but anthropomorphized nature created the disaster among the country's highest peaks—and then it sent that deadly combination of lake water and glacial ice crashing down out of a remote canyon above Huaraz. Yet nature concocted this deadly formula in the supposed indigenous homelands, where Indians watched it evolve and where the dairymaid returned to "her summits." Finally, Barrionuevo's story also presents a terrible, unnamable punishment: the transformation of Huaraz, a civilized city, into gravel. It was raw, untamed nature descending from the Andean highlands to obliterate the most modern, wealthiest, and most mestizo part of the region's most powerful city. Ultimately, it is a tale of revenge. The offended spirit, which left the valley and ascended to the highlands, returned to the valley floor to punish Huaraz. For what? Perhaps for exploiting indigenous labor because, in the end, the dairymaid returns to her summits "free of her burdens," the goods she produced for urban residents. Her story could, in this line of thinking, portray the outburst flood as revenge for the type of wretched abuses against Indians that renowned Peruvian author Clorinda Matto de Turner wrote about at the birth of indigenismo in the 1880s.[28] Barrionuevo's allegory laments the horrible treatment of oppressed Indians and suggested the flood freed them from those burdens.

Barrionuevo's story also suggests that legends can compare with—and even inform—Western scientific theories. They tell of similar processes through different means and with distinct messages. Scholars have increasingly tried to integrate folk knowledge and indigenous beliefs into Western science.[29] Barrionuevo's account, which by itself did not affect scientists' understandings, nonetheless captured the physical processes leading to the outburst flood—and this just weeks after the disaster, when scientists had not yet finished their studies of Lake Palcacocha and the flood's origin. More specifically, the dairymaid's account integrates climatic, geological, glaciological, and hydrological processes that scientists later learned were, in fact, interacting to cause the outburst flood. Some may not believe it was the sad mountain spirit or the weeping clouds that created the lake, but geologists, engineers, and Barrionuevo all suggested that climate change and weather patterns had melted the glacier, created the lake, and ultimately triggered the outburst flood.

[handwritten top margin: nature + culture dichotomies]

Julia Barrionuevo's fictional reflection, when combined with other acco[unts] of the flood, hints at ways in which educated urban residents blurred nat[ure] culture dichotomies to see the disaster as both social and environmental. Additional evidence also suggests how some residents saw the flood as disruptive to the region's hierarchy because it obliterated markers of social distinction.

The Andes Unchained: Social Disaster in Urban Huaraz

[handwritten margin: wealthy class — "equal" to others who lost everything]

Disaster aftermath can often present startling consequences for members of the wealthier classes who suddenly find themselves momentarily "equal" to other survivors who have lost everything. Disaster exposes wealthy survivors to the same vulnerability and precarious living conditions as the poor. A major post-disaster threat to middle- and upper-class victims is the unrestricted movement and social mobility of the lower classes into spaces previously reserved for them. In Huaraz, spatial mobility and the lack of physical barriers to demarcate space created a social disaster for urban survivors.

The transformation of thriving pre-disaster Huaraz into static nothingness dealt a particularly powerful blow because it did much more than just physically destroy buildings, streets, schools, hospitals, social clubs, infrastructure, and homes. Previously, the ordered urban environment had stood as the antithesis to wild nature. For many of Huaraz's middle- and upper-class inhabitants, the urban structures represented the triumph of civilized modernity over the back- *[handwritten margin: Civilized modernity]* ward Andean mountains. The outburst flood, as one survivor lamented, converted a vibrant city "into a pile of inert material that contrasts with the beautiful features" of the Callejón de Huaylas.[30] Some referred to Huaraz as "sick" after the disaster and grumbled that the "demented" Lake Palcacocha turned the city into a vacant land, a field (*campo*), or, as the disaster scar was called for decades, the "barren plain."[31] Reynaldo Coral Miranda, the young student described in the previous chapter who was doing homework at his parents' shop in Centenario when the flood approached, said that once this demented flood devastated the city, its survivors also became "maddened" and "crazed" (*enloquecida*). The disaster erased people's civility, urbaneness, and rationality.[32]

These descriptions of the disaster's effects reveal a deeper anxiety among residents: that modernization, education, technology, and wealth could not contain—or even withstand—the raw forces of nature. In mid-twentieth-century Peru, this realization conjured particularly potent fears because it eroded the very foundations of the socioeconomic hierarchy. Of course, one can easily imagine that survivors struggling after a catastrophe would feel betrayed and think that nature has conspired against them. And most disaster survivors want

[handwritten bottom margin: modernity can not w/ stand nature]

more than anything to return to their previous lives. However, in Peru in particular, the descent of raw nature from the wild, untamed heights to destroy a modern urban area represented a powerful transgression. The Peruvian social order hinged on maintaining rigid rural-urban and mountain-valley divides, as well as keeping wild nature in check to allow for progress and economic development. The flood eroded these markers of social distinction. Class and race boundaries suddenly seemed more porous than ever. Those at the top of the social hierarchy—and, perhaps more important, those in the middle—lost the physical structures of the urban area that had helped separate them from those at the bottom, the rural population referred to as indigenous in the 1940s.

One of the key ways that the outburst flood obliterated social boundaries was simply its origin in the high mountains and descent to the valley floor, as the numerous accounts, including Barrionuevo's, make clear. Height has always mattered in the Andes. Moving west to east, the Andes rise abruptly from the desert-like Pacific coast to the arctic-like mountain summits above 6,000 meters; the eastern slope then descends to the humid, tropical Amazon lowlands.[33] Over the last several thousand years, Andean societies learned to exploit various niches

FIGURE 2.2. Typical community interactions at the Yungay market, 1936.
Credit: Photo courtesy of Hans Kinzl Archive, Institute of Geography, University of Innsbruck, Austria.

within distinct elevational life zones and to redistribute goods to other areas that were higher or lower. John Murra famously labeled this system of ecological complementarity the "vertical archipelago."[34] Over time, and especially during the last two centuries, Peruvians came to equate elevation not just with ecology, agriculture, and economies but also with race, class, social status, and identity. By the late nineteenth century, most Peruvians, especially the coastal ruling classes in Lima, believed that the higher someone lived, the lower his or her social position. Peruvians divided the country, intellectually at least, between a creole/mestizo coast and an indigenous highlands.[35] These invented categories were not simply racial: Peruvians portrayed the coast as modern and civilized in contrast to the indigenous, backward, and poor highlands. Historical Indian uprisings in the Andes had provoked a lingering fear among the coastal elite, who consequently reinforced the imagined boundaries between coast and sierra. The massive Tupac Amaru uprising of the 1780s, the success of armed indigenous groups fighting Chileans in the 1880s War of the Pacific, and Pedro Pablo Atusparia's uprising in Huaraz in 1885 heightened those fears and exacerbated regional tensions.[36] In the early twentieth century, Peruvian scientists explained how indigenous people were more biologically fit to live at high altitude, thereby demonstrating that Indians, but not creoles, could thrive in the Andes.[37] Other factors helped divide the coast from highlands, but in the end, one of the most powerful forces separating the two regions was ignorance: coastal residents knew little about highland Peru, neither in the past nor today. Highland residents knew more about Lima because it was their capital city, and increasing twentieth century urban migration attracted highlanders to the coast.

Peruvians also conceptualized racial and class divisions through horizontal barriers: urban versus rural. Essentially, the rural world became the domain of Indians, and Indians became synonymous with the rural.[38] By the twentieth century, important intellectuals such as José Carlos Mariátegui and Luis Valcárcel had branded indigenous people as "an agricultural race."[39] By engaging in farming, living in houses with dirt floors, traveling on dirt roads, wearing sandals instead of shoes, cooking with clay pots, and building homes with adobe bricks, Indians supposedly maintained strong connections to the countryside, where nature and the earth existed in sharp contrast to the urban built environment and civilized customs.[40] The Spanish colonial legacy thus continued throughout Peruvian history. The upper classes maintained their status by avoiding manual labor, by inhabiting urban areas, by constructing second floors on their houses, and by building orderly towns and cities with straight streets.[41] Huaraz's modern district of Centenario exemplified these upper-class customs and structures in 1941. Disaster survivors thus, on some level, saw the flood as a rural—and thus Indian—invasion of the city.

breakdown of social boundaries [handwritten annotation]

elevation-determined [handwritten annotation]
urban + rural divide [handwritten annotation]

Huaraz citizens viewed the disaster as a breakdown of social boundaries because they saw identities through the same georacial binaries that existed throughout Peru. In Huaraz, however, they perceived them on a different scale. Whereas the coastal elite saw coast-sierra divisions, Callejón de Huaylas inhabitants saw both valley-highland elevational distinctions and urban-rural barriers, with rural inhabitants labeled not only as indigenous but also as a lower class. Rural residents who farmed and inhabited hamlets were, by definition, inferior indigenous people.[42] As one urban dweller explained at the time, the "indigenous race" lives in "rural hamlets, ranches, and high-elevation plains [*punas*]; mestizos, on the other hand, generally inhabit district capitals and the occasional hamlet of importance."[43] Of course, other factors beyond geography distinguished these identities, such as language, dress, education, literacy, and profession.[44] But even these characteristics became tied to elevation and rural-urban divides. If a rural farmer moved to the city, learned Spanish, dressed differently, and went to school, he lost some of his "Indianness" and became a *cholo*. Cholification—that is, the process of becoming less Indian—thus also implied social and spatial mobility. Consequently, rural-to-urban migration challenged the social status of existing *cholos* and mestizos.

Just before the Huaraz flood, migration patterns and fear of indigenous invasions made urban Callejón de Huaylas inhabitants particularly jittery about the social hierarchy. They continually worried that Indians from the hills would descend into the city and invade the urban space that had always represented mestizo and creole authority over the indigenous population. Referring to the appearance of Indians in towns for religious festivals, one scholar asserted that, for urban residents, this represented "menacing moments of invasion by the ponchoed Indians of the interior highlands."[45] More threatening in Huaraz, the specter of the 1885 Atusparia uprising, one of the country's most significant uprisings since independence, still loomed large. One resident even noted in the late 1930s that the uprising "put the social stability of the Department of Ancash in grave danger and was about to compromise the entire center of the republic."[46] During the 1930s, after President Leguía fell from power, Huaraz's upper classes grew more fearful of lower-class rural populations.[47] Additionally, in the decades leading to the 1940s, migration from the rural parts of Ancash to provincial capitals and Huaraz increasingly challenged urban residents' status above these newcomers.[48] Rural-urban migration threatened lower-status urban residents as well because they worried they might be lumped with the newcomers. As one scholar noted at the time about the 1950s Callejón de Huaylas, "the fear of being Indian is frequent" among urban mestizos.[49]

Given the ways in which the culturally constructed rural-urban, wild-civilized, indigenous-mestizo boundaries affected social standing, the 1941 flood's erosion of those barriers created anxiety among middle- and upper-class Huaraz survivors. Testimonials identified the flood as a treacherous invasion of Huaraz. Previously, writers from the Callejón de Huaylas suggested that both rural Indians and the mountain landscape should ideally remain docile and static. If natural features or Indians moved, descended, or stepped out of their submissive roles, they tipped the Andean social order and challenged the position of urban elites.[50] Almost invariably, urban people referred to the high mountain lakes that triggered the disasters as "traitors," thereby suggesting that nature had not simply caused calamity but had intentionally overstepped an assigned role. As one nervous Huaraz resident wrote disdainfully in a poem: "look at how the cruel Andean lakes/have tormented us/watch out Cuchillacocha don't go and/kill me/like the traitor Cojup."[51] Urban residents also described how lakes had "broken loose" from their high canyons or become "unchained" (*desencadenado*) from the mountains. Huaraz resident Mauro Mendoza believed that, before the "treacherous lake" Cojup caused the catastrophe, the lakes and glaciers had been "telluric forces repressed for centuries."[52] Dr. José Joaquín Sotelo, district attorney of the Superior Court of Lima, claimed that "the black forces of nature [were] unleashed in our path" because local people had not fully "subdued" the mountain areas.[53] The city people felt betrayed and under attack from recalcitrant lakes that had disobeyed urban authority.

Residents also portrayed the floods as a punishment. On the anniversary of the Huaraz disaster, a local inhabitant reflected, "One day like today, thirteen years ago, Huaraz suffered the most cruel and harsh punishment from the enraged Nature."[54] Another commentator felt Huaraz had "been cruelly flogged by the fury of nature turning tranquility and order into chaos and confusion."[55]

Huaraz residents felt so betrayed by the highlands that they developed (mostly uncorroborated) stories of "immoral" indigenous people sacking the city after the flood.[56] "While people in Huaraz cried out in terror," wrote one author disgustedly, "some Indians were looting. Then, below Patay, below Quinoacocha, even though the people were crying out to be saved, they say the looters did not rescue them, but rather they picked up whatever thing of value, but not cadavers nor those who were yelling to be saved."[57] A wealthy urban resident also noted how, during the early 1940s, Indians would sometimes descend from the hills and create a diversion, a panic that would spread through Huaraz. "They would arrive in the city yelling 'Here comes an outburst flood!' so that people would flee from their homes. Then they would loot their houses and stores." If they caught the culprits, he said, authorities would execute the Indians to make an example.[58] Another Huaraz man, Rufino Mendez Ramos, complained that looting began the same day as the outburst flood. He reported that Huaraz mayor Ernesto Salazar organized an assembly at 4 P.M., hours after the flood, to form an Urban Guard to work with the police to "guard the threatened population against unscrupulous people who wish to take advantage of every painful circumstance."[59] This example is the closest proof of looting I could identify, but the author makes no reference to the looters' race. Interestingly, these stories came primarily from testimonies about the flood recorded several years or decades afterward. A well-educated survivor who was nine when the flood destroyed Huaraz also claimed that Indians sacked the city after the outburst flood. "Why did they rise up?" he asked rhetorically. His answer echoed Barrionuevo's allegory: "Because they had grown tired of such abuse."[60] Survivors still say today that Indians descended to the ruined city immediately following the flood and began stealing from homes and shops.[61] They interpret the outburst flood as revenge for historical injustices committed against rural Andean inhabitants. The urban survivors did not blame rural residents or Indians for the flood itself, but their stories and memories conflated the destruction of the city by nature with the looting of the city by Indians. Discourse criminalized both glacial lakes and Indians.

At the root of urban concerns about Indian looters were beliefs that the flood disrupted the socioeconomic order.[62] Understanding this context of social disaster helps explain why Huaraz residents later rejected retaining walls and urban hazard zoning to keep people out of the floodplain. Reconstructing the city meant re-creating the physical characteristics that helped symbolize urban authority and social standing—as well as partially returning to a pre-disaster state. Huaraz residents' refusal to accept the government's plan to leave the destroyed part of Huaraz as a vacant hazard zone and their decision instead to advocate engineering projects to drain glacial lakes can be understood by recognizing many urban residents' anxiety about class and race relations, which hinged in part on the separation of rural from urban. Just as the Limeño elite had protested building restrictions against multistory buildings after the 1746 Lima earthquake—because they saw the suddenly forbidden second-story houses as literally and figuratively lifting them above the lower classes—the Huaraz upper and middle classes during the 1940s saw hazard zoning as an infringement on their ability to reconstruct the symbols that divided them from the rural, supposedly more natural indigenous population.

Chavín, 1945: Confirming a Pattern of Disaster

Glacial lake outburst floods continued to riddle Ancash. On January 17, 1945, another lake dam ruptured, this time inundating the town of Chavín de Huantar on the Cordillera Blanca's eastern slope. Like the 1941 Huaraz disaster, the Chavín outburst flood originated when mammoth ice blocks splashed into the precariously dammed glacial Lakes Carhuacocha and Ayhuinyaraju at the foot of Mount Huantsán, approximately 25 kilometers above Chavín. The moraine dams broke when waves lashed against them, and an estimated 1 million cubic meters of water, ice, and other debris immediately turned into a deadly outburst flood.[65]

Edilberto Lopez Illanes, who had recently returned to his hometown after being away for 15 years, remembered that morning vividly. At first he noticed that all the people around him had their heads raised and were staring toward the sky with an anxious, expectant look. "What are you looking at?" he asked. Then they all heard a distant, low rumble like "five hundred to a thousand fighter planes that approached slowly but terribly." A tremendous dust cloud rose up behind Mount Huachecza above the town, and suddenly some people darted over the crest of a hill in front of him. As they ran toward him they yelled in Quechua, "Here comes the mountain!" Lopez Illanes saw others waving and gesturing frantically with their arms, trying to tell everyone to get out of the way as disaster sped toward the town. "They were moments of terrible confusion and panic," he later lamented. "Men, women, children—old men and old women—rich and poor, some wearing only their underwear, fleeing toward the hills in search of safety and salvation." He found himself in a group of these bewildered residents on Shallapa Hill just above the town, watching awestruck as the catastrophe unfolded. "In these moments, man feels so small before the immense power of nature," he grieved. Some townspeople dashed about wildly trying to escape while others, unsure which areas were safe and which were not, locked themselves in their homes as the outburst flood blasted out of the hills and buried a significant portion of the town.[63]

From the hilltop, Lopez Illanes and other horrified survivors may have seen the group of politicians and academics swept away in the flood. This group had just assembled to determine how best to restore and maintain the famous archaeological ruins at Chavín. Participants in the meeting included Ancash Prefect Pedro Artola, his daughter Graciela, the director of the Colegion Nacional, Mariano Espinoza, and many other educators, authorities, and students. The Chavín settlement was established by one of Peru's oldest societies whose heyday spanned from approximately 900 to 200 B.C. Groups as far south as Nazca and Ayacucho and as far north as Cajamarca were influenced by important Chavín innovations in metallurgy, weaving, religious practices, stone carvings, and ceramics. The ancient urban center was situated at the confluence of rivers flowing down from the Cordillera Blanca's sacred Mount Huantsán.[64] Nearly three thousand years after Chavín was founded, it would turn out to be a tragic location.

As the flood poured through Chavín for nearly a half hour, it destroyed two-thirds of the town, the majority of the ruins and museum artifacts, and several other hamlets and small communities along the river below Chavín.[66] Local residents dug for days to extract bodies—including those of the prefect, government officials, intellectuals, and hundreds of others—from the muck that covered the town and the valley below. A few who were at the ruins escaped with their lives. Martín Flores somehow managed to summon lightning speed that allowed him to run from the ruins as mud, water, and debris lapped at his ankles. The prefect's chauffeur, Moises Olaza Sotelo, also saved himself—and the car—by driving out of the floodpath without a second to spare. Olaza later pleaded with Lima officials to reward him financially for saving the car.[68] Officials and witnesses estimated that the flood caused 500 deaths and 2 million soles' worth of damage. Fortunately, the famous Peruvian archaeologist Julio C. Tello had previously sent some artifacts to Lima to make replicas. These turned out to be some of the only ones preserved. [67] By early 1945, a dark shadow of grief and fear had descended on everyone living around the Cordillera Blanca. They all eyed the mountains anxiously, wondering which of the glacial lakes would next send down a lethal flood.

Shaping Western Science from the Andes

The 1945 Chavín flood received much less national attention than the 1941 Huaraz catastrophe, with only a few articles buried deep in Lima's newspapers and not even front-page coverage. Yet the less deadly 1945 disaster had a powerful influence within Ancash and on the history of glacier disaster prevention programs in the Cordillera Blanca. The Chavín flood made tens of thousands of people living below melting Cordillera Blanca glaciers wonder if their town would be next: if they would suddenly awake to the guttural roar of an outburst flood descending upon them and would lose their families, friends, and homes to similar cataclysmic events. As one writer observed in a Lima newspaper, "The Huaraz and Chavín catastrophes have created a state of collective anxiety in towns throughout the Ancash Department, and they demand that effective measures be taken to avoid new disasters."[69] The flood effectively mobilized the regional populations on the east and west sides of the Cordillera Blanca, especially in Huaraz and the Callejón de Huaylas.

Within days of the Chavín flood, angry and anxious residents gathered at town meetings, signed petitions demanding more scientific studies, and wrote opinion pieces that appeared in local and national newspapers. They demanded more information about glacier hazards and insisted that the national government drain every dangerous lake in the Cordillera Blanca. Just two weeks after the Chavín disaster, for example, water in the Chuchún River began to flow more vigorously through Carhuaz. Worried residents immediately went to the mayor, who in turn took his concerns directly to Peruvian President Manuel Prado. The mayor requested that the government drain glacial lakes above

Carhuaz.[70] This was not the first time Carhuaz residents had asked for government support to study, monitor, and drain glacial lakes. After the Huaraz disaster, they had made similar appeals to local and national authorities.[71] In Caraz, too, traumatized people who had demanded government action in 1942 redoubled their pleas for help.[72] In early February 1945, Lima's *El Comercio* published a petition signed by 50 Caraz residents, asking President Prado to drain the Cordillera Blanca's largest lake, Parón, which is directly above Caraz. These citizens believed Lake Parón posed one of the gravest threats to the region, primarily because of its sheer volume: it was several times larger than any other lake that had created an outburst flood.[73] "The town of Caraz is dismayed by the Huaraz and Chavín catastrophes," the petition read. "We again plead with the government, in an urgent manner, to send as soon as possible the personnel to drain the immense Lake Parón that poses a real, imminent threat of overflowing onto the entire population. Newspapers in Huaraz are describing in alarming detail the nature of this threat. This community finds itself in a panic, and we ask that you respond to our request to save thousands of lives and valuable property, returning once again the general tranquility that will come only after draining Lake Parón."[74]

FIGURE 2.3. Lake Parón above Caraz, 1932.
Credit: Photo courtesy of Hans Kinzl Archive, Institute of Geography, University of Innsbruck, Austria.

Residents in Huaraz were even more persistent and organized, and they also mobilized in 1945 to demand disaster mitigation. By February 1, 1945, just two weeks after the Chavín tragedy, Huaraz residents who had been marching in the streets to protest government inaction submitted a petition with 80 signatures—and many more promised to follow—to President Prado. They demanded that his government immediately drain Lakes Palcacocha, Cuchillacocha, and Shallap.[75] In a special January 30 meeting of "distinguished ladies" at the local chapter of the Club Huaraz, Carmela de Ramos Méndez explained insistently:

> Once again we see children's faces imprinted with terror, once again the dreams and tranquility have fled from our homes, again we have seen the lines of cadavers encased in mud and debris; again the disaster has leveled our homes, leaving orphans and widows.... To achieve peace and tranquility in our homes and to live safely in our beloved lands of Ancash, we come to the president to ask that he use all his power to ensure that his orders are carried out to achieve security for Huaraz, Carhuaz, Yungay, and all the towns of the Callejón.[76]

Huaraz residents became involved almost daily in public and official meetings with local, regional, and national government officials and engineers. Hundreds of people packed into these presentations and discussions about glacial lakes.[77] Representatives from such diverse entities as the Supreme Court, the Ministry of Development, the mayor's office, labor groups, cultural organizations, the prefect's office, churches, and even "a group of ladies" came out to hear speeches by engineers like Antonio Grüter, who had been working at lakes above Huaraz since 1942, and the national Water Division's director, Jorge Zegarra, who spoke about future disaster prevention plans for Huaraz. The Chavín flood had thrust scientists and engineers into prominent public positions. They suddenly found themselves presenting both their studies and their technical plans to a wide range of anxious residents, priests, local officials, government leaders, and members of social organizations and clubs. Glacier experts were now acting as intermediaries between the national government in Lima and the Callejón de Huaylas population.

Locals wanted all this information, but they also wanted to express their concerns and make their two major demands known. First, they wanted to know the results of previous lake studies regarding the degree of danger that glacial lakes posed. After the Chavín flood, many believed that authorities and experts hid the true dangers of these lakes. In fact, those suspicions were largely accurate. Engineers, ministers, and other government officials continually reported in newspapers and public meetings what became—and remained for several decades—an all too common mantra: "There is no danger." Locals had had heard this phrase repeatedly even before the Chavín disaster, and that sequence made them significantly more suspicious.

The technical reports, which were generally inaccessible to the public, reveal an entirely different expert perspective on glacial lakes in the 1940s. Engineers admitted that they did not know where glacial lakes existed or when a disaster would strike. Many experts kept asking for additional studies because they were not entirely sure how geological, geomorphologic, hydraulic, glaciological, or climatic forces actually interacted to create conditions for a glacial lake outburst flood. Many of these experts throughout the 1940s called for continued drainage of glacial lakes, suggesting that they were not satisfied with the degree of safety for valley residents. Victor Oppenheim, for example, recommended in 1945 and 1946 that the two most feared lakes above Huaraz—Palcacocha and Cuchillacocha—needed more draining and monitoring.[78] Luis Ghiglino pointed out that Lake Artesoncocha above Lake Parón was perhaps unstable, and an outburst flood from it could threaten Parón's natural dam.[79] Some of the conflicting reports about lake stability stemmed from scientists' disagreements. For example, Jorge Zagarra from the Ministry of Development and Public Works thought Oppenheim's report was "vague and obscure."[80] Officials may have also portrayed the lakes as stable to calm the public. Regardless of the motives behind these sharp discrepancies between the confident announcements of "no danger" and the hidden technical reports conveying uncertainty and lake instability, the local residents had by 1945 developed a strong interest in learning about the region's glacial lakes. And scientists, engineers, and policy makers in Lima were also learning about the Cordillera Blanca landscape and the highland population.

To ensure their safety, locals demanded that the national government drain lakes completely. They had grown tired of studies that warned of dangers but did not result in drainage projects. As one commentator wrote in a regional newspaper immediately following the Chavín disaster:

> We don't want study commissions anymore, which carry out their investigations and take off within twenty-four hours offering to inform us later. Then those reports lie dormant and are never divulged to the anxious populations that worry for their safety. In short, we don't want nor wish that the government deceive us. What we want is for [the government] to respond to the voice of the people, which is the voice of God, and these people want the complete drainage of their lakes without waiting for another rainy season and without doing more studies.[81]

In response, the prefect organized more town meetings and established a local group to monitor glacial lake control above Huaraz; it consisted of residents and officials representing the mayor's and prefect's offices. The prefect also mobilized religious leaders, teachers, mayors, and other local government officials to inform urban and rural residents about the status of glacial lakes above Huaraz and the ongoing engineering projects to drain them.[82] By March 1945, the national government had devoted nearly 60,000 soles to lake drainage projects above Huaraz.[83] No floods have since inundated the city, but glacial lakes kept bursting elsewhere and new ones continue to form.

The 1941 and 1945 glacial lake outburst floods in Huaraz and Chavín not only frightened and mobilized the regional population but also brought national attention to the problem of glacier retreat in the Andes. Never before had glacial lakes anywhere in the world killed so many people. Whereas other deadly glacial lake outburst floods, such as in Little Ice Age Europe or in the twentieth-century Himalayas, killed hundreds, these two Cordillera Blanca disasters took 5,500 lives.[84] Death and destruction descended on Ancash communities while fear hung in the air. Residents demanded immediate government intervention to protect them from future floods, and to a degree, they got it, though not in a comprehensive, organized, systematic, or efficient way. Consequently, they never believed the government's response was sufficient. For several decades— and even now—local residents persisted in their pleas for relief and protection from threatening glacial lakes. The state did in fact take several measures to prevent outburst floods following the Huaraz flood, though they were obviously not enough to avert the Chavín disaster. The influx of government officials and experts after 1941, the people's new relationship with the Andean lakes and glaciers, and the eradication of many physical markers that separated urban from rural, civilization from nature, mestizos from Indians, and coast from mountains created a host of other issues. In short, the floods—and the reactions to those floods—altered social relations, transformed power dynamics, and changed people's relationship with Andean environments and resources.

Though the Huaraz and Chavín glacial lake floods were particularly powerful events, they point to the broader significance of glaciers and lakes in Andean history. After all, glaciers shaped the past elsewhere in the Andes, too, as in the annual religious pilgrimage and collection of glacial ice on Mount Ausangate, the historical use of sacred glacier meltwater for irrigation, and the use of glacial ice for cold drinks in Lima before refrigeration existed.[85] In the Cordillera Blanca, glaciers became key historical actors in 1941 in part because of the physical destruction their melting caused, but also because they triggered important changes after the arrival of engineers and government officials.

Glacier retreat thus brought new historical actors—or stakeholders—into the Andes. This was part of a process some scholars refer to as the social production of landscape, with engineers and scientists playing important historical roles in the evolving relationships among natural sciences, engineering, environment, and government.[86] Climate, glacier retreat, lake formation, and moraine-dam failures were altering the historical trajectory of the region and changing diverse people's relationship with both the mountains and one another. The 1940s was only just the beginning of a long period of glacier disasters and government programs to prevent them.

3

Engineering the Andes, Nationalizing Natural Disaster

[handwritten annotation: in response to the 1950s flood, gov created the Control Commission of Cordillera Blanca Lakes — to conduct glacier studies + disaster mitigation projects]

The history of Cordillera Blanca glacial lake control and disaster management changed dramatically on the morning of October 20, 1950, when a catastrophic glacial lake outburst flood roared out of the Los Cedros Canyon. The flood destroyed the Chimbote-Huallanca railway line (again) and the nearly completed Cañón del Pato hydroelectric station, two high-profile state-funded projects run by the Peruvian Santa Corporation. In response, Peruvian President Manuel Odría created the Control Commission of Cordillera Blanca Lakes (or the Lakes Commission) to carry out glacial lake studies and conduct disaster mitigation projects. The enabling legislation directed the agency to avoid the "repetition of those outburst floods that can damage the current and ongoing works of the Peruvian Santa Corporation, as well as those of the Chimbote-Huallanca Railroad...avoiding at the same time damage to the populations of the Callejón de Huaylas."[1] The Lakes Commission was just the type of state agency that Ancash residents had pushed for (unsuccessfully) in the aftermath of the Huaraz and Chavín disasters. It was the destruction of a hydroelectric facility and its setback to national industrialization plans—rather than the deaths of thousands of Ancash residents in 1941 and 1945—that inspired the government's effective and far-reaching response to glacier retreat and glacial lake outburst floods in 1951.

[handwritten annotation: destruction of the hydroelectric facility]

Establishment of the Lakes Commission marked a significant shift away from the state's underfunded, piecemeal disaster prevention agenda of the 1940s. From 1951 to the late 1960s—at which point the Santa Corporation began to displace it as the region's preeminent disaster prevention entity—the Lakes Commission systematically studied Cordillera Blanca glacial lakes. It also developed innovative engineering techniques to drain and dam a dozen dangerous lakes. The Lakes Commission met a host of challenges in its disaster prevention programs: a fluctuating budget; a lack of detailed knowledge about the Cordillera Blanca; animosity between Callejón de Huaylas communities and Lima officials; and local residents who often disagreed with experts and officials about how best to prevent additional disasters. Moreover, the Lakes Commission grappled with a new glacial lake outburst at Lake Artesoncocha in 1951 and the near overflow of Lake Parón in 1952. The agency nonetheless made significant accomplishments in disaster prevention science, technology, engineering, and lake control—all with very little financial or technical assistance from outside Peru.

President Odría supported the Lakes Commission because he realized that to modernize Peru the government would have to contend with these recalcitrant glacial lakes that kept washing away hopes for economic development in the Andes. The Los Cedros flood struck during a worldwide era when dams and hydroelectric projects signified much more than just sources of water and energy. The Hoover Dam in the United States, Egypt's Aswan Dam, a series of dams in India, and many others fulfilled political as well as social and water-use agendas in the mid-twentieth century. Jawaharlal Nehru even referred to dams as "the Temples of Modern India."[2] Leaders of modernizing states became particular advocates of dams that they hoped would expand popular support and enhance their legitimacy.[3] Throughout the world, the post–World War II era was a time of "brute force" engineering to manipulate the natural world, of which hydroelectric and industrial projects were integral.[4] In Latin America, populist leaders also used engineering projects as a way to increase local support. Argentina's Juan Perón during the 1940s, for example, used post-earthquake disaster reconstruction and aid to bolster his political support.[5] At the same time, import substitution industrialization (usually referred to simply as ISI) offered a new economic model that promoted national self-sufficiency within Latin America.

President Odría understood these larger contexts for Cañón del Pato and the Santa Corporation, recognizing that they could boost his appeal and thrust Peru forward economically. He promptly enlisted scientists and engineers to put the country back on track after the Los Cedros disaster. But the evolution of flood control during the 1950s and 1960s was not simply a story of state-designed engineering practices imposed on local residents.[6] Nor was it a triumphant tale of experts engineering the Andes and manipulating the natural world to fulfill developers' or state agendas. Instead, the historical development of innovative science and technology to prevent glacial lake outburst floods involved continuous dialogue not only between humans and the physical environment, but also among local residents, engineers, water developers, state officials, and, occasionally, foreign scientists and mountaineers.[7]

Icons of Modernity: The Santa Corporation and Cañón Del Pato

The Los Cedros glacial lake catastrophe makes sense only after first recognizing the importance of the Peruvian government's Santa Corporation and its Cañón del Pato hydroelectric facility—and the influence of these icons on the politics of disaster prevention. Of course, part of the motivation for prompt state action stemmed from scientists' recognition that the 1950 glacial lake outburst flood revealed a clear pattern of Cordillera Blanca natural disasters, not just a fluke flood. Acknowledging the high likelihood of additional disasters, government officials saw the urgency of controlling the swelling glacial lakes beneath melting glaciers. But, as is generally the case with natural disaster response, scientific explanations and the environmental events themselves provided only partial motivation for government action. It was the confluence of science, politics, and economics that motivated government response to the 1950 flood. After all, a host of researchers had been warning the country about unstable glacial lakes for a decade. What was different about the Los Cedros disaster was its decisive impact on Lima policymakers and developers.

In the decades following World War II, many Latin American countries pursued an economic plan driven by ISI principles, which involved using natural resources and manufacturing goods within Latin America to avoid the previous reliance on foreign imports. It sought to end developing countries' global position solely as exporters of raw materials. Initially emerging during the global depression created by the 1929 economic catastrophe, ISI offered a way for Latin Americans to retain more autonomy and insulate their economies from fluctuations in international markets controlled by Europe and North America. Policymakers and economists, however, pursued ISI most systematically during the 1950s and 1960s, in response to various factors. First, Latin America was undergoing major demographic shifts by the mid-twentieth century: rapid urbanization and growing working class populations in the expanding cities provided a labor force necessary for industrialization. Second, Latin American economies improved during World War II, providing more capital to invest in industry than during previous decades. Finally, in 1948, the Argentine economist Raúl Prebisch advocated the theory and practice of ISI to the United

FIGURE 3.1. Cañón del Pato hydroelectric station, 2003.
Credit: Photo by Mark Carey.

Nations Economic Commission for Latin America. As director of this commission, Prebisch exerted considerable influence throughout Latin America. For the next several decades, Latin American nations adhered to ISI objectives, with countries like Brazil, Argentina, Mexico, and Chile making the most noteworthy advances.

Peru did not promote ISI as strongly as did its South American neighbors, but the country nonetheless encouraged industrialization and supported some development projects similar to ISI programs. The Santa Corporation was a classic example of an ISI-type project. During the 1940s, President Prado aspired to invigorate national industry more than his predecessors had (or successors would), and he created the Santa Corporation on June 4, 1943. The state-funded Santa Corporation, like the Amazon Corporation and other national programs, involved a comprehensive plan for economic development, self-sufficiency, and national modernization. Using the U.S. Tennessee Valley Authority as a model, the state created the Santa Corporation to "develop and exploit the mineral and industrial resources that come directly and indirectly from the Santa River region and its tributaries."[8]

The mission of the Peruvian Santa Corporation was, in short, to bring economic progress to the Ancash Department and to Peru as a whole.[9] As the corporation later explained, it was "a national company with the purpose of coordinating and promoting the development of a wealthy region of the country into a primordial source of energy."[10] Lima and Ancash residents, especially those who would be getting electricity for their homes and communities, saw the program's potential. The Huaraz newspaper *El Departamento* expressed continual support for hydroelectric development and coastal irrigation projects. In 1950, the paper referred to unused water flowing into the ocean as "wasted," asserting that Santa River valley irrigation and agriculture would help turn Chimbote into "one of the best ports on the Peruvian coast and, with time, it will undoubtedly be a port of enormous magnitude, not only in our country but in South America."[11] Another commentator believed the corporation's broad agenda would stimulate "progress not only for the Callejón de Huaylas but for the entire Peruvian economy. It signifies firm and secure steps toward competition with other countries."[12] Success of the Santa Corporation, however, hinged on completion of the Cañón del Pato hydroelectric station. Without this electricity from the glacier-fed Santa River, the company would have no energy to power the industrial factories in Chimbote, no electricity to light homes in the new urban zone of Chimbote, and no electrification in the Callejón de Huaylas to demonstrate Peruvians' ability to exploit water resources and modernize the country.

Cañón del Pato offered an ideal site to generate hydroelectricity because in this short canyon the Santa River valley narrows into a precipitous, winding gorge only a few dozen meters wide with nearly vertical walls that jut straight up hundreds of meters. In the course of 13 kilometers, the Santa River falls more than 500 meters through Cañón del Pato. In the early twentieth century, Santiago Antúnez de Mayolo identified the canyon as a lucrative site for hydroelectricity generation. In 1913, after studying engineering in France, he had returned to his hometown of Aija at the north end of the Callejón de Huaylas with a new perspective on the Santa River and Cañón del Pato. He mapped the narrow canyon, drew up preliminary plans for power generation, and even formed the Cañón del Pato Hydroelectric Company. The company never materialized, but Antúnez de Mayolo had publicized the canyon's hydroelectric potential, and he always remained cognizant of the Santa River's tremendous power. Others, too, recognized the potential value of the Santa's abundant water flowing through a steep, narrow canyon.

By 1940, water developers were again discussing construction of the hydroelectric station. Thirty-five lawmakers from the Peruvian congress spearheaded a national government plan to study the engineering project. The Peruvian government not only asked Antúnez de Mayolo to revise his technical plans for Cañón del Pato, but it also contracted Barton M. Jones, the engineer who oversaw construction of the Tennessee Valley Authority's Norris Dam. Both proposed to construct Peru's largest hydroelectric plant at the time, which would put at least 100 megawatts of electricity on line. By 1941, the wealthy Swedish investor Axel Wenner Gren, who was in Cusco for archaeological research, had also become intrigued with Cañón del Pato. He agreed to invest $15 million in the project, but his support evaporated in late 1941 when the United States froze his assets. It was then that President Prado decided the government should finance the project, but the Peruvian Santa Corporation was not actually created until 1943.[13]

Though President Odría pursued more traditional export-oriented economic policies than President Prado, Odría nonetheless supported the Santa Corporation and saw the importance of Cañón del Pato for Peru. It was, after all, his keen interest in the hydroelectric station that motivated his immediate and far-reaching response to the Los Cedros flood. Born into a military family in the Central Andes city of Tarma in 1897, Odría remained in Peru's armed forces throughout his career. His emergence as a hero during the 1941 border war with Ecuador helped win him an appointment in President Bustamante's cabinet in 1947. But Odría, and many others, soon turned against the president. In 1948, after leading the coup that toppled Bustamante's government, Odría named himself president, stalling elections until 1950. Inspired by Argentine President Juan Perón's populism and public works projects, Odría realized that he could increase his support among Peruvians—and thus exercise greater autonomy from the conservative oligarchy—by promoting public works and other social policies that appealed to the urban poor, the middle class, and other nonelite constituencies. He devoted particular attention and financial resources to the coastal agro-commercial sector. During his presidency, Odría focused on several specific projects, including enhanced irrigation works along the Quiroz River and in northern Peru generally, improved facilities and functioning of the port

Cañon del Pato power plant—step towards modernity

at Callao, road building along the coast and through the Andes, and funding for the Santa Corporation to complete both the Cañón del Pato hydroelectric station and the iron and steel factories in Chimbote.[14]

Even while supporting an export economy reminiscent of traditional liberalism rather than strict ISI policies, Odría nonetheless saw the Santa Corporation as a vital national project, especially in the last years of his presidency. What's more, because Odría encouraged laissez-faire export-led growth and started paying Peru's national debt for the first time since 1930, he provided an appropriate financial climate for foreign investment, in particular French funding for both the reconstruction of Cañón del Pato and the construction of a Chimbote steel mill. Though Odría's enthusiasm for the Santa Corporation waned from 1952 to 1954, he nonetheless revitalized the corporation's activities after 1954, when he appointed Max Peña Prado, a relative of former President Prado, as its director. It was this renewed dedication to the Santa Corporation, as well as a nudge from French funders, that ultimately stimulated completion of Cañón del Pato. When it opened in January 1958, it put 50 megawatts of electricity on line and immediately became one of the country's most important hydroelectric plants. The Chimbote steel mills, however, did not experience such success, and it was clear by the 1960s that they were not booming.[15] The Cañón del Pato power plant was no Aswan or Hoover Dam, but for Peru it represented an important step toward modernity.

Amid an international climate of ISI and "brute force" engineering to control nature and extract natural resources, the Santa Corporation inspired Lima and Ancash with hydroelectric and industrial fantasies.[16] Policymakers believed that the Los Cedros flood had dealt a significant blow not only to the country's ambitious industrialization and modernization programs, but also to Peru's global standing. Odría responded immediately. As a military leader, he possessed the concentrated political power to create legislation and fund a Cordillera Blanca natural disaster prevention agency to protect Santa Corporation interests in the future. With both power and will, he established a national government agency, the Control Commission of Cordillera Blanca Lakes, to oversee glacial lake studies, monitoring, and disaster prevention projects in Ancash. Political economy shaped the evolution of glacial lake science and engineering during the 1950s and after.

Knowledge and Science Converging at Lake Jankarurish

Well before the Los Cedros flood, Peruvian authorities had received warnings about Lake Jankarurish from local residents, mountaineers, and foreign scientists. Government officials relied on these unofficial reports because, although the 1941 and 1945 outburst floods had generated a few lake studies and reconnaissance trips, the Cordillera Blanca remained for most Peruvians a remote, unexplored region. And the Los Cedros Canyon was in one of the most isolated parts of the Cordillera Blanca. By the late 1940s, Limeño engineers' studies augmented local information and mountaineers' observations to persuade the national government to drain Jankarurish.

Lake Jankarurish, also called Lake Alpamayo in the mid-twentieth century, lies at the head of the Los Cedros Canyon, a curving valley that rises 20 kilometers and 2,000 vertical meters directly above Cañón del Pato. Located in the Santa Cruz District of the Huaylas Province, the Los Cedros Canyon was named for its great cedar forests. Those who lived, farmed, or tended livestock in the Los Cedros valley were classified on the 1940 census as indigenous: rural, Quechua-speaking, and illiterate. Indigenous people accounted for 84 percent of the Santa Cruz population at the time. With fertile soils and abundant water supplies for irrigation, the district supported sugar cane, flax (the plant used to make linen), yucca, fruit, corn, potatoes, wheat, and barley. Agricultural crops not consumed by local haciendas or independent farmers were generally exported to other Callejón de Huaylas towns or the coast. The district also supported ranching because alfalfa grew easily. By the mid-1940s, Santa Cruz exported between 1,000 and 2,000 cattle to Lima annually.[17]

Though the Los Cedros valley had relatively few population centers in 1950, it was home to many farmers and small-scale ranchers. On that October morning, many were probably feeding their cattle alfalfa, gathering potatoes, or doing chores around their stone homes when Lake Jankarurish bore down on them. In 1951, members of a Franco-Belgian mountaineering team met some of the survivors, residents of a small hamlet a few kilometers below Lake Jankarurish. "An Indian with green teeth and a mouth full of coca leaves bids us welcome," the climbers said. Two of them spent a night with the man's family, sleeping on sheep skins covering the frigid ground next to the entire family, who huddled together under a single poncho. The valley floor where the flood had passed was transformed into a desolate area, plowed out by the flood and topped with a layer of fine sand. Fertile soil and vegetation had been transformed into the bleak "haunt of frisking black bulls, who cast hostile looks at us," the climbers said.[18]

Before the flood, authorities had relied on these local farmers and community leaders for knowledge and information about melting Cordillera Blanca glaciers and lakes. Among those most knowledgeable about Lake Jankarurish were neighbors of the family these European climbers met. Residents of this small hamlet, called Alpamayo, at the head of the Los Cedros Canyon informed authorities in the late 1940s that the lake had been only a puddle 20 years before and had grown continuously since then. By the time government engineer Luis Ghiglino arrived at Alpamayo from Lima to verify local reports and check on the lake in October 1948, the puddle had transformed into a lake 500 meters long and 400 meters wide. Ghiglino recognized the potential danger of Jankarurish, noting in particular its weak moraine dam. Yet he concluded that the dam would only rupture catastrophically if "great blocks of ice" fell directly into the lake, which he thought unlikely.[19]

Residents of the region offered their own explanations for how Lake Jankarurish had formed and enlarged. Long ago, at the foot of Mount Huandoy in the Callejón de Huaylas, a prince named Alpachayllu reigned over a community of noble Indians. Alpachayllu lived a glorious life with his beloved and beautiful wife, Princess Alpamayo. One day a group of Indians from a small, unknown community visited the respected prince, asking if he would teach them how to work effectively and thus escape from their savage way of life. The noble Prince Alpachayllu accepted their offer and followed them to their community, leaving Alpamayo alone and sad. As soon as Alpachayllu reached the other community, they cast a spell on the magnificent leader to prevent him from ever leaving. The curse made him fall in love with a beautiful woman in their own community. Meanwhile, Princess Alpamayo, disgraced by her husband's infidelity, abandoned her community "like a spring flower burned prematurely by frost." She fled to an isolated, rugged place where she stayed and cried incessantly, suffering profoundly from such a cruel fate. Her tears continued to accumulate as she cried until, finally, they "turned into an immense lake." She then disappeared, leaving the lake behind.[20]

Regardless of how one explained the lake's formation, engineers determined in 1948 that Jankarurish could generate an outburst flood. That same year, European mountaineers seeking to climb Mount Alpamayo also noted the lake's instability. Lake Jankarurish lies at the foot of Mount Alpamayo along the approach climbers used, thus making the lake clearly visible to mountaineers. When a previous foreign expedition passed through the region in 1932, there was no lake at all. But when Austrian expedition members Hans Kinzl and Erwin Schneider reflected on their 1930s studies of the Cordillera Blanca, they underscored the problem with the region's glacial lakes in general and Jankarurish in particular. They explained how they had recognized by the late 1930s and 1940s that these lakes "spelt great danger not only to the high valleys, but also to the densely populated main valleys at the foot of the mountains." This became abundantly clear with the 1941 Huaraz disaster. In their book released just one month before the 1950 Los Cedros flood, the authors chose one specific lake among roughly 200 to warn readers about: Jankarurish. Their 1936 photograph of it showed the lake just beginning to form on top of the melting glacier tongue, the lowest section of a glacier. As the glacier continued retreating during the subsequent 14 years, the lake swelled as the melting ice created vacant space for water. "Nowadays," they reported in 1950, "the terminal moraine encloses a great expanse of water which constitutes perhaps the greatest danger to the main valley."[21] Climate change and glacier melting were again concocting a fatal formula.

Swiss mountaineers who tried to climb Mount Alpamayo in 1948 also recognized the danger. These climbers from the Swiss Academic Alpine Club of Zurich, led by Frédéric Marmillod, climbed several Cordillera Blanca mountains and made a nearly catastrophic attempt on Mount Alpamayo. The climbers had managed to negotiate a maze of crevasses and fragile seracs, but just before reaching Alpamayo's summit the team suddenly slipped when a cornice broke from under their feet. The climbers fell nearly 200 vertical meters but escaped with their lives.[22]

Beyond their perilous climb, the Swiss climbers also made observations and notes on the region's glacial lakes. In 1949, Alí de Szepessy Schaurek officially reported the group's conclusions to the Peruvian Institute of Geology in Lima. Szepessy warned in particular about the precarious condition of Lake Jankarurish and its high potential for causing an outburst flood. Because the glacier moraine damming the lake was so weak, Szepessy calculated that "an accident (earthquakes, avalanches of great masses of ice from the glacier, etc.) could destroy the dam. In this case, the whole lake would empty down the entire Los Cedros Canyon, onto the auxiliary electric plant at the foot of the valley and, after that, through Cañón del Pato."[23] Szepessy even went so far as to predict the precise disaster that unfolded in 1950. The Peruvian government did not wait while Jankarurish warnings accumulated. Rather, in 1949, it began draining Lake Jankarurish to avert disaster. Their goal was to lower its water level by several meters, thereby diminishing the likelihood of an outburst flood and reducing the amount of available floodwater in the event that the Jankarurish moraine dam did rupture. The choice to drain it suggests how social knowledge and politics infiltrated engineering projects: locals and mountaineers reported its instability, while the lake's position above Cañón del Pato stimulated action.

Draining Jankarurish, however, was no easy task. The project involved a labor force of between 50 and 100 men and large numbers of porters to transport equipment and materials to the glacial lake by foot or mule. This workforce generally consisted of a head engineer from Lima, foremen from Huaraz or coastal areas, and laborers (usually farmers, *campesinos*) who lived in the immediate vicinity of the lake project. Engineers and foremen referred to these laborers as *laguneros*, or lake people. Sometimes a rural farmer became something of a professional *lagunero*, gaining experience at one lake drainage project and then traveling to others because work in the Cordillera Blanca was so scarce. For example, in 1950, the Ministry of Development officials overseeing the Jankarurish project hired experienced laborers from Macashca near Huaraz, more than 125 kilometers from the Los Cedros Canyon. Foremen also traveled great distances to work at the lakes. Among them were the three Yanac brothers—Guido, Apolonio, and Pedro. The Yanacs lived on the coast before moving to the Callejón de Huaylas in the late 1940s.[24] They initially gained experience working as *laguneros* at Lakes Palcacocha, Shallap, Llaca, and Tullparaju near Huaraz where they lived. They quickly learned enough to manage the local day laborers. As foremen, they also acted as intermediaries between the laborers in the field and the engineers, scientists, and government officials based in Huaraz and Lima.

FIGURE 3.2. Workers digging out a glacial lake outlet, c. 1960.
Credit: Photo by the Comisión de Control de Lagunas de la Cordillera Blanca, courtesy of the Unidad de Glaciología y Recursos Hídricos.

All three Yanac brothers worked at Lake Jankarurish in the weeks leading up to the Los Cedros outburst flood. Apolonio and Pedro were at the lake the morning the moraine dam ruptured. They had been slowly, painstakingly lowering the lake level for months. Given the remoteness of Jankarurish and other Cordillera Blanca glacial lakes, they drained these lakes using only hand tools and materials they could carry on their backs or by mule. At Jankarurish and elsewhere, they constructed wooden floodgates for the lake's outlet stream, which they would put in place in the morning to stop the water flow out of the lake. Then, without water flowing in the streambed, laborers used shovels and pick axes to hack away at the soil, rocks, mud, and boulders, thereby lowering the lake's outlet stream throughout the day. In the evening, they would open the floodgates slightly, allowing some of the lake water to drain out into the now deeper outlet stream. A surge of water would rush out during the evening and night until the lake level matched the lowered streambed. Then they would repeat the process the next day. Men often labored with their ankles or even knees submerged in water. They were always in a frigid climate at high elevation, where the air is so thin that lowlanders gasp and clench their throbbing, oxygen-starved heads. By October 1950, after 18 months of digging and hacking, workers at Jankarurish had made significant progress, lowering the lake's water level approximately 15 meters.[25] Removing this water no doubt reduced the extent of the Los Cedros disaster, but it was not enough to prevent the catastrophe.

The Los Cedros Outburst Flood

According to witnesses, glacial ice and rocks crashed into Lake Jankarurish that October morning. The thunderous crack of splitting ice startled Apolonio and Pedro Yanac and the other 50 men working near the shore. When they heard the violent sound of crashing ice, they ran onto the moraine dam and watched helplessly as the nightmare unfolded in a matter of minutes. Moving glaciers periodically produce snow and ice avalanches on steep slopes. But this particular collapse of part of the glacier was not only large but also directly above the lake. When it splashed into Lake Jankarurish, it generated big waves that thrashed against the moraine dam containing the lake. Workers initially hoped the wooden floodgates they had installed to hold back lake water while they worked would contain the lake. But sloshing waves pushing immense icebergs quickly overpowered both the wooden floodgates and the moraine that had contained the lake during the previous decade.

The Yanac brothers and other horrified workers watched incredulously as ice and water acted with enormous, uncontrollable force. Realizing that they were losing the lake, panicked workers scrambled to pile rocks and debris in the drainage canal to plug the lake's exit. But neither the workers nor the moraine could hold back Jankarurish. Ultimately, the workers had to save themselves. Those at the lake, and those with enough time and foresight, fled to higher ground. As the moraine continued to deteriorate, the water level plummeted 25 meters, draining almost the entire lake as water spilled across the valley floor. In the labor camp a few hundred meters below the lake, some workers hurried frantically to their huts and living quarters, trying to save important items. In a matter of minutes, three and a half million cubic meters of water (nearly a billion gallons) spilled out of Lake Jankarurish and morphed into the infamous Los Cedros outburst flood.[26]

After demolishing the labor camp at Lake Jankarurish, the flood steadily gathered volume on its downhill course toward the Pacific Ocean. Unlike avalanches that can reach speeds above 200 kilometers per hour, outburst floods generally flow relatively slowly, like wet cement. In this case, the churning mixture of water, ice and snow—combined with rocks, trees, mud, buildings, bridges, livestock, and other debris—plowed down the river valley at just 20–40

FIGURE 3.3. Huallanca along the Santa River before the flood, 1948.
Credit: Photo by Peruvian Servicio Aerofotográfico Nacional.

kilometers per hour. The Franco-Belgian mountaineers described the flood's devastation when they visited ten months later: "When the glacial Lake Alpamayo burst its natural dam six million tons of water poured down the narrow valley, tearing rocks and soil from the banks, and flung itself into the bed of the Rio Santa, whose level rose in a few minutes by 300 feet [about 90 meters]. The road, the bridges, and several hydro-electric plants were carried away."[27]

Though the flood devastated the Los Cedros and Santa valleys, the bulk of the death and destruction occurred at Cañón del Pato and Huallanca. Shortly after 10 A.M., the flood plowed into the narrow Cañón del Pato where floodwaters washed away sections of the road and poured into both vehicle and railroad tunnels, corking them with packed mud, rocks, and other debris.[28] The flood destroyed 90 percent of the nearly completed hydroelectric station, including the intake dam, transformer, roads, bridges, tunnels, and other related components. Continuing downstream to Huallanca, it destroyed the hydroelectric power house and the administrative offices and housing units of the Santa Corporation. Huallanca had recently grown as a result of Cañón del Pato construction and its designation as the corporation's regional headquarters. In the mid-1940s, Huallanca had boomed, invigorating the entire Huaylas Province with new investments and jobs.[29] It was here, where Santa Corporation workers and towns-people lived, that most of the flood's 200 fatalities occurred.[30]

Beyond Huallanca, the outburst flood wiped out several parts of the Chimbote-Huallanca railroad, filling tunnels with debris and tearing up tracks. By the time the last remnants of Lake Jankarurish reached the Pacific Ocean—more than 150 kilometers from and 4,500 vertical meters below the glacier where the outburst flood originated—residents north of Chimbote noted increased water flow but reported no damage. Estimates reached U.S. $5 million for total reconstruction costs of Huallanca and Cañón del Pato.[31]

Blaming and Explaining the Flood

In the aftermath of the Los Cedros flood, some Peruvians blamed the workers at Lake Jankarurish—those striving to prevent catastrophe—for causing the outburst flood. Just as residents and experts sought explanations for the 1941 and 1945 outburst floods, they once again assigned blame, this time to people. Santiago Antúnez de Mayolo, for example, condemned the workers; the fore-man, Apolonio Yanac; and, most especially, the head engineer of the Jankarurish project, J. Elias Torres. He complained that the foreman had neglected "the precautions that such a delicate project demanded." He also lambasted Elias Torres, a Water and Irrigation Division engineer, for being in Huaraz, at least a day's trip from the lake, when the disaster occurred. Antúnez de Mayolo believed he should have been supervising at Jankarurish.[32] One lake worker also blamed the engineer, not because of faulty work, but because there was no communication system set up to warn people in Cañón del Pato and Huallanca about the start of the flood.[33] Huallanca had many telephones in 1950, but there were none at Lake Jankarurish.

While censuring the workers for carelessness, Antúnez de Mayolo never recognized the high vulnerability of Huallanca and Cañón del Pato—their dangerous placement on the glacier-fed Santa River—as contributing causes of the natural disaster. Yet, had the flood occurred a decade earlier, before the Santa Corporation existed, the flood might not have even warranted media attention in Lima, to say nothing of concentrated consideration and funding from the president of the republic. As scholars have shown for decades, it is this vulnerable construction that often makes disasters "unnatural," not natural.[34] But Antúnez de Mayolo, who had been dreaming about a hydroelectric plant at Cañón del Pato for nearly half a century, had placed his faith in technology to control and exploit the Santa River. So he pinned the blame on lake workers.

blamed the workers

Other technical analyses of the flood, however, vindicated these workers. Luis Ghiglino, who later became general manager of the Cañón del Pato hydroelectric station, knew more about Cordillera Blanca glacial lakes in 1950 than most other scientists or engineers. He had been studying them for nearly a decade and had first evaluated Lake Jankarurish in 1948. Within days of the disaster, he traveled to Jankarurish to investigate the Los Cedros outburst flood. Arriving at the head of the canyon, he found ice blocks littering the entire valley floor. Three kilometers below the lake, he found blocks up to a cubic meter. Blocks along the lake shore were as large as 120 cubic meters, and those floating in the remaining lake water were enormous icebergs reaching 18,000 cubic meters, the size of a modern-day container ship. These blocks of ice, Ghiglino concluded, could only have come from a huge avalanche or a large piece of the glacier breaking off and crashing into the lake, which would have created waves large enough to wash over and destroy the wooden floodgates. And once the water started running out the lake outlet and over the moraine, it would not have been possible to stop. In other words, just as witnesses explained, the outburst flood was attributable to the huge amount of glacial ice plunging into the lake, not the workers.[35] Besides, Ghiglino noted, workers had been opening the doors in this manner throughout their entire eighteen months of work on the project, with no ensuing flood.

glacier not the workers

Geologist Hans Spann and engineer Jaime Fernández Concha, who were leading members of the Geological Society of Peru, corroborated Ghiglino's findings. They too identified the glacial ice as the catalyst and reported that lesses at the lake saw waves approximately 1.5 meters high that ravaged the _____aine and floodgates. They went further to remove workers from any blame by insisting that the Jankarurish event was something "completely unknown" before it occurred. Previously no one had known about either the size of waves generated by falling ice or these waves' impact on the floodgates used for lake drainage projects. Spann and Fernández Concha believed the eyewitness workers' observations could actually contribute to the safety of future disaster prevention projects. No longer would lake drainage projects rely on wooden floodgates in such a manner. But Antúnez de Mayolo remained annoyed with this Ministry of Development report from Spann and Fernández Concha. Complaining that the authors blamed "only Nature," he wrote bitterly that "our detailed report that must be in the [Santa] Corporation archives explains [what really happened] without euphemisms or palliatives for God and the Devil to know."[36]

In the end, as with most disasters, the physical environment and social forces converged to create catastrophe. Climate change helped create the lake, and the falling ice from an unstable glacier triggered the flood. But it became a disaster because the hydroelectric plant was vulnerably located and because people inhabited the flood's path. Their placement had to do with history, economic development priorities, infrastructure planning, and human decision making at regional, national, and international levels.

The Lakes Commission in the Andes

The disaster aftermath was also driven by political, economic, and scientific forces. The almost religious devotion to developing Cañón del Pato blinded Peruvian developers and policymakers to the hydroelectric plant's highly vulnerable location on the Santa River. Glaciers and glacial lakes were becoming national obstacles to the country's economic development. Leaders turned to science and engineering—as societies do worldwide—to protect both the Santa Corporation and residents from future disasters.

But in 1950, several factors impeded swift action to contain glacial lakes. Continued climate change and glacier retreat through the mid-twentieth century meant that new glacial lakes kept forming and growing behind unstable moraine dams. Peruvian specialists also realized after the Los Cedros flood that neither national nor foreign scientists knew much about the multiple, interrelated environmental forces that created glacial lakes or triggered outburst floods. They would have to invent a new glacial lake classification scheme to determine lake stability. They would also need to create new engineering methods to safely drain and dam dangerous lakes. And they would need to do it quickly in the isolated Cordillera Blanca, where no roads existed to transport equipment or construction materials. As if the physical obstacles to travel and communication were not enough, there was also a psychological barrier between Lima and the Callejón de Huaylas. The French-Belgian mountaineering team mentioned above recognized this division in the early 1950s. "There are few inhabitants of Lima who travel in the interior" of Peru, they said, "and there are possibly more Peruvians who know Paris, New York, and Oxford than Huarás, 250 miles from their capital."[37] Whether these mountaineers knew of the famous Prussian geographer Alexander von Humboldt is unknown, but they reiterated his 1803 observation almost exactly: "Lima is farther from Peru than London," he wrote.[38]

President Odría recognized these obstacles, and on November 13, 1950, he appointed nine scientists, engineers, and government officials to a task force that would recommend specific measures to avoid outburst floods in the future. Specifically, Odría's Study Commission of the Santa Watershed sought first to understand "the phenomenon of Andean glacier retreat" and, second, to prevent "those outburst floods that can damage the works in progress of the Peruvian Santa Corporation, as well as those of the Chimbote-Huallanca Railroad."[39] The president gave this commission two months to visit the Cordillera Blanca region, compile data, and present a detailed report with recommendations for future action.

Two months only allowed the Study Commission to touch on the complexities of glacial lakes and outburst floods. In late 1950, nobody even knew how many lakes existed in the Cordillera Blanca. Researchers had only examined geomorphologic, geological, glaciological, and hydrological conditions at a handful of these lakes. Aerial photographs taken between 1948 and 1950 enriched specialists' knowledge of the Cordillera Blanca terrain and helped pinpoint glacial lake locations. But often, the mere identification of a lake did not provide conclusive evidence about its stability or potential for producing an outburst flood. Ascertaining those details required visiting the lakes on foot. These trips often entailed more than a day's walk up steep slopes, through dense vegetation, over precarious boulder fields, through raging streams, and around landslides— all at 4,000 to 5,000 meters above sea level. Worse, with new lakes forming every year at the foot of retreating glaciers, researchers had to maintain constant vigilance over the Cordillera Blanca's approximately 700 glaciers and 200 lakes spread over an area the size of Delaware. In early 1951, exasperated members of the Study Commission of the Santa Watershed recommended that Odría create a permanent government agency to study and monitor glacial lakes and to conduct engineering projects to prevent outburst floods.[40]

President Odría responded favorably to the commission's recommendation, and on February 20, 1951, he established Peru's first state agency charged
specifically and solely with analyzing glaciers and glacial lakes and taking measures to prevent future outburst floods.[41] The president appointed Pablo Boner
as head of this Control Commission of Cordillera Blanca Lakes and allocated
100,000 Peruvian soles for studies and projects at glacial lakes during 1951.[42]
This Lakes Commission established its central office in Lima and a branch
office in Huaraz to oversee projects in the Cordillera Blanca. Staff in Huaraz
included professional scientists and engineers, office personnel, 100–150
laborers (depending on the time of year), and various contractors who built
roads and labor camps at glacial lakes.[43]

Unlike the government's sporadic, poorly funded, and loosely organized
lake monitoring and drainage projects of the 1940s, the Lakes Commission of
the 1950s became a structured state agency that actively sought to prevent outburst floods throughout the Cordillera Blanca. In 1951, Lakes Commission managers identified three major problems they needed to overcome. First, the
commission needed a comprehensive glacial lake inventory to know where
Cordillera Blanca lakes existed and how many there were. Second, scientists and
engineers recognized the need for a classification system outlining specific characteristics to determine precisely which lakes were dangerous and which ones
were stable. Third, they needed to develop engineering plans to drain and dam
the dangerous glacial lakes, and they needed to overcome logistical and administrative obstacles to carry out what came to be known as "lake security projects."
Historians of science and technology have stressed Latin American advances in
the post–World War II period.[44] Few, however, have analyzed geology, glaciology, or hydrology. Yet, as the Lakes Commission would show, Peruvians also
excelled in their "creole science" beneath melting Andean glaciers.

A Glacial Lake Inventory

To identify the most pressing natural hazards, the Lakes Commission first
needed a detailed, complete inventory of the hundreds of glacial lakes hidden in
remote canyons, perched at extremely high elevations, and scattered throughout
the vast Cordillera Blanca. Aerial photographs from the Peruvian National Aerial
Photography Service offered an ideal starting point. Founded in 1942 within the
Aerial Photography Division of the Peruvian Air Force, this agency had taken
photographs in various parts of the country, including the Cordillera Blanca
from 1948 to 1950. In 1951 and 1952, Lakes Commission engineers and scientists began to analyze these photographs. Specialists were able to pinpoint lakes

with less reliance on local residents, mountaineers, or specific scientific expeditions that visited lakes in person. To find the glacial lakes growing most rapidly and thus posing particularly dangerous situations, Lakes Commission experts compared the service's images with thousands of photographs taken by the Austro-German expeditions of 1932, 1936, and 1939. To compensate for gaps in photographic coverage, they took more aerial photographs in August 1952.[45]

By 1953, the Lakes Commission had created a comprehensive glacial lake inventory of the Cordillera Blanca. This first inventory identified 223 total lakes in the Cordillera Blanca, with the majority (160) on the Santa River side.[46] Starting on the west side of the Cordillera Blanca, in the Santa River watershed, the Lakes Commission numbered these lakes beginning at "1"; on the east side, in the Marañón River watershed, they began numbering at 300. A lake's number code thus indicated geographical location as well as its name. A subsequent inventory that officials completed in 1962, again relying on both the photography service's aerial photographs and individual reconnaissance trips into the Cordillera Blanca, identified 263 lakes, an increase of 40 lakes in a decade.[47] On this second inventory, as well as subsequent ones, cartographers added letters to lake numbers when a new lake formed nearby or beneath the same glacier where a previous lake existed. For example, Lake Safuna on the 1952 inventory was Lake 29. When they discovered a new lake had formed above the previous lake, they called it Lake 29a, or Upper Lake Safuna, on the 1962 inventory.

 In recent years, social scientists have critiqued mapping, surveying, and photographic projects just like those the Lakes Commission carried out during the 1950s and 1960s. Scholars argue that maps produce power and that mapping has thus historically served the interests of empires and states or those who make the maps.[48] Peruvian engineers in the Cordillera Blanca no doubt expanded Lima's knowledge of and control over highland Ancash. Moreover, engineers' cultural impulse to quantify the environment with numerical depictions—rather than using local, historically grounded place names or relying on personal interaction with the environment—introduces a new way of understanding nature. For engineers and government officials, the supposedly objective quantification of physical environments often demonstrated the efficacy of Western science and engineering over local folk knowledge.[49] Mapping, surveying, and producing an inventory of Cordillera Blanca glaciers and glacial lakes followed a similar trajectory as these other historical cases worldwide. When the Peruvian government photographed every piece of a remote region and assigned numerical numbers to local place names, it also brought the arm of the state into secluded canyons and communities, which in turn yielded data to help the government control both territory and hydrology.

But the story in the Cordillera Blanca was more complex, and the turn to numbers less strict. Cordillera Blanca glacial lakes and glaciated mountains retained their mixed Spanish and Quechua names. *Cocha* means "lake" in Quechua (or *laguna* in Spanish); *raju* means "snow-covered peak" (*nevado* in Spanish). Tocllaraju thus means Trap Mountain: the Quechua word *toclla* means "trap" in English or *trampa* in Spanish. Laguna Cuchillacocha translates as Knife Lake.[50] Cordillera Blanca lake naming has involved Spanish and Quechua words as well as both local, scientific, and government naming practices. Though the numbering system remains today, few scientists, engineers, or residents refer to the numbers. In very few cases, such as Lake 69 or Lake 513a, people utilize these number names almost exclusively. Generally, though, the local place names remain in place, not only in common spoken usage but also in technical reports. In fact, Peruvian glacier expert Alcide Ames amended a 1980s national inventory to add local Andean names for glaciers and glacial lakes. Naming in Cordillera Blanca lake inventories demonstrated the hybridization of local knowledge and Western science. Just as local knowledge about Lake Jankarurish and other glacial lakes appeared in technical reports and scientific papers, local place naming has also remained integral to state maps and the Lakes Commission inventory. At the same time, though, the glacial lake inventory did enhance state knowledge of the region and its hydrological resources. This information later helped serve the related processes of national territorial integration and economic development in Ancash. The Santa Corporation and its successor Electroperú utilized the water data for decades. Lake inventories provided these state corporations with details about the best and safest places for reservoir construction, and runoff data contributed to their understanding of Santa River hydrology. The information therefore served state and development interests, which in the late 1990s transferred to the private company Duke Energy. But the details also saved countless lives by preventing glacial lake catastrophes.

The Politics of Disaster Prediction in Caraz

At the same time that Lakes Commission specialists analyzed photographs to create their lake inventory, they also came to realize—after narrowly avoiding a catastrophic outburst flood in late 1951—that a simple inventory plotting lake locations was insufficient. In July 1951, tragedy nearly struck at Lake Artesoncocha, surprising scientists and making them realize that they lacked comprehensive understandings of glacial lake dynamics. Lake Artesoncocha, like Jankarurish and so many of the dangerous Cordillera Blanca lakes, formed during the 1930s and grew rapidly through the 1940s.[51] Artesoncocha lies at the top of a short valley that rises above the head of Lake Parón, which lies directly above Caraz, one of the most populous towns in the Callejón de Huaylas. The largest Cordillera Blanca lake, Parón contained between 50 million and 80 million cubic meters of water in 1951, more than 20 times the amount of water in the Los Cedros flood.[52] To be sure, an outburst flood from Parón would have created a catastrophe of unimaginable proportions.

By the time the Lakes Commission was developing its glacial lake inventory in the early 1950s, Caraz residents had been worrying about an outburst flood from Lake Parón for more than a decade. Although technical studies of Parón in the 1940s suggested its moraine dam was secure, Luis Ghiglino had expressed concern about Lake Artesoncocha.[53] When he first visited Artesoncocha in 1947, he saw constant rockfalls and icefalls from the retreating glacier and worried about the lake's long-term stability. He also noted that Artesoncocha had space to grow into an enormous lake if the glacier kept melting.[54] A year later, he returned to the lake with Federico Stein. They concluded that "although Parón's dam is in good condition and not presently in danger of bursting, other agents could intervene in the future, one of those being the rupture of Lake Artesoncocha."[55] By 1951, Artesoncocha was three-quarters of a kilometer long and nearly a half-kilometer wide. If Artesoncocha produced an outburst flood, experts worried, the rush of water would inundate and possibly destabilize Lake Parón.

On July 17, 1951, Juan Pacheco, a watchman stationed at Lake Parón to monitor lake conditions, awoke to find that the lake had swelled dramatically, rising nearly a meter during the night. Pacheco also found "a great quantity" of trees and other floating debris jammed up against the moraine dam at the lake outlet. Pacheco and his companion were part of a government-funded surveillance program with teams placed at Parón the year before. Though hired to keep watch over the immense Lake Parón, the watchmen had not really expected to confront an imminent problem. Now, Pacheco and his companion worried about this mysterious influx of extra water and debris. Panicked by the prospect of an immediate outburst flood and scared for their own lives, the watchmen descended hurriedly to inform authorities in Caraz. There was no road to Parón in 1951, and the two watchmen had to descend carefully, negotiating the tangle of thicket and rough ground in the upper canyon. Finally, after hiking 30 kilometers and dropping 2,000 vertical meters from Lake Parón, the two watchmen reached Caraz, alerted local authorities, and immediately called engineers in Lima.[56]

Luis Ghiglino and geologist Hans Spann instantly recognized the gravity of the situation: the inundation into Parón could signify the first signs of an "unspeakable tragedy." Ghiglino and Spann prepared their materials and raced toward Caraz. It took a week. Once in Caraz, they lost an additional two days preparing the necessary food, supplies, and equipment for their expedition and finding enough mules to transport everything to Lake Parón. Finally, on July 28, they arrived at the lake. They found Parón in relatively stable condition, despite the influx of more than 1 million cubic meters of water. Given their previous studies and knowledge of Parón, they suspected the flood had originated at Lake Artesoncocha, above the upper end of Parón. Lake Parón stretches across the entire valley, walled in on both sides by sheer, towering cliffs. Geologist Parker Trask would later compare this valley to Yosemite in California, though in Parón's case the lake filled the entire valley floor. The vertical cliffs make stunning scenery, but they posed challenging obstacles for scientific research. Walking to Artesoncocha was impossible because of these cliffs lining both sides the lake. Instead, Ghiglino and Spann covered the three kilometer length of Parón by boat, brought to the lake by mule. Negotiating the trees and other floating debris—and worrying about a potential rupture of the lake—they maneuvered their rowboat to Parón's upper end. There they found a massive scar where the July 17 flood had erased all vegetation and left fine, light-colored sand and rocks spread out much wider than the streambed. The scar ran up the valley toward Artesoncocha, three kilometers above Parón.

Conditions at Lake Artesoncocha startled Ghiglino and Spann. The July inundation had clearly originated at Artesoncocha. Worse, the moraine dam barely contained the lake's remaining 4 million cubic meters of water. "Its rupture is imminent," they reported, "and the falling of just one block of glacial ice would be enough to trigger it."[57] Worse still, they believed Lake Parón might not be able to absorb a second outburst flood from Artesoncocha. Ghiglino and Spann were so worried about the situation they did not even stay long enough to take measurements or conduct detailed studies. Instead they hurried down and outlined several measures to "initiate immediately": draining Artesoncocha, lowering Parón's water level, and improving communications between the lakes and Caraz by building a road and running a telegraph line. Two months later, as engineers began their projects, another potential Artesoncocha nightmare began to unfold.

On October 27, 1951, just as the rainy season began, Lake Artesoncocha again burst through its moraine and sent 2.8 million cubic meters of water into Lake Parón.[58] A decade of debate about whether Parón's dam was stable was now being tested. Between July and October 1951, 4 million cubic meters of additional water—more than the total volume from Jankarurish in the Los Cedros flood—had inundated Lake Parón. Worse, as the rainy season wore on, Parón kept rising. The lake level rose to within ten centimeters of its brim. Lakes Commission engineers at Parón maintained constant radio contact with authorities in Caraz and with Santa Corporation officials at Huallanca and Cañón del Pato.[59] They had learned the value of communications after the Los Cedros disaster, when lake workers were unable to warn Santa Corporation officials about the impending flood.

Meanwhile, agitated residents in Caraz wondered what was happening at the lake that literally loomed over their heads. On January 31, 1952, many of these people attended a public meeting to hear reports from J. Elias Torres, the regional director of the Lakes Commission, and other Ministry of Development engineers from Lima who had just completed their technical analysis of Parón. These experts reassured the audience that, contrary to the rumors spreading through Caraz, Lake Parón offered no possible danger of an outburst flood. They disclosed details about the two recent outbursts from Lake Artesoncocha, but said these had only slightly raised Parón's water level. Besides, they had stationed guards at the lake with two radios to maintain direct communications between Parón and municipal offices in Caraz.[60] The engineers emphasized that people should not worry about Parón or an outburst flood. Residents, however, remained skeptical. They worried about a repeat of the mid-1940s when engineers had said no danger existed—and then the Chavín disaster occurred.

In fact, these experts' public declaration of safety and stability at Lake Parón contradicted their technical report produced for the Ministry of Development and Public Works. On January 23, 1952, just one week before their public meeting, the ministry's report called Lake Parón and other Cordillera Blanca glacial lakes a "situation of incessant danger." The report went on to suggest that the Artesoncocha outburst in the dry season had surprised experts because such an event had "never" previously occurred. Finally, quoting Pablo Boner, the Lima-based director of the Lakes Commission and one of the country's leading engineers, the report even acknowledged that "technically, it is impossible to consolidate the moraine dams that contain the lakes with 100 percent effectiveness due to the continually unstable condition of glaciers and, as a result, the persistent variation in the lake systems."[61] At the same time, ministry engineers told the public there was no danger. Within only a few weeks of their public statement about lake stability and safety for the Caraz population, the ministry and Lakes Commission sent emergency workers to Lake Parón, where they began frantically filling thousands of sandbags to construct a massive temporary retaining wall to hold back the dangerous lake.

Caraz residents must have detected the blatant contradictions. In early February 1952, at the height of the rainy season, the Caraz parish priest, Padre Araujo Ramírez, led 300 residents and local authorities on a 30-kilometer trek to Lake Parón. The group carried a statue of their venerated patron saint of Caraz, the Virgin of Chiquiaquirá. Placing the statue on the lake shore, the priest said mass in the frigid cold of the Cordillera Blanca. The priest then made his appeal

FIGURE 3.4. Investigating the high water level in Lake Parón, 1952.
Credit: Photo by the Comisión de Control de Lagunas de la Cordillera Blanca, courtesy of the
Unidad de Glaciología y Recursos Hídricos.

directly to God "for the entire Caraz population." He hoped that their visit had
awakened the spirit that could calm Parón in the same way that "Christ calmed the
sea at the request of his disciples."[62] Parón remained intact through the remainder
of that rainy season, and the emergency sandbag wall was never tested. By October
1952, a year after the second Artesoncocha flood, the lake level had dropped two
and a half meters below its brim. At that point, the Lakes Commission announced
that Parón's dam was "completely secure."[63] Some experts remained less confident about Parón, however.[64] The region had barely escaped tragedy.

Lake Artesoncocha's two floods perplexed engineers and revealed both the
challenges of accurate glacial lake classification and the politics of hazard assess-
ments. Government engineers suppressed information about lake instability.
They conveyed an attitude of control and a condition of environmental security
even though their own findings were inconclusive. Previous outburst floods had
all occurred during the wet season. As a result, most experts believed that precipitation contributed to lake instability and outburst floods. Artesoncocha defied this
theory by bursting at the height of the dry season, when Cordillera Blanca lake
levels were at their lowest. Artesoncocha's moraine dam failure also overturned

another previous assumption. Before 1951, scientists thought only steeply sloped moraines could rupture. Artesoncocha, on the other hand, had a very flat moraine, with a slope of just 11 percent. Ghiglino and Spann remarked that "until now, this type of lake dam was not considered to be in a precarious state."[65] Evidently, Lakes Commission experts needed new criteria to identify dangerous glacial lakes.

A Glacial Lake Classification System

Developing a glacial lake classification system required detailed knowledge of each lake's geomorphologic conditions, especially the positions of glaciers above each lake and the type of lake dam.[66] Though Peruvian engineers created their classification system in the early 1950s, authorities sought additional assistance from foreign experts trained in applied geology. In early 1952, Fernando Berckemeyer, the Peruvian ambassador to the United States, began searching for engineers who could help. He asked the Peruvian Consul General in San Francisco, who in turn suggested Parker Trask, a geologist and engineering researcher at the University of California at Berkeley. Trask was just the type of quick-learning applied scientist who could help Peruvian geologists and engineers. He accompanied Lakes Commission specialists and Santa Corporation officials through a comprehensive analysis of Cordillera Blanca glacial lakes in July and August 1952. They flew above every canyon of the range to observe existing lakes and scout for new ones. Trask also visited many of the lakes on foot, making his way systematically through the Cordillera Blanca from Lake Querococha in the south to Lake Parón at the north end of the Callejón de Huaylas. Access to lakes in the far north of the Cordillera Blanca remained difficult because the Los Cedros flood had destroyed roads, trails, bridges, and the Chimbote-Huallanca railroad.[67]

Partly with Trask's assistance, but mostly through the Lakes Commission's and other Peruvian specialists' own accomplishments and insights, the Lakes Commission finalized its lake classification system by 1953, just in time to categorize all 223 lakes in the Cordillera Blanca inventory. The system identified several characteristics to determine lake stability: whether the lake was touching the glacier, the type of lake dam (rock, gravel, or moraine), and the slope of the lake dam (steep or gentle). They determined that lakes touching a glacier with a steeply sloped moraine dam were the most precarious, whereas those with a gently sloped rock dam and not touching glacial ice were the most stable lakes. Trask made further distinctions by recognizing that all lakes with more than 5 million cubic meters of water posed risks for local residents and infrastructure simply because of the scale of destruction that would result from an outburst flood with so much water. He also explained that lake dams formed of glacial ice were particularly dangerous because they could melt or move. Using

FIGURE 3.5.   Lake Rajucolta (1.5 km. long) with glacier tongue touching lake, 2003.
Credit: Photo by Mark Carey.

this classification system, the Lakes Commission identified 35 unstable lakes, 25 of which required immediate control. The classification system remains a powerful tool today to evaluate new and expanding glacial lakes worldwide.[68]

Draining and Damming

Along with the completion of lake inventories and classification systems, the Lakes Commission also began "lake security projects," the partial draining and damming of the region's most unstable lakes. First, they lowered lake levels either by digging open canals through relatively stable moraines or by constructing drainage tunnels under the more unstable moraine dams, such as at Lake Tullparaju in the 1950s and at Lakes Safuna Alta and Parón in subsequent decades. Second, the Lakes Commission built cement or earthen dams at lake outlets to strengthen existing moraines. These artificial dams, usually 8 to 20 meters high, helped prevent the erosion of natural moraines containing lakes. Engineers designed them to withstand waves created by giant chunks of glacial ice crashing into lakes. At the base of each concrete dam, engineers also installed a drainage pipe two or three meters in diameter to allow constant lake draining and thus avoid filling the lake beyond that point. Engineers did not, however, design these dams to regulate water flow or to hold back water in a reservoir. They were security dams.[69]

FIGURE 3.6. Lake Cuchillacocha with security dam, 2008.
Credit: Photo by Jeffrey Bury.

Beyond technical problems involving retreating glaciers and dangerous lakes, the Lakes Commission also faced administrative and management issues in the 1950s and 1960s. Management conflicts arose partly because the national government was unwilling to relinquish control of state agencies to satellite offices in the highlands. From the outset, the Lakes Commission managers in Lima oversaw Cordillera Blanca research and engineering projects. Even the Huaraz office engineers were from Lima originally. Management of the Lakes Commission did not shift to an Ancash resident until the Santa Corporation's Glaciology and Lakes Security Office took over in 1966. Through the 1950s and much of the 1960s, professional engineers and bureaucrats from Lima over-saw the Lakes Commission, its lake inventories and classification system, its engineering projects, and its financial and technical resources. In 1953, for example, when President Odría restructured the commission, he assigned engineers with high-level bureaucratic positions to run the Lakes Commission from Lima, while placing other well-known Lima experts in the Huaraz office. Jaime Fernández Concha, head of the Geology Division of the Ministry of Development's National Institute of Mining Research and Development, became the executive member of the Lakes Commission, and César Sotillo, head of the Mining Division of the Ministry of Development's National Institute of Mining Research and Development, became the commission's advising member. In Huaraz, José Ayllón supervised the office, Daniel Delgado acted as assistant manager, and Armin Hoempler worked as the cartographer.[70] The bulk of the labor force for lake security projects, however, consisted of Ancash residents, mostly from the Callejón de Huaylas and surrounding communities. The workforce of between 100 and 150 laborers also fluctuated seasonally, slowing progress on trail building, labor camp construction, and disaster miti-gation projects. With decisions emanating from Lima, passing through a Huaraz office manager, and reaching the lakes by way of an engineer who had given directions to the foreman responsible for overseeing both daily opera-tions and the dozens of laborers, there were many misunderstandings, road-blocks, and detours—as well as power struggles and incompetence. Even the Huaraz newspaper *El Departmento* argued that the Lakes Commission regional office should exercise greater autonomy from Lima. One writer urged the com-mission's director and president to live and work in Huaraz, where they could carry out disaster prevention measures more quickly and efficiently.[71]

In subsequent years, Lakes Commission engineers themselves echoed these sentiments for independence from Lima. Luis Ghiglino, for instance, noted in 1962 that the technical experts should not be confined to Lima and that the executive director should work from the Huaraz office to ensure safe execution of delicate lake security projects. There was not sufficient expertise in geology, glaciology, cartography, or climatology, Ghiglino maintained, to understand adequately the evolving complexity of glacier and glacial lake dynamics. Without well-trained scientists and engineers working constantly in the Cordillera Blanca, the Lakes Commission, he believed, ran the risk of simply draining lakes rather than also increasing scientific understandings of the complex relationships among climate, glaciers, geology, and hydrology.[72] Later, in 1962, the Lakes Commission manager of the Huaraz office, Miguel Elías Pizarro, offered different reasons to enhance his office's autonomy. If his office was not so encumbered by "administrative bureaucrats" from the Irrigation Division of the Ministry of Development, he asserted, the Lakes Commission would be able to complete necessary work more efficiently. Elías Pizarro also maintained that more autonomy from Lima would help keep the regional population calm. With potential floods and frequent false alarms, he wanted to be able to distribute information to the public in a timely manner without first seeking approval from Lima officials.[73] That struggle persists today.

By the late 1960s, the Lakes Commission had completed two dozen engineering projects to stabilize remote glacial lakes, significantly reducing the risk of outburst floods. In spite of shortages of money, scant information, limited scientific knowledge, and few technological resources, the Lakes Commission pioneered new scientific research, invented new technologies, and implemented new engineering designs. It created an applied strategy to engineer the Andes. Almost certainly, government efforts prevented additional outburst floods, saved lives, and protected infrastructure. Local people mostly supported these projects. Their primary complaints centered on sharing information about lakes with the public, draining lakes faster, and draining more lakes. They thus challenged the Lakes Commission's speed and diplomacy rather than its fundamental approach to disaster prevention.

The number of Cordillera Blanca lakes doubled to more than 400 in the half century after the first inventory was completed in 1953. After the Los Cedros disaster, smaller floods burst out of these precarious glacial lakes, but none caused more than a handful of deaths or major infrastructure damage. The Lakes Commission deserves significant credit for its successful fight against melting ice. The institution's activities declined during the 1960s, however, because of budget cuts and reduced political support. By 1968, the Santa Corporation's new Glaciology and Lakes Security Office had eclipsed the Lakes Commission. President Velasco officially dissolved the commission in 1971, leaving Cordillera Blanca disaster prevention in the hands of the state hydroelectric company, Electroperú, which succeeded the Santa Corporation.[74] Politics and economics would then influence science and engineering in new ways to shape the course of disaster mitigation.

Historians have often overlooked the contributions of Latin American states to public security, usually characterizing them as interventionist entities using science to impose their power on people and remote regions.[75] But Lakes Commission achievements indicate how the Peruvian government protected people from environmental hazards. Climate change and glacier disasters affected the state's role in the Andes, though mid-twentieth-century economic development and Peruvian politics also influenced institutional responses. An outcome of this increased state presence in the Cordillera Blanca was the transfer of responsibility for disaster prevention from locals to the nation-state. President Prado initiated this process in the 1940s, but Odría and the Lakes Commission carried it out. This nationalization of natural disaster is not to suggest that local actors had no say in the process or its outcome. Many groups—from local farmers and foreign mountaineers to Limeño geologists—shaped the particular glacier science and glacial lake engineering that occurred during the 1950s and 1960s. Glacial lake engineering protected people while serving state and economic development interests.

Even with much local support for state-controlled lake engineering projects, Lakes Commission activities in the 1950s and 1960s laid the groundwork for future problems. As lakes became more secure, people ignored other Cordillera Blanca glacier hazards—hazards that would in subsequent decades unleash deadly catastrophes. As local residents pleaded for and then received national assistance to prevent floods, they became more dependent on the national government to continue glacial lake monitoring and keep the lakes secure. Finally, the intrusion of the hydroelectric industry into glacial lake management brought other stakeholders into the management of land, water, natural resources, and disaster mitigation programs. Environmental change—the dynamic and interrelated effects of climate change, glacier retreat, glacial lake formation, and outburst floods—brought the state to places it had barely been, to landscapes that were little studied, and to natural resources only barely tapped even by locals.

4

High Development
Follows Disasters

In early 1952, following the two Artesoncocha glacial lake outburst floods, the water level in Lake Parón rose to within centimeters of its brim. But when the Ministry of Development and Public Works investigated the precarious lake situated above the city of Caraz, engineers focused their study as much on water resources as on the hazard. Their memorandum lamented diminished water flow in the Santa River and expressed the hope that the ministry could transform Lake Parón into a regulated reservoir to increase hydroelectricity generation and expand coastal irrigation projects.[1] This was not the first time that engineers and scientists sent from Lima to inspect Cordillera Blanca hazards also examined economic opportunities. Engineers who examined glacial lakes brought with them the development fantasies that had inspired Limeño policymakers and developers for more than a century: the hope of exploiting Andean natural resources to promote national economic development and modernization. After 1951, the Lakes Commission became the vehicle that merged disaster prevention with Peru's economic development agendas. The agency was the foundation for "disaster economics" to play out: that is, economic development that directly and indirectly followed the science, technology, engineering, and policies implemented after catastrophes and to prevent additional disasters.

In the 1950s and 60s, the Lakes Commission provided a springboard for comprehensive economic modernization plans in Ancash.

While studying hazards, it also carried out projects related to hydroelectricity, irrigation, tourism, road building, and job creation. The Santa Corporation and its successor, Electroperú, would later intensify their commitment to these projects. But from 1951 to the late 1960s, the Lakes Commission initiated and implemented the institutional link between catastrophes and economic development—the process of disaster economics.

Scholars have scrutinized the economic dimensions of natural disasters in other contexts by explaining how disaster relief often favors the wealthy while neglecting the poor or showing how disasters have historically stimulated development, especially since the 1980s.[2] Others recognize that after the late nineteenth century, the global capitalist economy turned "useful" natural resources and crops into commodities to buy and sell on world markets.[3] These developers often relied on local peasant populations for the necessary labor. Most existing studies that examine historical patterns of capitalist resource extraction, engineering projects, and state expansion conclude that these processes produced significant negative repercussions for both local people and environments. Quantifying and controlling the environment often corresponded with colonial or state projects to subjugate landscapes and people.[4]

In the Cordillera Blanca, these power imbalances and nation-building agendas were also inherent in government-funded Lakes Commission projects. Yet local people frequently supported and benefited from these programs, or they evaded or rejected aspects they did not endorse.[5] Many chose to work at the glacial lake security projects, content that they could earn some cash. Local residents used roads and trails to transport their goods or themselves, and an increasing number worked in tourism. From 1951 to 1970, disaster mitigation, economic development, and state building projects were thus not simply imposed from above against local wishes. They were part of a dialogue among various social groups about water use, road and trail building, tourism, and labor.[6]

Modernity and the Lakes Commission Mission

The quest to integrate the Peruvian economy, extract natural resources from the Andes, modernize the highland labor force, and link the national territory has driven Peruvian policymakers and entrepreneurs since the formation of the republic and the spread of nineteenth-century liberalism. By the 1920s, President Leguía became a particular advocate of uniting and building the country through infrastructure, transportation networks, radio stations, irrigation canals, and ports while simultaneously tying Peru's economy to global markets. Leguía's goal was, as he explained, to transform Peruvians from "an apathetic, backward and colonial people into a nation of today, entrepreneurial, progressive and modern, which knows how to use technology to subdue nature."[7] His legacy influenced state policy for the next several decades, particularly during Odría's presidency.

Many Callejón de Huaylas residents shared this interest in modernization and economic development. During the 1950s, for example, the Huaraz newspaper *El Departamento* devoted a daily column to development and economic issues. Columnists consistently demanded improvements in the region's drinking water, sewage systems, roads, hospitals, schools, and energy supplies (electrification). In Huaylas, residents responded positively not only to the electricity that the Cañón del Pato hydroelectric plant would provide, but also to the opportunity to work there and participate in such a monumental engineering project.[8] Rural inhabitants also expressed an interest in greater modernization and access to goods during the 1950s. As one resident explained about his rural community, "I wish Vicos could be like Carhuaz—with many houses, plantations of trees, open streets, and also that there would be shops with the articles we need most in every house such as coca, salt, chili peppers, sugar, candles, kerosene."[9] Though Andean residents had suffered through economic development agendas since the Spaniards arrived in the sixteenth century and even under the expansive Inca Empire, they were not always opposed to the modernization campaigns that the national government advocated and that the Santa Corporation—and then the Lakes Commission—implemented after the 1950s.

The early mission of the Lakes Commission reveals its combined focus on water use, coastal economic development, and disaster prevention. The agency's predecessor, the temporary study commission, consisted of infrastructure planners and developers. Some members were from the Geological Institute of Peru, the Ministry of Development, and the Santa Corporation, while others came from various ministry divisions related to railroads, roads, and irrigation. In its enabling legislation and technical reports about glacial lakes, the commission often noted the need to protect agriculture and industry without mentioning the affected people or local communities.[10] Yet Lakes Commission staff such as Jaime Fernández Concha, Hans Spann, Luis Ghiglino, Oreste Massa, and J. Elias Torres scoured the Cordillera Blanca to find potentially dangerous lakes. In 1953, Elias Torres traveled several days to Lake Purhuay on the east side of the Cordillera Blanca at the request of local authorities in Huari. Located in the Marañón River watershed, this lake had no effect on Santa River infrastructure.[11] In another case, Fernández Concha made monthly trips to Huaraz and Cordillera Blanca lakes during 1952 and 1953—a time when roads were poor or nonexistent, when travel to lakes involved entire days on horseback and much hiking and camping, sometimes in freezing rain. Most glacier experts dedicated themselves to controlling lakes, and they realized that their work saved human lives as well. Their backgrounds and worldviews, however, had trained them to see environments as economic potential for infrastructure, public works, dams, railroads, bridges, and roads.

When the Los Cedros outburst flood destroyed the hydroelectric station at Cañón del Pato, the damage struck a particular nerve among Peru's development-minded classes. It decimated the nearly constructed hydroelectric plant and thus represented a setback to the entire Santa Corporation mission and bespoke the unreliability of Cordillera Blanca glacial lakes. The corporation could not modernize Peru with so many lakes threatening its energy source. As a result, when the corporation's president of the board and director of management sat down with the seven other architects of the Lakes Commission in late 1950, they discussed these development plans and insisted that the government write them into policy. Two Ancash senators encouraged them, writing to the president that "Ancash has been endowed with enormous material wealth and is in a privileged position to exploit it. The unequivocal proof for this lies in the projects of Cañón del Pato and the Santa [Corporation], which have made a great step toward affirming our economic liberation and relieving our subordination to foreign industrial markets."[12]

The Lakes Commission emerged with an enduring connection to the Santa Corporation and hydroelectricity generation at Cañón del Pato. Sometimes this link hindered disaster prevention and the protection of Ancash populations. Other times it was the existence of the hydroelectric plant that justified Lima's investment in disaster prevention, which helped secure vulnerable people regardless of the underlying motivation. Three cases illustrate these various connections between hydroelectricity and Cordillera Blanca lake hazards: Lake Tullparaju illuminates conflicts between water use interests and disaster prevention agendas; Lake Safuna suggests a preference to protect infrastructure over people; and Lake Parón indicates how hydroelectric interests justified a lake drainage project. I'll consider each of these in turn.

Water Use or Disaster Prevention: The Debate at Tullparaju

Sometimes the government's interest in increasing water use projects jeopardized disaster mitigation. This trend dates back to the early years of the Santa Corporation, when Swiss geologist Arnold Heim told corporation officials about the likelihood of an outburst flood affecting the Cañón del Pato hydroelectric station. According to Heim, he reported directly to both the Santa Corporation president, Fernando C. Fuchs, and the Geological Institute director, Jorge Broggi, on September 12, 1947, that glacial lakes posed "an immense threat to the power plant." Heim referred to the Cañón del Pato project as hopeless, and he said its success was "impossible" because of the various environmental hazards surrounding it. Heim even claims these officials asked him to keep his conclusions quiet to avoid public outrage over Santa Corporation programs.[13] He notes that he sent his report to the Ministry of Development, but faith in hydroelectricity and the quest to modernize blinded officials to the hazards—a hazard that became reality with the Los Cedros flood.

Debate about glacial Lake Tullparaju above Huaraz exemplified these conflicts between water use and disaster prevention a decade later. Tullparaju lies

FIGURE 4.I. Avalanching snow on Mount Tullparaju (with lake at bottom), undated.
Credit: Photo courtesy of Hans Kinzl Archive, Institute of Geography, University of Innsbruck, Austria.

at the head of the Quilcayhuanca Canyon, 28 kilometers above the city of Huaraz. Though the lake barely existed in the mid-1930s, by 1945 it had morphed into a rapidly growing glacial lake with "an extremely weak dam and a considerable quantity of water."[14] In response, the Ministry of Development and Public Works lowered Tullparaju several meters in 1948. But the lake kept expanding during subsequent years, motivating the Lakes Commission to initiate another Tullparaju security project in 1953.[15] On June 18, 1954, avalanching glacial ice crashed into Lake Tullparaju, nearly producing an outburst flood and, in the process, destroying the partially completed lake security project. It inspired the Lakes Commission to install a telephone line from Huaraz to the Quilcayhuanca Canyon entrance, where a watchman stood guard.[16] This was one of the only early warning systems ever installed in the Callejón de Huaylas. And it only existed for a few years.

The Tullparaju security project was nearly finished when, on December 8, 1959, a glacier again sent ice and snow plunging into the lake. Waves once more damaged the newly constructed dam and drainage canal.[17] Late that night, lights in Huaraz flickered as the electricity supply suddenly became intermittent. Concern among Huaraz residents turned to alarm when the river level suddenly rose—and kept rising. Thinking an outburst flood was racing toward town, families emptied their homes, carrying whatever possessions they could as they fled to higher ground. A flood did not arrive that night, but the Quilcay River water level did not diminish the following day. The increased water flow from the Tullparaju overflow continued to generate "a serious and generalized climate of alarm among Huaraz residents."[18] Damián Michelena, head of the Construction and Control Department of the national government's Water Division, told *El Comercio* that "if the artificial control dam had not existed, a true outburst flood would have started," inundating Huaraz while residents slept. On Saturday, December 12, the Ancash prefect in Huaraz ordered the evacuation of the two hundred homes most directly in the path of a potential outburst flood.[19]

Resolving Tullparaju pitted water use arguments against safety concerns. Government officials in Lima had immediately dispatched two engineers to Huaraz. Once they saw Lake Tullparaju, they argued that the city's safety could be ensured only by completely draining the lake. Huaraz residents agreed.[20] In a public town meeting on December 12, furious residents charged the Lakes Commission with corruption, negligence, and mismanagement because the agency had failed to drain all the dangerous glacial lakes. They proposed that a joint commission made up of the Santa Corporation, the Peruvian army, and government engineers should drain *all* remaining unstable lakes in the Cordillera Blanca. Ministry of Development engineers concurred that drainage of Tullparaju was the only way to "eliminate all future danger for the city of Huaraz."[21]

Developers interested in water use argued otherwise. They asserted that lake drainage would impinge on irrigation, hydroelectricity generation, and industrial production and should not be done. As one water use advocate maintained:

> It is a shame, truly—although in certain ways inevitable given the neglect of economic planning—that one arrives at the extreme of wasting a substantial volume of water, a volume that, well exploited and effectively-channeled, could irrigate vast spaces that are uninhabited, unproductive today precisely because of the lack of water. Additionally, it should not be forgotten that water in Peru puts in motion great hydroelectric stations, which the iron and steel industries of Chimbote depend upon to function. The hydroelectric station and heavy industry exist because of water from the Cordillera [Blanca]. Thus to carelessly utilize that water will result, in truth, in a travesty of grave consequences for the development of basic national industries.[22]

Other prominent scientists, such as Jorge Broggi, asserted that the drainage of Lake Tullparaju was a mistake because it would diminish Santa River water flow into Cañón del Pato. Santiago Antúnez de Mayolo, who had originally proposed the hydroelectric plant at Cañón del Pato, was blunter, saying it was "stupid and crazy to proceed with the drainage of lakes situated above Huaraz." Instead, he argued that glacial lakes should be managed solely by the Santa Corporation.[23] Amid local residents' fear of disaster, government authorities and water developers jockeyed for control of the water. Finally, the "energetic intervention" of Ancash Deputy David T. Izaguirre and other deputies and senators expanded Lakes Commission funding by several million soles, allowing it to continue lakes security projects without caving to water use advocates.[24] Engineers never drained Tullparaju completely, but in the early 1960s the Lakes Commission did finally lower its water level.[25]

The Tullparaju debate reveals additional issues embedded in glacial lake management. For one, different government agencies disagreed about how best to control glacial lakes. Various congressmen, hydraulic engineers, state institutions, and local residents all offered different suggestions. There was no single "state view" of the glacial lakes or water control objectives. Yet the seemingly divergent solutions for Tullparaju produced the same outcome: enhanced human control over Cordillera Blanca water. Further, debates among engineers from Lima showed how little influence Huaraz residents had. Decisions about lake control were mostly in the hands of Lima policymakers and glacier experts.

Protecting Hydroelectricity Above All

President Fernando Belaúnde and his Acción Popular party renewed interest in economic development after he took office in 1963. Belaúnde tried to realize "The Conquest of Peru by Peruvians"—the title of a book he had written in 1959—by uniting the country and connecting the coast with the jungle through trans-Andean roads that would enable transportation, communication, and economic development. Economic crisis in 1967, however, thwarted his plans: drought on the coast caused agricultural decline; the Peruvian *sol* was devalued from 27 to 39 per dollar; the trade deficit increased for three consecutive years; and foreign investment declined.[26] The crisis paralyzed many public works projects and heightened unemployment. Belaúnde saw Cañón del Pato as a way to help jump-start the economy with expanded hydroelectricity generation, irrigation, and industrial development in Chimbote. Lake Safuna threatened those aspirations.

Located at the base of Mount Pucahirca (6,020 meters), Lake Safuna at 4,363 meters had grown dramatically during the 1950s and 1960s.[27] In mid-1966, Santa Corporation engineers compared their recent photographs of glacial Lake Safuna with aerial photographs taken in 1950 and 1961. They determined "with great alarm the tremendous variation in the lower glacier of Mt. Pucahirca Norte, where Lake Safuna has formed over a very short time period."[28] Because Safuna lies at the head of the Quitaracsa Canyon, which empties into the Santa River at Huallanca (location of the Cañón del Pato hydroelectric power house), an outburst flood from the lake would have destroyed the Santa Corporation's capacity to generate hydroelectricity. Consequently, the corporation contracted two French firms to help study this dynamic glacial lake. The world-renowned glaciologist Louis Lliboutry led the French consultants between 1967 and 1969.[29] Meanwhile, conditions at Lake Safuna worsened so that on June 16, 1967, the Peruvian government declared a state of emergency for Quitaracsa Canyon.[30] By mid-1967, Quitaracsa Canyon occupied the national spotlight because it threatened a major hydroelectric plant. While a dozen other glacial lakes remained uncontained by the Lakes Commission, political pressure and Santa Corporation resources shifted the national focus to Lake Safuna, which primarily threatened infrastructure rather than populations.

From 1967 to 1969, preoccupations about Safuna led the Santa Corporation and French firms to partly drain the unstable glacial lake. Work conditions at

Safuna presented life-threatening challenges. Lliboutry reported that when he went out onto the lake to conduct studies, researchers had a rubber boat, the only type of boat that mules could carry to the remote lake. Lliboutry was exasperated that, to overcome the layer of ice on the lake, they "attempted to protect the rubber boat with a wooden bow to convert it into an icebreaker!"[31] Fortunately, they completed their studies without incident. By 1969, engineers lowered the level of Lake Safuna first by pumping water out and then by drilling a 150-meter tunnel through the moraine so that new water entering the lake would drain through the tunnel without raising the lake level.[32]

Disaster Prevention to Develop Lake Parón

Long considered a potentially dangerous lake, Parón was still not drained or artificially dammed in the late 1960s. Engineers finally started draining it in 1967, when the Santa Corporation determined the lake could serve as a natural reservoir to help regulate Santa River water flowing into Cañón del Pato. From the Santa Corporation's perspective, Parón offered an ideal way to expand Ancash water use for hydroelectricity generation and coastal irrigation. If regulated, the lake could add significantly to water flow in the dry season, when flow rates dropped from 400 to 4 cubic meters per second.[33] Draining Parón, however, would prove to be the most expensive, technically demanding, and time-consuming lake security project in Cordillera Blanca history.

Engineers ultimately decided to drill a 1.2-kilometer tunnel into Parón's lakebed through the base of a solid granite mountain. Identifying the exact place where the drainage tunnel would connect with the lakebed presented a unique challenge in the history of glacial lake engineering: it required scuba diving to a depth of 60 meters in a glacial lake at 4,200 meters above sea level. In late 1967, Santa Corporation and French scientists working amid Peru's highest glaciated peaks teamed up with an unlikely collaborator, the Peruvian navy.[34] Lieutenant José Jeanneau Gracey, the navy's most distinguished scuba-diving specialist and a graduate of the U.S. Marine Corps Deep Sea Diving School, planned and directed scientific explorations on the floor of Lake Parón. As head of the Scuba Department in the Peruvian navy at Callao, Jeanneau had faced many challenges during his career. Parón, he later said, was among his most rewarding.

Jeanneau immediately recognized a host of obstacles making the mission to Parón complicated and dangerous. The lake's remote location meant that there was no nearby medical help, no transportation for equipment, no compressed air, no recompression room, and no laboratory for analyzing gases.

What's more, diving 60 meters into a lake whose surface was at 4,200 meters meant that descent and ascent rates, proportions of oxygen and nitrogen, quantities of gas, and other technical aspects of the dive needed to be determined with great precision before entering the water. Lieutenant Jeanneau selected another navy scuba diver, Alfonso Román, to help him, and the two worked with a third diver, the French scientist Bernard Schneider from the consulting firm Coyne et Bellier in Paris. While Román selected the expedition's equipment, Schneider gathered data and soundings of Parón's lakebed, and Jeanneau made the necessary calculations for such an unusual dive. He contracted Hannes Keller, a Swiss mathematician, to develop an equation to calculate underwater pressure in the lake and determine the rates at which divers would have to descend and ascend in the lake.

In the first test run by the two professional divers Jeanneau and Román, they found the lake water a few meters below the surface in "total darkness," and their instruments were not working well. Realizing a potentially dangerous situation, the divers surfaced immediately. But the wind and current had drifted their raft 25 meters away, and by the time they swam to it, Jeanneau said, "I felt the sensation that my lungs had collapsed and that all the air I could bring into them was not sufficient to breathe." After more adjustments and preparation, they successfully dived the following day and continued diving daily. After four days, the three divers had explored most of the northwest wall of the lakebed. Then, on the fourth day, they plunged down to discover what they had hoped to find all along: a sheer rock portion of the lakebed. This uniform section would be the ideal place to connect the tunnel with the lake and to begin draining Lake Parón.[35]

Financial and technical obstacles made drilling Parón's tunnel even more difficult than locating its connection point with the lake.[36] After beginning in 1968 and drilling 1,060 meters of the total 1,200 meters that would ultimately be done, tunnel work stalled for a decade because of problems with the contractor and lack of government funds. In 1984, the Parón project finally resumed under the direction of engineer César Portocarrero.[37] After completing the drainage tunnel and connecting it to the lake, technicians lowered the water level approximately 45 meters, removing 58 million cubic meters of water.[38] The fact that Parón was not drained until 1984—while a dozen other lakes were drained, dammed, or repaired during the 1970s—suggests that the tunnel and drainage project was not necessarily to avert an imminent threat but rather was useful for hydroelectricity generation at Cañón del Pato and large-scale coastal irrigation projects. In 1990, Electroperú estimated that Parón's contribution as a reservoir to regulate water flow in the Santa River would bring an additional $3 million per year in revenue from Cañón del Pato.[39] Parón was more than a disaster mitigation project; it was an investment in hydropower and irrigation.

Hydroelectricity: The View from the Callejón de Huaylas

It was not only engineers, scientists, and government officials who pushed for Santa Corporation and Lakes Commission development projects in the region. Many urban middle- and upper-class residents also supported economic expansion in the region. In 1953, Alberto Carrillo Ramírez, a resident of the Bolognesi province in Ancash, lamented the "industrial misery" of his province.[40] Others from Yungay complained about the "marked industrial backwardness" in the region and noted specific natural resources that should be exploited, such as Lake Llanganuco for tourism and the Santa River for hydroelectricity and industry.[41] Other longtime residents of the area supported hydroelectric development because the projects provided jobs and the electricity lighted their homes. One rural resident in his seventies appreciated the Santa Corporation because without it "there is no electricity.... Not a single plant or merchant can work."[42] A host of local people consistently argued that the Santa Corporation, hydroelectricity, and irrigation would bring "high development" to Ancash and Peru.[43]

Yet tensions arose among locals about the distribution of Cañón del Pato electricity. When the plant began operating in 1958, the first electricity went directly to the coastal city of Chimbote and the much-talked-about industrialization projects—rather than to the Callejón de Huaylas communities where the water that ran the facility originated. In 1960 and 1961, Huaylas residents began to work out a contract with the Santa Corporation to get electricity in their community to replace the ailing generator and to supply electricity to everyone in the district, not just those in town. After all, the high tension line that transported power from Cañón del Pato to Chimbote had passed through the district of Huaylas but did not deliver any electricity there. Landowners had not been compensated for the use of their land—neither for the line and towers nor for the Santa Corporation's use of landowners' and communities' roads and trails to construct and maintain the high tension line to Chimbote. Locals felt justified in their demands for electricity. The Huaylas mayor first went to the Santa Corporation in 1957 to request electricity. The corporation rejected his proposal, but another mayor again pleaded for electricity in 1959. People in Huaylas were interested enough in receiving electricity that when an agreement with the company and the community was established by December 1959, the community volunteered to do all the work to build the lines to carry electricity there from Cañón del Pato. In other words, the Santa Corporation provided the energy, but residents working through their community leaders and volunteer work units did the rest. Overall, electrification was something that Huaylas (and other communities) wanted. In some cases, men 60 years old and older were volunteering to dig post holes for the electric lines. By the end of 1960, the lines were completed, and in January 1961 Huaylas celebrated the arrival of electricity there and in the surrounding areas.[44]

Other Callejón de Huaylas residents supported greater exploitation of the Santa River and hoped to receive electricity from Cañón del Pato. Before the station's electricity extended into the Callejón de Huaylas, only larger towns had power—and they received it from generators that operated for only three or four hours in the evening. By the 1960s, the Santa Corporation had installed power lines up the Callejón de Huaylas, but the company passed Yungay without providing electricity for residents, moving on directly to Huaraz. Yungay residents were so angry and so eager to acquire electricity that they threatened to blow up a Santa Corporation transformer and power line if the corporation did not electrify Yungay. Within a few weeks, Yungay had received electricity.[45]

Development through Roads and Trails

When the Lakes Commission began constructing dozens of roads and trails in the 1950s, this opening of the Andes had monumental implications, diverse meanings, and far-reaching consequences for a host of different groups—on local, national, and international levels. The quest to penetrate the Andes with roads, trails, and railroads has a long history in Peru. Whether to oversee the Inca Empire in the fifteenth century or to extract agricultural goods in the eighteenth century, such routes were always vital for Andean travel, transportation, shipping, and communication. They also symbolized progress and modernization. And like the construction of dams and the taming of rivers, road building, many people argued, proved humans' ability to dominate the natural world and to bring civilization to remote places and peoples. The Incas built 40,000 kilometers of roads through the rugged Andean terrain, relying on a labor draft, the *mit'a*. Andean roads that contributed to bureaucratic efficiency and the distribution of goods and services thus emerged long ago and through forced labor. In the 1920s, President Leguía rejuvenated road construction projects and recreated a labor draft (*Conscripción Vial*) to complete them.[46] But by the late 1920s, this labor draft had become a national symbol of corruption, leading President Luis Miguel Sánchez Cerro to promptly abolish it when he became president in 1930.

But interest in road building continued. In Ancash and the Callejón de Huaylas, development-minded residents wanted roads that linked the region to the nation. By the mid-twentieth century, a main highway ran through the

Callejón de Huaylas along the Santa River connecting Huaraz, Carhuaz, Yungay, Caraz, and Huallanca. Only a few roads in the mid-twentieth century extended into the Cordillera Blanca uplands from the Santa River. Engineers in Huaraz remarked that roads could bring "momentous consequences" for the region while also fulfilling a "patriotic dream." A Huaraz newspaper claimed that new Andean roads would solve Peru's greatest problems.[47] But roads did not appear overnight. It took from 1927 to 1942 to complete the road connecting the town of Huaylas with the rest of the Callejón de Huaylas.[48] In the 1950s and 1960s, many Ancash residents and Lima politicians advocated construction of a trans-Andean highway to connect the coast and Callejón de Huaylas with the Amazon. Commentators claimed it was a "magnificent project," a "patriotic dream" that would have monumental consequences "not only for the adjacent provinces and mountainous region but also for the entire department [of Ancash]."[49] Trails (caminos de herradura) were also extremely important for smaller communities because, in the absence of roads, they were essential for transportation and communication. Each indigenous community was responsible for monitoring, maintaining, and repairing the trails in its territory. Though a twenty-first century tourist might consider them quaint or scenic trekking routes, trails in Ancash served vital economic needs. They have also been the primary way scientists and engineers reach glacial lakes for research.

Glacier monitoring and glacial lake engineering projects depended on the existence of roads and trails into Cordillera Blanca canyons. Glacier experts often spent days trying to reach the Cordillera Blanca glacial lakes, which were generally perched between 4,000 and 4,700 meters above sea level, more than 20 kilometers from the closest roads, and up to 2,000 vertical meters above local towns. Dense vegetation, boulder fields, and landslide debris clogged the steep, narrow canyons leading to many glacial lakes.[50] In 1951, a Lakes Commission official described the route to one Cordillera Blanca lake as arduous and perilous, complaining especially about the route above the Ulta Canyon entrance:

From there, the trail becomes abominable because of erosion caused by outburst floods, which have completely destroyed the trail that follows along the base of the canyon. It is in such a way that one has to make the major part of the journey by foot [instead of by horse], with great difficulty for the loaded mules.

After four kilometers of walking in the Ulta Canyon, one arrives at the Paccha Canyon, within which Lake Unucocha is found. There is no trail to the lake, so one has to pass by extremely abrupt places where it is even difficult to walk. The equipment and materials are carried on the backs of peons, making the journey a great risk for them. One practically has to climb a staircase that rises a thousand meters from Ulta to the start of Paccha, where the terrain is more normal and climbs gradually for two kilometers.[51]

Many other Cordillera Blanca glacial lakes were similarly perched in isolated places that required comparably harrowing journeys—and an enormous amount of time and energy—to reach.

FIGURE 4.2. Mules loaded with scientific equipment for Cordillera Blanca research, 2008.
Credit: Photo by Paul Illsley.

The Lakes Commission built and improved some 200 kilometers of Cordillera Blanca trails and roads during the 1950s and 1960s.[52] Most of the new trails covered from 15 to 30 kilometers and climbed steeply into Cordillera Blanca canyons. They often rose from the banks of the Santa River at 2,500 or 3,000 meters elevation to 4,000 or 4,500 feet above sea level at the foot of alpine glaciers and the shores of dangerous glacial lakes. After the 1950 Los Cedros flood, President Odría ordered the reconstruction of destroyed roads. He appointed Juan Quiroga, a high-ranking official in the national Department of Roads, to the 1950 Study Commission of the Santa Watershed.[53] But in most cases, the Lakes Commission could only afford to build trails, not roads, to Cordillera Blanca lakes. Though roads would have no doubt enabled quicker completion of glacial lake security projects, the trails nonetheless provided a degree of accessibility.[54] Through the 1950s and after, the new roads and trails also served the regional population and government by improving transportation, communication, tourism, water use, glacier and lake monitoring, and disaster mitigation. In many ways, it was the Lakes Commission that initially "opened up" the Cordillera Blanca and broadened interaction between local communities and outsiders.

Sometimes the Lakes Commission built roads instead of trails because government engineers realized they would serve other purposes as well, such as tourism at Lake Llanganuco. According to the 1953 lake inventory, Llanganuco was not among the most dangerous glacial lakes in the Cordillera Blanca.[55] But as one commentator suggested in 1951, a tourist hotel, boat launch, and "magnificent road to access the lake" could transform Llanganuco into a terrific economic asset for the entire Yungay province.[56] The Lakes Commission teamed up with the Santa Corporation to complete the Yungay-Llanganuco road in 1959. At its inauguration ceremony, authorities boasted that the road had "national importance" for boosting international tourism and for providing "multiple benefits: tourist, scientific, commercial, and industrial."[57] The Lakes Commission's involvement in the Llanganuco road at a time when dozens of other unstable glacial lakes existed, most without road access, also showed the agency's broad priorities beyond disaster mitigation and the way in which it actively carried out disaster economics.

In the 1960s, two Peace Corps volunteers working on tourism and conservation in the Cordillera Blanca observed that lakes control projects enhanced physical security of inhabitants, whereas the Llanganuco and other access routes offered economic security.[58] In the cases of Lakes Parón and Llanganuco, the Lakes Commission constructed roads with an explicit goal of hydroelectricity generation and tourism. After all, the Lakes Commission never considered building roads to the small glacial lakes that were unfit to be reservoirs or unlikely to attract tourism. Lakes Commission access routes into the Cordillera

Blanca remain important today as thousands of people use the roads and trails daily. As one Vicos elderly man put it, "life is easier" with the road.[59]

Tourism

As scientists and engineers explored remote glacial lakes, most recognized the region's stunning beauty. The Cordillera Blanca boasts hundreds of turquoise-colored glacial lakes at the foot of craggy glaciers and majestic peaks that tower over the Santa River valley. The Cordillera Blanca also contains Mount Huascarán, the highest mountain in Peru and one of the highest in the Western Hemisphere. Glacier experts helped publicize the scenery and adventure terrain to audiences in Peru and abroad. A visit there, one engineer wrote, "will leave the traveler with memories that will be difficult to erase in the course of a lifetime."[60] International scientists also praised the region's unsurpassed beauty. The Austrian geographer-mountaineers Hans Kinzl and Erwin Schneider, who visited the Cordillera Blanca several times between 1932 and 1970, described the range as one of the most stunning in the world, reminiscing in 1950: "The Cordillera Blanca has captured our hearts. We had the privilege of resting on some of its peaks—happy almost beyond words and with no further desire."[61] These scientists and engineers became boosters for tourism in Ancash.[62]

Peruvians also promoted Cordillera Blanca tourism because it was potentially profitable.[63] Their quest paralleled worldwide twentieth-century growth of tourism in general and mountaineering in particular. In the 1950s, the trend among Westerners and the wealthy—those who had the money for leisure travel—increasingly focused on new, "uncharted" areas, such as the Himalayas, Arctic, Antarctic, and Andes.[64] The novelty of Peru attracted a few mountaineers to the Cordillera Blanca during the first half of the twentieth century. Annie Smith Peck was among the early pioneers of Andean mountaineering. A U.S. college professor turned women's suffrage advocate, Peck became the first to climb Huascarán's lower north peak (6,655 meters) in 1908.[65] Austrian and German mountaineers generated more publicity for the Cordillera Blanca in 1932 when they became the first to climb Mount Huascarán's higher south peak (6,768 meters).[66] In Ancash, residents promoted tourism through the 1950s and 1960s. Doctor Guzmán Flores proclaimed in 1962, "We are clearly convinced that stimulating tourism in Yungay will elevate the economic standard of living not only in our province but also in all of Peru."[67]

FIGURE 4.3. German and Austrian mountaineers in the Cordillera Blanca, 1932.
Credit: Photo courtesy of Hans Kinzl Archive, Institute of Geography, University of Innsbruck, Austria.

The Lakes Commission helped turn dreams about tourism into reality. The new roads and trails provided access routes for tourists seeking out canyons, glacial lakes, and glaciated peaks. So important were these new roads that in 1963 the Automobile Club of Peru featured the Callejón de Huaylas and Lake Llanganuco among its most favored destinations.[68] The Lakes Commission also transformed labor camps built for lakes security projects into tourist lodging. Jorge Broggi had urged the Peruvian government to invest in workers' quarters for the execution of disaster prevention projects at lakes because the buildings could later "serve for those who wish to practice mountaineering."[69] In the 1950s, Lakes Commission directors Elias Torres and then José Ayllón granted permission to the Cordillera Blanca Mountaineering Group to use labor camps for climbing expositions, where mountaineers demonstrated how much fun the sport could be while teaching skills to those attending.[70] Some of the buildings remain in use, such as the one at Lake Llaca that is now a lodge, training center, and outpost for mountaineering search-and-rescue operations.

Beyond building infrastructure during the 1950s, Lakes Commission officials explicitly supported tourism and mountaineering through advocacy, publicity, and participation in climbing groups. After César Morales Arnao and others founded Peru's first mountain-climbing club in 1952, this Cordillera Blanca Mountaineering Group teamed up with the Lakes Commission to promote tourism in the region.[71] On June 4, 1953, the two groups organized a public celebration and glacier-naming ceremony at glacial Lake Legiacocha. The event, hosted by Elias Torres, included skiing and mountain-climbing demonstrations, as well as an afternoon *pachamanca*, a traditional Peruvian meal of potatoes, corn, pork, and other foods cooked slowly underground. The Lakes Commission prepared the *pachamanca*, gave welcoming speeches, and offered space for guests at the Lake Legiacocha labor camp, constructed in 1951 to house workers for the lake security project. The following day, participants traveled to Cañón del Pato and Huallanca, where they toured the hydroelectric station.[72] But the highlight of the two-day event was the christening of "Glacier Miró Quesada," named for the prominent Lima family that owned Peru's most widely read newspaper, *El Comercio*.[73]

The Lakes Commission also supported tourism and mountaineering by indirectly training some of the most important mountaineers in Peruvian history, the Yanac brothers. Pedro, Apolonio, and Guido Yanac had several years of experience working on glacial lake security projects when they began wandering in the nearby mountains and climbing peaks "for something to do." Lakes Commission work had trained them well for high elevation, extreme weather, a lack of oxygen, and an ability to scale precipitous glacier-covered slopes. The Yanac brothers reached the summit of Mount Huascarán, which no Peruvians had ever done before, in August 1952 and proved to the world that Peru's peaks were not just the domain of foreign mountaineers.

Yet tourism did not always bring glory and celebration. The potential for economic profit meant that tourism sometimes distracted engineers and politicians from their mission to control dangerous glacial lakes. Parker Trask, the University of California geologist who studied Cordillera Blanca glacial lakes in the early 1950s, suggested that lake drainage for security should be curbed because it would destroy the lake's beauty. He concluded that large lakes with more than 5 million cubic meters of water could produce catastrophic outburst floods and thus posed the greatest threats to people and infrastructure below. He then contradicted his own analysis by asserting in his technical report that Lake Parón should *not* be drained too much because of its beauty and tourist potential. "Certainly the lake should not be lowered considerably because it is one of the most honorable [lakes] in the world. The Llullan Canyon that leads to it is as magnificent as Yosemite Valley in California, and, with time, it could become one of the most valuable tourist attractions in Peru."[74] Kinzl and Schneider also complained that the government lowered lake levels "without paying heed to scenic beauty."[75]

The government's withholding of information about dangerous lakes—because such information could scare away tourists—showed a more dangerous side of tourism promotion in the Cordillera Blanca. In August 1962, when the project to partially drain Lake Tullparaju was still not finished, the prefect of Ancash visited the lake and announced publicly that it "is not dangerous."[76] He expressed frustration with those who had "divulged alarming, unfounded news about the possible overflow of Lake Tullparaju," not necessarily because they were wrong, but rather because the reports "drive away the tourist population and cause financial damage because the news echoes in the press of the capital city [Lima]."[77] The prefect's hurried suppression of information about potential threats from Tullparaju does not suggest a cover-up, but his reassuring statement was certainly premature. The Lakes Commission did not complete the Tullparaju security project until 1964.[78]

Tourism has generated mixed outcomes worldwide—whether in Tanzania's Arusha National Park or California's Yosemite.[79] Far from the clean, unproblematic "industry without smokestacks" that some hail it to be, tourism in the Cordillera Blanca produced ambiguous effects.[80] Lakes security and other projects stimulated the regional economy and left the Cordillera Blanca with much more infrastructure than before 1950, but this development sometimes eclipsed disaster mitigation efforts.

Work and Security

A long-standing dream of the Andean elite was to use Indian labor to develop the region, rule the people, and expand the economy. In the nineteenth century, liberals saw labor as critical to the development of capitalism. Through wage labor, Andean subsistence farmers would theoretically transition from backward Indians to effective producers and consumers. In the mid-twentieth-century Callejón de Huaylas, wage labor barely existed for rural populations. Instead, most inhabitants had their own plots of land and were subsistence farmers. Some worked on haciendas in exchange for a plot of land to farm. Occasionally, these residents worked on large-scale state projects such as at Cañón del Pato, and 2,000 or 3,000 residents of Yungay even worked on the guano islands during the 1950s.[81] The Lakes Commission expanded labor opportunities—and worked to inculcate some of the values that the elite associated with wage labor—by hiring local farmers to build roads and trails and to conduct lake security projects. For these residents, lake work offered one of the few opportunities to earn extra cash.

Each Lakes Commission glacial lake project—some of which lasted for months, others for years—required professional scientists and engineers, as well as scores of laborers who worked as masons, rock and dirt haulers, pipe-layers, carpenters, cooks, mule drivers, and assistants to the geologists, surveyors, engineers, and other professionals. As many as fifty people worked on individual lake projects. During the 1950s, the Lakes Commission hired perhaps a thousand Ancash residents to work at its various projects throughout the Cordillera Blanca, usually relying on local communities near lakes for the bulk of the labor force. Although a steady crew of Huaraz-based foremen, engineers, and technically trained staff emerged in the early 1950s, the agency contracted a substantial portion of new local laborers every time it started a different project.[82] Given the wide distribution of lakes security projects throughout the Cordillera Blanca, the Lakes Commission hired local residents from dozens of communities.

The Lakes Commission sought to transform these workers into hardworking wage laborers who would both complete lakes security projects and advance developers' economic agendas. An inconsistent labor supply for Lakes Commission projects continually vexed government officials and demonstrated that rural residents were not simply puppets of the state. Two commission managers griped in 1955 that the labor force was extremely unstable, just as it was "at all development projects in the sierra."[83] Other Lakes Commission administrators demanded that their employees be more punctual, work a full day, and stay

on the job throughout their workday.[84] Complaints grew particularly voci.
around harvest times, when a large number of laborers left the lakes proje
tend their crops. Not surprisingly, some laborers also left when the governn
failed to pay them; this was the case with workers at Lake Ishinka who walked
off the job in November 1953. To compensate for these walk-offs, Lakes
Commission officials in Huaraz—acting as intermediaries between the state
and its subjects—insisted that Lima distribute money more promptly. In July
1953, the commission developed a system by which its accountant actually went
directly to the lakes to pay workers every 15 days, a system that also compelled
laborers to remain on the job until that fifteenth day. In addition to these efforts
to mold laborers' work habits, the commission also regulated their free time by
banning alcohol at labor camps because, according to project managers, it led to
conflicts and fights.[85] Instead of liquor, engineers brought soccer balls to the
labor camps so workers could play after their shifts. Lakes Commission officials
were not the only ones hoping for a better trained, more efficient, and more
productive labor force in the countryside. The local elite also scoffed at rural
subsistence farmers who did not work for wages in industry because of their
"primordial preoccupation to satisfy the immediate needs of their stomachs."[86]
Another local resident generalized that rural people were "backward" and lacked
initiative and therefore needed training in wage labor.

According to José Ayllón, Lakes Commission director in 1953, the stipula-
tions imposed by his agency, which penalized those workers not remaining on
the job until the fifteenth day but rewarded workers who remained a full month
with a bonus, have "given us complete success because we have seen for the
month of July that the quantity of people at the projects has increased rapidly."[87] Of course, the "success" was for the Lakes Commission, not those laborers who may have worked for ten days but then needed to leave for family
reasons or to harvest crops. The Lakes Commission also imposed specific hours
employees had to work.[88] They had to be on the job at a minimum from 8:30 in
the morning until 12:30 and from 3 to 6 P.M. on weekdays, and from 8:30 A.M.
to 1 P.M. on Saturdays. Of course, many jobs went over these hours. Nevertheless,
the focus on the clock and specific hours differed from many rural farmers'
labor patterns. Lakes Commission staff extended credit to its employees at the
lakes projects as well.[89] The commission even established small "stores" at the
labor camps so that workers could use money they had not earned yet.[90] By
allowing workers to buy goods on credit, the commission effectively bound
workers to the lake projects and indirectly spurred consumer habits. Although
probably not part of a conscious "civilizing" or capitalist mission, Lakes
Commission engineers and administrators nonetheless helped imbue rural
people with wage-labor behaviors and beliefs.

paternalism —like killing for
coal

Sometimes, however, local residents challenged state plans. When the Lakes Commission tried to rescue an archaeological artifact lost in the Chavín outburst flood, for example, local residents refused to work because of cultural beliefs. The 1945 flood had devastated the ancient Chavín ruins and buried one of the museum's most important relics, the Condor of Chavín sculpture. In November 1953, the Lakes Commission sought to recover the sculpture. On his first trip to Chavín, José Ayllón left Chavín empty-handed after relentless rain impeded the search. Three weeks later, Ayllón learned that the rain had ceased and that the Mosna River water level had dropped. When he returned to Chavín in December to resume the search, he found local authorities reluctant to cooperate and local residents unwilling to work, even when he offered increased wages. Locals refused because they believed the sculpture did not want to be found. In fact, they claimed that, when the commission began its search, the Condor of Chavín cried out from the depths of the river, pleading with the mountains to help halt the search. In response, the skies released rain, which had thwarted the first search, while the mountains prepared a fatal flood. Continuing the search, locals maintained, "would bring an immediate outburst flood." Mystified and frustrated after his fruitless hunt for laborers in Chavín, Ayllón traveled many kilometers to the town of Purhuay, where he did finally hire workers. As soon as they began digging for the lost sculpture, torrents of rain fell, and the river rapidly grew to double the size it had been when they started. Ayllón abandoned the project. Local residents meanwhile demonstrated that cultural beliefs could outweigh their drive to earn money.[91]

Despite obstacles encountered in Chavín, the Lakes Commission did affect hundreds of wage laborers in and around the Cordillera Blanca. Just as previous governments had implemented labor drafts to build roads—and simultaneously civilize the rural populations—the Lakes Commission, in a much less intrusive way, helped inculcate Ancash residents with capitalist ethos and work habits.

In early 2004, a handful of *laguneros* recounted how they saw the lakes projects primarily as one thing: a job. These "lake people" were men who worked intermittently on Lakes Commission projects during the 1950s and 1960s. They had lived for decades in the Callejón de Huaylas and had seen firsthand the devastation and death caused by glacial lake outburst floods. As they worked as *laguneros,* their families and communities resided in the valley below the expanding lakes. But none acknowledged their role in reducing threats of outburst floods from glacial lakes. When asked directly if the government increased people's security by draining nearby lakes, their answers invariably emphasized their own specific work hauling rocks, driving mules, or digging trenches, as well as the new government-constructed roads and trails that connected upland communities with lowland cities along the Santa River.

FIGURE 4.4. Workers digging a lake drainage canal and tunnel, c. 1960.
Credit: Photo by the Comisión de Control de Lagunas de la Cordillera Blanca, courtesy of the
Unidad de Glaciología y Recursos Hídricos.

Security for *laguneros* focused on economics, especially wages and infrastructure, not necessarily protection from glacial lake outburst floods.[92]

Lakes Commission programs to contain glacial lakes during the 1950s and
1960s merged intimately with economic development in the Ancash
Department. The commission became a springboard for transforming rural
farmers into wage laborers, exploiting natural resources, building infrastructure, enhancing communications, utilizing technology, and expanding tourism. The physical environment—climate, glaciers, glacial lakes, and
floods—was one of the major forces driving these historical changes. Local

people also benefited from the state's increased presence in the Cordillera Blanca. Their support for various Lakes Commission programs reveals complex state-society relations: the government was not simply intrusive, and local populations did not always oppose state projects, even ones that enhanced Lima's authority in Ancash.

Ultimately, the Lakes Commission's development mission initiated two long-term trends. The regional population came to depend on the state for economic support and disaster prevention. Additionally, the commission's economic development programs created a link that later hydroelectric companies managing disaster mitigation would further cement: the connection of glacier and glacial lake research to water use, instead of glacier hazards.

5

In Pursuit of Danger: Defining and Defending Hazard Zones

On January 10, 1962, an avalanche from Glacier 511 on Peru's highest mountain, Huascarán, swept into the Callejón de Huaylas, leveling a half-dozen communities, destroying the town of Ranrahirca, and killing approximately 4,000 people. *National Geographic* writers assessing the aftermath described it as "the weight of 1,200 navy destroyers combined [that] crashed wildly into a troughlike gorge."[1] Triggered by nearly a century of climate change that had melted and fractured Glacier 511, the Ranrahirca tragedy was a new type of Cordillera Blanca climate catastrophe: an avalanche (landslide) rather than a glacial lake outburst flood. Some worried that Ranrahirca might not be an isolated event—that Glacier 511 could produce more disasters or that deadly avalanches could come from other retreating Andean glaciers. Their concerns were realized on May 31, 1970, when a massive earthquake dislodged Glacier 511. The ensuing avalanche killed an estimated 15,000 people, and the combined death toll from the earthquake and avalanche reached 70,000, making it the most deadly disaster in the Western Hemisphere's history.

Glacier experts and other government officials recognized that the only way to escape these deadly avalanches in the future would be to get out of the way in advance. Hazard zoning, which had faded as a disaster prevention program during the 1940s and 1950s, reemerged in 1962 and even more in 1970 as a key strategy to keep people safe from Cordillera Blanca glacier disasters. President Juan

FIGURE 5.1. Ranrahirca avalanche scar, 1962.
Credit: Photo by Peruvian Servicio Aerofotográfico Nacional.

Velasco also continued glacial lake security projects and glacier research during the 1970s. More than any of his predecessors since 1941, he also attempted hazard zoning in the Callejón de Huaylas. Given that the earthquake and avalanche had leveled so many structures, relocation did not require moving intact cities. Rather, reconstructing Huaraz, Yungay, and Carhuaz in safer areas involved rebuilding already destroyed cities in new locations.

Hazard zoning, however, failed in the 1970s, just as it had after the 1941 outburst flood in Huaraz and the 1962 avalanche in Ranrahirca. Opposition to what locals considered an intervening state—which began conducting disaster prevention programs in people's communities rather than at isolated glacial lakes—explains some of the resistance to relocation. But many locals also saw hazard zoning as simply a pretext for Velasco's government to dismantle the existing class-race structure, which the region's wealthier classes resented bitterly.[2] By trying to implement Velasco's agenda of social equality while distributing disaster aid and reconstructing the Callejón de Huaylas, government officials made the aftermath intensely political. But glacier experts were not simply state bureaucrats or pawns carrying out Velasco's plans on the ground,

rebuilding destroyed cities in new locations

hazard zoning failed

as scholarship on nation building and disaster studies often assume
many engineers and scientists in the Callejón de Huaylas worked vi$
prevent additional glacier disasters.

The 1970s hazard zoning and disaster prevention plans were part of a longer story about climate change, glacier hazards, state rule, local defiance of
government authority, and the social construction of science and technology in
the Andes. Moreover, just as local residents contested state rule, glacier experts
also made decisions and pursued agendas outside the Velasco mission. Many
disaster studies portray locals in vulnerable positions as being pushed into
marginal places by wealthier groups, a neglectful state, or by other forces
beyond local control. These social dimensions of disaster vulnerability no doubt
exist but can too often depict vulnerable populations as passive victims without
control over their destinies.[3] They also do not adequately consider the active
ways in which experts try to protect populations and how they mediate between
centralized states and various local populations. The state is more complex,
experts are more diverse, and political processes entail more dialogue than
disaster scholarship often acknowledges.[4] Of course, Callejón de Huaylas residents are not alone in their habitation of hazard zones. People live on river
floodplains in Brazil, the sea coast in Bangladesh where monsoons inundate
the population, and in California where earthquakes, fires, landslides, and a
vast number of potential disasters lurk. For these and other societies worldwide
that grapple with potential disasters, this Peruvian hazard zoning history is
enlightening because it explains how and why people refuse to move, even
when they recognize their vulnerability and understand the risk of disaster.

Avalanche at Ranrahirca: The New Glacier Threat

By 1962, residents of the Callejón de Huaylas knew that glacial lakes threatened them. Few, however, recognized that calamity could come directly from
glacial ice. Just before 6:15 P.M. on January 10, 1962, Glacier 511 on the north
peak of Mt. Huascarán slid off the upper mountain. One witness thought he
saw a low cloud, but then he realized the cloud was "flying" downhill—toward
the valley town of Ranrahirca and a half-dozen communities above it. Those
who did not see it heard the terrifying roar of the approaching mass of glacial
ice, snow, rocks, mud, and other debris. Some said the avalanche sounded like
"ten thousand wild beasts" or hundreds of airplanes flying over Mt. Huascarán.
One survivor likened it to an earthquake, which made "a rumble in the walls of
the belly." In the village of Huarascucho, Juan Mallqui Rodríguez darted out of
his house when he heard the roar. After looking to Huascarán and seeing the

descending avalanche, he ran up the hill, yelling and warning others to flee. Most paid no attention, though, and two women simply told him that " 'the snow on Huascarán always falls like that.' " It did, but not on this cataclysmic scale. Other oblivious inhabitants also ignored neighbors' warnings. Party guests in Ranrahirca continued to sing and laugh, thinking that Lamberto Guzmán Tapia was joking when he screamed "Avalanche! Save yourselves!"[5] Most people, however, never had a chance: within four minutes the violent mass from Huascarán had descended to the valley floor.

Like the previous glacial lake outburst floods, the avalanche destroyed everything in its path. Ranrahirca, the second-largest town in the province of Yungay, experienced the greatest loss of life with the near-complete annihilation of all 2,900 inhabitants. The avalanche also obliterated pastures; agricultural plots of potatoes, barley, wheat, and alfalfa; forests of *quenua* and *alisos*; dozens of huts used by shepherds; bridges; and irrigation canals. Ranrahirca survivor Ricardo Olivera Mejía later recovered his town's public clock tower. It still read 6:15 when he excavated it from what survivors called the "barren plain."[6]

Many small towns also disappeared, including Pacucco, Shacsha, Yanama Chico, Matacoto, Armapampa, Chuquibamba, Caya, Encayor, and Uchucoto. Huarascucho, a community of 600 inhabitants approximately one kilometer up valley from Ranrahirca, was one of the destroyed towns. Huarascucho residents were primarily artisans, bricklayers, pottery makers, and carpenters who did specialized work in the churches of Yungay and other Callejón de Huaylas towns. By the early 1960s, Huarascucho had become famous for its flowers, which were used—ironically enough—primarily for the region's funerals. Although townsmen worked for part of the year on Peru's guano islands off the Pacific Coast, they were at home in January when the avalanche swept the town away.[7] Glacier 511 also destroyed Huarascucho's agricultural plots, its school, the San Ignacio Hospital, and the Catholic and Presbyterian churches. Little remained of Huarascucho or any of the other towns in its path. Damage estimates soared into the tens of millions of soles.[8]

Grief and suffering descended on the survivors who had witnessed the cataclysmic event. Injuries were few: the avalanche either killed people or left them completely unscathed. One journalist reported that only two dozen people were hospitalized.[9] Survivors often blamed the "damned" mountain as they lamented their terrible losses and gazed across the milewide "barren plain" that was once a thriving river valley of rich agricultural fields, pastures, and towns. One survivor wrote in anguish:

> Ah, friend, hold me, the pain is killing me
> the Ranrahirca avalanche has terminated everything.

With sentimental tears and crying in hopeless despair
I look for my beloved beings,
Without anyone to look after me and without any hopes
I look for my beloved beings.[10]

Despite their suffering, survivors remained determined to rebuild and persist. As Ranrahirca survivor Alberto Romero Leguia insisted, "Huascarán has been terrible. Its destructive force has been like the fury of God, but as long as there is one survivor, Ranrahirca has not died. Today they cry for their dead…but at dawn tomorrow they will begin to work, and what used to be gardens will once again be gardens."[11]

The avalanche occurred because Glacier 511 had fractured, and the steeply sloped bedrock was too unstable to prevent the glacier from sliding. Glacier melting had also lubricated the bedrock underneath the ice with water. Avalanches from Mount Huascarán had probably occurred long before the twentieth century (in Quechua, *Ranrahirca* means "pile of thrown stones," suggesting to many a history of avalanches in that valley).[12] But after the Spanish conquest of Peru, people increasingly inhabited the avalanche path on the valley floor. When the glacier broke away from the mountain in 1962, it crashed into the lower Llanganuco Valley and Ranrahirca River. Like many high-speed debris flows, the Huascarán avalanche actually jumped. At points the avalanche even floated because of the air pocket trapped beneath it. In the upper canyon, trees directly in the path of the avalanche lost all their bark and foliage from the blast of wind, while the avalanche passed directly over the treetops. The initial avalanche on the glaciated slope of Mt. Huascarán contained more than 2.5 million cubic meters of glacial ice and rock, a volume that increased as it descended and picked up more rocks, water, mud, sand, and other debris.[13] Unlike glacial lakes that engineers could drain, avalanches on the Ranrahirca-Glacier 511 scale were uncontrollable. Protecting people thus required moving them out of the path of potential avalanches.

Hazard Zoning before 1970

Authorities and engineers had been advocating hazard zoning in the Callejón de Huaylas since the 1940s, as I discussed in chapter 1. Following warnings from geologists like Jorge Broggi, who had recommended that Huaraz residents rebuild higher and outside the Lake Palcacocha flood path, authorities and experts in 1941 prohibited reconstruction in the *cono aluviónico* (the Huaraz flood path). Expert advocacy for hazard zoning continued thereafter. In August

Lakes Commission engineer Jaime Fernández Concha worked with ɪz's Mariscal Luzuriaga School to determine a safe place for construction. chosen site," he pointed out in a summary of their meeting, "is completely out of range of all possible destruction from outburst floods."[14] But the school's solicitation of input from Lakes Commission engineers was an exceptional case. Most ignored or opposed zoning. Lima officials, however, continued to advocate hazard zoning in Huaraz. In 1959, the Ministry of Development explained in an official memorandum published in Lima's *El Comercio* that Huaraz need not be entirely relocated "but rather the recommendation is that all city expansion be in zones not exposed to these natural phenomena," the glacial lake outburst floods.[15] Despite well-intentioned proposals, zoning policies proved largely unsuccessful—and were generally unenforced in the 1940s and 1950s.

Huaraz residents settled and built in the *cono aluviónico* for several reasons. Many inhabitants saw glacial lake outburst floods as isolated events. Local books and newspaper articles published during the 1950s generally referred only to the 1725 avalanche that destroyed the town of Ancash and the 1941, 1945, and 1950 outburst floods. Many more outburst floods had occurred in the Cordillera Blanca since the late nineteenth century, but most local residents did not seem to know about them.

Faith in science and technology led many to believe the government had the capacity to contain glacial lakes. Societies worldwide have used technological barriers such as dikes and levees to hold back floods or stop tsunamis. Others have relied on science to predict hurricanes or provide tornado forecasts.[16] Peruvians were thus not alone in their continual preference for glacial lake engineering instead of hazard zoning.[17] During the 1940s and 1950s, many urban residents believed that experts could effectively drain all the glacial lakes. As one commentator declared just six months before the 1950 Los Cedros outburst flood, "studies done with determination and exactitude" and works done to "impede natural phenomena" would prevent future outburst floods. "With such projects," the author concluded, "man imposes his science and his will one more time to triumph over the [natural] elements."[18]

Many urban residents also remained in vulnerable locations because of their cultural and economic attachment to the places they lived. They wanted to rebuild their destroyed cities in their precise locations. They lamented lost buildings and places, such as the eucalyptus-lined Raimondi Avenue. The devastated area, many maintained, had been the heart of the city.[19] An article in *El Departamento* noted that construction in the hazard zone was a positive step toward "achieving the existence of order and urban harmony in the structures of the outburst flood zone."[20] In addition to cultural and emotional attachment, economics motivated people to inhabit vulnerable locations. For centuries, urban Callejón de Huaylas residents had lived, worked, and socialized in towns and cities along the Santa River. Roads, public services, markets, bureaucratic headquarters, and entertainment had thus become centralized in Huaraz, Carhuaz, Yungay, Caraz, Recuay, and other riverbank towns. Relocation of the population centers and their tens of thousands of inhabitants was not practical, reasonable, or affordable.[21] But in Huaraz, the 1941 outburst flood had completely leveled the floodplain. The city had to be rebuilt. And although the ban on reconstruction in the floodplain indicated authorities' intentions to rebuild in safe areas, many people nonetheless wanted to recolonize the floodplain because they wanted to recover their lost property. Others saw the vacant land as an economic opportunity.[22] In 1956, urban residents even formed the Association of Flood Zone Property Owners to "restore the urbanization of this important sector of the city." They argued that regaining their land and reurbanizing such an "important sector of the city" was vital not only to their own interests but also to general recovery from the 1941 disaster.[23]

Huaraz inhabitants' refusal to obey hazard zoning laws suggests that fear of glacier disasters was not their most pressing concern; restoration of the socioeconomic order that the flood decimated was more urgent.[24] Without a powerful urban core zone and the concomitant symbols of progress, modernity, and urbanity, many urban middle- and upper-class residents believed they could not restore the social order. They were aware of the risks but rebuilt Huaraz in the hazard zone anyway. The Ranrahirca avalanche, however, was a new glacier hazard without the comparably easy lake drainage solution. Nevertheless, it inspired only limited attention to hazard zoning—and continued opposition.

Government response to the Ranrahirca tragedy was slow and embedded in the processes of disaster economics that had been ongoing since the 1950s. On February 9, 1962, a month after the avalanche, Peruvian President Manuel Prado established an Inter-Ministerial Council for the Defense and Rehabilitation of the Callejón de Huaylas that worked alongside the Lakes Commission.[25] The Inter-Ministerial Council's duty was to investigate glacier threats "with the objective of studying all geological, energy, industrial, communication, monitoring, defense, rehabilitation and tourism problems in the region." Beyond the political objectives, the rehabilitation plan also proposed scientific solutions to the glacier problem, such as placing Cordillera Blanca observation stations that could maintain radio contact with Callejón de Huaylas towns and warn people with alarms if an avalanche or outburst flood occurred. Neither the Lakes Commission nor any other entity implemented these early warning or evacuation plans, nor did many state-sponsored glacier studies ensue.

Overall, the Peruvian government did little in the wake of Ranrahirca to help survivors, rebuild towns, or prevent future natural disasters. Residents complained bitterly, demanding aid for reconstruction and a more systematic approach to disaster prevention.[26] More authoritarian governments like those of Odría and Velasco responded to catastrophes more quickly and energetically than did the democratically elected administrations of Prado and Belaúnde. Of course, the scale of the disaster and what was destroyed also influenced the degree of state response. Disasters at Ranrahirca and Chavín affected places less important—at least for Lima policymakers and the Ancash ruling classes—than the floods that devastated Huaraz and Cañón del Pato.

Within the Callejón de Huaylas, the Ranrahirca avalanche fed anxiety about future disasters. Within a month of the avalanche, false alarms about impending glacial lake outburst floods spread through Huaraz and Marcará. Tensions were high enough that *El Departamento* was even recommending criminal punishment for whoever started the rumor of a flood in Huaraz on February 6, 1962.[27] Lakes Commission director Miguel Elías Pizarro saw that the new avalanche threat created a need for hazard zoning.[28] This time some residents supported the experts. Transplanted residents in Lima, for example, formed the Ancash Rehabilitation and Defense Committee to protect the population from future floods. It recommended "the relocation of population centers found along the Cordillera Blanca slope to places such as hilltops and plateaus."[29] A few weeks later, *El Departamento* suggested that Callejón de Huaylas towns were "badly located." The article explained that the Incas had lived on the hills overlooking the Santa River. They lived high to avoid floods, to leave valleys free for farming, and to have more hours of sunlight. The article concluded, "It is recommended with good reason that populations should imitate those ancestors who, from experience, defended themselves from nature's fury. One should take note of these studies and opinions for Ancash today."[30]

But not everyone agreed that hazard zoning was a good idea. The day after the Ranrahirca disaster, but before the newspaper had time to report on the catastrophe, *El Departamento* ironically printed an article recommending that Huaraz expand "horizontally" into Centenario, precisely the area destroyed by the 1941 flood. The newspaper never mentioned floods, the hazard zone, or potential disasters.[31] Just as during previous decades, most Callejón de Huaylas residents preferred glacial lake and glacier control to hazard zoning.[32] As Huaraz Mayor Augusto Soriano Infante summarized at a public town meeting in February 1962, the community demanded more Cordillera Blanca studies, completion of engineering projects at glacial lakes, and the formation of a Geological Commission staffed with foreign scientists who could help prevent future disasters. The mayor never mentioned hazard zoning as a possible solution.[33]

Disaster and Velasco

At 3:23 P.M. on Sunday, May 31, 1970, a massive earthquake off Peru's north-central coast thrashed the Ancash Department, especially the Callejón de Huaylas. At a circus in Yungay, the shaking earth frightened children, who clung to the nearest adults. In Huaraz, a man watched stunned as the undulating earth sent a pickup truck galloping sideways up a steep hill. Houses and buildings collapsed everywhere. People who had been listening intently to their radios as Mexico played Russia in a World Cup soccer match ran from their homes in fear. Huaraz resident Benjamín Morales was driving with his mother when they saw adobe houses begin to fall apart. Once it became too difficult to drive, they parked and waited, listening to terrifying sounds like "a stampede of elephants" and watching horrified as the world fell down around them.[34] Hugo Córdova Milla was working underground in the Powerhouse Machine Room of the Cañón del Pato hydroelectric power plant when the earth began to shake "horizontally and vertically to such magnitude that we were jerked and tossed."[35] Eventually, he and his coworkers escaped through a tunnel, only to find their homes in ruins. At a party in Huaraz, a young boy, Lucho Olaza, disobeyed adults who insisted he hide

FIGURE 5.2. Yungay before the avalanche, 1954.
Credit: Photo courtesy of Hans Kinzl Archive, Institute of Geography, University of Innsbruck, Austria.

under a desk when the trembling began. Instead he sprinted into the streets and emerged miraculously unscathed. These were lucky survivors.[36]

Ranked in the top 20 most deadly earthquakes in world history and the most deadly in the Western Hemisphere, the 7.7 Richter magnitude earthquake left 70,000 dead and 50,000 injured.[37] A half-million people became homeless after the earthquake destroyed 186,000 buildings, which accounted for 80 percent of structures in the affected region. The earthquake demolished 65,000 square kilometers of Peru, an area larger than West Virginia. It caused an estimated $800 million in damage, devastating houses, shops, schools, bridges, roads, water, sewage systems, and the hydroelectric plant at Cañón del Pato, which supplied much of the region's electricity.[38]

In Yungay, the trembling ground had barely ceased when a low, distant rumble emerged from the Cordillera Blanca. Many of the survivors say they knew from the sound that the earthquake had shaken loose a large portion of Glacier 511 on Mount Huascarán. In those terrifying moments, a heavy cloud of dust billowing after the earthquake obscured most Yungay residents' view of the Cordillera Blanca. Professor Pelayo Aldave Tarazona ran "terrified" toward the cemetery, which was on a hill overlooking the town. His friend yelled at him, "Get up...run...the avalanche is on top of us!" He arrived at the cemetery as the avalanche passed within meters, ripping cadavers from the ground and creating a gruesome scene of scattered skeletons and terrified survivors. Geologist Mateo Casaverde was driving through Yungay with a French geologist, Gerard Patzelt, when the earthquake startled them. They abandoned their vehicle when it began "jumping vertically." Then they "heard the low frequency noise, something different than the earthquake," and they saw the clay-colored cloud growing over the Cordillera Blanca indicating that "Huascarán was coming down." They scrambled to the top of the cemetery just in time to watch "a giant wave" approximately 30 meters high careen down the hill and wipe away Yungay.[39] In total, the glacier avalanche from Mt. Huascarán killed 15,000 people, a significant portion of the 70,000 total deaths.

Political circumstances shaped Peruvians' reactions to the 1970 earthquake and avalanche. At that time, Peru was ruled by General Juan Velasco Alvarado, who had seized power in a 1968 coup that ousted President Fernando Belaúnde Terry. Velasco's "revolutionary government" sought far-reaching social, economic, political, and even cultural changes, including accelerated economic growth, redistribution of income and wealth, integration of the indigenous population into mainstream Peruvian society, and, essentially, the fabrication of a new Peruvian identity free from the country's long-standing racial and class divisions.[40] As Velasco proclaimed, "We are in the midst of a revolutionary process which implies redoing all the reality of the world in

FIGURE 5.3. Aerial view of 1970 avalanche from Mount Huascarán.
Credit: U.S. Geological Survey Photographic Library/Photo by Peruvian Servicio Aerofotográfico
Nacional.

which we were born."[41] Plans for such sweeping changes fell short in many ways because his top-down approach alienated so many people and because his reforms did not go far enough for any one group. Most significantly, the Peruvian economy faltered under the revolutionary government. Agricultural and industrial productivity fell, real wages declined, unemployment rose, inflation climbed, the national debt skyrocketed, and racism continued. Nevertheless, his presidency did alter the traditional social landscape of Peru through land reform and a new ideological discussion about the place of lower classes and Indians in society.[42]

Once he provided urgent disaster relief for Ancash, Velasco saw the catastrophe as an opportunity to construct his new Peruvian society in the demolished region. His Commission for the Reconstruction and Rehabilitation of the Affected Zone (CRYRZA), which he established immediately following the earthquake and avalanche to oversee aid distribution, became the vehicle for implementing those plans.[43] Managers of CRYRZA sought to implement this agenda, and they issued a statement asserting, "The earthquake of the 31st of May 1970 confirmed the unequal and unjust socioeconomic and political order existing in the Affected Zone, a situation that as revolutionary Peruvians we have the obligation to change through the tasks of Reconstruction and Rehabilitation."[44] Velasco's government tried to remake Huaraz by appropriating all downtown land and property, only to move slowly with reconstruction and to give land to those who previously did not own it.

FIGURE 5.4. Former Yungay city center obliterated by avalanche, 1970.
Credit: U.S. Geological Survey Photographic Library/Photo by George Plafker.

Wealthier urban classes criticized Velasco's programs because relief workers adhered to the government's agenda for promoting socioeconomic equality. In Yungay, a resident quipped in reference to the arrival of CRYRZA, "First the Earthquake, then the avalanche, and then...the disaster!"[45] As survivors increasingly saw the president's reconstruction strategy as interventionist and threatening, they turned against the government, opposed its projects, and lumped all government engineers and officials into one unappealing category with CRYRZA. This view simplifies and overlooks the role of glacier experts during the 1970s.

Science and Technology Deployed

While CRYRZA directed relief and reconstruction in Callejón de Huaylas communities, the Santa Corporation's Glaciology and Lakes Security Division significantly expanded the work it had been doing since Benjamín Morales began directing this new division in 1966. Morales was a Huaraz native who grew up in the Callejón de Huaylas and survived both the 1941 Huaraz outburst flood and the 1970 earthquake. As a boy, Morales became intrigued by the Cordillera Blanca peaks partly through his family's interactions with mountain climbers. His brother César founded Peru's first mountaineering club in 1952, and a year later they climbed one of the region's highest peaks, Mount Hualcán. Morales developed a passion for the Cordillera Blanca and wrote his early 1960s university thesis on its glaciers. From 1962 to 1966, he studied glaciology in Switzerland. Then he returned to Peru to become the first director of the Santa Corporation's Division of Glaciology and Lakes Security, and in 1967 he established the National Glaciology Institute.[46]

By the early 1970s, the Santa Corporation had officially absorbed the Lakes Commission. When President Velasco nationalized the electricity-producing industry in 1973, the new state-owned Electroperú took over both the Santa Corporation and the Glaciology and Lakes Security Division. With a surge in support and funding from the Velasco administration, the division was able to increase the number of glacier studies and expand Cordillera Blanca monitoring. He also devoted attention both to new glacial lake hazards and the previously drained glacial lakes to ensure that the projects remained intact.[47] Within days of the May 31 catastrophe, Peruvian officials also asked the United Nations Educational, Scientific, and Cultural Organization (UNESCO) to coordinate research on the region, requesting that French glaciologist Louis Lliboutry return to Peru to lead new studies. On June 5, less than a week after the earthquake and avalanche, the Peruvian Aerial Photography Service photographed Cordillera Blanca glaciers and lakes. Morales flew additional helicopter missions with Lliboutry on June 9–10.[48] During these flyovers, Morales and

Lliboutry determined that the earthquake had damaged dams and drainage canals associated with previous lakes security projects.

For the next several years, the Santa Corporation and then Electroperú conducted the region's most comprehensive and intensive disaster prevention agenda yet. Whether it was the immediate emergency drainage of upper Lake Llanganuco in June 1970 or the numerous lake security projects during subsequent years, the glaciology office was able to contain a dozen Cordillera Blanca lakes by 1978.[49] They also investigated glacier hazards, including a crevasse on Mount Huascarán Norte (6,654 meters) that took engineers into a life-threatening situation in August 1973. A year earlier, mountaineers had reported that this yawning gap in the glacier was on the verge of catastrophic rupture. Benjamín Morales examined the mountaineers' photographs, compared them to aerial photographs of previous decades, and declared the crevasse to be normal and nonthreatening. However, to inspect the crevasse firsthand and to determine its stability, the glaciology division engineer Marino Zamora led a dozen engineers, mountaineers, and porters to the upper slopes of Huascarán.

What began on August 14, 1973, as a productive expedition nearly turned into tragedy. Amid blowing wind and 30 centimeters of fresh snow, two rope teams reached the summit of Huascarán Norte after six days. As Marino Zamora, another glaciology division engineer Marco Zapata, and three professional climbers descended from the peak, they lost their way in near-whiteout conditions. Stranded in the freezing darkness, the group spent a long, miserable night clinging for life at 6,400 meters as they exercised to prevent hypothermia. The long-awaited morning did not bring the hoped-for clarity of view, but they saw that they had stopped their descent only a few paces before plunging into a gaping crevasse. Despite 70 centimeters of new snow and continued cloudiness, the group managed to descend through the course of the day. It was a narrow escape. They never saw the large crevasse on Huascarán Norte. Instead—and just as Morales did in late 1972—Zamora analyzed the next best available information (the aerial photographs) and concluded that the crevasse "has not evolved and has preserved its form without alteration. As a result, it is not an immediate threat."[50] Active efforts to engineer unstable glacial lakes and investigate some glacier hazards revealed the ways in which glacier experts in the 1970s both continued pre-1970 programs and expanded them to better safeguard the regional population.

Zoning the Clean Slate

Glacier experts also advocated the relocation of Cordillera Blanca towns and cities that were vulnerable to avalanches and outburst floods. Though locals opposed top-down intervention from the national government, glacier experts' recommendations to rebuild destroyed communities in new places were based on their long-standing devotion to preventing tragedy, rather than adherence to Velasco's social-political agenda. Immediately following the 1970 Yungay disaster, Morales argued that "the catastrophes produced by avalanches from hanging glaciers such as Huascarán will be periodic events, which is to say that they will occur again in the future. This type of phenomenon has no solution; there are no measures to avoid them or control them. Consequently, populations located below glaciers with these characteristics must be relocated."[51] Scientists from the UNESCO commission agreed.[52]

Glacier experts and government officials proposed three distinct relocation plans for the provinces of Yungay, Huaraz, and Carhuaz. They planned to relocate Yungay, Ranrahirca, and Mancos to the Tingua area, which was 15 kilometers from the destroyed part of Yungay and much less vulnerable to avalanches and outburst floods. According to UNESCO, relocation was necessary because the bedrock on Mount Huascarán remained unstable and could trigger more avalanches.[53] "There is an absolute probability that this phenomenon will occur again," UNESCO concluded. "It is not possible to predict when, but one can definitely say that [an avalanche] will happen."[54] Peruvian authorities followed the recommendation to relocate and proposed reconstructing the three towns in Tingua.[55] Survivors became angry when they heard the plans.

Experts also worried that parts of Huaraz could be destroyed by glacial lake outburst floods, and they suggested that reconstruction and future development occur in safer areas north of the city.[56] Experts from UNESCO urged residents to rebuild on higher ground, leaving floodplains along the Quilcay and Santa Rivers free of settlement—just as Peruvian glacier experts had been advocating since 1941. Many residents rejected the plan, construing it as an imposed Velasco agenda rather than a safety precaution.[57]

Glacier experts and UNESCO indicated that Carhuaz was vulnerable to both glacier avalanches and glacial lake outburst floods. In July 1967, members of the Hualcán Mountaineering Club reported a gigantic, half-kilometer-long fissure in one of the glaciers. Carlos Villón, president of the club, feared the fissure could break apart and create an avalanche that would crash into Lakes Cochca or Yanahuanca and cause an outburst flood. Geologists from the 1970 UNESCO team noted these same dangers on Mt. Hualcán, asserting that the *development of Carhuaz in its present site must not be considered.*[58] Government officials proposed Huáchac as the new site for Carhuaz, where 80 hectares of safe, protected land could support a population of up to 14,000 inhabitants.[59]

Relocation proposals in the 1970s represented a shift in the long-term trajectory of disaster mitigation beneath melting Cordillera Blanca glaciers.

Previously, glacier experts had advocated zoning, but not so comprehensively and with such vigorous campaigns. Recognizing the limitations of glacier studies and glacial lake control, glacier experts in the 1970s expanded their disaster prevention mission to include the relocation of the region's most vulnerable populations. Despite experts' good intentions, locals resisted the comprehensive approach to vulnerability reduction and instead demanded more technological control of glacial lakes.

Contested Science

Conflicts over the scientific knowledge that justified hazard zoning followed during the 1970s, as did a quest for credibility by the glacier experts seeking both to preserve their power and calm the public. To defend their monopoly over the production of scientific knowledge, glacier experts often went to great lengths to maintain their credibility. One way experts maintained their privileged position was by assuming that common people did not know or could not understand scientific concepts or environmental processes. A CRYRZA technician, for instance, expressed this attitude when he asked rhetorically, "What does the public understand about technical details?"[60] Division of Glaciology and Lakes Security engineers echoed these sentiments when they labeled local residents as superstitious, uninformed, or backward.[61] Experts sometimes explained their exclusive right to produce science based *not* on their technical data but rather on their experience. For example, in late 1972 an independent geologist, Leonidas Castro, confronted the government over its proposal to relocate the town of Carhuaz. In response, Benjamín Morales sent a report to Luis La Vera Velarde, president of CRYRZA, that critiqued Castro's conclusions point by point. Morales offered few technical or scientific reasons for why Carhuaz needed to be relocated. Instead he accused Castro of basing his position on "sentimental arguments and nothing technical." He went on to insist that Castro "had never in his life climbed on any Cordillera Blanca glaciers" and subsequently did not know about glacier problems, glacier research, or glacier behavior.[62]

Glacier experts also sought to retain authority by being more transparent and demonstrating their ability to tame nature. In the 1970s, the glaciology office began staging inaugurations for completed lake security projects. On October 22, 1974, and November 26, 1974, Benjamín Morales hosted inaugurations at Lakes Shallap and Palcacocha, respectively.[63] Hundreds of local residents and authorities trekked to the mountains for these ceremonies. They sang Peru's national anthem, and dignitaries from high level positions in the

Civil Defense, Ministry of Energy, Electroperú, local and regional authorities, and the Division of Glaciology and Lakes Security gave speeches and boasted about how the projects contributed to "the tranquility of the city of Huaraz because they have eliminated a serious threat of an outburst flood from this lake that was seriously affected by the May 1970 earthquake."[64] To impress their audience with scientific and technological prowess, engineers spoke about project details and statistics. Then they gave tours of the new dams, tunnels, and drainage canals. After speeches and tours, the inauguration culminated when the Division of Glaciology served a traditional *pachamanca* meal.

In addition to inaugurations for engineering projects, the Glaciology Office also began producing and distributing glossy pamphlets to showcase their work.[65] Filled with photographs of cement dams and artificially bounded lakes, these pamphlets depicted glacial lakes as oversized bathtubs or water in culvert pipes rather than as the unruly, treacherous lakes that had killed thousands. These materials boosted engineers' credibility and showcased effective state projects because these images of the completed lakes security projects allowed the press—and thus the public—to see the fruits of science, technology, and

FIGURE 5.5. Inauguration of Glacial Lake Llaca Security Project, 1977.
Credit: Photo by Programa de Glaciología y Seguridad de Lagunas, INGEOMIN, courtesy of the Unidad de Glaciología y Recursos Hídricos.

Velasco's projects. As officials told newspaper reporters after they inaugurated Lake Palcacocha, "This is one more thing the Revolutionary Government is doing...in the Department of Ancash."[66] Proving scientists' ability to manipulate and dominate nature could only help solidify their authority and relevance to human security.

Local residents, however, often contested scientists' conclusions and the supposed experts' right to exclusive control over the scientific data. As Huaraz author Marcos Yauri Montero explained, a psychosis emerged in Huaraz because they lacked access to the glaciological and seismological information that was used to tell them where they could or could not live, or what type of house they could or could not construct. Without that data, Yauri Montero confessed, people felt "constantly threatened and, above all, impotent."[67] A mathematics professor from Huaraz also complained about people's uninformed state, declaring that "if all knowledge is an instrument of power, science is more powerful than everything else."[68] One way residents tried to dethrone scientists was by gaining access to the information that scientists and state officials shared. In June 1970, for example, after Yungay residents learned about the rapidly filling Lake Llanganuco, Yungay mayor José María Lobina Falcón demanded that authorities conduct technical studies and disclose the results to relieve insecurities among survivors.[69]

Others tried to compile their own data about glacial lakes and possible outburst floods. In March 1971, residents of Huaraz organized town meetings and a group, the Defensive Front of the Callejón de Huaylas against the Threat of Outburst Floods, so that they could acquire and distribute information about the dangers of the lakes above Huaraz. The regional newspaper *El Diario de Huaraz* participated in these information-sharing campaigns by publishing data and sponsoring informational meetings.[70] In July 1970, two Huaraz mountain climbers spent five days in the Cordillera Blanca to collect and share information. Residents were thirsty for the details because they worried about the lakes. One woman in Huaraz exclaimed, "We live constantly aware of those lakes. Every day I think of them, that one could come down."[71] Such nervous residents therefore supplied the mountaineers' gear, food, and logistical support so that they could examine Lakes Llaca, Cuchillacocha, Palcacocha, Perolcocha, and Shallap.[72] The following year, Huaraz residents went to check on lakes themselves. On Saturday, January 9, 1971, at the height of the rainy season, more than 200 people left the city at 3 A.M. to "verify their true level of danger" at the glacial lakes.[73] Hugo Ríos, president of the Revolutionary Civic Union, led the expedition that sought to overcome the dearth of lake information available in Huaraz. If residents themselves could gain an understanding of the lakes—especially if they could prove the lakes were not threatening—then locals would possess the capacity to challenge forced relocation from hazard zones.

Local residents not only sought improved access to scientific information; they also worried about who produced it, believing that Lima technocrats were inherently biased against the Callejón de Huaylas. For example, many people in Huaraz saw the arrival of scientists and engineers as yet another intervention of *Limeños* in the highlands.[74] One Callejón de Huaylas resident categorized Lima technicians and government officials as outsiders with inflated salaries who "lacked a deep appreciation for the region, a love for it, or a will to serve the people."[75] Many complained that government officials treated survivors callously, without respect for their grief over the loss of families, friends, homes, and their entire community.[76]

To challenge Lima's presence in the region and to reduce the state's monopoly on scientific information, residents sometimes contracted their own scientists to study glacier hazards. In early 1971, Huaraz residents organized a town meeting to discuss glacial lake threats. They invited independent scientists to demystify the technical aspects of the government information.[77] It was soon after that meeting that Carhuaz residents who refused to relocate hired geologist Leonidas Castro to evaluate Mount Hualcán. His report, contradicting government officials by suggesting that there was no danger from either outburst floods or avalanches (and hence that it was not necessary to relocate Carhuaz), was endorsed by another local scientist, Augusto Calvo, dean of Huaraz's Engineering University. Calvo concluded that authorities could direct reconstruction and future development to the northern district of Carhuaz, which offered protection from potential glacier hazards.[78] Residents were relieved by these scientists' announcements. As Carhuaz inhabitant Carlos Vinatea Quevedo recalled, "It would have been a terrible thing to uproot an entire community."[79] Some went even further in their challenges to science and technology. The well-known Ancash scholar of history, anthropology, and literature, Marcos Yauri Montero, for example, argued that science and technology had produced the Titanic and the 1970 earthquake. Both were massive failures and severe catastrophes. He thus proposed the integration of science with humanism to illustrate that relocating towns was not possible because they were too meaningful to the people living there.[80]

Claiming the Hazard Zone

Immediately following the May 1970 disaster, Callejón de Huaylas survivors assembled in refuge camps and focused on securing food, water, shelter, clothing, and health care.[81] By August 1970, government officials turned their attention away from survival needs and toward long-term relocation and recon- struction. By then, many victims had already fled the region. Of the approxi- mately 27,000 survivors of the earthquake and avalanche in the entire province of Yungay, an estimated 4,000–5,000 of them moved to Lima right after the May 31 devastation.[82] Many of the emigrants were wealthier people who could afford to leave after the devastation. Emigration to Lima was highest from Huaraz, where those with access to transportation and social networks that extended beyond the Callejón de Huaylas were most likely to leave.[83] For those who stayed, the government's plan to impose hazards zones was unacceptable, even though the glacier experts with the most experience in the Cordillera Blanca believed the relocation of certain cities offered the safest solution to the decades-long problem of glacier disasters. Removing people from potential flood and avalanche paths would have been the most effective way to eliminate their vulnerability to those hazards.

Many survivors, however, challenged relocation on the same basis they had challenged hazard zoning since 1941: because social, cultural, and eco- nomic forces bound them to the urban space they previously inhabited. In Yungay, the avalanche had buried thousands of people. Without a proper burial and with so many lost family members, survivors wanted to remain close to their dead.[84] Yungay survivors also opposed relocation to Tingua because Mount Huascarán anchored them to the region. As one commentator explained, "Most struggle to live and die on these prodigal lands because, although Huascarán and the lakes threaten us…they have spirits that attract and capti- vate everyone who lives here and sees them."[85] Carhuaz residents also identi- fied "mi pueblo" and "mi tierra" as motivating factors that kept them in place. Cosme Blas Torres Palomino, a Carhuaz resident who fought relocation during the 1970s, referred nostalgically to his old city and its central plaza, and its beautiful location below the Cordillera Blanca. He remains proud of all the people who said they "will not move from Carhuaz," and he boasts about their efforts to "rehabilitate" the city through "the work of everyone who came out to raise up Carhuaz to return to be what it was before and what it will be in the future."[86] Others in Carhuaz echoed these sentiments and resisted relocation to Huáchac.[87]

Many believed the state had an obligation—and the capacity—to protect them from glacial lakes. In Huaraz, urban residents demanded that the national government use the 83 million soles appropriated to drain the lakes and defend the population. As one commentator insisted, they must "drain the dangerous lakes or the money will not be well spent. There is no other alternative."[88] Instead of moving out of the way, Huaraz residents came to rely on the

Glaciology Office that had worked so successfully to keep the lakes in the mountains.[89] Moving, many believed, would be redundant if the state contained the glacial lakes. Evidently, many did not recognize the new threat of glacier avalanches.

While many residents believed the state could help protect them from calamity, others saw earthquakes and avalanches as simply beyond their control. Religious followers suggested that God inflicted the damage as punishment for people's sins. Others contended that France had caused the earthquake because it detonated an underwater atomic bomb on May 30, 1970. The bomb produced enough force, many Peruvians maintained, to shift the earth and generate the earthquake.[90] Some residents identified the culprit as the U.S. space agency NASA because it had sent astronauts into space. The astronauts' transgression against *chukaro* (raw nature) disrupted the earth's balance of forces and produced the catastrophe. By explaining disasters as products of these supernatural, foreign, or external forces, many Callejón de Huaylas residents placed the blame for natural disasters elsewhere and thus ignored how their own living conditions and choices of community location made them vulnerable to these hazards in the first place. Fate excused their culpability. As Hugo Ramírez noted, "Towns continue moving forward in pursuit of their goals, only to fall again later and then start to move forward, falling again, and starting over again."[91] Destruction and reconstruction were part of life and out of residents' control.

But there was more to staying put than cultural forces that tied people to their homeland or worldviews that explained culpability. Urban residents' quest to maintain their privileged social status above the rural population also impelled people to support the traditional status quo and, therefore, to resist relocation. In the first year after the disaster, the population of Yungay Norte, for example, rose from several hundred survivors to 2,000 as rural residents descended to Yungay Norte to collect relief aid.[92] A similar downward migration occurred in Huaraz as well. This influx of rural people threatened the urban elite because government officials and CRYRZA representatives distributed aid equally among all survivors.[93] A surviving Yungay woman captured the rural-urban rift when she grumbled that "The people of the heights, the Indians, never had anything, so why should they get help? On the other hand, we, the real Yungainos, have lost everything, so we should get more."[94]

In addition to status, economic concerns also drove Yungay elites to protest relocation to Tingua. They feared that Tingua would never attain the economic prominence that had enabled the town's traditional economic control over the surrounding province. Others worried that the proposed site was unsuitable for future development. Complaining to a national newspaper in

November 1970, Yungay residents demanded that the national government "give more attention to future considerations, such as population, production, design of the city, and communication and transportation."[95] In subsequent weeks, local authorities from Yungay insisted that CRYRZA expand its studies to offer concrete plans for the future development of Tingua.[96] Interestingly, Yungay residents barely mentioned safety from glacier hazards as a consideration in either Tingua or Yungay Norte.

The potential for future tourism was another economic concern for Yungay residents who defended their homeland. Prior to 1970, the Yungay province had become a principal tourist destination in Peru. In late 1970, Yungay survivors believed tourists would come to see the avalanche site as well as Huascarán and Llanganuco.[97] Devotion to tourism meant that as quickly as Yungay Norte leaders built public schools and hospitals, they also reopened the road to Lake Llanganuco.[98] At the same time, a prominent Yungay leader, Pedro Maximo Angeles, pleaded with the College of Architects of Peru to design the new Yungay with engineering plans that "make the Province of Yungay a worldwide tourist attraction."[99] Tingua simply did not offer the proximity and access to Mount Huascarán and Lake Llanganuco that Yungay did.

Relocation in Huaraz also threatened the material well-being of inhabitants. Urban landowners complained because the state usurped land to widen streets, to restrict building, and to enforce hazard zoning. Government expropriation of land affected all economic classes and racial groups because, after the earthquake, officials bulldozed all remaining structures from the downtown section of Huaraz. CRYRZA oversaw the repartitioning of all lands. Residents thus lost power as well as land.[100] As a result, many Huaraz inhabitants attempted to intervene and maintain their land holdings. On November 7, 1971, for instance, 2,000 men and women in Huaraz simultaneously delimited and claimed their plots in the city by inscribing their names in the ground. The plan did not work. As Huaraz journalist, teacher, and longtime resident Olimpio Cotillo Caballero griped, when they returned to mark their plots, the police came and forcibly evicted them. In the end, "almost nobody received a plot of land in the same place as before." Huaraz became "an urban experiment" because of the dislocation and chaos involved in reapportioning lots to former residents.[101] Even worse for those who had held the largest plots of land, CRYRZA redistributed land through a lottery, and nobody could get more than anyone else. Officials often gave land to previous landowners first, but nobody could get more than 200 or 250 square meters because Velasco's mission was both equality and the toppling of oligarchy.[102] To Huaraz residents who had lived in the floodplain, hazard zoning bore an uncanny—and unacceptable—resemblance to the repartitioning of downtown land.

FIGURE 5.6. Houses along the Santa River, evidence of failed zoning in Huaraz, 2003. Credit: Photo by Mark Carey.

Urban survivors from Yungay also protested relocation because it signified their subordination—and power loss—to the central government. Yungay landowners also worried that Velasco's agrarian reform program sought to eliminate the traditional landed aristocracy, redistribute wealth, and enhance agricultural productivity. Urban survivors in Huaraz even went so far as to blame agrarian reform for the earthquake: "The president is to blame for this earthquake. He and this Agrarian Reform have caused all of this. They should kill him; they should throw him out."[103] Relocation and hazard zoning, many Callejón de Huaylas residents believed, also resembled Velasco's agrarian reform.[104] Economically, landowners did not receive full compensation for their land both because they received the (undervalued) self-declared tax value and because of rapid inflation. Socially and politically, the national government eroded landowners' traditional power over rural laborers and status as the dominant social group.

In contrast to scholarship that explains disaster vulnerability through the lens of external economic or political forces, these cases indicate that Callejón de Huaylas residents chose to remain inside the hazard zone—against the will of government officials and glacier experts. Although urban elites generally led resistance, other social groups participated in the campaign against reloca-tion, including the lower economic classes in both rural and urban areas. For example, some rural communities supported reconstruction in Yungay Norte from the outset. Others, however, yielded only after the Yungay elite persuaded the mayor of the district of Yanama, Isidro Obregón, to reject the Tingua relo-cation plan by pledging Yungay leaders' willingness to build a long-awaited road across the Cordillera Blanca at Punta Olímpica.[105] Yungay leaders also needed to persuade the new immigrants in Yungay Norte to resist relocation to Tingua. To accomplish this, leaders ensured that those in the relief camp had sufficient food and shelter.[106] Providing immediate needs linked residents to Yungay Norte and demonstrated leaders' effectiveness, thereby generating political support for Yungay elites. These recent arrivals became a force against government officials as they too resisted government relocation plans.

Successful resistance to relocation should not suggest that residents were unafraid of glacier avalanches and outburst floods. Many wondered if Huascarán would again break apart, and some local beliefs suggested that the Cordillera Blanca consisted of volcanoes of water that could erupt at any point. Jet air-planes even scared people because the noise sounded like an avalanche. Everyone was profoundly aware of the glacial lakes that loomed over their heads.[107] Given that fear of glacier disasters was acute, people's rejection of relocation suggests not that they were uninformed or oblivious, but rather that other risks—of losing social status, wealth, or power—ranked higher than the risk of an avalanche or outburst flood.

Peruvian responses to attempted hazard zoning beneath melting glaciers from the 1940s to the 1970s illustrates how economic, social, cultural, scientific, political, and environmental forces affect the success (and failure) of govern-ment efforts to prevent glacier disasters. Many Callejón de Huaylas residents rejected relocation because they believed it would jeopardize their social status, economic potential, or political autonomy. They insisted instead that science and technology deployed against the ice and lakes could save them. Most locals conflated hazard zoning with President Velasco's broader political agendas, which threatened to displace local elites and restructure the social landscape of highland Peru. Velasco was the Peruvian president who most actively and com-prehensively tried to reduce people's vulnerability to glacier hazards, but people opposed his measures—more than those of his predecessors—because they saw his larger social and political objectives as too intrusive. In trying to imple-ment what would have been the most comprehensive and effective way to reduce residents' vulnerability to glacier hazards, Velasco became the president who generated the most widespread and bitter local resistance to relocation plans since 1941. As glacier experts tried to mediate these opposing views, ence became a contested medium. Hugo Ramírez, a native of Recuay, celebrated local resistance to relocation, and he captures the essence of the struggles over scientific knowledge and the hazard zoning conflict more broadly:

> And this was the drama of Ancash in 1970: They discussed at great length the new location of destroyed towns. The love for homeland and the rigid, cold science congealed in distinct forms. Each struggled to impose its authority on the other, but in the end what should have triumphed did in fact triumph: human will. And thus the majority of towns, among them Huaraz, came to rebuild themselves in the same places of their destruction.... [T]hey will be there forever, suffering, stoic, crying through their destiny. And that is the beauty of it, the poetry, the immortality of a people.[108]

But in resisting relocation through this poetry of the people, the residents of Huaraz, Yungay, and Carhuaz created enduring legacies. On the one hand, they challenged authoritarian state power and participated in political processes. They also shaped the evolution of scientific and engineering approaches to disaster mitigation. They turned Callejón de Huaylas flood control programs into strictly technoscientific projects that lacked community participation. Disaster prevention thereafter had no human dimension. Glacier experts had advocated community involvement in hopes it would reduce local vulnerability by keeping residents out of possible flood and avalanche paths in the first place. Most disaster scholarship suggests that vulnerable populations are either forced into hazard zones or abandoned by the state. The Callejón de Huaylas history reveals a vulnerable people not simply as passive victims pushed into precarious situations.[109]

Ultimately, these technoscientific solutions to environmental hazards created local dependency on the very state the residents tried to keep out of their communities. They rejected hazard zones because of their desire to maintain their autonomy, keep the state at bay, and preserve power. But their choices produced the opposite result: they became highly dependent on the state to keep studying and monitoring glaciers and draining dangerous glacial lakes. By choosing lake drainage as the preferred solution to prevent outburst flood catastrophes, local residents rejected the solution that would have made them independent of the national government, which was relocation of their communities outside hazard zones. The state retains the power to end those programs with the stroke of a pen, as it did with President Fujimori's neoliberal reforms in the 1990s. Resistance to relocation plans—in large part because they wanted to remain independent of Lima—bound them to the state, a potentially precarious situation given Peru's lack of resources.

6

The Story of Vanishing
Water Towers

Glaciers have become an icon for global warming in part because
they are vanishing water towers. As ice disappears, so do water
supplies. From the Andes and Alps to the Himalayas and Rockies,
glaciers store water for societies to use. More important, glaciers
regulate water flow throughout the year. In temperate zones, they
release water during warm summer months, while in tropical
regions like the Andes, glaciers discharge water year-round. In Peru,
non-glacier-fed rivers often dry up when the rainy season ends. The
Santa River maintains a higher level of dry season (May to
September) water flow than other rivers in the country that do not
have the heavily glaciated Cordillera Blanca as the water source.
Complete glacier loss will likely affect not only Peruvians but also
hundreds of millions of people worldwide who use water from
mountain glaciers. At first glance, the issue of melting glaciers and
vanishing water seems straightforward: glacier runoff is almost the
only dry-season water supply on the Pacific side of the Cordillera
Blanca, from the Callejón de Huaylas to Chimbote.[1]

The discourse about vanishing water towers, however, is not so
simple. For one, loss of glacier volume is not necessarily an objective,
timeless, or inherently bad phenomenon. Glaciers always move,
sliding on their bedrock and changing size as a result of
geomorphologic and climatic conditions. Today people tend to
lament glacier loss, but previously many worried about the opposite.
From the fifteenth to the nineteenth century, most Europeans feared

advancing glaciers that periodically crashed into the communities, overtook their pastures and barns, destroyed crops, or created glacial lake outburst floods.[2] The early-nineteenth-century Swiss would have warmly embraced glacier melting to protect themselves, their food, and their property. Today's lament for lost ice thus raises questions about who is most affected by it, whose water is disappearing, who is managing the glacial water, and who has the political authority to maintain access when water supplies dwindle with likely global warming in the future.[3] In other words, power dynamics and societal issues underlie the scientific story of vanishing glaciers' effect on water.

Many narratives we take for granted have embedded power dimensions that put certain groups in control of managing landscapes and resources. Discourses about deforestation in the Amazon and land management in Africa, for example, have empowered empires, states, or the ruling classes. These narratives often pinpoint subsistence farmers or small-scale ranchers as the ones causing environmental degradation, thereby implying that states and experts should manage natural resources instead of local people.[4] In a few cases, such as rubber tappers in Brazil or indigenous groups fighting oil companies in Ecuador, local groups have seized international environmental discourse to pursue their own goals of labor and land rights.[5] In all cases, social relations and power imbalances shape stories about the environment, which in turn affect resource management policies.

The glacier narrative portraying the ice as vanishing water towers has also carried an embedded assumption about who has the right to the ice and how glaciers should be managed. This narrative could have taken a different turn. Consider some counterfactual questions. How would glacier science and subsequent discourse about melting Cordillera Blanca ice have evolved if Cañón del Pato did not exist, if the government had never formed the Santa Corporation, if the Santa River flowed gently to the coast with no option for hydroelectricity generation, or if climate and geography put glaciers on the eastern Andean slope, the opposite side from Lima? Would disaster prevention programs, glacier science, and national discourses about Andean ice have followed differently and with different social actors? Definitely. The energy industry shaped glacier science and played a vital role in constructing narratives about glaciers as vanishing water towers. State power companies conceived, funded, and conducted many glacier studies done by Peruvians, as opposed to international researchers studying glacier-water dynamics. The Santa Corporation, Electroperú, and Hidrandina carried out disaster prevention projects in the Cordillera Blanca, but they simultaneously did studies of hydrological resources. The Lakes Commission initiated this during the 1950s. In the 1960s, however, this hydroelectric hegemony was not yet as solidified as it became by the end of the 1980s. The "glaciers as vanishing water towers" narrative contributed to that transformation of glaciers from natural hazard to natural resource. Analyzing glacier science and discourse from the 1960s to 1980s provides a fascinating history of the relationship between environmental discourse and management.

Vying for the Right to Represent Ice

The 1962 Ranrahirca disaster raised questions about whether it was a fluke avalanche or the beginning of a trend. Two North American mountaineers, David Bernays and Charles Sawyer, held that it could be the latter and suggested later that year that another catastrophe from the same Glacier 511 could again devastate the Callejón de Huaylas. An avid climber with worldwide experience, Bernays was an electronics engineer from Florida. Sawyer was a geophysics graduate student at the Massachusetts Institute of Technology. They climbed several Cordillera Blanca peaks in mid-1962, including a first ascent of Mt. Tullparaju above the dangerous glacial lake that engineers were actively draining.[6] The mountaineers also spent several weeks on Mount Huascarán. Upon descending from that excursion, they warned Callejón de Huaylas authorities that another avalanche even larger than the Ranrahirca disaster could follow someday because of the loose bedrock under melting Glacier 511. On September 27, 1962, the local newspaper *El Expreso* exaggerated their findings in a story topped with the headline "Dantesque Avalanche Threatens Yungay." Regional newspapers picked up the story, and the news spread throughout the Callejón de Huaylas. The "mountaineers and scientists," as *El Departamento* referred to them, provided "a dramatic revelation that a gigantic avalanche three times larger than that of Ranrahirca threatens to dislodge, putting in danger Yungay, Mancos and the proposed site where they [authorities] plan to rebuild the devastated Ranrahirca." The news story concluded, "It is hoped that authorities take preventative measures to save the lives of the flourishing Callejón de Huaylas populations."[7]

But instead of following with studies or taking measures as newspapers implored, regional leaders clamored to silence the North Americans and halt dissemination of their conclusions. Authorities in Yungay, for example, issued a warning for people who might spread the U.S. mountain climbers' findings: "Return to your homes with your faith placed in God," the official statement read. It continued by announcing that anyone who spoke in favor of the Americans' conclusions would be charged under the Penal Code for "disrupting public tranquility."[8] The Ancash prefect asked Miguel Elías Pizarro, director of the Lakes Commission, to provide an "expert" analysis. Elías Pizarro's statement in early October—which was not apparently based on any scientific studies—dismissed the American mountaineers' statements as outlandish, hurried, and uninformed. As he wrote in a Huaraz newspaper, "Any ice avalanche coming from Huascarán would only affect the already razed area of the Ranrahirca valley without affecting the indicated populations [of Yungay and Mancos]." Elías Pizarro sharply criticized Bernays and Sawyer, writing bitterly, "This office deplores one more time the dissemination of this false information without first obtaining proof from worthy or credible sources, thereby creating, for no reason whatsoever, unrest and intranquility for the populations that are not threatened."[9] Huaraz residents later recalled that authorities even said they would imprison Bernays and Sawyer if they did not recant their initial warnings.[10]

On October 10, two weeks after the initial news story in *El Expreso*, David Bernays appeared at a public meeting in Huaraz. According to *El Departamento*, he called the Callejón de Huaylas media coverage exaggerated. Bernays apparently did warn about the "crevasses that signify a certain danger, but very remote because it is not possible to determine precisely when the avalanche could happen, because it could be within dozens or hundreds of years just as it could be very soon." The audience also asked about dangers from Lake Tullparaju, and Bernays apparently replied that "danger does not exist" there. He witnessed the "magnificent works the Peruvian engineers were conducting" at Tullparaju, which "when concluded will leave the entire Huaraz area totally secure from possible outburst floods."[11] That same month, the *Peruvian Times* printed a brief report in which Bernays and Sawyer clarified that "it is absolutely impossible to predict either *when* or *how large* such an avalanche will or could be. There is no basis for the widely circulated reports that such an avalanche will be either inevitable or three times as large as the last one." They did nonetheless point out that the Ranrahirca avalanche did not reduce the threat of a future avalanche because so much rock and ice remained on the mountain. Moreover, they observed that villages along the 1962 avalanche path remained vulnerable and "there may be a very remote danger to Yungay, as a sufficiently large avalanche might be able to spill over the hill Southeast of the town." They concluded that this was "only a preliminary report" that relied on minimal data.[12]

The mountaineers had little else to say about Huascarán. Bernays subsequently wrote many articles about his Peruvian climbs, including a detailed account of his Tullparaju climb.[13] None discuss the Huascarán situation or any of his interactions with authorities in Yungay or Huaraz. Was the commotion over the avalanche warning so unimportant and uninteresting that he would ignore it, even though he described his climbs in extensive detail? The lack of historical records about the public meetings and authorities' responses leaves a critical gap in the analysis of this event. But other evidence raises additional questions about what was at stake with glacier science in the early 1960s. And regardless of the mountaineers' findings, it was not their responsibility to conduct additional studies on the stability of Mount Huascarán.

But no state agency made a systematic investigation of Glacier 511—or hazards from any of the range's 700 glaciers. The 1962 avalanche was a new phenomenon in the Cordillera Blanca, and it would have been reasonable to research glacier stability, especially considering the mountaineers' conclusions and the great successes of glacial lake control that helped avert outburst floods after 1950. Nevertheless, through the 1960s, Peruvian glacier experts did not study glacier physics, bedrock stability, or relationships between bedrock and glaciers. They could not envision the 1970 catastrophe.

Disregard for the mountaineers' observations reveals how glacier experts struggled to defend their monopoly on Cordillera Blanca research and to preserve their right to "speak for the ice." When Elías Pizarro wrote that he "deplores one more time the dissemination of this false information without first obtaining proof from worthy or credible sources," he not only contradicted himself (because he did not first obtain proof for his denial of the danger), but he also hinted at his weakened power over glacier studies and information. The mountaineers both generated public angst and infringed on his domain. Struggles for control of glacial lake information had been ongoing since 1941. In the aftermath of each new disaster or false alarm, local residents insisted that the government divulge data about lakes and hazards. They asked for lists of the most dangerous glacial lakes, information about rain's effect on lake stability, and details of government expenditures on Cordillera Blanca disaster prevention projects. Government engineers' responses varied. In the case of Lake Parón in 1952 and after the 1962 mountaineers' warnings about Huascarán, the Lakes Commission hid information from the public or failed to investigate potential hazards. But after the 1959 near catastrophe from Lake Tullparaju, the Ministry of Development responded to angry public requests for details about completed lakes projects by revealing information on the status of fourteen glacial lake security projects, published in *El Comercio* on December 14, 1959.[14]

The Ranrahirca tragedy and two subsequent false alarms of outburst floods descending on Huaraz and Marcará in February 1962 exacerbated tensions over glacier and glacial lake information.[15] Some locals blamed the Lakes Commission for the Glacier 511 disaster, charging that the agency had not previously warned the population or even kept the avalanche from occurring in the way that it prevented outburst floods. Director Elías Pizarro dismissed this reaction as part of the population's "state of collective psychosis." He became increasingly defensive throughout the early 1960s. He even tried to justify his office's monopolization of glacier research "so as not to unproductively distract our normal work and to give authority solely and exclusively to the information that emanates from this Public office."[16] Less exclusive Lakes Commission control might have helped calm the public.[17] On the other hand, disasters compel victims to blame the government, regardless of state actions. There was little Elías Pizarro could have done in 1962 to quell public attacks on his office. He published numerous reports in regional newspapers and wrote in February 1962 that his "door is open" both for further suggestions about preventing glacier disasters and for residents to have a personal tour of the commission's lake security projects. He rightly scoffed at a local suggestion that a hundred men with buckets could drain Cordillera Blanca glacial lakes. And when complaints surged that the Lakes Commission should have prevented the Ranrahirca disaster, Elías Pizarro accurately pointed out that his predecessors never established a commission for "Control of Cordillera Blanca *Glaciers* and Lakes."[18] The emphasis had always been on glacial lakes. Glacier 511 was thus a new, unanticipated threat.

Though the commission had done—and continued doing—a host of engineering projects to stabilize glacial lakes, the false alarms and the Ranrahirca disaster pitted the community against the Lakes Commission. Local residents writing in regional and national newspapers lambasted the agency through the 1960s. As one person griped in 1965, the Lakes Commission "has become a bureaucratic entity that does nothing technical."[19] Both the glacier experts and the locals seemed to provoke the deepening tension. Residents were quick to blame the Lakes Commission for every hazard and disaster, which was obviously unfair because climate change and glacier retreat created the hazards that endangered communities that Spaniards had founded in the sixteenth century. Yet the commission withheld data about lake hazards, often stressing that "there is no danger"—only to have another disaster devastate the region a few years later.

At the root of these conflicts that flared after Bernays and Sawyer climbed Huascarán was the issue of who controlled science and information—who had the power to represent glaciers. Elías Pizarro did not conduct his own studies of Glacier 511 to verify or contradict the developments that the mountaineers found alarming. He pounced on them to try to keep control of glacier knowledge. In the early 1960s, the Lakes Commission did not have the local support, the political backing, or the financial resources to possess that power. That declining Lakes Commission authority helped usher in expanded control for the Santa Corporation, which had more political power in Lima and local support in Ancash. By the early 1970s, the Santa Corporation and its successor, Electroperú, had acquired the right to represent the ice.

More important, the 1962 warnings had not been enough to prevent the loss of life in the 1970 avalanche. As survivor Lamberto Guzmán Tapia lamented, "The disaster was predicted, but the warning was not taken into account. Since they predicted it, thousands of lives could have been saved and Yungay would not have disappeared."[20] Such sentiment simplifies the story, because the avalanche would have occurred regardless and residents likely would have refused to move out of the way in advance given the regional population's incessant rejection of hazard zoning since 1941. His accusation nonetheless illustrates a common no-win situation for governments and how they have to predict disasters with perfect accuracy or face public outrage: a lack of evacuation measures or hazard zoning when disaster strikes generates blame; evacuation when no disaster comes yields a costly public relations nightmare. Government leaders worldwide can be held to standards that require environmental omniscience.

Science and Economics Converge on the Glaciers

As Cordillera Blanca glacier and glacial lake research increasingly shifted to the Santa Corporation after the late 1960s, the studies' focus also switched from a primary concentration on hazards to an agenda that investigated both glacial hazards and resources. From the outset in 1966, the corporation's Division of Glaciology and Lakes Security had a strong emphasis on water use, in particular on the expansion of hydroelectricity generation at Cañón del Pato. The hydroelectric station at Cañón del Pato had opened in 1958 with a 50-megawatt capacity, and the station increased output to 100 megawatts in September 1967.[21] To reach its ultimate electricity generation objective of 150 megawatts, the Santa Corporation began in 1967 to search the Cordillera Blanca for potential sites to construct reservoirs, where the corporation could expand and regulate Santa River water flow.[22] Glacier studies contributed to these plans, and the Division of Glaciology and Lakes Security gathered data "with the objective of acquiring more knowledge about our water reserves in order to exploit water for electricity and irrigation."[23]

The Santa Corporation created its Division of Glaciology and Lakes Security in 1966 under the leadership of Peruvian glaciologist Benjamín Morales. Within a year, the better funded Glaciology Division became more active than the Lakes Commission in Cordillera Blanca research and glacial lake engineering. The

Glaciology Division devoted considerable attention to future water use and energy production. As Morales noted in a report summarizing the division's first two years, one of the Santa Corporation's "principal concerns" was studying reservoirs along the Santa River because some of its future projects to expand energy production would "depend directly on the possibility of hydrological regulation by being able to store [water] in the high valleys of the Cordillera Blanca. Consequently, another one of our principal activities has been to systematically explore the Cordillera Blanca from the South to North to study the possibilities for damming lateral valleys." After many reconnaissance trips, the Santa Corporation suggested twelve canyons as possible sites for future reservoirs that could be used to regulate water flow in the Santa River. Some glacial lakes, they noted, proved too dangerous for large dams and reservoirs, such as Lake Shallap and the lakes in Carhuaz's Ulta Canyon that had too many hanging glaciers to make reservoirs safe.[24] The specific cases of disaster prevention projects at Lakes Safuna and Parón, as well as the general direction of glaciology research in the late 1960s, demonstrate the corporation's dual focus on water use and disaster prevention.

Hydroelectric interests motivated both the Santa Corporation's glacial lake engineering projects and its study of glaciers. When it began studies in 1966, it investigated ablation, mass balance, glacier tongue positions, and regional climatic change. These topics reflected the water use orientation. Ablation studies, for example, allowed the Santa Corporation "to know the volume of water melting from glaciers and flowing into valleys below, and in what seasons that volume is greatest."[25] Mass balance helps determine whether a glacier is generally getting larger or smaller because it accounts for both accumulation and melting. The corporation also gathered climatic data throughout the Cordillera Blanca. In particular, its specialists wanted to learn about past and future snowfall, the primary ingredient for glacier making. It had installed 18 weather stations by the late 1960s, the majority along the Santa River and at lakes Conococha, Querococha, Llanganuco, and Parón. In the early 1970s, engineers installed additional pluviometric stations at Glaciers Broggi and Yanamarey to understand better the effects of temperature and precipitation on glacier retreat.[26] The mapping of glacier tongues—the lowest portion of a glacier—also yielded information about glacier size and behavior. By the early 1970s, the Santa Corporation was plotting locations of four glacier tongues—Safuna, Broggi, Uruashraju, and Yanamarey—in distinct Cordillera Blanca zones from the extreme north to south.[27] Peruvians' glaciological studies demonstrate how Andean researchers developed and maintained research agendas on their own terms, independent of international glaciologists' expertise in Europe and North America.[28]

Studies of ablation, mass balance, climatic conditions, and glacier tongue positions could have been the first steps toward understanding glacier hazards—a reasonable assumption given the 1962 avalanche. Glacier physics are complex and the analysis of mass balance in particular is a fundamental requisite for understanding glacier behavior generally. But Peruvian engineers' studies on these topics seem to have been directed toward more utilitarian and economic concerns. Disaster economics was actively playing out with the Santa Corporation because its glaciology office officially integrated glacier research and disaster mitigation with economic development—something the Lakes Commission encouraged but did less systematically. The research also began the process through which Andean glaciers transformed from hazards to vanishing water towers. As the corporation became *the* entity conducting glacier research and carrying out disaster mitigation in the Cordillera Blanca after the early 1970s, when the government dissolved the Lakes Commission, the Santa Corporation benefited from the discursive construction of glaciers that justified its own control over Cordillera Blanca hydrology.[29]

A National Inventory of Glaciers

An important step in the historical construction of glaciers as vanishing water towers was the quantification of glaciers through inventories. Since the 1970s, the surface area of Cordillera Blanca glaciers has declined, as revealed by a rather constant rate of loss of mass balance and the retreat of glacier tongues.[30] But quantifying these processes over the last decades has also contributed to the discursive construction of glaciers as hydrological resources. The inventories serve an important role in understanding glacier-water relationships, but they also provided that data to particular groups, such as government agencies, hydroelectric companies, and large-scale irrigators, rather than to individual Callejón de Huaylas farmers.

The Santa Corporation and Electroperú played a vital role in defining and quantifying glaciers throughout Peru. In 1988, Alcides Ames of the Glaciology and Lakes Security Unit compiled the first "glacier inventory" of Peru. Ames began informal work on the inventory during his initial days as a glacier expert in the early 1960s. After 1978 he devoted significant attention to the inventory, relying on his excellent skills as a cartographer and superb knowledge of the Cordillera Blanca and other mountain ranges. Although Ames and other collaborators were hampered by shortages of money and resources—such as the lack of computers, which forced Ames to do all calculations by hand—they completed the inventory in 1987. Ames's leadership and tenacity kept the project on track.

This Peruvian glacier inventory accumulated data never before collected in the Andes, and it contributed to international programs including the World Glacier Inventory. The study compiled data to map glaciers' edges, latitude and longitude, elevations, ablation zones, and total surface area. Ames underscored the purpose of the inventory in its opening sentences: "Water is a resource closely bound to the progress of civilization, both to satisfy its vital needs and to produce food, energy and other uses. Where there is plenty of this element, peoples develop and grow; where it lacks, people languish and become extinct."[31] The emphasis on water resources of course paralleled Electroperú's broader mission: hydroelectricity generation. Quantifying glaciers expanded company knowledge about the water supplies that produced energy. As Benjamín Morales explained in the inventory, "During those years, groups of technicians from Huaraz went out to know the characteristics of the 20 ice-covered cordilleras of Peru, in what is considered an unprecedented effort in the research work of the water resources of the Peruvian Andes."[32] The fact that experts based glacier classifications on glacier type—instead of creating an index of stability or likelihood of producing avalanches—reveals the focus on glaciers as bodies of ice that stored water. In fact, the overall orientation of the inventory suggests that its purpose was to quantify water resources.

The inventory can be analyzed in several ways. It has heightened Peruvian knowledge about scarce Andean water supplies. This information has helped electrify homes and promote industry and agriculture. More recently, the data have helped national and international studies of global climate change. But the inventory provided data primarily for Electroperú, the Huaraz-based power company Hidrandina, and the national government. What had for entrepreneurs and ruling coastal classes been "vacant," "frigid," or "white" lands became organized, classified, and ordered space from which to extract natural resources.[33] This could be seen as part of long-term global processes whereby states gained knowledge and power over remote regions and resources, whether Prussian forests or the boundaries of Mexico.[34] Rural inhabitants who practice irrigation rituals and maintain spiritual connections with glacier water have ascribed meanings to glaciers different from those emerging from the quantified inventory circulating among scientists, economic developers, and policymakers. It is often the data, numbers, and statistics that generate policies regarding water use and environmental management.[35] The quantification of glacial ice supplies also helped define glaciers as utilitarian water towers. Local people obviously benefited from expanded water use, but state-run power companies and the Peruvian government controlled the information—at least until Duke Energy took over Cañón del Pato in the late 1990s. Through Peruvian glaciology, the state-run Electroperú expanded its control over one of the last Andean frontiers, the glaciated peaks. As scholars have shown in many world regions, the power to define nature and control the discourse often determines who gets to use nature and for what purposes.

From Hazard to Resource

New agencies managing Cordillera Blanca disaster prevention projects after the 1980s further shifted the management of glaciers from hazards to resources. The names of these state agencies illustrate the transformation. President Odría established the Control Commission of Cordillera Blanca Lakes in 1951, an agency with a clear disaster mitigation mission. The Santa Corporation's Division of Glaciology and Lakes Security Program displaced the Lakes Commission in the early 1970s. The new name, which continued while Electroperú and other agencies ran it in the 1970s and 1980s, was a rhetorical shift that nonetheless continued to emphasize its role in research and disaster prevention. But the transition had shifted oversight from the Ministry of Development and Public Works to the Ministry of Energy and Mines, suggesting a new orientation toward resource extraction rather than public works. From 1986 to 1990, the agency became the Glaciology and Hydrology Unit under management of Hidrandina. "Lakes security" vanished from its name. Then, from 1990 to 1997, when the agency moved back to Electroperú, it adopted the name it retains today: the Glaciology and Hydrological Resources Unit. Since 2001, the office has been in the Ministry of Agriculture, first within the National Institute of Natural Resources and then, since 2008, part of the National Water Authority.

The new terminology was reflected in the agencies' mission statements as well. In 1987, the Glaciology and Hydrology Unit's mission had a clear water-use emphasis. "All the planned activities," the mission statement read, "are oriented toward the evaluation of the alpine zone's hydrological resources with the objective of regulating water flows to exploit it for electricity generation, as well as the security of hydroelectric facilities."[36] By 1995, the Glaciology and Hydrological Resources Unit framed its mission by noting that "glaciers are the continent's freshwater reserves that constitute natural reservoirs and regulate the flow of water in rivers during the dry season." Its objectives were: (1) "to apply the knowledge from Glaciology toward the better use of Hydrological Resources"; (2) "to recommend alternative projects to exploit the High Mountain Hydrological Resources"; and (3) "to carry out security Studies and Projects at lakes."[37]

Electroperú, Hidrandina, and the Glaciology and Hydrology Unit were now putting activities and programs behind the discursive conceptualization of

Andean glaciers as water towers. Glacier experts in the 1980s focused on glacier monitoring, conducting more water use studies at the largest glacial lakes,
and constructing reservoirs to control Santa River water flow specifically at
Lakes Parón, Cullicocha, Auquiscocha, and others. After Lake Parón had been
partially drained in 1985 to reduce the threat of an outburst flood, engineers
and policymakers proposed moving into the next phase of the Parón project:
installing valves at the opening of the lake drainage tunnel to control water flow
leaving the lake and thus in the Santa River. They hoped that after installing
these they would be able to increase the amount of water in the lake during the
rainy season to release it under their control during the dry season, when the
hydroelectric facility and irrigators most needed the water downriver. In a
strange reversal, after 45 years of local demands and expert efforts to drain Lake
Parón to reduce the threat of an outburst flood, water developers—with the
help of the glacier experts—in the late 1980s were trying to put water back in
the lake. They estimated that after installing these valves, their increased ability
to regulate the Santa River would earn Electroperú an additional U.S. $1 mil-
lion–$3 million annually at Cañón del Pato.[38] They hoped to build other reser-
voirs at Lakes Cullicocha, Santa Cruz, Rajucolta, and Querococha.[39] The
glaciology office also continued its hazard reduction programs, though without
the dedicated focus and resources that had characterized the 1970s.[40] Residents
and regional officials kept demanding such projects to protect the population.[41]
The glaciology office kept reporting for Huaraz that "it has been clarified with
exactitude that no danger of possible lake outburst floods exists around our
city."[42] The emergency situation at Lake 513a would soon show that risks to
regional populations persisted even though disaster prevention programs
occurred with only marginal support from Lima.

The Gamble at Lake 513a

By 1985, when Lake 513a became an imminent threat to Carhuaz and the
Callejón de Huaylas, glacial lakes worldwide were becoming increasingly dangerous. That same year, for example, the famous Tsho Rolpa glacial lake caused
an outburst flood in Nepal.[43] Lake 513a is at the base of Mt. Hualcán above the
city of Carhuaz. Residents of the Hualcán village have long believed that dangerous winds could descend from glacial ice on Mt. Hualcán and that enchanted
lakes could harm the people. Lake Yawarqoca (Bloody Lake), named for the red
water that people claimed to see there, was one of these enchanted lakes.
Nobody went near the lake for fear of its malevolent spirits. As locals explain, a
woman carrying her baby once went right up to the water because she did not

know about the spirits. Immediately, the water "came up high and covered up the two. After a few days, the body of the woman, carrying her baby, appeared. They had been changed into stone. When the people came to learn what had happened, they brought up a priest to bless it. Now it is tame." According to testimonies, the lake remained dangerous during the new moon, and residents thus preferred to stay away from it or, if necessary to go near it, stopped at a shrine nearby to pray beforehand.[44]

Carhuaz residents also worried about Mount Hualcán's glaciers and lakes. In 1953, engineers partially drained Lake Cochca, and in the late 1960s mountaineers pointed out potential glacier hazards on Mt. Hualcán. Avalanches from the unstable glacier, they worried, could crash into Lakes Cochca and Yanahuanca, thereby creating a glacial lake outburst flood. By the 1970s, authorities and experts were concerned enough about unstable Hualcán glaciers and glacial lakes that they tried to relocate the city of Carhuaz to keep it out of potential flood and avalanche paths. It was an opportune moment to move Carhuaz, authorities argued, because the 1970 earthquake had destroyed much of the city and because glacial hazards still existed. Residents resisted—and won. Yet, by refusing to relocate, they remained in the hazard zone. Thus, when researchers on a routine inspection in 1980 first noticed a new lake forming at the base of Glacier 513a, residents were well aware of the glacier hazards hanging over their heads.[45]

By 1985, the lake was large and unstable. The experts' detailed study found that Lake 513a had swelled to three-quarters of a kilometer long, a quarter-kilometer wide, and 120 meters deep.[46] In 1988, glaciology unit engineers César Portocarrero and Andrés Huamán believed the situation had escalated into an emergency for Carhuaz's 25,000 residents. They discussed the problem with two foreign scientists doing independent research projects in Peru at the time, British geophysicist John Reynolds and Italian physical geographer Georg Kaser from Austria's University of Innsbruck. These specialists identified two related problems that made Lake 513a particularly threatening. First, the lake had space to grow much larger and was supplied by a large glacier that produced abundant meltwater. Second, the moraine dam holding back the lake had an ice core, a remnant of the glacier—what glaciologists call "dead ice"—that was now melting rapidly inside the moraine. As the ice inside the moraine melted, the dam holding back Lake 513a kept sinking. As fast as the lake level rose, the height of the lake dam simultaneously fell. Between 1985 and 1988, the moraine dam had sunk an astonishing four meters, at an estimated average rate of 11 centimeters per month. Experts estimated the lake dam would fail within months, sending an outburst flood into urban Carhuaz.[47] Kaser and Reynolds suggested evacuating Carhuaz while the lake remained unstable.

Regional authorities, however, insisted that the people would not obey and would instead become angry about such a proposal that reminded them of their fight against hazard zoning in previous decades.[48]

Only one solution seemed a practical option: drain the lake immediately. Experts hoped that if they lowered the lake level by at least 8 meters, but preferably 12, they could avert disaster. In October 1988, Peruvian engineers Marino Zamorra, César Portocarrero, Andrés Huamán, and Marco Zapata installed an eight-inch-diameter pipe to siphon water out of the lake. By Christmas they had pumped out approximately 1 million cubic meters of water, but because of the constant influx of both glacier meltwater and precipitation, the lake level had not dropped at all. Engineers realized they needed to install an additional pipe to increase the rate of water discharge. But funding evaporated amid the Peruvian government's extreme financial difficulties, especially the country's 2,000 percent inflation rate. Recognizing the likelihood of an impending disaster for Carhuaz and the entire region, Reynolds traveled to Lima to visit the British ambassador, who agreed to help fund the lake drainage project, as did private donors in Austria. In January 1989, engineers installed the second drainage pipe at Lake 513a. With two siphons running constantly, the lake's water level finally fell. They continued draining the lake with siphons for the next year and a half.

While the siphons helped avert an immediate catastrophe, they did not offer a long-term solution of lake stability. Thus, in mid-1990, engineers proposed to dig an open drainage channel through the moraine to keep the lake level down. As they planned for this project into 1991, enlisting support from the national government's Civil Defense, the feared scenario occurred: an ice avalanche crashed into the lake and triggered an outburst flood. Water spilled out from the lake, spread out across the floor of the upper canyon, and began racing downhill toward Carhuaz. Fortunately, the moraine dam did not disintegrate completely, and only some of the lake water burst out through the opening. The valley floor was wide enough to dissipate much of the floodwaters, so the flood caused only minimal damage and no deaths. It did, however, destroy bridges and irrigation canals, which created a scare among residents. It was a narrow escape, and no doubt the diligent efforts to drain the lake from 1988 to 1991 had prevented catastrophe. But the small 1991 outburst flood from Lake 513a also demonstrated its continued instability and threat to local communities.

Beyond money shortages and the rapidly changing physical environment that vexed engineers at the lake, Shining Path (Sendero Luminoso) violence in the late 1980s and 1990s also slowed progress. Shining Path was a Maoist organization formed by Abimael Guzmán in the early 1970s as the Communist

Party of Peru. In 1980, the guerrilla group began fighting violently against the Peruvian state and other forces it saw as oppressive to the country's poor. The brutal conflict originated near Huamanga (Ayacucho), but through the course of the 1980s spread throughout the country. Widespread violence, especially in rural parts of the Andes but increasingly in urban areas and into Lima, persisted into the 1990s, until the Peruvian government captured Guzmán in 1992. The Shining Path movement waned in subsequent years, but between 1980 and 2000 approximately 70,000 people died in the struggle.[49] Though Ancash and the Cordillera Blanca region were less affected than many other parts of Peru, the region did not escape terrorism, especially in the years around 1990. Continuous threats of violence affected both residents and glacier experts. Rumors spread that Shining Path members had transformed former labor camps at isolated glacial lakes into hideouts. Not surprisingly, engineers in the Glaciology and Hydrological Resources Unit became more apprehensive about some of their fieldwork. They tried to dissuade foreign scientists and engineers from conducting research in the Cordillera Blanca or even helping them with the Lake 513a project, which was mostly secure by 1989 but required ongoing drainage to stabilize the lake dam. Through 1990 and 1991, the proposed project to construct a drainage canal from the lake thus lagged. As John Reynolds explained at the time, "Even though funding could be made available through international aid, the presence of Maoist terrorists in the area has made it highly unlikely that any further remedial action can be taken until the political problems have been resolved."[50] Consequently, it would take several more years for engineers to complete the security project at Lake 513a.

Once engineers with the glaciology unit finally resumed their work to make the lake safe for Carhuaz residents, they met still more obstacles. First, access to Lake 513a required hiking a steep, rough trail. Hauling equipment was extremely difficult, sometimes requiring up to 60 porters. A second obstacle was the technical challenge of draining Lake 513a. The lake proved particularly problematic because of its ice-cored moraine dam. Experts used a Norwegian technique that was different from any used at the 30 other Cordillera Blanca glacial lakes the glaciology office had drained since the 1940s. They had drilled four drainage tunnels by 1994 and removed between 6 million and 7 million cubic meters of water—an amount comparable to that released in the 1945 Chavín and 1950 Los Cedros outburst floods. They lowered the lake far enough that it was dammed behind granodiorite bedrock instead of an unstable moraine. Carhuaz residents could feel more secure about glacial Lake 513a.

But Lake 513a was not the only hazard in the 1990s. Georg Kaser estimated that "five to ten similar situations could develop within the next few years."[51]

John Reynolds argued that because of "the continuation of glacier recession and lake development through global warming, there is an urgent need for a national government strategy for glacier hazard assessment and mitigation." He also maintained that lake security projects and glacier monitoring would ultimately be much cheaper than disaster relief, and it would save lives.[52] Peruvian glacier expert Alcides Ames, with experience in the Cordillera Blanca since the early 1960s, also recognized the continued importance of both glacial lake monitoring and disaster mitigation.[53] But fulfilling these objectives that foreign and national glacier experts outlined would prove difficult.

Draining Lake 513a took nine years. At a similar emergency situation at a glacial lake on the Italy-Switzerland border in 2002, authorities and experts responded within 24 hours, setting up a drainage system and a communications network that eliminated the threat within weeks, even allowing tourism to boom at the lake several months later.[54] Things in Peru moved more slowly, in part due to economic woes and Shining Path activity.

And yet, while Carhuaz residents wondered whether they would live through another weekend, the state managed to fund water *use* projects in the Cordillera Blanca. In 1989, the operating budget for "urgent" glacial lake security projects at Lake 513a and Lake 69 was just slightly higher than the amount allocated to the glaciology office to transform Lake Parón into a water-regulating reservoir that would increase hydroelectricity generation and expand irrigation projects.[55] Engineers installed water-regulating control valves at Lake Parón in 1992, two years before they secured Lake 513a. Energy needs were growing in Peru, and Electroperú could help meet them with increased electricity generation at Cañón del Pato. But were these energy needs more acute than the need to head off potential catastrophe in Carhuaz?

Tension between disaster prevention imperatives and water use interests was obviously nothing new in the Cordillera Blanca. It had been evolving since 1941 and then became much more forceful after the Santa Corporation and its successors managed glacier science after the 1960s. But scientific depictions of glaciers increased hydroelectric hegemony in the region, and the lack of a major catastrophe in the 1980s and 1990s helped water use interests prevail over disaster prevention.

While the Santa Corporation—and later Electroperú and Hidrandina—did protect people from glacial lake outburst floods, the hydroelectric companies' increasing monopolization of glacier research meant water developers acquired the authority to define glacial ice primarily as a water tower. After the 1960s, glacier experts produced their glaciological and hydrological data for the hydroelectric company. Once President Fujimori privatized Cañón del Pato in 1996, that information began benefiting Duke Energy, a private company based in the United States and responsible to shareholders rather than the Peruvian public.

Long-term, detailed documentation of glacier melting also led to a "glacier narrative" that told of retreat, loss, decline, and future tragedy from water loss. Global warming concerns perpetuate and strengthen this narrative of loss. Yet there are problems with this urgent doomsday scenario. Studies still do not offer precise estimates about how much water will actually flow down the Santa River if all or some of the Cordillera Blanca glaciers disappear or when glaciers will begin to release less water under specific future climate change scenarios. There is another problem with the glacier narrative. Cordillera Blanca glaciers affect water *availability*, but in many ways it is people who affect the amount of water *used*. Water use obviously depends upon water availability; but use also depends on technology, human ingenuity, population, and other factors. In the case of Peru's glaciers—and those elsewhere in the world—there is no doubt that glaciers have retreated. Yet, as glaciers shrank during the last half century, the use of glacial water has actually increased. This trajectory runs contrary to the embedded but obviously too simplistic assumption in the "glaciers as vanishing water towers" narrative that less ice would mean less water to use.

Specifically, two areas of water use have increased since the glacier narrative of loss became etched in Peruvians' minds during the 1960s. Hydroelectricity output at Cañón del Pato has risen steadily. When it opened in 1958, its capacity was 50 megawatts; then it increased to 100 megawatts in 1967, to 150 in 1982, to 200 in 1999, and to 256 by 2002.[56] Duke Energy continues to search for sites to build reservoirs and expand hydroelectricity generation. In the last half century, hydroelectric capacity increased both through the installation of more equipment at Cañón del Pato and through the construction of reservoirs in the Santa River watershed. Coastal irrigation projects that arose during the last three decades to boost agricultural production in the Pacific lowlands also increased Santa River water use. The Chavimochic and Chinecas projects were the largest enacted; others remain under consideration. Far from suffering negative consequences of persistent glacier retreat, these large-scale water users in the Santa River watershed have continued to expand water use as glaciers melted.

The glacier narrative that emphasizes loss and decline thus fails to yield a comparable reality when actual water use is considered. Nevertheless, the narrative carries an implicit assumption that less ice means reduced water use. Given the overall importance of glaciers for water availability, the past trend could change with continued glacier melting in the future. If glaciers continue to melt, it is likely that water availability and use will decline.

Ice as vanishing water towers is not the only glacier narrative. Glaciers also represent natural hazards, scientific laboratories, mountaineering terrain, recreation playgrounds, spiritual centers, and scenery. The water source, however, has increasingly taken precedence and priority in terms of management and policy. Peruvians of course benefit from Cañón del Pato hydroelectricity and coastal irrigation. At the same time, glacier experts and the various hydroelectric companies that constructed the glacier-water discourse also promoted increased Peruvian state control over one of the most remote Andean regions, the glaciated peaks.

7

The Risk of Neoliberal
Glaciers

When President Alberto Fujimori implemented his neoliberal reforms that privatized Peru's hydroelectric industry during the 1990s, Cordillera Blanca disaster prevention programs suffered markedly. By selling the Cañón del Pato hydroelectric plant to Egenor (Northern Peru Electric Generation Company), which the U.S.-based Duke Energy then consolidated, the state-owned Electroperú withdrew from the Santa River watershed. As it withdrew in late 1996 and 1997, Electroperú closed the Glaciology and Hydrological Resources Unit. Suddenly, the state agency charged with monitoring and mitigating glacier hazards became a victim of the neoliberal agenda to reduce public spending. For Ancash residents, privatization meant increased vulnerability to glacier and glacial lake hazards. And the hazards remained as Andean and worldwide glacier retreat and ensuing glacial lake formation persisted after the 1980s.

As local vulnerability to glacier hazards increased, Egenor nearly doubled its use of Santa River water, which comes primarily from Cordillera Blanca glacier meltwater. The energy company also began building new reservoirs at Cordillera Blanca lakes to boost electricity generation at Cañón del Pato. In one case, Duke Energy even tried to add water to Lake Shallap, which the state had previously drained to prevent an outburst flood. As local residents pleaded with the government to remove water from glacial lakes, Egenor was trying to fill them higher than ever.

Privatization meant that Egenor began managing the Cordillera Blanca as a "neoliberal waterscape," which consists of glacial lakes, reservoirs, rivers, and streams. Glaciers play a vital role in the waterscape by providing a major water source and, perhaps even more important, regulating water flow throughout the year. To generate more electricity at Cañón del Pato, the company tried to increase Santa River water flow, which sometimes involved managing the river's tributaries right up to the glacial ice. Egenor, of course, did not (and does not) want an outburst flood. But its management of the waterscape has focused on maximizing profits at the hydroelectric station. The type of broadly based disaster prevention programs that state agencies since the Lakes Commission had conducted—which tackled some glacial lake hazards that may not have even affected Cañón del Pato—was not in the private company's interest. Duke Energy bought access to Peru's vanishing water towers, not a responsibility to protect the region's populations. Neoliberal privatization provided the legal and political framework for Santa River water use interests to potentially eclipse local safety issues—the more insidious part of "disaster capitalism" that Naomi Klein and others have discussed.[1]

Peruvians, of course, were not the only ones to experience what scholars often refer to as the "neoliberalization of nature" in recent decades.[2] As Ancash residents watched Duke Energy transform hydroelectricity generation and manage the region's waterscape, people elsewhere in Peru and Latin America also underwent similar neoliberal transitions. In Cajamarca, the privatization of mining transformed land tenure patterns, while neoliberalism led to more open access to fisheries off the Peruvian coast. In cities like Guayaquil and Cochabamba, residents saw their urban water supplies privatized. In Chile and Mexico, privatization allowed more open access to forests and agricultural lands, among other resources.[3] Many argue that neoliberalism intensified vulnerability to disasters by increasing poverty, by siphoning labor and food production into exports rather than family livelihoods, and by pushing people onto marginalized land susceptible to flooding or landslides.[4] As one of the most important political and economic transformations in recent decades, neoliberalism has generated far-reaching changes worldwide. Yet, the understanding of how neoliberalism affects human-environment relations remains relatively understudied compared to the analysis of issues such as unemployment, poverty, income distribution, social equality, and the quality of democracy.[5] Examining Peru's Cañón del Pato and Duke Energy in the context of climate change and glacier retreat not only illuminates these neoliberal processes, but also exposes the gap that usually exists between neoliberal doctrine and on-the-ground implementation.

Neoliberalism, Fujimori, and Duke Energy

When Alberto Fujimori began his decadelong presidency in 1990, he had bigger disasters to worry about than a potential flood from glacial lakes such as Lake 513a. The two most pressing national problems revolved around the foundering economy and bloody civil unrest that had increasingly plagued Peru since 1980. The Peruvian economy spun out of control in the late 1980s under President Alan García. Economic catastrophe only encouraged Shining Path terrorism, which Fujimori subdued in 1992 after capturing Guzmán and other terrorist leaders.[6] The president accomplished this in part because of his expanded powers following his April 1992 self-coup, which allowed him to rule for the next eight years as an authoritarian populist. During that time, his popularity rose alongside his increasingly centralized power because he helped stabilize the economy.

Fujimori followed neoliberal doctrine to deregulate, privatize, and open the Peruvian economy. Neoliberalism had been transforming economies and governments worldwide since the 1970s, and increasingly so by the 1990s after the collapse of the Soviet Union.[7] In Latin America, it replaced the post–World War II model of import substitution industrialization. Fujimori began implementing neoliberal reforms immediately after taking office, pursuing them even more aggressively as his centralized power expanded. He reduced the size of the national government, slashed price subsidies, limited social spending, raised interest rates, increased taxes, deregulated financial and labor markets, decentralized services, allowed more free trade, and started paying Peru's national debt.[8] But democracy and human rights suffered.[9] There were other social costs—such as disaster and climate vulnerability—that have gone largely unanalyzed.

Privatizing the public sector, especially communications and energy, was particularly important to Fujimori. He believed that President Velasco had begun the expansion of the Peruvian government into a colossal bureaucracy that became increasingly inefficient, ineffective, and expensive. Indeed, by 1990 the Peruvian state had become one of Latin America's largest and weakest. Instead of generating revenue, public sector industries between 1985 and 1990 cost the national government $1.6 billion. The electricity industry was particularly prone to losing government money, given its large bureaucracy, corruption, lack of transparency, and inefficient expenditures and investments. Because of the financial liability of state-owned companies and the neoliberal dogma of deregulation and privatization, President Fujimori began liquidating state-owned companies as soon as he took power.[10]

Seeing Electrolima and Electroperú as two of the most important state-owned energy companies to privatize, the government implemented the 1992 Electric Concessions Law to begin that process.[11] The Cañón del Pato station became one of the hydroelectric plants targeted for privatization. In April 1996, President Fujimori and Daniel Hokama, the minister of energy and mines, approved the measure to sell Cañón del Pato to Egenor. The U.S. company Dominion Energy acquired the majority of Egenor in 1996.[12] Through a complicated process involving political policies, stockholder decisions, and economic agreements, Duke Energy had by 1999 acquired the principal share of Cañón del Pato. A Fortune 500 company based in Charlotte, North Carolina, Duke Energy now produces roughly 4,000 megawatts of energy in Central and South America, specifically in Argentina, Brazil, Ecuador, El Salvador, Guatemala, and Peru. By 2002, the company held 99 percent of Egenor and in Peru was called Duke Energy International Egenor, known interchangeably in the country as either Duke or Egenor. Duke Energy ranks among the largest private energy companies in Peru, and its principal electricity generation station is Cañón del Pato.[13]

Privatizing the electricity industry generated mixed results for Peruvians. On the one hand, Peru's electrification index (percentage of people with electricity) rose from 48.4 percent in 1992 to 70 percent in 1998. Also, the number of households with electricity rose from 1.8 million in 1992 to 2.9 million in 1998.[14] While sounding like positive accomplishments, these statistics fail to mention that prices for residential power rose substantially during the 1992–1997 period, without a similar rise in income.[15] Beyond rising prices, Peruvians and others also complained about privatization more generally, arguing that it limited public spending on social programs and public works projects and diminished their control over resources and agendas previously managed by the state.[16] It was the elimination of one such social program—the Glaciology and Hydrological Resources Unit—that irritated Ancash residents living beneath melting Cordillera Blanca glaciers.

The Fate of Glaciology in the Privatized Andes

The glaciology unit, originally scheduled to close by October 1996, maintained a small staff until it officially disintegrated in March 1997.[17] Fujimori's neoliberal agenda was generating far-reaching implications for Callejón de Huaylas residents: they suddenly found themselves without the state agency that had been working to prevent glacier and glacial lake disasters for a half century. The glaciology office had in the past been unstable, had moved among several agencies, had its budget slashed, and had increasingly pursued water use interests instead of disaster mitigation. Nevertheless, the state had been funding and maintaining a specific agency for decades.

Local residents, regional leaders, glacier experts, and an increasingly active Lima-based environmental community concerned with global warming did not stand by idly as Electroperú got out of the disaster prevention business. In fact, even before the Glaciology and Hydrological Resources Unit was shut down, these groups began protesting the closure and insisting on alternative plans to keep the office open. A group of Ancash mayors explained in January 1997, for example, that after 50 years of protecting the region's inhabitants, the glaciology office must continue "to maintain control of the lakes and consequently provide security to the populations surrounding the entire Cordillera Blanca."[18] By March 1997, Ancash President Fredy Moreno Neglia had also become concerned. In a letter to Electroperú's director, Jesús Beutis, the president explained that Cordillera Blanca glaciers were important nationally and that glacial lakes put Ancash in "permanent danger" of outburst floods. He praised the historical accomplishments of Electroperú (and its predecessor, the Santa Corporation) not only for protecting Ancash residents, but also for advancing national and regional economic development and distributing electricity to Peruvians. Its work "cannot be interrupted," the Ancash president concluded.[19]

Electroperú actually began discussing the glaciology office's future as soon as the state privatized Cañón del Pato in 1996. The energy company weighed four options: fund the glaciology office even though Electroperú had no Santa River operations; close it completely; transfer it to another government ministry; or transfer it to a private organization. Electroperú recognized the agency's importance and believed its equipment and its archive, with thousands of technical reports, remained useful for future disaster prevention and water resource management. But the office had an estimated annual budgetary need of 1.7 million Peruvian soles, and Electroperú could not maintain it. Consequently, company managers saw a transfer as the best solution. Transferring it to the Water Division of the National Institute of Natural Resources (INRENA) within the Ministry of Agriculture would keep the glaciology office within the national government, which Electroperú viewed as favorable because it was legally created as a national state agency. But Electroperú worried that under INRENA's control, information would not be standardized with the hydroelectric industry. Alternatively, Electroperú saw advantages to private operation of the Glaciology and Hydrological Resources Unit. In particular, the company's 1996 report on the fate of the unit concluded that private management would allow "the intervention of Electroperú" and other electric companies to direct the institute's research and maintain access to its data. The disadvantage of this solution, they projected, would be its tenuous funding, which could cause "grave damage to the development of water use projects and the production of hydroelectric energy." Electroperú considered handing over the glaciology office to the Geological Mining and Metallurgical Institute, the Ancash government, Civil Defense, and Huaraz's "Santiago Antúnez de Mayolo" National University.[20] Although Electroperú searched for a new home for the glaciology office, its objective did not revolve around glacier hazards or the protection of local populations. Instead, Electroperú saw the Glaciology and Hydrological Resources Unit as a tool of the hydroelectricity industry.

Like many local residents, glacier experts also opposed the closing of the unit and, in some cases, sought to continue its existence in a new form if necessary. Alcides Ames, one of the country's leading glacier experts, with 40 years of experience working in the Cordillera Blanca, expressed considerable apprehension about closing the office. He argued that "the continuous attentive observation of existing lakes as well as of developing proglacial lakes is of major importance especially in the Cordillera Blanca where human activities are in the immediate neighbourhood of hazardous proglacial lakes."[21] César Portocarrero, who previously directed the Glaciology and Hydrological Resources Unit, proposed transferring it to a private organization that he was forming called the Institute of Hydrology and Glaciology. Also in late 1996, Benjamín Morales, the first director of the Santa Corporation's glaciology office back in the 1960s, also saw the need to maintain an organization charged with Cordillera Blanca research and disaster prevention. Morales announced in January 1997 that he and his colleagues had formed a new organization that could take over glacier and glacial lake monitoring, the Andean Glaciology and Geoenvironmental Institute. His institute was formed "with the objective of continuing and expanding research on hydrological resources from glaciers and lakes located in the country's 20 glaciated mountain ranges."[22] These glacier experts, along with Marco Zapata, who had by the late 1990s become one of the most prominent glacier experts in Peru, knew more about Andean glacier hazards than anyone on earth. They vehemently opposed the permanent closing of the government's Glaciology and Hydrological Resources Unit. But they also had personal interests in seeing the agency continue. Some observers even suggested that these glacier experts' infighting and competition helped derail discussions about the future of the glaciology office.

Other national agencies also became involved in the fate of glaciological research. In the mid-1990s, the Peruvian government formed the National Climate Change Commission to implement specific programs to combat global warming. This work increasingly fell under the auspices of Peru's National Council for the Environment (CONAM) during the late 1990s. The

Peruvian government created CONAM in 1994 to serve as the "national environmental authority," and it is governed by a board of national, regional, and local government officials as well as private sector specialists and university academics.[23] In early 1997, Patricia Iturreguia, a well-established CONAM climate change expert, wrote to Electroperú on behalf of the council and the National Climate Change Commission. She asked that the energy company transfer the glaciology office's information and equipment to Morales's Andean Glaciology and Geoenvironmental Institute, which would join CONAM and other collaborating national campaigns to combat climate change.[24] The involvement of CONAM and the National Climate Change Commission indicated that, by 1997, glacier hazards had become a national problem tied to the issue of global warming. Further, national and international awareness of global warming was helping the case for Cordillera Blanca disaster prevention.

The various debates about the fate of the Glaciology and Hydrological Resources Unit in 1996 and 1997 showed that Cordillera Blanca glaciers had become part of a global discussion. People and groups in England, Austria, and the United States were now deciding what melting Andean glaciers represented and how they would be managed. This globalizing trend represented a broader shift internationally, whereby glacier retreat shifted from a local issue to a global debate. Mountaineers now worry about glaciers on Mt. Everest, trekkers lament the loss of Kilimanjaro ice, government officials express concern (or joy) about the disintegration of Arctic ice, environmentalists worry about melting glaciers in Glacier National Park, and ski resorts everywhere worry about losing ski terrain. The Cordillera Blanca glaciers also shifted from a local concern to a global discussion. They represented a threat, to be sure, but the discussions also centered on opportunities. Groups had something to gain in the Cordillera Blanca: hydrological data for hydroelectricity, climate data for understanding global warming, power by controlling the agency and its mission, political support from local constituents, or personal safety. But as all these social groups debated the issue in 1997, sudden climatic shifts and glacial lake changes once again made nature a potent historical actor shaping policy and science.

The Never-Ending Hazards

The Callejón de Huaylas has not suffered any major glacier-related catastrophes since 1970, though climate change and ensuing glacier retreat have continued to create dangerous conditions—and near disasters—at Cordillera Blanca glacial lakes. By the late 1980s, after nearly five decades of engineering projects to reduce glacier hazards and prevent glacial lake outburst floods, experts had completed 25 glacial lake security projects. Five additional disaster prevention projects were also under way. Meanwhile, glaciers kept retreating, and unstable moraine-dammed glacial lakes kept forming and enlarging. Surveys showed an increase from 314 Cordillera Blanca lakes in 1983 to 374 in 1997, an astonishing rise considering they numbered only 223 in the first lake inventory completed in 1953.[25]

These glacier and glacial lake trends were part of a global phenomenon.[26] In fact, by the 1990s, glacier retreat had become for most scientists and observers in the world a clear sign of global warming—whether it was melting glaciers in the Andes or the shrinking Greenland ice sheet. Dangerous glacial lakes were also forming elsewhere, most notably in the Himalayas, where particularly damaging glacial lake outburst floods occurred in Nepal in 1977 and 1985.[27] In 2003, the International Center for Integrated Mountain Development and the United Nations Environment Program, working with several other organizations, completed an inventory of glacial lakes in Nepal, Bhutan, Tibet, and Pakistan. They concluded that Nepal had 20 dangerous glacial lakes, Bhutan had 24, Tibet had 24, and Pakistan had 9.[28] Glacial lakes have also formed in other world regions, creating dangerous conditions in Europe and North America as well. On the Italian-Swiss border region in 2002, for example, a glacial lake at the base of Belvedere Glacier expanded rapidly and threatened to inundate the Macugnaga community. Fortunately, engineers drained it quickly. Dozens of other glacial lake outburst floods have occurred elsewhere in the Alps.[29] In British Columbia, Canada, at least nine moraine dams have burst since the nineteenth century, most in the last few decades.[30] Glacier and glacial lake hazards have formed in recent decades—and in many cases triggered disasters or required emergency lake-drainage projects—in North America, Europe, Asia, and South America. Peruvians may have felt the catastrophic effects of these glacial lakes before any other world region and in much deadlier ways, but the problems unfolding in the Cordillera Blanca have become global issues.

El Niño and Precarious Lakes

In 1997, an outburst flood, an El Niño event, and the emergence of three new unstable glacial lakes suddenly made the fate of the Glaciology and Hydrological Resources Unit an urgent issue. First, the natural dam holding back Lake Pacliashcocha in the Honda Canyon above Carhuaz, Marcará, Vicos, and other smaller communities burst in January 1997. The ensuing small-scale flood dramatically confirmed the existence of persistent glacial lake hazards in the region. Many Quechua-speaking residents, who referred to the Honda Canyon as the "deep broken place," had long feared spirits from the glaciated peaks and water from the valley's glacial lakes.[31] Their concerns became reality as the flood destroyed bridges, roads, trails, and agricultural land and killed livestock that grazed near the river. Fortunately, no people died.[32] News of the event spread quickly. Local authorities in many Callejón de Huaylas communities subsequently demanded specific measures to drain and contain Pacliashcocha. Their concerns about this specific lake only invigorated broader quests to keep the glaciology office active.

A few months later, scientists began predicting a major El Niño event to affect Peru in late 1997 and 1998. El Niño events, known technically as El Niño-southern oscillation, occur when trade winds blowing west across the tropical Pacific Ocean ease up. As less warm sea surface water blows west across the Pacific, the normally cool sea surface temperature off the Peruvian coast warms, which cuts off the nutrient-rich upwelling. El Niño events thus change water temperatures and shift ocean currents, often wreaking havoc on Peru's fishing industry. Inland temperatures and precipitation patterns also fluctuate and vary. El Niño events generally produce increased rainfall on the coast and diminishing precipitation in the highlands. During El Niño, Puno can suffer drought while Trujillo drowns. Peru has always suffered from El Niño events, and scientists in June 1997 began predicting a particularly devastating one.[33] President Fujimori listened.[34] He assembled a task force of policymakers and scientists to prepare a national plan to help avoid devastation from predicted heavy rains and floods. Fujimori secured $150 million from the World Bank to help prepare the country.[35]

Following the mid-1997 El Niño prediction, glacier experts, policymakers, and local residents grew more concerned about Cordillera Blanca glacial lakes. Scientists now recognize complex and dynamic interactions among climate change, atmospheric humidity, snowfall, El Niño events, and glacier behavior. In 1997, they believed El Niño would immediately exacerbate glacier melting.[36] Electroperú responded by authorizing 162,000 Peruvian soles for the temporary continuation of the glaciology office, though with a skeletal staff.[37] Further, Electroperú ordered the completion of both a Cordillera Blanca glacial lake inventory and a study of 31 specific lakes deemed potentially dangerous or historically unstable. They hoped to identify prospective problems before the onset of El Niño. And they did. The lake inventory revealed that many more glacial lakes existed in the Cordillera Blanca than experts expected, pointing to the dynamic, unpredictable nature of the alpine environment.[38] At the same time, Morales's institute conducted a glacier report that showed marked Andean glacier retreat.³⁹ The 31-lake study found three potentially dangerous lakes: Lake Pacliash in the Ishinka Canyon just north of Huaraz; Lake Pacliashcocha in the Honda Canyon above Vicos and Carhuaz; and Lake Arhuaycocha in the Santa Cruz Canyon near Caraz.⁴⁰

The identification of these three lakes following the early 1997 outburst flood and as an El Niño event approached caused an outcry from local residents and authorities. Those inhabiting the valleys below Lakes Paclishcocha and Pacliash understood the magnitude of these predictions because they had recently seen glacial lake outburst floods come through their communities. The Lake Pacliashcocha flood had only months before provoked anxiety in Vicos, Marcará, and Carhuaz. In the Ishinka Canyon below Lake Pacliash, residents also remembered a glacial lake outburst flood that ripped down the valley in 1982 and an earlier one in 1952.⁴¹ In 2004, residents of the Ishinka Canyon's Collón community could still describe the 1982 outburst flood in vivid detail. Their community, however, lies above the riverbanks. They heard the raucous roar of the passing flood but survived. One resident lamented that fishing was never as good after the flood.⁴² Their historical experiences in Ishinka Canyon merged with new anxieties in 1997, when Electroperú identified Lake Pacliash as a large, unstable glacial lake that could swell and collapse from the accelerated glacier retreat and precipitation changes associated with the approaching El Niño.

Fear of floods spread to Huaraz, and a panic broke out there in 1998. One evening while students were in class at the Ancash National University in Huaraz, an administrator arrived at the classroom door asking urgently to speak with the professor. She became quite animated and agitated when the professor only halfheartedly began making his way toward the door. After a very brief discussion, the professor quickly came back in the classroom announcing firmly that "an outburst flood is coming." The entire classroom emptied. The university campus sits on the 1941 flood path close to the Quilcay River. Students and professors ran through the campus, but as one student later said, none of them really knew where to go. While students scrambled on the campus, a young man in downtown Huaraz emerged from his shop when he heard commotion on the streets. People had been watching the rising water level in the Quilcay River all day. Somewhere, somehow, from someone, a rumor emerged and exacerbated the anxiety building in the region for months: the rising water level signaled an approaching outburst flood. The shopkeeper described the scene as "extreme panic." People carrying suitcases, televisions, and other household "essentials" clogged the streets. A family near the Soledad church went out on their fourth-floor balcony to see if they could make sense of the situation. They only saw chaos. Police and authorities were scarce.

Nobody seemed to know what to do—neither the police nor the newscasters on television reporting the situation live.[43] In the end, no outburst flood appeared. Huaraz remained intact, at least physically.

The closing of the glaciology office, the El Niño scare, and the continued uncertainty about Lakes Pacliash, Pacliashcocha, and Arhuaycocha made people throughout the Callejón de Huaylas jittery about their safety. Some international research on Cordillera Blanca glaciers continued in the late 1990s by scientists such as Georg Kaser, Bryan Mark, Bernard Pouyaud, and others. But their primary interests were not glacial lake hazards, though Kaser had helped at Lake 513a. Local concerns thus arose and persuaded an Ancash congresswoman to petition the national government to reinstate the glaciology office.[44] Many other Peruvians, including glacier experts and regional authorities, put pressure on Electroperú and the government to keep the glaciology office staffed. President Fujimori, who was by late 1997 allocating significant resources for El Niño preparation, gave a tepid response. In October he issued a 120-day national state of emergency for Ancash. It stipulated that Electroperú use its own operating budget—and work with Civil Defense—to contain the three lakes.[45] Glacier experts working on a contractual, short-term basis implemented several strategies to protect the population, including installing radio-equipped watchmen at the three dangerous lakes, doing helicopter surveillance of these and other Cordillera Blanca lakes, and immediately starting to drain Lakes Arhuaycocha, Pacliashcocha, and Pacliash.[46] Fortunately, predictions about the devastating effects of El Niño on unstable lakes did not play out: the three lakes did not produce any outburst floods, though it took three years to drain them.

By the time engineers had completed the three lake security projects, a new government was in power in Peru. President Toledo's government reestablished a Glaciology and Hydrological Resources Unit, this time under INRENA and the Ministry of Agriculture instead of a hydroelectric corporation within the Ministry of Energy and Mines. The new glaciology office opened in 2001, but the staff, which numbered 74 in 1987, was cut to five.[47] This small but dedicated staff, headed by Marco Zapata, has nonetheless continued to do important work on glacial lake security, water use, and global warming issues related to glacier retreat and glacier hazards. They have also collaborated with a host of international scientists—especially from Austrian, French, and US research centers—doing an ever-increasing number of studies on tropical glaciers.

Fujimori's neoliberal reforms no doubt diminished Cordillera Blanca disaster prevention programs in the late 1990s. It even seemed as if privatization would end state support for monitoring and mitigating glacial lake hazards. But local residents, glacier experts, environmental groups, and regional authorities prevented the state's complete abandonment of glacial lakes. Fujimori's own increasingly populist policies and his personal interest in combating the 1997–1998 El Niño also made Lima aware of Cordillera Blanca glacier retreat. Ultimately, the El Niño event and the rapidly changing glacial landscape became powerful reminders of the perils of neoliberalism and the reasons for national governments to continue funding social programs like disaster prevention.

Duke Energy's Dam Projects

By the early twenty-first century, while Ancash residents advocated the draining of Cordillera Blanca glacial lakes to keep them safe, neoliberal reforms had created a political-economic-legal framework for Duke Energy to construct new reservoirs. This process by which neoliberalism promoted reservoir construction was also taking place in Bolivia, and worldwide from Brazil to India, where local residents fought aggressively against these new water-regulating reservoirs.[48] Duke Energy was not the first entity to propose and construct reservoirs in the Cordillera Blanca.[49] In fact, the original Cañón del Pato privatization concession stipulated that its new owner would have to increase electricity output by a total of 100 megawatts at the two hydroelectric stations that Egenor acquired in 1996, Cañón del Pato on the Santa River and the much smaller plant at Carhuaquero on the Chancay River in Cajamarca. The goal was to boost Cañón del Pato by at least 90 megawatts and Carhuaquero by 10. Duke adhered to the concession, investing $90 million between 1999 and 2002 to upgrade Cañón del Pato from 150 to 256 megawatts. Also, in 1999, Duke petitioned the Ministry of Agriculture to expand its use of Santa River water from 48 cubic meters per second to 79.[50] Even after meeting the concession requirements, however, Duke Energy continued its quest to manage the Santa River and manipulate the Cordillera Blanca waterscape. The company wanted more control over water flow. It needed more dams and reservoirs.

By 2001, plans were under way to transform Lakes Aguascocha, Shallap, and Aquiscocha into water-regulating reservoirs. Duke chose the three lakes because they were able to store significant amounts of water, were economically and logistically feasible, and were safe from avalanches, thus limiting the possibility of outburst floods. Reports indicate that Duke Energy was aware of glacial lake and glacier hazards but did not find them significant at these specific lakes. For Auquiscocha, for example, the Duke assessment concluded: "In general the glaciers are found to be moderately stable. In the event that they produce probable avalanches of snow, these will first affect Lake Chequiacocha, which will be able to mitigate their effects." For Lake Shallap, the studies observed that nearby glaciers "do not show indications of instability." The report did, however, assert that Shallap's proposed dam "must be secure and appropriate to resist the effects of probable avalanches of snow that can fall into the lake and/or be caused by seismic activity."[51] To Duke, glacial hazards either did not exist, were not cause for alarm, or could be mitigated by effective engineering.

Local residents saw Duke's dam projects differently—as they had with previous reservoir proposals. Many had opposed Cordillera Blanca reservoirs since the 1980s, when Hidrandina and later Electroperú planned to build them. By the time Egenor took over Cañón del Pato in 1996 and proposed to build new reservoirs, residents were already leery. They also seemed to distrust a foreign company more than Electroperú.[52] Thus, as Duke Energy initiated reservoir construction plans, locals throughout the region escalated their opposition to the three projects, especially those at Lakes Auquiscocha and Shallap, because each lake's specific history turned people against Duke.[53]

Located above the city of Carhuaz and the community of Shilla, Lake Auquiscocha is a large lake that water developers and the glaciology office had long hoped to transform into a reservoir.[54] But the local population did not always welcome outsiders warmly. A confrontation erupted over a rain gauge that the glacier experts had installed to monitor precipitation patterns just below melting glaciers. Rural farmers complained that the rain gauge caused the drought. To make it rain, they removed it. A few days later, when glaciology office personnel arrived at the lake to collect their monthly data, they could not find the instrument. Descending from the lake on their way back to Huaraz, they met a local man who told them who had taken it. Back in Huaraz, the glaciology office director told the technicians to install a new rain gauge near the lake, which they went back to do the following day, taking the Carhuaz subprefect with them. When community members saw another rain gauge in the vehicle, they became angry. They swarmed the Jeep, captured the four men, and destroyed the new rain gauge. They let the driver go so that he could inform authorities that they had taken hostages and convey their terms of release: they demanded that Marino Zamora, then head of the glaciology office, personally return to the community and promise to keep these drought-inducing rain gauges out of the area. A few hours later, Zamora arrived with other members of his office and the prefect, the highest authority in Ancash. As a precaution, the unnerved prefect took 20 police officers with the returning delegation.

Approximately 80 local residents had gathered to speak with authorities when they arrived around 5 P.M. Zamora negotiated the release of the three hostages by agreeing not to install a rain gauge. The prefect then drafted a decree, which they all signed. Locals released the hostages, and the authorities were about to leave when the police officers suddenly appeared—unexpectedly and unnecessarily, and without an order to do so. Insulted and alarmed, community members turned belligerent. The glaciology staff and authorities jumped in their vehicles and fled while a "rain" of rocks flew at them. They escaped unharmed, but the previously tense situation ended even worse. The glaciology office never again tried to install a rain gauge near the lake.[55] But the animosity remained when Egenor began surveying the lake in the late 1990s.

Residents near Lake Auquiscocha had other reasons to fight the proposed reservoir as well. Locals believed the lake was enchanted, and because of its malicious spirits the lake "wanted" to overflow. As local resident María Apolinario told anthropologist William Stein in the 1950s:

They think that Awkish Qoca, which is above Hualcan, can burst. There are some people who go up there to get [glacial] ice. They see that the lake is full of mist. The water wants to spill over. That is why people believe that it can burst out without warning. Every time that people come near the lake, it turns into blood and a rainbow forms. The water begins to rise up. The people who go to see it do not come close because it is very dangerous.

One time it did come over. A voice was heard in the lake. It was the voice of a woman, calling out, saying that if they did not have a mass given, all the water would come out. Then the people who had their chakra nearby brought the priest to have a mass for them. Since that time, the water has gone down a little. Many people are now saying that it wants to come out again.[56]

Historical forces and social circumstances at Lake Auquiscocha made the proposed reservoir deeply problematic for Duke. If locals saw Auquiscocha as enchanted and likely to rise up and come out—as they likely did because these views remain common throughout the Callejón de Huaylas—then Duke's proposal to add additional water to the lake could have provoked considerable anxiety and fear. What's more, the interest in turning the entire lake into a technologically managed system likely inflamed historical tensions that ignited over a rain gauge less than a decade before. Rural communities and Carhuaz mayor José Mejía Solórzano mobilized against Duke's proposed project. The company did not try for long to overcome these powerful obstacles. It abandoned the Auquiscocha reservoir in 2002, turning its attention instead to Lake Shallap above Huaraz.

Lake Shallap is one of the Cordillera Blanca glacial lakes that engineers have recognized as a potential threat to Huaraz since 1941. Two issues made locals and experts worry about it. First, the retreating glaciers above the lake descend down steep slopes, increasing the likelihood of avalanching ice that would splash into the water. Second, water leaving Lake Shallap flows directly into the Quilcay River that runs through the heart of Huaraz. Engineers first began draining the lake in 1942, constructing an artificial security dam in the 1950s, and rebuilding it after the 1970 earthquake.[57] In addition to conducting security projects, glacier experts had repeatedly determined that Lake Shallap was too risky to serve as a reservoir. Morales, for example, inspected the lake in 1966 and concluded that there was "no possibility" for reservoir construction anywhere in the Shallap Canyon.[58] Even when Electroperú and the glaciology office conducted more elaborate studies in 1989 and 1990, engineers still did not consider Lake Shallap a suitable lake.[59]

Duke Energy reversed these earlier apprehensions about the lake's suitability for a reservoir. By 2001, the company was increasing the height of the security dam, hoping to raise the Shallap lake level by 10 meters. The raised water level would add an additional 2 million cubic meters of water to the lake, enough to generate an extra 1.8 megawatts of electricity at Cañón del Pato.[60] To complete the project, Duke complied with a host of bureaucratic obligations, completed an environmental impact statement, and got official approval from the Ministry of Energy and Mines, the Ministry of Agriculture, and Huascarán National Park because Lake Shallap lies within park boundaries. In early 2003, the project was under way. Once again, environmental events turned local people against the project by reminding them of persistent lake and glacier hazards above Huaraz.

NASA Provokes the Palcacocha Nightmare

Duke Energy's Lake Shallap project progressed with little local awareness until early 2003, when it burst into public view after a near catastrophe spilled out of Lake Palcacocha. On March 19, 2003, Huaraz residents awoke to a city without running water. After several hours, much longer than the usual interruption, residents and authorities grew concerned. They also discovered distressing changes in the Quilcay River: it was cloudy, filled with sediment, and was running much higher than the previous day. As workers made their way up the Quilcay River to investigate the city's water treatment plant, farmers on their way down told them that an ice avalanche into Lake Palcacocha the night before

FIGURE 7.1. Lake Palcacocha with two security dams in foreground, 2003.
Credit: Photo by Mark Carey.

had triggered a small outburst flood. The surging water, filled with sediment
from the flood's turbulence, had clogged the water treatment plant. Suddenly,
the nightmare from 1941 filled everyone's mind. Was Palcacocha again about
to inundate Huaraz?

Authorities called an emergency meeting. A few hours later, members of
the regional government, Civil Defense, the glaciology office, the prefect, the
Huaraz mayor, the Ancash president, and many others met to discuss
Palcacocha and develop a plan of action. Using an airplane loaned by the Barrick
mining company, experts flew up the Cojup Canyon that same afternoon.
Blocks of glacial ice covered 70 percent of Lake Palcacocha and one of the security dams was destroyed. The lake had evidently overflowed. To gather additional information, authorities sent a delegation of engineers and authorities
directly to the lake. Meanwhile, Ancash President Fredy Ghilardy held a press
conference to convey the situation and advise residents that he was putting the
city on alert. Huaraz remained without water for a week as experts swarmed
Palcacocha to assess its stability and determine the cause of the mini-flood.
Residents waited anxiously to hear the results.

FIGURE 7.2. Lake Palcacocha security dam damaged by overflowing water, 2003.
Credit: Photo by Mark Carey.

By the end of March, 10 days after the Palcacocha overflow, the glaciology office explained publicly what had happened. A landslide from the steeply sloped moraine slid into the lake and created eight-meter-high waves that washed over the security dam and then sloshed around in the lake bed like ocean waves in a swimming pool.[61] Half of the auxiliary security dam eroded away completely, but it withstood the force long enough to keep most of the water in the lake. The water that did escape damaged Huaraz's water treatment plant and covered parts of the upper Cojup Valley. But the lake's two security dams probably prevented a catastrophe in the city. Six decades of glacial lake security projects in the Cordillera Blanca had paid off in just this one case of disaster averted. Nevertheless, Huaraz could not yet rest peacefully because potential problems still lurked at Palcacocha. The security dams needed repairing, and experts worried that icebergs floating in the lake could block the outlet stream, thereby damming the lake and adding more water to the unstable situation.

A few weeks later, while Palcacocha concerns still festered, NASA, the U.S. space agency, turned that anxiety into panic. In an April 11, 2003, press release,

NASA announced that Lake Palcacocha posed more serious threats to Huaraz than people even contemplated. According to ASTER satellite images taken in 2001 and 2003, an "ominous crack" had formed in a Mt. Cupi glacier directly above Lake Palcacocha. "Should the large glacier chunk break off and fall into the lake," NASA warned, "the ensuing flood could hurtle down the Cojup Valley into the Rio Santa Valley below, reaching Huaraz and its population of 60,000 in less than 15 minutes." Mt. Cupi and Lake Palcacocha, NASA concluded, were a "disaster-in-the-making."[62] Stunned by the already tense situation in the valley, people wondered whether (and when) the glacier and lake would crash down on them. They feared a disaster more deadly and destructive than the 1941 flood. Huaraz radio stations were soon telling residents to pack their most valuable belongings and to sleep in their clothes so they could flee the flood rapidly. "We were all very worried in my family," a resident told the BBC in an October 9, 2003, broadcast. "We packed suitcases with clothes and blankets."

Although NASA's press release said that the agency was "assisting Peruvian government officials and geologists in monitoring a glacier that feeds Lake Palcacocha," most Peruvian glacier experts, including the Glaciology and Hydrological Resources Unit, had no idea that NASA had found the problems or that NASA was going to post such a high-profile, alarming press release. Peruvians thus condemned NASA for its "apocalyptic" claim, which Peruvian scientists and the press called "alarmist." Experts also criticized the way NASA handled such a delicate situation. The report lacked corresponding field studies to verify the problem noted in the satellite image. The space agency failed to communicate with Peruvian experts or government officials before generating widespread panic in Peru. Most important, NASA had its facts wrong: the supposed "ominous crack" in the glacier was a rock cliff.[63] Georg Kaser, who had been researching Cordillera Blanca glaciers for fifteen years at that point, and Christian Georges, both from the University of Innsbruck's Tropical Glaciology Group, concluded after a careful study that NASA's warning lacked "any realistic reason and can only be understood to be a rash misinterpretation of satellite images."[64] Other international experts in glacier hazards also believed NASA made a "serious misinterpretation" of the situation, though they agreed that Palcacocha "is not, however, without hazards."[65]

Local residents' frustration with NASA's report stemmed not only from the panic it generated and the seemingly inaccurate scientific analysis, but also because of its timing. The agency released it less than a month after the Palcacocha overflow and just days before the Easter holiday, a time when Peruvians from Lima and elsewhere generally flock to the Callejón de Huaylas. Despite local and national efforts to reassure tourists about the safety of Huaraz, the Easter 2003 tourism season was poor for business.[66] El Comercio reported that only 6,000 visitors made it to Huaraz, instead of the anticipated 18,000. "Those who decided not to visit the Ancash capital," the newspaper concluded, "had been influenced by the news that NASA disseminated, which was subsequently echoed in various forms throughout Peru."[67]

The NASA debacle opens an illuminating window on twenty-first-century Cordillera Blanca glacier hazards. On the one hand, Peruvian glacier experts and authorities may have responded to NASA hastily and turned the potential glacier hazard into a political rather than environmental issue. Of course, NASA made its report political by interfering in another country. But Peruvian responses also centered on personal attacks, the economics of Easter tourism, and the power to control information. More important, though, Peruvian glacier experts' confident claims that "no danger existed of any kind" mostly came before they had completed scientific analyses of both the Mt. Cupi glacier and Lake Palcacocha.[68] Even after experts visited the site and analyzed historical photographs of the supposedly threatening glacier, they still operated with a wrong assumption about the amount of water in Lake Palcacocha. As Benjamín Morales explained to the Lima newspapers *Correo* and *La Republica* on April 15, 2003, "Today there is very little water [in Palcacocha], which could not produce a catastrophe of the type [NASA] predicts." But Morales and others drew their conclusions based on the most recent study, conducted in 1974. Not until October 2003, six months after NASA's announcement, did experts learn that Palcacocha actually contained approximately 3.7 million cubic meters of water—nearly eight times the amount they assumed when they called NASA's claims "alarmist" and "apocalyptic."[69] The amount of lake water may not have mattered, as Kaser and Georges argued compellingly, because NASA had been wrong about glacier instability above the lake. Its analysis focused solely on the supposed glacier crack, not the lake. But Morales and the media had argued passionately that the amount of water in Palcacocha did matter, and that neither the glacier *nor* the lake posed a threat precisely because the lake contained so little water.

On the other hand, the NASA report was problematic on various fronts even beyond its inaccuracy. Ostensibly about the Mt. Cupi glacier crack, the NASA press release actually reads like a sales pitch for ASTER satellite images. The report devotes more attention to general ASTER capabilities than to Peru, Huaraz, or the glacier above Palcacocha that could affect 60,000 people. Half of the report discusses potential uses of these satellite images, including "monitoring glacial advances and retreats and potentially active volcanoes; identifying crop stress; determining cloud morphology and physical properties; evaluating wetlands," and many other uses unrelated to Huaraz. In fact, NASA provided no detailed analysis of the glacier's "ominous crack" except to say that the images showed its existence. Several Peruvian scientists believed NASA had simply wanted to generate attention for its ASTER program. On April 24, 2003, the prestigious scientific journal *Nature* criticized NASA for generating alarm in Peru. A news brief reported that, in response to questions about the press release identifying threats to Huaraz, NASA explained that the agency sought to demonstrate the value of remote sensing and the circulation of satellite images in monitoring glacier hazards worldwide. *Nature* was quite critical of NASA: "Earth-observation experts have questioned whether it was responsible to do this, as the glacier posed no immediate threat. José Achache, director of the European Space Agency's Earth Observation Programmes, says it is 'not ethical for an agency to refer to threats to people's lives as a means of demonstrating the relevance of Earth-observation satellites.'"[70] The space agency appears to have tried to capitalize on the already traumatized people of Huaraz. That trauma backfired not only against NASA but also against Duke Energy.

Fighting Globalization at Lake Shallap

Anxiety about the Palcacocha mini-flood and the NASA news increased local residents' awareness of unstable Cordillera Blanca glaciers and glacial lakes. As a result, the Huaraz population turned against Duke Energy's Lake Shallap reservoir project. Benjamín Morales, who was at the time hoping to become the Huaraz mayor, used the Palcacocha incident to express concern about the Shallap reservoir. "The threat of an outburst flood is not so much from Lake Cojup [Palcacocha]," he wrote in a newspaper, "but rather from Lake Shallap. That is the real danger." Morales identified two critical problems that he believed endangered the Huaraz population. First, Shallap's dam that Duke was modifying was originally built as a security dam—not to hold back water in a reservoir. Second, adding water to a previously drained lake with retreating glaciers above it ran the risk of creating a devastating outburst flood. The only solution, Morales concluded, "is to paralyze the Lake Shallap project."[71] Other experts agreed.[72] A representative from Duke Energy maintained, however, that Shallap did not—and would not—contain enough water even to reach Huaraz in the event that the reservoir dam failed. For him, the question of a catastrophic outburst flood was moot.[73]

By October 2003, locals considered the Shallap reservoir as one of several issues instigated by the national government and Duke Energy that threatened their security, their livelihoods, and their autonomy.[74] A July 2003 article in a local Huaraz magazine excoriated Duke Energy, not just for its proposed reservoir but also for treating farmers poorly, for greedily taking water from the Lake Parón watershed, for failing to meet environmental regulations, and generally for treating the regional population poorly in its "lucrative business."[75] In early October, an estimated 30,000 people packed into downtown Huaraz in what newspapers called a protest of "historic" proportions. As Huaraz Mayor Lombardo Mautino rallied the crowd from a podium in the city's main plaza, he outlined the protestors' three main demands: finalizing studies for the Casma-Huaraz highway; abandoning the Lake Shallap reservoir and repairing the security dams at Lake Palcacocha; and allocating the promised $7 million to the National University "Santiago Antúnez de Mayolo" in Huaraz.[76] Thousands of residents and high-level local and regional government officials had turned out in part to oppose the Shallap reservoir. The huge protest spurred additional opposition from residents, government offices, and technical institutions throughout the region.

By early 2004, concern about Shallap had evolved into regional, national, and international discussions about a private company's right to access natural resources and reshape the Cordillera Blanca waterscape. Suddenly this glacial lake was at the center of national debates not only about how neoliberalism was playing out, but also about citizen participation in a democratic government, the state's involvement in the economy, social welfare programs, access to natural resources, and environmental management. These debates involved a foreign energy company, diverse Peruvian residents, scientists and engineers, attorneys and judges, mountaineers, environmental groups, and politicians at all levels of government. Eventually, in 2004, the Peruvian Supervising Institution of the Investment in Energy, which was established in the late 1990s to oversee the energy industry, intervened against Duke at Lake Shallap. The Shallap project, the agency concluded, could not "verify the stability of the dam and reservoir." Juan Cardich, a representative of Duke Energy, responded by saying that the company had indeed followed all the necessary steps and requirements, both legal and technical. Moreover, he pointed out that "Huaraz already has a water deficit, a problem that will later spread throughout the Callejón de Huaylas. With lake reservoirs, we all benefit because the water that is being stored will be able to improve water distribution in the dry season, benefiting Huaraz [and] communities surrounding the projects."[77] Despite Cardich's optimism, Duke abandoned the project, leaving the Shallap dam as a security dam. In two out of the first three reservoir construction cases that Duke pursued, local residents had successfully fought its projects. Indeed, neoliberalism was playing out much differently in Peru than its theorists would have anticipated.[78]

Duke Energy, however, was mobile and flexible. It turned its attention to another reservoir construction project at nearby Lake Rajucolta (Figure 3.5). The glaciology office first recommended using Rajucolta as a reservoir in 1973, even though the lake had produced a major outburst flood with "many deaths" in 1883.[79] It reiterated the prospects for a Rajucolta reservoir in 1974 but recognized the instability of overhanging glaciers descending into the lake itself.[80] The report indicated that Huaraz would be unaffected by a Rajucolta outburst flood, which, by 2003, made it appealing to Duke Energy. Before initiating the project, the energy company estimated that a reservoir there would allow Cañón del Pato to boost electricity generation by 4 megawatts. It was an important, potentially lucrative lake to dam. Its location away from the highly charged political environment of Huaraz—and the lingering bitterness over Shallap and Palcacocha—allowed Duke to proceed with the Rajucolta reservoir with little local interference.

Neoliberal reforms and the privatization of Cañón del Pato led to significant changes in the management of the Santa River watershed and Cordillera Blanca glacial hazards. The state disaster prevention agency, though reopened in 2001, never regained the status, budget, and support it had in previous periods. Local vulnerability to glacier disasters thus increased after privatization. Management of the Santa River waterscape also transferred to foreign hands. Duke Energy, however, was not the first entity to see glaciers and glacial lakes as water resources. While many scholars are quick to blame recent resource depletion and landscape consumption on neoliberalism, privatization in the Santa River watershed only accelerated processes that had begun decades before. As a more authoritarian leader, Fujimori had the centralized power to implement his agenda, just as Presidents Odría and Velasco had done following the 1950 and 1970 disasters.

But neoliberalism did not proceed smoothly because the theory collided with historical reality. When Duke tried to expand Santa River water flow and manipulate the Cordillera Blanca waterscape into an environment designed to promote electricity generation, local people resisted. History thus made it nearly impossible for the state to abandon disaster prevention and for Duke Energy to manage the waterscape uncontested. History had also, ironically, helped Duke because the company utilized glacial lake engineering projects, hydrological information, and Cordillera Blanca access routes to increase the company's use of Andean water supplies. Understanding neoliberalism at the ground level requires attention to these historical forces and the numerous competing visions of landscapes.

Diverse social groups' interactions with the Cordillera Blanca during the last two decades illuminates larger issues involving the intersections of neoliberalism, climate, landscape, science, resource use, and society.[81] Neoliberalism exacerbated vulnerability to environmental hazards. Various interacting social forces also affected the evolution of science. Tourism in Huaraz, Duke Energy profits, publicity for NASA satellite images, and local political issues influenced glacial lake research. Further, local residents continued to influence environmental management decisions, even while international forces brought a range of other social groups to share decision making. By the twenty-first century, the solution had become part of the problem: more disaster prevention brought more outsiders, more economic development, and less local control. The situation became acute when privatization brought a U.S. company responsible to shareholders, not the public good or local safety, into the Santa River watershed. These interactions among nature, neoliberalism, and society in the Andes represent larger processes unfolding elsewhere in Latin America and beyond, where the privatization of water and energy brings social groups into conflict with one another and with dynamic physical environments.

Conclusion

The effect of melting glaciers on water supplies has become an urgent issue worldwide. Achim Steiner, the United Nations undersecretary general and executive director of the UN Environment Program, recently exclaimed that everyone must recognize the critical problems caused by vanishing glaciers worldwide. "Millions if not billions of people," he said in 2008, "depend directly or indirectly on these natural water storage facilities for drinking water, agriculture, industry and power generation during key parts of the year." The head of the World Glacier Monitoring Service, Wilfried Haeberli, added that glacier retreat has accelerated considerably since 1980, making the diminishing water supplies even more alarming.[1] Andean countries in particular worry about how future glacier retreat will affect water supplies for tens of millions of inhabitants, especially in cities like Quito, La Paz, and Lima.[2] Andean nations also depend on glacier runoff to generate energy. Hydroelectricity is their primary energy source, and glaciers are often critical for its generation because they regulate water flow throughout the year, as Cordillera Blanca glaciers do for the Santa River and Cañón del Pato.

Scientists have increasingly turned their attention to Andean glacier-water relationships, shifting from their previous emphasis on climate and hazards. Their studies show how glaciers regulate water flow, releasing runoff even during the dry season when non-glacier-fed rivers on the western slope of the Andes have little or no water.

The contribution of glacier runoff to rivers is thus significant. In specific Santa River tributaries in the Cordillera Blanca valleys, glacier runoff can account for between one-third and two-thirds of river flow. Glaciers contribute as much as 66 percent of the water in the Santa River when it leaves the Callejón de Huaylas and flows into Cañón del Pato. A growing portion of that glacier water is not replenished during the year by additional precipitation that turns to glacial ice because, overall, glaciers are shrinking with global climate change. At some future time—depending on climatic conditions and the extent of continued glacier retreat—the glaciers may release less water. Scientists suggest we are dangerously close to that point. And the trend will continue as long as glaciers keep retreating. If glaciers disappear altogether, the Santa River will likely have significantly less water flowing, especially during the dry season, and shortages will undoubtedly generate conflicts among water users.[3]

World Bank and University of Massachusetts researchers have recently estimated the economic effects of water loss from future Andean glacier retreat, including potential costs at the Cañón del Pato hydroelectric plant. A 50 percent reduction in Cordillera Blanca glacier runoff, they estimate, would reduce Cañón del Pato energy generation from 1,540 annual gigawatt-hours to 1,250, while complete glacier loss would reduce it to 970 gigawatt-hours. The authors extrapolate potential financial burdens on the Peruvian energy sector and electricity consumers, estimating costs at the low end of $60 million annually for price increases with reduced glacier coverage and as high as $1.5 billion per year for rationing costs once all Peruvian glaciers disappear.[4] Their calculations helped motivate a new World Bank project in the Andes. They also reveal a larger historical transformation: melting Andean ice now has a price.

Concerns about Andean glacier melting have accelerated and spread so broadly that, in May 2008, the World Bank helped finalize—and became the largest contributor—to a $33 million project called "Adaptation to the Impact of Rapid Glacier Retreat in the Tropical Andes."[5] Recognizing both the likelihood of future glacier retreat and the vulnerability of Andean economies, energy supplies, and human populations, the bank plans to implement adaptation measures and pilot programs to reduce costly effects of climate change and glacier retreat in Peru, Ecuador, and Bolivia. The project has three major objectives: "(a) the effective integration of the implications of glacier retreat into regional and local development planning, particularly in glacier basins; (b) the inclusion of glacier retreat impacts in local development projects and programs; (c) the collection of data on glacier dynamics to improve policy decisions." To carry out these objectives and foster adaptation measures, the World Bank is targeting specific issues, including Quito's metropolitan water supply, agriculture and food security in Peru, watershed management on the Bolivian Plateau, and the implementation of a "climate observation network" to collect data and provide early warnings about "extreme climate events." In Peru, the project will focus on the Mantaro valley. Though the Cordillera Blanca has many more glaciers, Mantaro glaciers supply significant water and energy for Lima, where a third of Peru's population now lives. Mantaro valley agriculture also supports Lima's population. The broad scope and ambitious plans for integrated water-shed management—from glacial ice to kitchen faucets to electricity to watch soccer on television—offer exciting prospects for future climate change adaptation.

History also raises crucial concerns about these current and future plans to grapple with glacier retreat—not just in Peru but in Bolivia, Ecuador, Colombia, Nepal, India, Russia, Switzerland, the United States, and scores of other coun-tries where people live near or depend on water from melting mountain gla-ciers. Climate-glaciers-water-society dynamics are of course distinct in Peru and for tropical glaciers. This case of nearly 70 years of adaptation to glacier retreat and climate disasters nonetheless yields several broadly applicable conclusions.

Local residents living close to glaciers or directly in glacially fed watersheds endure the highest cost of glacier retreat because they often pay with their lives, their families, and their communities. Lost hydroelectricity or diminishing water can affect people beyond the region, but those vulnerable to glacier disas-ters and those who lose control of their glaciers because of increased outside management suffer the most. With Peru's coast-sierra divisions and with the largest cities concentrated on the coast, future glacier retreat stands to affect highland populations most severely not only through potential floods or ava-lanches but also through lost energy generation from a destroyed or declining hydroelectric plant that would likely maintain power in Trujillo and Chimbote while Huaraz and Yungay literally go dark and fester with sanitation problems.[6]

But this history is not a lament for passive victims who lost control of their lives or succumbed helplessly to the forces of climate change, disasters, envi-ronmental destruction, economic modernization, nation building, and global-ization. Callejón de Huaylas residents did endure hardship and loss of life caused by these forces. However, they responded in ways that shaped their future, and they benefited from disaster economics—the economic develop-ment that directly and indirectly followed climate catastrophes and disaster prevention programs. The three dozen glacial lake security projects undertaken in the Cordillera Blanca since the 1941 Huaraz flood have no doubt saved thou-sands of lives and averted countless tragedies. Hydroelectricity and other devel-opment projects helped justify government expenditures for disaster prevention in a relatively remote part of Peru—providing greater motivation for state action than the deaths of thousands in Chavín and Ranrahirca. People throughout the region also used—and still rely on—the electricity generated at Cañón del Pato. They further benefit from the roads, trails, and other infrastructure that have boosted the regional economy and quality of life. Disaster prevention and economic development thus provided benefits for many local residents. But those new opportunities do not make up for Ancash residents' suffering cataclysmic death and destruction from melting glaciers. Their lost lives far overshadow any economic losses to energy production, irrigation, or infrastructure.

Glacier retreat brought new historical actors—scientists, engineers, water users, tourists, the nation-state, and most recently, the World Bank—to a region these groups previously had little knowledge about or control over. Each group brought its own ideas about how to define, manage, and utilize the glaciated landscape. Power dynamics among the groups influenced management policies and whose vision for the Andes, its glaciers, and its water ultimately won out. Urban residents' fear of populations descending from "the heights" drove them to rebuild destroyed cities in hazard zones and to reject state-mandated hazard zoning to keep their autonomy from what they perceived to be an interventionist state. Complex historically produced social relations—rather than ignorance—influenced how distinct groups responded to glacier retreat and explains why the most vulnerable urban populations continued to rebuild in hazard zones. Local residents consequently do not always want the programs that policymakers believe will most reduce their vulnerability to climatic or other environmental hazards. Social conflicts may be more urgent to people than potential floods or even water-shortage issues that experts see as most pressing.

The success of the World Bank's Andean project and other climate adaptation programs worldwide will depend as much on understanding social relations and power dynamics as on deciphering how many cubic meters of water per second will flow out of the Mantaro valley's Huaytapallana Glacier in 2025.[7] Local resistance to adaptation measures may have as much to do with *who* is proposing them as with *what* the plan recommends. Even when experts, policymakers, and local groups agree on the problem, they might disagree about specific mitigation strategies and solutions. Further, local choosing of a more socially palatable solution for the short term may ultimately make them more vulnerable and dependent on state science and technology in the long run. Ironically, then, opposition to hazard zoning to preserve community autonomy later leads to greater reliance on the same entity they opposed in the first place: the state. This process occurred in the Callejón de Huaylas when residents rejected hazard zoning in the 1970s but, as scares at Lakes Palcacocha and

Shallap illustrate, they are dependent on state-funded glacier monitoring and glacial lake control to protect them from disasters.

Whereas many scholars demonstrate how government management of land, resources, flora, and fauna expanded state authority and promoted nation-building agendas, fewer have revealed how the changing physical environment itself influenced state hegemony or political processes.[8] Climate change and glacier disasters brought a host of state institutions to Ancash, in many cases for the first time. But increased state presence did not simply represent the expansion of unwanted government authority imposed from above.[9] Instead, many residents saw clear roles for government, believed state institutions could and should help them, and invited the national government into the Cordillera Blanca region. Disasters may seem somewhat unique in that people have a personal stake in surviving, but disaster prevention is like many public services and corresponds with the welfare state more broadly. Although authoritarian regimes exhibited greater capacity to respond to catastrophes, their initiatives generated greater opposition. The most decisive transitions in government action in Ancash occurred in 1941, 1950, 1970, and 1996. With the exception of the 1941 Huaraz disaster that first triggered state responses during Prado's democratic regime, the others all occurred when authoritarian governments held power. This suggests increased capacity for authoritarian leaders to respond—whether helping prevent floods through Odría's Lakes Commission in the 1950s, impinging on regional autonomy through Velasco's 1970s hazard zoning, or increasing local vulnerability through neoliberal reforms that closed the glaciology office in the 1990s. But authoritarian leaders also generated more local resentment than democratically elected officials. President Velasco did more for disaster prevention in the Callejón de Huaylas than any other Peruvian leader. Yet he inspired the most resistance because his relocation proposals challenged the regional elite and threatened to dismantle existing class-race hierarchies. Disaster mitigation was always a political process as much as it was about science and engineering.

Socio-geographical divisions in Peru persist, and highland populations have increasingly lost control of their resources or at least progressively shared resource management decisions with an increasingly coast-oriented national and international community. Like landscapes in the U.S. West, the African Serengeti, and the Amazon rain forest, the Cordillera Blanca became a landscape for consumption—whether by a tent-carrying trekker, an agroindustrial coastal irrigator, a Huaraz hotel owner, or a multinational energy company. Global climate change and glacier retreat did not exactly put the Cordillera Blanca on the map—Austrian and German mountaineers and cartographers did that in the 1930s. But climate change made government officials, water developers, tourists, and scientists look at that map for the first time, study it, redefine it, redraw it according to their growing body of information, and then use their new "maps" to steer Peruvian development through the twentieth century and into the twenty-first. These different groups strove not just to protect people from potentially perilous melting ice but also to expand state power, bolster the national economy, and ultimately to control and consume the Andes. Local residents contributed to these ongoing processes by insisting on certain types of science and engineering, demanding some government programs (while rejecting others), and advocating for some development projects, thereby sharing the benefits from modernizing campaigns in hydroelectricity, infrastructure, and tourism. But all stakeholders and historical actors are not created equal. The state and water developers accumulated power over time, taking on increasingly dominant roles in the management of the Cordillera Blanca landscape, glacial lakes, and water. The UN Human Development Office worries that diminishing Andean water supplies in the future will disproportionately affect the urban and rural poor through rising prices, inequitable access, lack of legal protections, and countries' favoring of large-scale and industrial water use over local needs.[10] History suggests that the UN is right to raise these concerns. We may only be partway through the tragic, contested story of glacier retreat that began with the 1941 Huaraz disaster and continues into the twenty-first century.

When residents of the Cruz de Mayo community seized Duke Energy's Lake Parón reservoir in July 2008, they clearly demonstrated that these tensions have already ignited. Residents complained that Duke had mismanaged the lake, lowering its level below the intended design, diminishing water quality, and releasing Parón's water at night, when farmers could not use it for their crops. Local groups merged with environmental and church organizations to fight for control of Parón. Discussions continued for months and were complicated because so many state agencies have authority at the lake. Duke Energy owns rights to the reservoir, but it lies in Huascarán National Park in the province of Huaylas and within the Ancash region; the ministries of agriculture, energy and mining, and environment all have authority at Parón as well. Historical responses to glacial lake outburst floods are responsible for bringing some of these state, private, and nongovernmental organizations into the Cordillera Blanca. Locals thus increasingly contend with a host of other groups and entities to manage the glacier-fed lake and river. Most of these groups can exert significantly more political power than can residents of Cruz de Mayo or even Caraz. Many locals feel that they are losing control as glaciers retreat, water supplies decline, and a foreign company manages the water. The Lake Parón conflict remains unresolved and highly contentious.

As is obvious from the Andean example, climate scientists and hydraulic engineers do not simply carry out objective research and implement uncontested projects. Instead, glacier experts serve as intermediaries among social groups. They produce science and technology in response to economic and political forces as well as in the context of distinct environmental circumstances. Their advances in glacial lake engineering and tropical glaciology were dependent not just on their skill but also on social relations, politics, national economic models, and foreign interests. They negotiated with llama herders, held town meetings in Callejón de Huaylas communities, planned the Cañon del Pato hydroelectric facility, shared data with irrigators, spread Cordillera Blanca information to university and government colleagues in Lima, and reported to the Peruvian president. A disaster or false alarm affected science, technology, and engineering in the Andes—as did a new president, local demands for certain projects, racism, coast-sierra divides, and the government's neoliberal transition. Duke Energy abandoned its proposed reservoirs at Lakes Shallap and Auquiscocha because of political and economic issues, not necessarily scientific or technological conclusions. Current policies and climate adaptation agendas, however, often lack this conception of expertise. Climatology, hydrology, and civil engineering are only part of the adaptation equation because the actual implementation of pilot programs will follow much negotiation among the various stakeholders. The World Bank's adaptation measures will work best by deciphering whose vision is most powerfully influencing their studies and proposed projects. Recognizing this social and historical construction of expertise—as well as seeing scientists and engineers as stakeholders rather than objective producers of information—could help smooth the implementation of climate change and glacier retreat adaptation measures in Peru and elsewhere.

In this process, certain social groups exert more power over science, technology, disaster prevention programs, and climate change adaptation agendas than others. Since 1941, local residents have generally demanded more state presence, not less, consistently requesting glacial lake security projects and glacier monitoring. The state's inconsistent, often tepid response reveals how deep fissures in Peruvian society affected disaster prevention programs: coastal economic development projects rather than humanitarian issues usually influenced government policy, except in 1970 when the sheer scale of the destruction made the earthquake-avalanche an international spectacle. Disaster economics, then, was not simply a story of the state and economic development versus local residents, as researchers often assume when they fail to examine local perspectives in their analyses of risk, vulnerability, global warming, and the history of science and technology. Nevertheless, the discursive construction of the Cordillera Blanca as a site for tourism paved the way for creating Huascarán National Park in 1975, which displaced local management of the region. The hydroelectric company influenced decades of glaciological and hydrological research, turning glaciers into vanishing water towers and using government money to acquire data that helps the now-privatized energy industry. Scientists and engineers ask certain questions and try to resolve certain issues with their research. Increasingly, these questions have centered on the concerns of the energy and water industries. While many benefit from electricity and food production for national consumption or international export, these questions guiding glacier research also serve certain sectors most directly, often those with the most money and power. Asking who has the political capacity to influence present-day engineers and to shape future climate science will tell us as much about the types of adaptation projects implemented than will the results of scientific studies.

Climate change and glacier retreat adaptation programs can stimulate new economic development, which then requires more science, technology, engineering, and policies to protect it. A cycle emerges as disaster economics play out: technoscientific solutions to climate change and natural hazards create new vulnerabilities—not simply in the way a levee heightens vulnerability because it can rupture, but because disaster prevention programs help open regions to new economies of consumption such as hydroelectricity, irrigation, and tourism. As societies grow more tied to these new developments, the stakes of glacier retreat also grow—as does the need for still more disaster prevention programs. Technology begets technology. The World Bank project calls for the use of drought resistance seeds, for example, to ensure food security in Peru. Selling seeds could be a boon for seed producers (disaster economics), while local populations and agroindustrial producers may become dependent on the new seeds, thereby heightening their vulnerability to future climate change and increasing their dependency on seed suppliers and possible state or nongovernmental organization subsidies. Recognizing evolving patterns in Cordillera Blanca glacier disaster adaptation may alert planners to future cycles in the Mantaro valley and beyond.

Finally, water use is more cultural, political, economic, and social than hydrological, environmental, or climatic. Certain physical restraints on water availability matter, of course, because not all world regions have the same access to water. In the Santa River watershed, water use has skyrocketed since the 1940s even as glacially fed water availability did not fluctuate so dramatically. Hydroelectricity generation, for example, increased from zero to over 250 megawatts. A significant jump in generation occurred after Duke Energy began operating the plant in the late 1990s, suggesting that neoliberal policies more

than water supplies influenced energy production on the Santa River. T
coastal irrigation projects that water tens of thousands of hectares wit
from Cordillera Blanca glaciers have appeared only in the last 25 years, precisely the era of accelerated glacier retreat. These points should not suggest that
glacier retreat is irrelevant; water supplies matter immensely. Rather, adaptation to glacier retreat and climate change hinges as much on culture, technological innovation, politics, economics, and social relations as it does on science
and environmental change—even though societies prioritize science rather
than society in their analysis of climate change. Climate and glaciers shaped
modern Peruvian history, but only by interacting with other social, political,
economic, and cultural forces.

Appendix

APPENDIX TABLE 1. Selected Cordillera Blanca Glacial Lake Security Projects

Lake Name	Year Completed	Project Type	Province
Safuna	1969	Tunnel	Pomabamba
	1973	Tunnel #2	
Jankarurish	1950*	Drainage canal	Huaylas
Rajucocha/Cullicocha	1950s	Tunnel	Huaylas
	1992	Reservoir†	
Parón	1952	Sandbag wall (temp. dam)	Huaylas
	1984	Tunnel	
	1992	Reservoir†	
Llanganuco	1970	Drainage canal	Yungay
Lake 69	1980s	Drainage canal	Yungay
Hualcacocha	1960s	Drainage canal	Carhuaz
	1976	Drainage canal, dam	
Cochca	1953	Drainage canal	Carhuaz
Lake 513a	1994	Tunnels	Carhuaz
Pacliashcocha	2000	Drainage canal	Carhuaz
Llaca	1953	Drainage canal, dam	Huaraz
	1977	Repaired canal, dam	
Palcacocha	1942	Cleared lake outlet	Huaraz
	1950s	Drainage canal, dam	
	1974	Repaired canal, dam	
	1974	Drainage canal, dam #2	
Cuchillacocha	1943	Drainage canal	Huaraz
	1950s	Drainage canal, dam	
	1973	Repaired canal, dam	
Tullparaju	1948	Drainage canal	Huaraz
	1953–1964	Tunnel, dam	
Shallap	1948	Drainage canal	Huaraz
	1950s	Drainage canal, dam	
	1974	Repaired canal, dam	

*Drainage project in progress when the 1950 outburst flood destroyed it, making it unnecessary.
† Reservoirs at Lakes Parón and Cullicocha refer to water–flow regulated dams.

APPENDIX TABLE 2. Glacier–Related Disasters in Cordillera Blanca History

Date	Type of Disaster and Origin	Damaged Area
6 Jan 1725	Avalanche/GLOF, Huandoy	Ancash destroyed; 1,500 deaths
10 Feb 1869	GLOF	Monterey; houses damaged; 11 deaths
24 Jun 1883	GLOF, Rajucolta	Macashca destroyed; many deaths
22 Jan 1917	Avalanche, Huascarán Norte	Ranrahirca, Shacsha
13 Mar 1932	GLOF, Solteracocha	Bolognesi province
20 Jan 1938	GLOF, Artesa	Carhuaz; Ulta Canyon damaged
1938	GLOF, Magistral	Conchucos; houses, bridges damaged
20 Apr 1941	GLOF, Suerococha	Cordillera Huayhuash; farms damaged
13 Dec 1941	GLOF, Palcacocha (Cojup)	Huaraz destroyed; 5,000 deaths
17 Jan 1945	GLOF, Ayhuiñaraju, Carhuacocha	Chavín and ruins destroyed; 500 deaths
20 Oct 1950	GLOF, Jankarurish, Los Cedros	Hydroelectric destroyed; 200 deaths
16 Jul 1951	GLOF, Artesoncocha	Drained into Lake Parón; no damage
28 Oct 1951	GLOF, Artesoncocha	Drained into Lake Parón; no damage
6 Nov 1952	GLOF, Milluacocha	Ishinka Canyon; farms damaged
18 Jun 1954	GLOF, Tullparaju	Damaged ongoing lake control project
8 Dec 1959	GLOF, Tullparaju	Damaged ongoing lake control project
10 Jan 1962	Avalanche, Huascarán	Ranrahirca and valley; 4,000 deaths
19 Dec 1965	GLOF, Tumarina	Carhuascancha Canyon; 10 deaths
31 May 1970	Avalanche, Huascarán	Yungay; 15,000 deaths
21 Dec 1979	GLOF, Paccharuri Canyon	Vicos; livestock killed, trail, farms damaged
14 Feb 1981	GLOF, Sarapococha	Cajatambo; bridge, highway damaged
31 Aug 1982	GLOF, Milluacocha	Carhuaz; trails and bridges damaged
16 Dec 1987	Avalanche, Huascarán	Yungay; livestock killed, road damaged
20 Jan 1989	Avalanche, Huascarán	Yungay; livestock killed, farms damaged
Jan 1997	GLOF, Pacliashcocha	Carhuaz; bridges, roads, pastures
20 May 1997	GLOF, Artizón Baja	Huaylas; Santa Cruz trail damaged
2002	Lake overflow, Safuna	Pomabamba Province; livestock killed
19 Mar 2003	Lake overflow, Palcacocha	Lake security dam partially destroyed
16 Oct 2003	Avalanche, Hualcán	Carhuaz; 9 glacial–ice collectors killed

GLOF = Glacial lake outburst flood

APPENDIX TABLE 3. Government Entities Conducting Glacier and Glacial Lake Projects

Year	Entity Name	Agency Oversight	Government Ministry Responsible
1941–50	No specific entity	Water and Irrigation	Development Division
1951–71	CCLCB	CCLCB	Development and Public Works; Agriculture (after 1968)
1966–73	Division of Glaciology and Lakes Security	CPS	Energy and Mines
1967	ING	ING	Council of Cultural Development
1973–77	Construction Unit No. 16, Glaciology and Lakes Security Program	Electroperú	Energy and Mines
1977–79	Glaciology and Lakes Security Program	INGEOMIN	Energy and Mines
1979–81	Glaciology and Lakes Security Program	INGEMMET	Energy and Mines
1981–86	Glaciology and Lakes Security Unit	Electroperú	Energy and Mines
1986–90	Glaciology and Hydrology Unit	Hidrandina	Energy and Mines
1990–97	Glaciology and Hydrological Resources Unit	Electroperú	Energy and Mines
2001–08	Glaciology and Hydrological Resources Unit	INRENA	Agriculture
2008–	Glaciology and Hydrological Resources Unit	ANA	Agriculture

Abbreviations:

ANA = National Water Authority
CCLCB = Control Commission of Cordillera Blanca Lakes
CPS = Peruvian Corporation of the Santa
ING = National Institute of Glaciology
INGEOMIN = National Institute of Geology & Mining
INGEMMET = National Institute of Geologic Mining & Metallurgy
INRENA = National Institute of Natural Resources

Notes

INTRODUCTION

1. Richard Black, "Media Attacked for 'Climate Porn,'" BBC News, 2 Aug. 2006, online at http://news.bbc.co.uk/1/hi/sci/tech/5236482.stm (accessed 6 June 2008).

2. Exceptions that do examine glacier-society relations include Carey, "The History of Ice"; Cruikshank, *Do Glaciers Listen?*; Knight, "Glaciers: Art and History"; Orlove, Wiegandt, and Luckman, eds., *Darkening Peaks*; Pyne, *The Ice*; Spufford, *I May Be Some Time*; Wilson, *The Spiritual History of Ice*.

3. Alley, *The Two-Mile Time Machine*; Bowen, *Thin Ice*.

4. For recent examples, see Adger et al., "Are There Social Limits to Adaptation to Climate Change?"; Crate and Nuttall, eds., *Anthropology and Climate Change*; Daniels and Endfield, "Narratives of Climate Change"; Hulme et al., "Unstable Climates"; Strauss and Orlove, eds., *Weather, Climate, Culture*.

5. Liverman, "Conventions of Climate Change"; Miller and Edwards, eds., *Changing the Atmosphere*; Oels, "Rendering Climate Change Governable"; Okereke, Bulkeley, and Schroeder, "Conceptualizing Climate Governance."

6. Recent analyses of climate history include Carey, "Beyond Weather"; Davis, *Late Victorian Holocausts*; Diaz and Stahle, "Climate and Cultural History"; Endfield, *Climate and Society*; Fleming, Jankovic, and Coen, eds., *Intimate Universality*; McIntosh, Tainter, and Keech McIntosh, eds., *The Way the Wind Blows*; Pfister, "Climatic Extremes, Recurrent Crises."

7. Studies drawing lessons for today from past human-climate interactions include Diamond, *Collapse*; Linden, *The Winds of Change*. McNeill critiques Diamond in "Diamond in the Rough."

8. Ames Marquez and Francou, "Cordillera Blanca glaciares"; Bode, *No Bells to Toll*; Carey, "Living and Dying with Glaciers"; Fernández Concha, "El problema de las lagunas"; Hegglin and Huggel, "An Integrated Assessment of Vulnerability"; Huggel, Haeberli, and Kääb, "Glacial Hazards"; Lliboutry et al., "Glaciological Problems...I. Historical Failures"; Oliver-Smith, *The Martyred City*; Reynolds, "The Identification and Mitigation of Glacier-Related Hazards"; Vilímek et al., "Influence of Glacial Retreat on Natural Hazards"; Young and Lipton, "Adaptive Governance"; Zapata Luyo, "La dinámica glaciar en lagunas."

9. For example, Stern, "Paradigms of Conquest"; Ortner, *Life and Death on Mt. Everest*, chap. 1.

10. On experts in history, see Cueto, "Social Medicine and 'Leprosy'"; Mitchell, *Rule of Experts*; Nash, "The Changing Experience of Nature"; Reuss, "Seeing Like an Engineer."

11. On the status of Cordillera Blanca and Andean glaciers, see Casassa et al., "Current Status of Andean Glaciers"; Georges, "20th-Century Glacier Fluctuations"; Kaser and Osmaston, *Tropical Glaciers*; Mark, "Tracing Andean Glaciers"; Racoviteanu et al., "Decadal Changes in Glacier Parameters"; Silverio and Jaquet, "Glacial Cover Mapping"; Vuille et al., "Climate Change and Tropical Andean Glaciers"; Vuille, Kaser, and Juen, "Glacier Mass Balance Variability in the Cordillera Blanca."

12. Grove, "Glacier Fluctuations and Hazards"; Huggel, Haeberli, and Kääb, "Glacial Hazards"; Richardson and Reynolds, "An Overview of Glacial Hazards"; Tufnell, *Glacier Hazards*.

13. Anthropologists provide excellent analyses of the 1970 earthquake and avalanche in Yungay and Huaraz. I build on their research to show, in part, that the 1970 event and responses to it were just one chapter in a longer story. See Bode, *No Bells to Toll*; Oliver-Smith, *The Martyred City*; Oliver-Smith, "Peru's Five-Hundred-Year Earthquake."

14. Taype, "Los desastres naturales." For other studies of disasters, climate, and El Niño in Peruvian history, see Cushman, "Enclave Vision"; Glantz, *Currents of Change*; Huertas Vallejos, *Diluvios andinos*; Orlove, Chiang, and Cane, "Forecasting Andean Rainfall and Crop Yield"; Sánchez, "Clima, hambre y enfermedad"; Seiner Lizárraga, *Estudios de historia medioambiental*; Zapata Velasco and Sueiro, *Naturaleza y política*.

15. Barbara J. Fraser, "Church Sees Latin American Glaciers as Symbols of God, Source of Life," Catholic Online 2007, http://www.catholic.org/international/international_story.php?id=25939 (accessed 6 June 2008).

16. "Solo seis mil visitantes fueron a Huaraz informa Cámara de Turismo," *El Comercio*, 21 April 2003.

17. Steinberg, *Acts of God*; Maskrey, ed., *Los desastres no son naturales*.

18. For these regional and racial divisions in Peruvian history, see Contreras and Cueto, *Historia del Perú contemporáneo*; de la Cadena, *Indigenous Mestizos*; Larson, *Trials of Nation Making*; Orlove, "Putting Race in Its Place."

19. McCook, *States of Nature*. For "science on the periphery," see George Basalla, "The Spread of Western Science," *Science* 156, no. 3775 (1967): 611–622; Cueto, *Excelencia científica*; Saldaña, *Historia social de las ciencias*.

20. Clague and Evans, "A Review of Catastrophic Drainage of Moraine-Dammed Lakes"; Reynolds, Dolecki, and Portocarrero, "The Construction of a Drainage Tunnel"; Richardson and Reynolds, "Degradation of Ice-Cored Moraine Dams."

21. On historical environment-economy connections, see Brannstrom, ed., *Territories, Commodities, and Knowledges*; Castro Herrera, "The Environmental Crisis"; Evans, *Bound in Twine*; McNeill, *Something New under the Sun*; Santiago, *The Ecology of Oil*; Sedrez, "Environmental History of Modern Latin America"; Soluri, *Banana Cultures*; Tucker, *Insatiable Appetite*.

22. Gootenberg, *Imagining Development*; Jacobsen, *Mirages of Transition*; Larson, *Trials of Nation Making*; Mallon, *The Defense of Community*; Nugent, *Modernity at the Edge of Empire*; Thorp and Bertram, *Peru 1890–1977*; Poole, *Vision, Race, and Modernity*; Thurner, *From Two Republics to One Divided*.

23. On historical explorations of the Cordillera Blanca, see Ames Marquez and Francou, "Cordillera Blanca glaciares"; Byers, "Contemporary Landscape Change"; Grötzbach, "Tourism in the Cordillera Blanca"; Lefebvre, "L'invention occidentale de la haute montagne"; Morales Arnao, *Andinismo en la Cordillera Blanca*; Neate, *Mountaineering in the Andes*; Walter, *La domestication de la nature*.

24. My conceptualization of nature's agency and human-environment interactions over time draws on literature in both environmental history and science and technology studies (STS), including Asdal, "The Problematic Nature of Nature"; Cronon, ed., *Uncommon Ground*; Gade, *Nature and Culture in the Andes*; Latour, *Science in Action*; Maskrey, ed., *Los desastres no son naturales*; Mitchell, *Rule of Experts*; Nash, "The Changing Experience of Nature"; Soluri, *Banana Cultures*; Stepan, *Picturing Tropical Nature*; Sutter, "Nature's Agents or Agents of Empire?"; Steinberg, *Acts of God*; Taylor, "Unnatural Inequalities"; White, *The Organic Machine*; Worster, *Nature's Economy*.

25. Walker, *Shaky Colonialism*; Healey, "The Fragility of the Moment"; Bode, *No Bells to Toll*; Berke and Beatley, *After the Hurricane*; Stonich, "International Tourism and Disaster Capitalism."

26. Liverman, "Conventions of Climate Change," 280–281; Oels, "Rendering Climate Change Governable"; on the economics of climate change more broadly, see Stern, *The Global Deal*.

27. Klein, *The Shock Doctrine*; Schuller, "Deconstructing the Disaster," 20.

28. On Cordillera Blanca-Santa River hydrology, see Kaser et al., "The Impact of Glaciers on the Runoff"; Mark, McKenzie, and Gómez, "Hydrochemical Evaluation of Changing Glacier Meltwater"; Mark and Seltzer, "Tropical Glacier Meltwater Contribution to Stream Discharge."

29. Huaraz and Callejón de Huaylas histories include Alvarez-Brun, *Ancash*; Doughty, *Huaylas*; Gonzales, *Huarás*; Stein, *Hualcan*; Thurner, *From Two Republics to One Divided*; Yauri Montero, *Ancash o la biografía de la inmortalidad*.

30. Examples include Craib, *Cartographic Mexico*; Gordillo, *Landscapes of Devils*; Poole, *Vision, Race, and Modernity*; Stepan, *Beginnings of Brazilian Science*; Swyngedouw, *Social Power and the Urbanization of Water*; Wisner, "Risk and the Neoliberal State."

31. Centeno and Silva, eds., *The Politics of Expertise*; Craib, *Cartographic Mexico*; Cueto, ed., *Saberes andinos*; Mitchell, *Rule of Experts*; Stepan, *Beginnings of Brazilian Science*; Prakash, *Another Reason*; Burnett, *Masters of All They Surveyed*.

32. On the limits of history of science scholarship for Latin America, see Fisher and Priego, "Ignorance and 'Habitus.'"

33. For a recent assessment of glacial lake outburst flood vulnerability in Huaraz, see Hegglin and Huggel, "An Integrated Assessment of Vulnerability."

34. For the social and historical construction of science and technology, see Hård and Jamison, *Hubris and Hybrids*; Bijker, *Of Bicycles, Bakelites, and Bulbs*; Latour, *Science in Action*. For locals inhabiting hazards zones worldwide see Nathan, "Risk Perception, Risk Management"; Davis, *Ecology of Fear*, 66–67; Orsi, *Hazardous Metropolis*, 104–106; McPhee, *The Control of Nature*, Part III; Oliver-Smith, "Traditional Agriculture"; Bode, "Disaster, Social Structure"; Carey, "The Politics of Place."

35. Most scholars argue that the typical binary division of urban *mestizos* versus rural indigenous people is a misleading categorization that falsely essentializes racial and ethnic groups in the Callejón de Huaylas and Andean Peru. See Stein, *Deconstructing Development Discourse in Peru*, 39–40; de la Cadena, *Indigenous Mestizos*.

36. On the relationship between environmental narratives and power, see Bravo, "Voices from the Sea Ice"; Daniels and Endfield, "Narratives of Climate Change"; Davis, *Resurrecting the Granary of Rome*; Fairhead and Leach, *Misreading the African Landscape*; Martinez-Alier, "Ecology and the Poor"; Weiner, "A Death-Defying Attempt"; Zimmerer and Bassett, eds., *Political Ecology*; Radkau, *Nature and Power*.

37. Gunewardena and Schuller, eds., *Capitalizing on Catastrophe*; Klein, *The Shock Doctrine*; Steinberg, *Acts of God*; Varley, ed., *Disasters, Development, and Environment*.

38. Max Weber's definition remains useful: the state is "a human community that (successfully) claims the *monopoly of the legitimate use of physical force* within a given territory" (emphasis in original). States, then, acting through what we call "politics," seek to control "the distribution of power, either among states or among groups within a state" (Weber, "Politics as a Vocation," 78).

39. Bode, *No Bells to Toll*; Oliver-Smith, *The Martyred City*.

40. Foucault, *Discipline and Punish*; Scott, *Seeing Like a State*; Drake and Hershberg, eds., *State and Society in Conflict*; Andermann, *The Optic of the State*.

41. For simultaneous local support and rejection of Peruvian state programs, see Harvey, "The Materiality of State-Effects"; Nugent, *Modernity at the Edge of Empire*; Mallon, *Peasant and Nation*; Burt, "Contesting the Terrain of Politics."

42. Ramos Guardia, "El Callejón de Huaylas"; Phol, "El 'Callejón de Huailas'"; Zapatel, *Vialidad y Turismo en el Perú*.

43. Vivanco and Gordon, eds., *Tarzan Was an Eco-Tourist*. On the link between tourism and climate change, see essays in Hall and Higham, eds., *Tourism, Recreation, and Climate Change*.

44. Ellis, *Vertical Margins*; Ortner, *Life and Death on Mt. Everest*; Schrepfer, *Nature's Altars*; Isserman and Weaver, *Fallen Giants*.

CHAPTER I

1. Fernández Concha, "El problema de las lagunas"; Lliboutry et al., "Glaciological Problems. I"; Zapata Luyo, "La dinámica glaciar." For glacial lake hazards outside Peru, see Clague and Evans, "A Review of Catastrophic Drainage"; Grove, "Glacier Fluctuations and Hazards"; Kattelmann, "Glacial Lake Outburst Floods"; Mool, "Glacial Lakes"; Richardson and Reynolds, "Degradation of Ice-Cored Moraine Dams"; Richardson and Reynolds, "An Overview of Glacial Hazards"; Janský et al., "The Evolution of Petrov Lake"; Breien et al., "Erosion and Morphology."

2. For technical descriptions of the outburst flood, see David Torres Vargas, "Informe preliminar sobre algunas lagunas de la Cordillera Blanca" (Lima, October 1942), File I-GEOL-003 in Biblioteca, UGRH; Alberto Giesecke and Luke Lowther, "Informe sobre el aluvion de 13 de Diciembre de 1941" (Lima, 1941), File # I-GEOL-003 in UGRH; "El InformeTécnico: 8 millones de metros cúbicos de agua, incrementados por toneladas de piedra y agua se precipitaron desde las alturas sobre Huaraz," El Comercio, 16 December 1941, 5; Moisés Rajavinschi, "Copia del informe emitido por el Ingeniero don Moisés Rejavinshi [sic] comisionado por el Concejo para estudiar las condiciones actuales de las lagunas de Cojup y Quillcayhuanca" (Huaraz, 1942), Ministerio del Interior, Prefectura, File 425, Folio 302, in AGN; M. Zegarra, "Sobre la catástrofe de Huaraz: Informe técnico del origen de ésta," El Comercio, 21 December 1941, 3; Unidad de Glaciología y Recursos Hídricos, "Estado situacional de la laguna Palcacocha" (Huaraz: Marzo, 2003), in UGRH; Vilímek et al., "Influence of Glacial Retreat."

3. Larson, Trials of Nation, chap. 1; Orlove, "Putting Race in Its Place"; Thurner, From Two Republics.

4. Klinenberg, Heat Wave; Kelman, A River and Its City; McPhee, The Control of Nature; Walker, Shaky Colonialism.

5. Gridilla, Huaraz, o apuntes y documentos, 51. Lima at the time (1700), one of the largest cities in South America, had a population of 37,000. See Walker, Shaky Colonialism, 58.

6. Thurner, From Two Republics, 23.

7. Mangin, "Estratificación social en el Callejón de Huaylas." Scholars now understand that Peruvian racial categories have always been more social than racial and are thus imagined or imposed classifications. See de la Cadena, Indigenous Mestizos.

8. Progresos del Perú, 1933–1939, durante el gobierno del Presidente de la República General Oscar R. Benavides (Buenos Aires: Editorial Guillermo Kraft, 1945), 56–60.

9. Republica del Perú, Censo national de población de 1940. Vol. 3: Departamentos: Lambayeque, Libertad, Ancash (Lima: Dirección de Estadística, 1947), 5, 22.

10. Coral Miranda, El aluvión de Huaraz, 34–35.

11. Stowe, "El desastre de Huarás," 43.

12. Interview by author, Unchus, 2003.

13. Stowe, "El desastre de Huarás," 43.

14. Coral Miranda, El aluvión de Huaraz, 36.

15. Fernández, 13 de Diciembre de 1941, n.p.; "Instantes supremos de angustia vivió Huaraz el día 13 de Dicmbre. de 1941," Noticias é Informaciones, 10 January 1942, 1.

16. "Huaraz sufrio grandes daños por el desborde del río Quilcay," *El Comercio*, 14 December 1941.

17. Fernández, *13 de Diciembre de 1941*.

18. Comisión Liquidadora de la Corporación Peruana del Santa, "Memoria general de la Corporación Peruana del Santa, años 1943–1974" (Lima, 1980), Caja 058347, no. 6 in Electroperú-FS, Lima, 19; Alberto Giesecke, "La tragedia de Huaraz del 13 de Diciembre de 1941," unpublished testimonial in author's possession.

19. J. A. Broggi, "Informe preliminar sobre la exploración y estudio de las condiciones de estabilidad de las lagunas de la Cordillera Blanca" (Lima, July 1942), File I-GEOL-001 in UGRH; Ministerio de Fomento y Obras Públicas, "Memorandum del Ministerio de Fomento y Obras Públicas solicitando la contracción de una comisión de expertos" (Lima, 23 January 1952) in appendix A of Trask, "El problema de los aluviones," 66–72; Coral Miranda, *El aluvión de Huaraz*; Prado, *Acción del Presidente Prado*.

20. "Huaraz está enfermo," *Noticias é Informaciones* (Huaraz), 10 January 1942, 1–2.

21. For a compilation of these December 1941 articles, see Prado, *Acción del Presidente Prado*, 131–157.

22. Prado's trip to Huaraz was reported in numerous *El Comercio* articles, 14–16 December 1941, and in *Acción del Presidente Prado*, 25–55. *La República* quoted on p. 48.

23. Klarén, *Peru*, 242–244, 281; Kristal, *The Andes Viewed from the City*, 189–190.

24. Contreras and Cueto, *Historia del Perú*, 253–254.

25. Fleming, *The Callendar Effect*, chap. 5.

26. F. E. Matthes, "Report of Committee on Glaciers, April 1939," *Transactions of the American Geophysical Union* 20 (1939): 518–523. Also see Grove, *The Little Ice Age*, 3–4.

27. Cox et al., "The Study of Threatening Glaciers: Discussion"; Mason, "The Study of Threatening Glaciers." For disasters from advancing glaciers, see Grove, "Glacier Fluctuations and Hazards," 351–367; Wiegandt and Lugon, "Challenges of Living with Glaciers"; Ladurie, *Times of Feast, Times of Famine*, chaps. 3 and 4.

28. Kinzl, "La ruptura del lago glacial."

29. Weart, "Spencer Weart on Depicting Global Warming," 11.

30. Alberto Giesecke and Luke Lowther, "Informe sobre el aluvion de 13 de Diciembre de 1941" (Lima, 1941), File I-GEOL-003 in UGRH; personal communication with Alberto Giesecke, Lima, February 2004.

31. Rajavinschi, "Copia del informe emitido por el Ingeniero."

32. Guardia Encargado de Pareja, "Dá cuenta del resultado obtenido en la comisión a la Laguna de 'Cojup,'" (Huaraz, 14 November 1942), Ministerio del Interior, Prefectura, File 425, Folio 485, in AGN; Oppenheim, "Sobre las lagunas de Huaraz."

33. Lorenzo Sousa Iglesias, Prefecto del Departamento, Letter to Señor Director de Gobierno, Lima (Huaraz, 15 July 1942), in Ministerio del Interior, Prefectura, File 425, Folio 302, in AGN.

34. J. A. Broggi, "Informe preliminar sobre la exploración," 9.

35. J. A. Broggi, Letter to Luís Chavez Badani, Director de Aguas e Irrigación (Lima, 21 July 1942), File I-GEOL-001 in UGRH; J. A. Broggi, Letter to Sr. Director de Aguas e Irrigación (Lima, 26 August 1942), File I-GEOL-003 in UGRH.

36. Broggi, "La desglaciación andina"; Broggi, "Informe preliminar sobre la exploración."

37. Heim, "Observaciones glaciológicas"; Indacochea and Iberico, "Aluvionamiento de Chavín"; Oppenheim, "Sobre las lagunas de Huaraz"; Spann, "Informe sobre el origen de la catástrofe."

38. Kinzl, "La ruptura del lago."

39. Isidro Espejo Luna, Letter to Ministro de Fomento (Cajatambo, 26 May 1941), Aguas de Regadío, File RF DA 4, CA 87, Do. 247, in AGN; "Avalancha en el río Pativilca," La Vida Agrícola: Revista de Agricultura y Ganadería 18, no. 210 (1941): 462; Ames Marquez and Francou, "Cordillera Blanca glaciares," 56–57; Zapata Luyo, "La dinámica glaciar," 49; Ames, "A Documentation of Glacier Tongue Variations," 4. Though some cite a 1702 flood, an extensive search in numerous archives never yielded specific descriptions or references to an early 1700s disaster in the Callejón de Huaylas, including a search of Catholic church visitas to Huaraz in the early and mid–1700s, held at Lima's Archivo Arzobispal.

40. Broggi, "La desglaciación andina"; Kinzl, "La ruptura del lago glacial"; Kinzl, "Los glaciares de la Cordillera Blanca"; Kinzl, "Aufgaben und Reisen des Geographen"; Kinzl, "Gletscherkundliche Begleitworte."

41. Grove, Little Ice Ages; Wiegandt and Lugon, "Challenges of Living with Glaciers"; Fagan, The Little Ice Age, chap. 7; Cruikshank, Do Glaciers Listen?; Ladurie, Times of Feast, Times of Famine.

42. Georges, "20th-Century Glacier Fluctuations"; Kaser and Georges, "Changes of the Equilibrium-Line Altitude"; Morales Arnao, "Desglaciación y disminución de recursos hídricos," 7; Kaser and Osmaston, Tropical Glaciers, 26.

43. Dyurgerov and Meier, "Twentieth Century Climate Change"; Oerlemans, "Extracting a Climate Signal."

44. Craib, Cartographic Mexico; Mitchell, Rule of Experts; Nash, "The Changing Experience of Nature"; Scott, Seeing Like a State.

45. Subprefecto de Carhuaz Torres Ramos, Telegram from Torres Ramos to Lorenzo Sousa Iglesia, Prefecto del Departamento (Carhuaz, 30 December 1942), Ministerio del Interior, Prefectura, File 425, Folio 11, in AGN.

46. Subprefecto Lucar, Caraz, Telegram to Mendez Muñoz, Director Gobierno diputado Capitán (Caraz: 16 January 1942), Ministerio del Interior, Prefectura, File 425, Folio 11, in AGN.

47. Antonio Grüter, Jefe de la Comisión del Estudio Lagunas, "Cumplo con informar el resultado de nuestro estudio en la región de la laguna de Parón" (Caraz, 15 November 1942), Ministerio del Interior, Prefectura, File 425, Folio 485, in AGN.

48. For example, see Luis A. Ghiglino, "Informe de los estudios de la laguna de Parón" (Lima, 18 October 1947), File 70I 27.720 in Biblioteca de Electroperú, Lima; Luis A. Ghiglino and Federico Stein, "Estudios de las lagunas de Parón, Querokocha,

Conococha y Aguash situados en la Cordillera Blanca" (Lima, 31 December 1948), File 701 27.720 in Biblioteca de Electroperú, Lima.

49. Telegram from Subprefect of Carhuaz Torres Ramos to Ancash Prefect Lorenzo Sousa Iglesia (Carhuaz, 8 January 1942), Ministerio del Interior, Prefectura, File 425, Folio 11, in AGN.

50. Indacochea and Iberico, "Aluvionamiento de Chavín," 27.

51. Luis A. Ghiglino, "Informe de los estudios practicados en la Laguna de Janca-Rurush" (Lima, 28 October 1948), File 701 27.720 in Biblioteca de Electroperú, Lima.

52. Broggi, "Informe preliminar sobre la exploración," 9–10; J. A. Broggi, Letter to Sr. Director de Aguas e Irrigación (Lima, 26 August 1942), File I-GEOL-003 in UGRH, 1–3.

53. Torres Vargas, "Informe preliminar sobre algunas lagunas," 2.

54. J. A. Broggi, Letter to Luís Chavez Badani, Director de Aguas e Irrigación (Lima, 21 July 1942), File I-GEOL-001 in UGRH; Broggi, "Informe preliminar sobre la exploración," 3. Kinzl made a similar pro-mountaineering argument in his 1940 article "Alpinismo-Andinismo."

55. Ueda Tsuboyama, *Historia del Cuerpo de Ingenieros.*

56. López-Ocón Cabrera, "El nacionalismo," 124; Orlove, "Putting Race in Its Place."

57. Gamio, "Viajando por el Perú."

58. Broggi, "La desglaciación andina," 17.

59. Indacochea and Iberico, "Aluvionamiento de Chavín"; Oppenheim and Spann, "Investigaciones glaciologicas"; Guardia Encargado de Pareja, "Dá cuenta del resultado obtenido"; Rajavinschi, "Copia del informe emitido por el Ingeniero"; Comisión de Estudios Cuenca del Santa, "Informe de la Comisión de Estudios Cuenca del Santa" (Lima, 1951), in UGRH; Spann, "Informe sobre el origen de la catástrofe."

60. Broggi, "Informe preliminar sobre la exploración," 11.

61. Davis, *Ecology of Fear;* Glantz, *Currents of Change;* Steinberg, *Acts of God;* Walker, *Shaky Colonialism.*

62. "La reconstrucción de Huaraz," *El Departamento,* 7 June 1945, 2; "La reconstrucción de la zona del aluvión," *El Departamento,* 21 July 1945, 2; "Obras públicas que requiere Huaraz," *El Departamento,* 2 August 1956, 3; Irving, "Lo que el pueblo de Huaraz debe conocer en torno al plano regulador," *El Departamento,* 10 November 1952, 3.

63. Coral Miranda, *El aluvión de Huaraz.*

64. "Asociación de Propietarios de la Zona Aluviónica," *El Departamento,* 12 April 1956, 2.

65. "Edificaciones en El Aluvión," *El Departamento,* 11 August 1951, 2.

66. "Obras públicas que requiere Huaraz," *El Departamento,* 2 August 1956, 3; "En torno al vaciado de las lagunas de la Cordillera Blanca," *El Departamento,* 9 March 1945, 3; "Urbanisación de la zona del aluvión," *El Departamento,* 7 January 1956, 2.

67. "Centenario de la creación de la provincia de Huaraz," *El Departamento,* 3 January 1956, 2.

68. See, for example, "La seguridad de Huaraz," *El Departamento*, 19 June 1943, 2; "Las obras de defenza de la ciudad de Huaraz," *El Departamento*, 16 September 1943, 2; Moisés Estremadoyro and Gonzalo Salazar, "Especificación de las obras que deben ejecutarse de acuerdo con los respectivos proyectos en las obras de defensa de Huaraz y el desagüe de las lagunas," *El Departamento*, 9 September 1943, 3; Lorenzo Sousa Iglesias, "En torno a las obras de defensa de la ciudad de Huaraz," *El Departamento*, 22 November 1943, 2–3.

69. "En torno a las obras de defenza y encausamiento del río Quilcay," *El Departamento*, 23 June 1943, 3.

70. H. Ochoa, "Algunos problemas locales," *El Departamento*, 18 December 1943, 2.

71. "Con motivo del desagüe de la laguna de Cuchilla-Cocha ayer a las 5 de la tarde hubo alarma en la población," *El Departamento*, 17 November 1943, 3.

72. Manuel Prado, *Mensaje del Presidente del Perú, Doctor Manuel Prado y Ugarteche, ante el Congreso Nacional, el 28 de Julio de 1945*, online at http://www.congreso.gob.pe/museo/mensajes/Mensaje-1945-4.pdf (accessed 27 June 2008), 112.

73. Schiebinger and Swan, eds., *Colonial Botany*; Drayton, *Nature's Government*; Lafuente, Elena, and Ortega, eds., *Mundialización de la ciencia*; Clement, "El nacimiento de la higiene urbana"; Parker, "Civilizing the City of Kings"; Wilson, "Indian Citizenship and the Discourse of Hygiene."

CHAPTER 2

1. De la Cadena, *Indigenous Mestizos*; Stein, *Countrymen and Townsmen*; Walton, "Human Spatial Organization in an Andean Valley."

2. Thurner, *From Two Republics*, 130; Méndez Jurado et al., eds., *Monografía de la provincia de Huaylas*, 20; Carrillo Ramírez, *Ensayo monográfico*, 21.

3. Walker, "The Upper Classes and Their Upper Stories."

4. Kelman, *A River and Its City*, chap. 3.

5. Bode, "Disaster, Social Structure, and Myth"; for Yungay, see Oliver-Smith, *The Martyred City*.

6. Maskrey, ed., *Los desastres no son naturales*; Gade, *Nature and Culture in the Andes*; Cronon, ed., *Uncommon Ground*; Steinberg, *Acts of God*.

7. For "the engineer as negotiator," see Reuss, "Seeing Like an Engineer."

8. Sherbondy, "Water Ideology in Inca Ethnogenesis"; Gelles, *Water and Power in Highland Peru*; Sikkink, "Water and Exchange."

9. Gose, "Segmentary State Formation."

10. Polia Meconi, *Las lagunas de los encantos*.

11. Gose, *Deathly Waters and Hungry*, 126–129; Pantoja Ramos, Ripkens, and Swisshelm, *Cuentos y relatos en el quechua de Huaraz*, 237–241; "La laguna de Purhuay," in Yauri Montero, *Leyendas ancashinas*, 70–71; Walter, *La domestication de la nature*, Part 1; Bode, *No Bells to Toll*, chap. 11.

12. Camino, *Cerros, plantas y lagunas poderosas*, 116.

13. Stein, *Hualcan*, 305.

14. Interview by author, Vicos, 2004.

15. Yauri Montero, *Leyendas ancashinas*, 54.

16. Ibid., 55–56.

17. Carranza Calvo et al., eds., *Huandoy y Huascarán*, 44–45.

18. Fernández, *Antología de la tradición*, 108–112. Also see Yauri Montero, *Leyendas ancashinas*, 70–71; Stein, *Hualcan*, 305.

19. Bode, *No Bells to Toll*, 148; personal communication with anthropologist Doris Walter, October 2002, Sion, Switzerland.

20. Pantoja Ramos, Ripkens, and Swisshelm, *Cuentos y relatos en el quechua*, 237–241.

21. Walter, *La domestication de la nature*, 108–111.

22. Yauri Montero, *Leyendas ancashinas*, 63.

23. On enchanted lakes in Peru, see Camino, *Cerros, plantas y lagunas poderosas*; Polia Meconi, *Las lagunas de los encantos*.

24. One the local construction of environmental knowledge, see Cruikshank, *Do Glaciers Listen?*; Gordillo, *Landscapes of Devils*; Raffles, *In Amazonia*.

25. Julia de Barrionuevo, "Causa la inundación un 'Encanto,'" *Noticias é Informaciones*, 10 January 1942, 3.

26. See, for example, García, *Making Indigenous Citizens*; Tamayo Herrera, *Liberalismo, indigenismo y violencia*; Graham, ed., *The Idea of Race*.

27. Kristal, *The Andes Viewed from the City*.

28. Clorinda Matto de Turner, *Aves sin nido: Novela peruana* (Lima: Imprenta del Universo de Carlos Prince, 1889).

29. Cruikshank, "Glaciers and Climate Change," 391; Menzies, ed., *Traditional Ecological Knowledge*.

30. Coral Miranda, *El aluvión de Huaraz*, xi.

31. "Huaraz está enfermo," *Noticias é Informaciones*, 10 January 1942, 2; Fernández, *13 de Diciembre de*; César Valverde Tito, "La tragedia de mi pueblo," *La Hora*, 13 December 1954.

32. Coral Miranda quoted at length in Fernández, *13 de Diciembre de 1941*.

33. Pulgar Vidal, *Geografía del Perú*.

34. Murra, "El 'Archipiélago Vertical' Revisited"; Van Buren, "Rethinking the Vertical Archipelago." On Andean agriculture and pasturing see Zimmerer, *Changing Fortunes*.

35. Larson, *Trials of Nation*, 150; Orlove, "Putting Race in Its Place."

36. Mallon, *The Defense of Community*, 91; Thurner, *From Two Republics*.

37. Cueto, "Andean Biology in Peru."

38. Orlove, "Down to Earth"; Poole, *Vision, Race, and Modernity*.

39. de la Cadena, "Silent Racism," 155–156.

40. Orlove, "Down to Earth."

41. Bauer, *Goods, Power, History*, chap. 3.

42. Mangin, "Estratificación social en el Callejón de Huaylas," 181–183; Oliver-Smith, "Traditional Agriculture, Central Places, and Postdisaster Urban Relocation."

43. Carrillo Ramírez, *Ensayo monográfico de la Provincia de Bolognesi*, 21; Buse, *Huarás Chavín*, 55.

44. Stein, *Countrymen and Townsmen*, 36–46; Allan Holmberg, "Some Relationships between Psychobiological Deprivation and Culture Change in the Andes" Paper presented at the Cornell Latin American Year Conference, Cornell University, Ithaca, NY, 1966, 14.

45. Larson, *Trials of Nation Making*, 177–178.

46. Barrionuevo, ed., *Ancash Actual*, 41. Also see Thurner, *From Two Republics*, 103–104.

47. Gonzales, *Huarás: visión integral*, 26–27.

48. Méndez Jurado et al., eds., *Monografía de la provincia de Huaylas*, 20; Carrillo Ramírez, *Ensayo monográfico de la Provincia de Bolognesi*, 21–22; Stein, *Countrymen and Townsmen*, 7–8; Walton, "Human Spatial Organization in an Andean Valley," 20–50.

49. Mangin, "Estratificación social en el Callejón de Huaylas," 182.

50. For example, Barrionuevo, ed., *Ancash Actual*; Méndez Jurado et al., eds., *Monografía de la provincia de Huaylas*, 10; Victor Ramos Guardia, "El Callejón de Huaylas: Futuro centro de turismo y de estaciones termales," in *Ancash Actual*, 52–53; Victor Crúz Dextre, "Del ambiente ancashino," in *Ancash Actual*, 25–26.

51. Emilio Montes, "Catásrofe de Chavín" (uncited newspaper clipping from 1945), in Ministerio del Interior, Prefectura, File 465, Folio 182, in AGN. Also see "Decimo doloroso aniversario," *El Departamento*, 13 December 1951, 2; Buse, *Huarás Chavín*, 60; "A trece años del aluvion de Huaraz," *La Hora*, 14 December 1954, 3.

52. Mauro G. Mendoza, "Prólogo," in Coral Miranda, *El aluvión de Huaraz*, vi–vii.

53. Fernández, *13 de Diciembre de 1941*.

54. "La catástrofe de Huaraz," *La Hora*, 13 December 1954, 2.

55. Fernández, *13 de Diciembre de 1941*.

56. For example, "Con motivo del desagüe de la laguna de Cuchilla-Cocha ayer a las 5 de la tarde hubo alarma en la población," *El Departamento*, 17 November 1943, 3.

57. Pantoja Ramos, Ripkens, and Swisshelm, *Cuentos y relatos en el quechua*, 17.

58. Interview by author, Lima, 2004.

59. Fernández, *13 de Diciembre de 1941*.

60. Interview by author, Lima, 2003.

61. Every urban Huaraz resident I interviewed about the 1941 disaster—more than a dozen survivors in total—complained about Indians descending into the city to loot.

62. "13 de Diciembre de 1941," *El Departamento*, 13 December 1955, 2. Also see the speech by Dr. Miguel A. Morán quoted in Justo Fernández, *13 de Diciembre de 1941*.

63. Edilberto Lopez Illanes, "Como se produjo la catástrofe de Chavín," *El Comercio*, 28 January 1945, 7. Also see Marcelino Flores Garcia, "Chavín, después del aluvión: versión de la tragedia (conclusión)," *El Comercio*, 6 February 1945, 2; Samuel Ordóñez del Rio, "La tragedia en Chavín: Pobre Rúben," *El Comercio*, 2 February 1945, 7.

64. Tello, *Chavín*; Burger, *Chavín and the Origins of Andean Civilization*; Contreras, "Reconstructing Landscape at Chavín de Huántar."

65. Indacochea G. and Iberico M., "Aluvionamiento de Chavín"; Spann, "Informe sobre el origen de la catástrofe."

66. Pedro Allemant Oliva, "La tragedia de Chavín: Pedro Artola del Pozo," *El Comercio*, 25 January 1945, 2; "Fueron hallados los restos del Sr. Pedro Artola, Prefecto de Ancash," *El Comercio*, 28 January 1945, 13; "Un alvión destruyó el distrito de Chavín: Desaparecen casas y personas," *El Comercio*, 17 January 1945, 1; Marcelino Flores Garcia, "Chavín, antes del aluvión, parte II," *El Comercio*, 30 January 1945, 5.

67. Tello, *Chavín*, 362–363.

68. Moisés Olaza Sotelo, Letter to Prefecto del Departamento de Ancash (Huaraz, 9 April 1945), in Ministerio del Interior, Prefectura, File 465, Folio 182, AGN; Alfredo de Orbegoso, Prefecto del Departamento de Ancash, Letter to Señor Director General de Gobierno, Lima, (Huaraz: 9 April 1945), in Ministerio del Interior, Prefectura, File 465, Folio 182, AGN.

69. "Las lagunas del Departamento de Ancash," *El Comercio*, 30 January 1945, 2. Also see "Comenzó el rescate de los que perecieron en Chavín," *El Comercio*, 20 January 1945, 15; Juan Valjean, "La catástrofe de Chavín," *El Comercio*, 20 January 1945, 20.

70. "Inquieta en Carhuaz el crecimiento de un río," *El Comercio*, 4 February 1945, 13.

71. Subprefecto de Carhuaz Torres Ramos, Telegram to Lorenzo Sousa Iglesia, Prefecto del Departamento (Carhuaz: 30 December 1942), Ministerio del Interior, Prefectura, File 425, Folio 11, in AGN.

72. Antonio Grüter, Jefe de la Comisión del Estudio Lagunas, "Cumplo con informar el resultado de nuestro estudio en la región de la laguna de Parón," (Caraz: 15 November 1942), Ministerio del Interior, Prefectura, File 425, Folio 485, in AGN; Subprefecto Lucar, Caraz, Telegram to Mendez Muñoz, Director Gobierno duputado Capitán (Caraz: 16 January 1942), Ministerio del Interior, Prefectura, File 425, Folio 11, in AGN.

73. Technical reports on Parón include Luis A. Ghiglino, "Informe de los estudios de la laguna de Parón" (Lima, 18 October 1947), File 70I 27.720, in Biblioteca de Electroperú, Lima; Luis A. Ghiglino and Federico Stein, "Estudios de las lagunas de Parón, Querokocha, Conococha y Aguash situados en la Cordillera Blanca" (Lima, 31 December 1948), File 70I 27.720, in Biblioteca de Electroperú, Lima.

74. José Terry et al., "Se solicita en Caraz el desagüe de la laguna Parón," *El Comercio*, 29 January 1945, 11.

75. "El desague de las lagunas Cojup, Cuchillacocha y Shallap: La importante reunión de ayer en la prefectura," *El Departamento*, 1 February 1945, 2; "Comenzó el rescate de los que perecieron en Chavín," *El Comercio*, 20 January 1945, 15; "El Meeting de ayer," *El Departamento*, 22 January 1945, 3.

76. "En torno al desague de las lagunas," *El Departamento*, 2 February 1945, 2–3.

77. "El Meeting de ayer," *El Departamento*, 22 January 1945, 3; "En torno a las lagunas de la Cordillera Blanca," *El Departamento*, 24 November 1945, 2; "Exposición del Director de Aguas en Huaraz," *El Comercio*, 2 February 1945, 15; "La amenaza de las lagunas de la Cordillera," *El Comercio*, 29 January 1945, 11.

78. "Exposición del Director de Aguas en Huaraz," *El Comercio*, 2 February 1945, 15; Oppenheim, "Sobre las lagunas de Huaraz."

79. Ghiglino, "Informe de los estudios de la laguna de Parón"; Ghiglino and Stein, "Estudios de las lagunas de Parón."

80. "El desague de las lagunas Cojup, Cuchillacocha y Shallap: La importante reunión de ayer en la prefectura," *El Departamento*, 1 February 1945, 2.

81. "Una Catástrofe mas en Ancash," *El Pueblo (Seminario Informativo Independiente)*, 21 January 1945, 2.

82. "Se van a desaguar las lagunas," *El Comercio*, 9 February 1945, 4.

83. Manuel Gonzales Ramírez, Prefecto Accidental de Ancash, "El desague de las lagunas," *El Departamento*, 22 March 1945, 3.

84. Fagan, *The Little Ice Age*; Grove, "Glacier Fluctuations and Hazards"; Hambrey and Alean, *Glaciers*; Richardson and Reynolds, "An Overview of Glacial Hazards"; Tufnell, *Glacier Hazards*.

85. M.E. Gentile Lafaille, "Una Lima que no se va: los refrescos del Siglo XVII," *Boletín de Lima* 19, no. 4 (1982): 10–14; Locke, "Catholic Icons and Society"; Sallnow, *Pilgrims of the Andes*, chap. 1; Reinhard, "Sacred Landscape."

86. Braun, "Producing Vertical Territory." Michel Foucault and Bruno Latour have examined these issues broadly, and Marcos Cueto has called for more of this research in the Andes (see the introduction to his *Saberes andinos*).

CHAPTER 3

1. Resolución Suprema No. 70, 20 February 1951.

2. Quoted in Arundhati Roy, *The Cost of Living* (New York: Modern Library, 1999), 13.

3. McNeill, *Something New under the Sun*, 157–159.

4. Josephson, *Industrialized Nature*.

5. Healey, "The Fragility of the Moment."

6. One might suspect such a state-imposed agenda based on existing scholarship related to Scott, *Seeing Like a State*.

7. Here I draw on Mitchell, *Rule of Experts*, 27–31.

8. Quoted from the law to create the Corporación Peruana del Santa, Lima, 9 June 1943; also see Corporación Peruana del Santa, *Corporación Peruana del Santa: Planta Siderúrgica y Central Hidroeléctrica* (Lima: Iberia S.A. Industria del Offset, 1958).

9. David Dasso, *Observaciones al informe presentado por los auditores a la Comisión Parlamentaria Investigadora de la Corporación Peruana del Santa* (Lima: Torres Aguirre, S.A., 1945); Comisión Mixta Parlamentaria, *Informe sobre las actividades de la Corporación Peruana del Santa* (Lima: Salas é Hijos, 1945); Comisión Liquidadora de la Corporación Peruana del Santa, "Memoria general de la Corporación Peruana del Santa, años 1943–1974" (Lima [1980]), Caja 058347, No. 6 in Electroperú-FS, Lima; Corporación Peruana del Santa, "Primera Memoría" (1943), File O 352.43 M in BNP; Corporación Peruana del Santa, "Segunda Memoría" (1944), File O 352.43 M in BNP.

10. Corporación Peruana del Santa, *Corporación Peruana del Santa*.

11. "Irrigación de tierras en Chimbote," *El Departamento*, 11 March 1950, 2.

12. "Corporación del Santa," *La Hora*, 22 July 1954, 2; "La Corporación Peruana del Santa," *El Departamento*, 22 July 1954, 2.

13. Corporación Peruana del Santa, *Corporación Peruana del Santa*; Santiago Antúnez de Mayolo, "La caida de agua del Cañon del Pato" (Lima, 1941), File Ancash 00038, Biblioteca del Instituto Riva Agüero, Lima; Antúnez de Mayolo, *Relato de una idea*; Ramírez Alzamora, *Santiago Antúnez de Mayolo*.

14. Guerra Martiniére, *Manuel Odría*, 94, 103; Thorp and Bertram, *Peru 1890–1977*, 257, 269, 407; Masterson, *Militarism and Politics in Latin America*, chap. 6.

15. Thorp and Bertram, *Peru 1890–1977*, 269.

16. Josephson, *Industrialized Nature*.

17. Méndez Jurado et. al., eds., *Monografía de la provincia de Huaylas*, 299–302; Republica del Perú, *Censo national de población de 1940*. Vol. 3: *Departamentos: Lambayeque, Libertad, Ancash* (Lima: Dirección de Estadística, 1947).

18. Kogan and Leininger, *The Ascent of Alpamayo*, 83–84.

19. Luis A. Ghiglino, "Informe de los estudios practicados en la Laguna de Janca-Rurush" (Lima, 28 October 1948), File 70I 27.720 in Biblioteca de Electroperú, Lima, 1–2.

20. Yauri Montero, *Leyendas ancashinas*, 21–22.

21. Kinzl and Schneider, *Cordillera Blanca*, 25–26.

22. Neate, *Mountaineering in the Andes*, 4–5.

23. Szepessy Schaurek, *Contribución al conocimiento de las lagunas*, 3.

24. Interview by author, Huaraz, 2004.

25. Luis A. Ghiglino, "Expedición de estudio a la Laguna de Jancarurush efectuada entre el 22 y 26 de Oct. de 1950" (Lima, 28 October 1950), File 70I 27.720 in Biblioteca de Electroperú, Lima, 1.

26. Descriptions of the outburst flood appear in "Cómo se produjo el aluvión en Huallanca," *El Comercio*, 22 October 1950, 5; "El aluvión en Huallanca," *El Comercio*, 29 October 1950, 13; "Se intensifican los trabajos de auxilio y reparación en la zona afectada por el aluvión de Huallanca," *El Comercio*, 24 October 1950, 7; "Testigo presencial del desborde 'Los Cedros,'" *El Departamento*, 23 October 1950, 3; Ghiglino, "Expedición de estudio a la Laguna de Jancarurush efectuada entre el 22 y 26 de Oct. de 1950"; Hans J. Spann and Jaime Fernández Concha, "Informe sobre el origen del aluvion de la quebrada de Los Cedros" (Lima, 3 November 1950), File I-GEOL-003 in UGRH; Trask, "El problema de los aluviones."

27. Kogan and Leininger, *The Ascent of Alpamayo*, 79.

28. Trask, "El problema de los aluviones," 28.

29. Méndez Jurado et al., eds., *Monografía de la provincia de Huaylas*, 150; Doughty, "Engineers and Energy."

30. "El Doctor Hans J. Spann nos formula declaraciones después de haber volado sobre la zona afectada," *El Comercio*, 23 October 1950, 5; "El Señor Senador por Ancash, Alejandro Roel declara sobre la catástrofe de Huallanca," *El Comercio*, 26 October 1950, 11; Comisión de Estudios Cuenca del Santa, "Informe de la Comisión de Estudios Cuenca del Santa" (Lima, 1951), File I-GEOL-003 in UGRH.

31. Antúnez de Mayolo, *Relato de una idea.*

32. Ibid., 89–90.

33. Interview by author, Huaraz, 2004.

34. Maskrey, ed., *Los desastres no son naturales*; Steinberg, *Acts of God*; Wisner et al., *At Risk.*

35. Ghiglino, "Expedición de estudio a la Laguna de Jancarurush efectuada entre el 22 y 26 de Oct. de 1950."

36. Antúnez de Mayolo, *Relato de una idea,* 90.

37. Kogan and Leininger, *The Ascent of Alpamayo,* 37.

38. Alexander von Humboldt, Guayaquil, to Don Ignacio Checa, Governor of the Province of Jaén de Bracamoros (Peru), 18 January 1803, in *Cartas Americanas: Alejandro de Humboldt,* ed. Charles Minguet (Caracas, Venezuela: Biblioteca Ayacucho, 1980), 106–107.

39. Resolución Suprema No. 259, 13 November 1950.

40. Comisión de Estudios Cuenca del Santa, "Informe de la Comisión de Estudios Cuenca del Santa" (Lima, 1951), File I-GEOL-003 in UGRH.

41. Resolución Suprema No. 70, 20 February 1951.

42. Comisión de Estudios Cuenca del Santa, "Primera Sesión: Comisión de Estudios Cuenca del Santa" (Lima: 2 March 1951), File I-GEOL-003 in UGRH.

43. Oreste Massa G., Jaime Fernández Concha, and César Sotillo P., "Informe sobre las actividades de la Comisión de Control de las Lagunas de la Cordillera Blanca" (Lima, 26 September 1953), File I-MEM-005 in UGRH, 1.

44. McCook, *States of Nature*; Saldaña, *Science in Latin America*; Cueto, *Saberes Andinos.*

45. Trask, "El problema de los aluviones," 11.

46. J. Fernández Concha and A. Hoempler, "Indice de lagunas y glaciares de la Cordillera Blanca" (Lima, May 1953), File I-INVEN-011 in UGRH.

47. Hugo Gálvez Paredes and Alcides Ames Márquez, "Indice de lagunas y glaciares de la Cordillera Blanca, 1962" (Huaraz, March 1965), File I-INVEN-013 in UGRH.

48. Harley, "Deconstructing the Map"; Wood, *The Power of Maps*; Craib, *Cartographic Mexico*; Burnett, *Masters of All They Surveyed.*

49. Nash, "The Changing Experience of Nature"; Porter, *Trust in Numbers.*

50. To be precise, Laguna Cuchillacocha is redundant because the common practice of preceding the lake name with the word "Laguna" duplicates the Quechua suffix "cocha," which also means lake. Nevertheless, this redundancy remains common practice.

51. Kinzl and Schneider, *Cordillera Blanca,* 26.

52. Studies vary widely on Parón's water volume in 1951. See Jaime Fernández Concha and Aquiles Bottger, "Reconocimiento del dique de la laguna Parón" (Huaraz, 8 August 1951), File I-GEOL-007 in UGRH; Luis A. Ghiglino, "Informe de los estudios de la laguna de Parón" (Lima, 18 October 1947), File 70I 27.720 in Biblioteca de Electroperú, Lima; Trask, "El problema de los aluviones," 5; "Algo más sobre la laguna de Parón," *El Departamento,* 6 February 1952, 2.

53. Ghiglino, "Informe de los estudios de la laguna de Parón"; Luis A. Ghiglino and Federico Stein, "Estudios de las lagunas de Parón, Querokocha, Conococha y Aguash situados en la Cordillera Blanca" (Lima, 31 December 1948), File 701 27.720 in Biblioteca de Electroperú, Lima; Antonio Grüter, Jefe de la Comisión del Estudio Lagunas, "Cumplo con informar el resultado de nuestro estudio en la región de la laguna de Parón" (Caraz, 15 November 1942), Ministerio del Interior, Prefectura, File 425, Folio 485, in AGN, Lima.

54. Ghiglino, "Informe de los estudios de la laguna de Parón," 4.

55. Ghiglino and Stein, "Estudios de las lagunas de Parón, Querokocha, Conococha y Aguash," 6.

56. Luis A. Ghiglino, "Memorandum" (Huallanca, 24 July 1951), File 701 27.718 in Biblioteca de Electroperú, Lima.

57. Luis A. Ghiglino and Hans J. Spann, "Informe: Ruptura Laguna Artesoncocha" (Huallanca, 30 July 1951), File 701 27.718 in Biblioteca del Electroperú, Lima, 2.

58. Jaime Fernández Concha, Oreste Massa G., and Juan Quiroga, "Informe sobre la laguna de Parón" (Lima, 10 October 1952), File I-GEOL-014 in UGRH, 7.

59. J. Elias Torres, "Informe sobre la laguna de Parón" (Huaraz, 31 March 1952), File I-GEOL-008 in UGRH, 1–2.

60. "Algo más sobre la laguna de Parón," El Departamento, 6 February 1952, 2.

61. Ministerio de Fomento y Obras Públicas, "Memorandum del Ministerio de Fomento y Obras Públicas solicitando la contracción de una comisión de expertos" (Lima, 23 January 1952), in appendix A of Trask, "El problema de los aluviones," 66–72.

62. "Visita a Laguna de Parón," El Departamento, 11 February 1952, 1.

63. Fernández Concha, Massa G., and Quiroga, "Informe sobre la laguna de Parón," 8.

64. Damián Michelena M., "Informe No. 173 del Ministerio de Fomento y Obras Públicas, Dirección de Aguas e Irrigación," (Lima, 14 February 1953), File I-MEM-005 in UGRH.

65. Ghiglino and Spann, "Informe: Ruptura Laguna Artesoncocha," 3.

66. On the classification system, see Fernández Concha, "El problema de las lagunas"; Gálvez Paredes and Ames Márquez, "Indice de lagunas y glaciares"; Jorge Matellini, "Conclusiones de la comparación de las fotografías de la Cordillera Blanca, Año 1948–1962" (Lima, 4 January 1965), File I-VARIOS-007 in UGRH; Trask, "El problema de los aluviones."

67. "El control de las lagunas de la Cordillera Blanca y la Corporación Peruana del Santa: Un notable geólogo norteamericano inspecciona las lagunas," El Departamento, 18 August 1952, 2.

68. Massa G., Fernández Concha, and Sotillo P., "Informe sobre las actividades de la Comisión," 4; Trask, "El problema de los aluviones," 28–29; Matellini, "Conclusiones de la comparación de las fotografías," 1–3; Kaser and Osmaston, Tropical Glaciers, prologue; Clague and Evans, "A Review of Catastrophic Drainage of Moraine-Dammed Lakes"; Richardson and Reynolds, "Degradation of Ice-Cored Moraine Dams."

69. Elías Pizarro, "Trabajos de la Comisión," 57–60.

70. Oreste Massa G. and Jaime Fernández Concha, "Informe sobre los trabajos efectuados por la Comisión Control Lagunas Cordillera Blanca" (Lima, January 1955), File I-MEM-005 in UGRH; Massa G., Fernández Concha, and Sotillo P., "Informe sobre las actividades de la Comisión."

71. "Comisión de Control de Lagunas," El Departamento, 15 June 1953, 2.

72. Luis A. Ghiglino, Jefe General de la Central Hidroeléctrica del Cañón del Pato, Letter to Jorge de las Casas, Gerente General de la Corporación Peruana del Santa (Huallanca, 6 April 1962), File 701 27.720 in Biblioteca del Electroperú, Lima.

73. Elías Pizarro, "Trabajos de la Comisión," 61.

74. Decreto-Ley No. 19242, Lima, 28 December 1971; Decreto-Ley No. 19521, Lima, 5 September 1972.

75. For good analyses of states and science, see Andermann, The Optic of the State; Craib, Cartographic Mexico; Cueto, "Social Medicine and 'Leprosy.'"

CHAPTER 4

1. The report is reprinted in appendix A of Trask, "El problema de los aluviones."

2. Davis, Ecology of Fear; Klein, The Shock Doctrine; Landis, "Fate, Responsibility, and 'Natural' Disaster."

3. Castro Herrera, "The Environmental Crisis"; McNeil, Something New under the Sun; Tucker, Insatiable Appetite.

4. This literature is vast. See Langston, Forest Dreams, Forest Nightmares; Prakash, Another Reason; Evans, Bound in Twine; Brannstrom, ed., Territories, Commodities, and Knowledges.

5. Harvey, "The Materiality of State-Effects"; Nugent, Modernity at the Edge of Empire; Mallon, Peasant and Nation.

6. Jo-Marie Burt argues for the need for "analyses of state-society relations that are historically grounded and that examine these relationships in a multiplicity of arenas" ("Contesting the Terrain," 222).

7. El Comercio (Lima, 21 July 1929), quoted in Atwood, "Democratic Dictators," 157.

8. Doughty, "Engineers and Energy in the Andes," 369–373; Doughty, Huaylas, 185.

9. Patch, "Life in a Peruvian Indian Community," 17.

10. Resolución Suprema No. 259, 13 November 1950. Also see Comisión de Estudios Cuenca del Santa, "Actas de la reunión de la Comisión de Estudios Cuenca del Santa, 10 de Agosto de 1951" (Lima, 1951), File I-GEOL-003 in UGRH; Comisión de Estudios Cuenca del Santa, "Informe de la Comisión de Estudios Cuenca del Santa" (Lima, 1951), File I-GEOL-003 in UGRH.

11. J. Elias Torres, "Inspección a la laguna de Purhuay" (Huaraz, 12 March 1953), File I-GEOL-017 in UGRH.

12. E. Silva y Elguera and Alejandro Roel, "Documentos parlamentarios. Importante pedido de los Senadores por Ancash sobre el aluvión de Los Cedros," *El Departamento*, 10 November 1950, 3.

13. Heim, *Wunderland Peru*, 180–181.

14. Hans J. Spann, "Infrorme sobre algunos limnos glaciares sobre Huaras y Caras," (Lima [1945]), File I-GLACIO-001 in UGRH, 3.

15. Jaime Fernández Concha and César Sotillo P., "Informe sobre las obras de consolidación de la laguna Tullparaju," (Lima, 18 January 1954), File I-GEOL-018 in UGRH, 1.

16. Comisión de Control de Lagunas de la Cordillera Blanca, "Informes mensuales de los años 1951–1952–1953–1954" (Huaraz, 1951–1954), File I-MEMORIAS-004 in UGRH, January 1954; Oreste Massa G. and Jaime Fernández Concha, "Informe sobre los trabajos efectuados por la Comisión Control Lagunas Cordillera Blanca" (Lima, January 1955), File I-MEM-005 in UGRH, 2.

17. Ministerio de Fomento, "Comunicado del Ministerio de Fomento sobre obras de defensa hechas en Ancash," *El Comercio*, 15 December 1959, 1, 18; "Un millón ciento cuarenta mil soles para los desagües de las lagunas en Ancash," *La Hora*, 13 May 1957, 1.

18. "Crecida de laguna mantiene clima de alarma en Huaraz," *El Comercio*, 11 December 1959, 1, 12.

19. "Disminuye peligro de desborde del río Quilcay en Huaraz," *El Comercio*, 10 December 1959, 1; "Crecida de laguna mantiene clima de alarma en Huaraz," *El Comercio*, 11 December 1959, 1, 12; "Desagüe total de laguna Tullparaju para salvar Huaraz de aluviones," *El Comercio*, 12 December 1959, 1–2; "Estado de obras de defensa causa zozobra en Huaraz," *El Comercio*, 12 December 1959, 1, 14.

20. "En mitin y Cabildo abierto, Huaraz censura negligencia y engaño sobre sus defensas," *El Comercio*, 13 December 1959, 1, 19.

21. "Desagüe total de laguna Tullparaju para salvar Huaraz de aluviones," *El Comercio*, 12 December 1959, 1–2.

22. "Defensa de la riqueza acuífera," *El Comercio*, 15 December 1959, 3.

23. "Problema de las lagunas de Huaraz está siendo mal encarado por autoridades," *El Comercio*, 16 December 1959, 1, 16.

24. "Reunión en la Cámara de Diputados esta mañana: Fondos para defensa de Huaraz," *El Comercio*, 18 December 1959, 1.

25. Elías Pizarro, "Trabajos de la Comisión."

26. Contreras and Cueto, *Historia del Perú contemporáneo*, 291–304.

27. Lliboutry, Morales A., and Schneider, "Glaciological Problems," 276; Ames Marquez and Francou, "Cordillera Blanca glaciares en la historia," 52.

28. Benjamín Morales A., "Estudios glaciológicos-geológicos efectuados en la Cordillera Blanca entre Enero de 1966 a Diciembre de 1967" (Pati, December 1967), File I-GLACIO-049 in UGRH, 2.

29. Corporación Peruana del Santa and República Francesa, "Estudio de las cuencas Parón y Safuna en la Cordillera Blanca" (Paris, February 1967), File IRN. 05.392 in Biblioteca de Electroperú, Lima, 1; Coyne et Bellier, "Peligro de las lagunas

de Safuna: Visita del Ingeniero J. Grador en los días 19 y 20 de Abril 1967" (Paris, 12 May 1967), File 70I 27.826 in Biblioteca de Electroperú, Lima; Coyne et Bellier, "Lagunas de Safuna: Informe de la misión de Julio de 1967" (Paris, 21 August 1967), File # 70I 27.821 in Biblioteca del Electroperú, Lima; Lliboutry, "Informe preliminar sobre los fenómenos glaciológicos," 21.

30. Decreto Supremo No. 45-F, "Declaran en emergencia zona de influencia de lagunas de la Quebrada de Quintaracsa [sic]," 16 June 1967; "Declaran en Emergencia Zona de influencia de lagunas de la Quebrada de Quintaracsa," El Peruano, Lima, 24 June 1967; "Piden fondos para expertos que ven peligro por desbordes de lagunas," La Cronica, 7 July 1967.

31. Lliboutry, Morales A., and Schneider, "Glaciological Problems," 276.

32. Lliboutry, "Informe preliminar sobre los fenómenos glaciológicos," 21; "Ejecutarán obras del túnel de drenaje de la laguna Safuna Alta," El Peruano, Lima, 18 July 1968. Even in 2003, technicians "lost" a half day of work waiting for a coating of ice to melt off Lake Palcacocha. It had mostly cleared when two technicians jumped in their rubber boat, hoping the remaining layer of ice and floating icebergs would not puncture their vessel. Neither did, and they successfully, though carefully, completed the lake measurements.

33. For advocates of Parón's exploitation, see Diez Canseco, La red nacional de carreteras, 132; Luis A. Ghiglino and Federico Stein, "Estudios de las lagunas de Parón, Querokocha, Conococha y Aguash situados en la Cordillera Blanca" (Lima, 31 December 1948), File # 70I 27.720 in Biblioteca de Electroperú, Lima.

34. Luis Salazar R., "Memorandum de la Corporación Peruana del Santa: Programa de trabajos sub-lacustres en laguna Parón" (Lima, 23 November 1967), File # Caja 058347, No. 1 in Electroperú-FS, Lima, 1–2.

35. Jeanneau Gracey, "A 200 pies de profundidad."

36. Coyne et Bellier, "Lagunas Parón y Safuna: Relación de la misión en el Perú de los Ingenieros Grador y Pautre en Junio de 1968" (Paris, 1968), File # IRN 05.401 in Biblioteca de Electroperú, Lima, 1; Corporación Peruana del Santa and República Francesa, "Estudio de las cuencas Parón y Safuna," 14; Personal communication with César Portocarrero, Huaraz, February 2004.

37. Electroperú, "Afianzamiento hídrico río Santa: Proyecto laguna Parón" (Huaraz, 1990), File # I-VARIOS-498 in UGRH, 3–4.

38. Unidad de Glaciología e Hidrología Hidrandina S.A., "Información de la Unidad de Glaciología y Seguridad de Lagunas y del Proyecto Parón" (Huaraz, 1987), File # I-MEM-020 in UGRH, 2–4.

39. Electroperú, "Afianzamiento hídrico río Santa," 7.

40. Carrillo Ramírez, Ensayo monográfico, 38, 39.

41. Leoncio Guzmán Flores, "Realidad económica de Yungay: La industrial-ización en Yungay," in Libro de oro de Yungay, ed. Carrión Vergara, 346.

42. Interview by author, Unchus, 2004.

43. Alberto Carrión Vergara, "Rasgos de pluma sobre Yungay," Forjando Ancash (Vocero del Club Ancash), 30 June 1959, 19; "Comisión de Control de Lagunas," El Departamento, 15 June 1953, 2.

44. Doughty, *Huaylas*, 168–173.

45. Oliver-Smith, *The Martyred City*, 69.

46. Diez Canseco, *La red nacional de carreteras*; Zapatel, *Vialidad y Turismo en el Perú*; Pereyra Chávez, "Los campesinos y la conscripción vial"; Doughty, *Huaylas*, 161.

47. "Carretera Huaraz-Huari," *El Departamento*, 6 February 1956, 2; Pedro G. Villón et al., "Informe sobre el camino por Quillcay-Huanca," *El Departamento*, 4 February 1956, 3.

48. Doughty, *Huaylas*, 165.

49. Pedro G. Villón et al., "Informe sobre el camino por Quillcay-Huanca," *El Departamento*, 4 February 1956, 3.

50. On access to Cordillera Blanca lakes, see Jaime Fernández Concha and Aquiles Bottger, "Reconocimiento del dique de la laguna Parón" (Huaraz, 8 August 1951), File I-GEOL-007 in UGRH; Ghiglino and Spann, "Informe: Ruptura Laguna Artesoncocha."

51. Aquiles Bottger, "Estudio de la laguna Huallcacocha, Quebrada de Ulta, Carhuaz," (Huaraz, 5 December 1951), File I-GEOL-010 in UGRH, 1.

52. See, for example, Massa G., Fernández Concha, and Sotillo P., "Informe sobre las actividades de la Comisión."

53. Resolución Suprema No. 259, 13 November 1950.

54. Massa G. and Fernández Concha, "Informe sobre los trabajos," 1–2; Massa G., Fernández Concha, and Sotillo P., "Informe sobre las actividades de la Comisión," 1; Trask "El problema de los aluviones," 51.

55. Fernández Concha and Hoempler, "Indice de lagunas y glaciares de la Cordillera Blanca."

56. "El Nevado Huascarán," *El Comercio*, 2 August 1951, 11; Isaías L. Izaguirre, "Llanganuco," *La Hora*, 15 July 1954, 2.

57. "La carretera a las lagunas 'Llanganuco' abre nuevas posibilidades al turismo en el Callejón de Huaylas," in *Libro de oro de Yungay*, ed. Carrión Vergara, 321; Alberto Carrión Vergara, "Rasgos de pluma sobre Yungay," *Forjando Ancash (Vocero del Club Ancash)*, 30 June 1959, 19.

58. Curry Slaymaker and Joel Albrecht, "Proyecto: 'Parque Nacional Huascarán': Informe elevado al Servicio Forestal y de Caza del Ministerio de Agricultura por voluntarios del Cuerpo de Paz de Los Estados Unidos de Norte América" (Lima, November 1967), File I-VARIOS-008 in UGRH, 23.

59. Interview by author, Vicos, 2004.

60. Ignacio Amadeo Ramos, "Turismo," *Informaciones y Memorias de la Sociedad de Ingenieros del Perú* 43, no. 10 (1942), reprinted in Carrión Vergara, ed., *Libro de oro de Yungay*, 313–317.

61. Kinzl and Schneider, *Cordillera*, 34.

62. Izaguirre, "Llanganuco," 2.

63. Phol, "El 'Callejón de Huailas,'" 347–349; Gamio, "Viajando por el Perú"; "El andinismo y el desarrollo económico del país," *Boletín de la Sociedad Geográfica de Lima* 73, no. 3 (1956): 61–64.

64. Vivanco and Gordon, eds., *Tarzan Was an Eco-Tourist*; Ortner, *Life and Death on Mt. Everest*.

65. Peck, *A Search for the Apex of America*; Ellis, *Vertical Margins*; Morales Arnao, *Andinismo en la Cordillera Blanca*; Ricker, *Yuraq Janka*.

66. Borchers, *Die Weisse Kordillere*; Kinzl, "Las tres expediciones"; Kinzl, "Los glaciares de la Cordillera Blanca"; Kinzl and Schneider, *Cordillera Blanca*.

67. Leoncio Guzmán Flores, "Realidad económica de Yungay: La industrialización en Yungay," in *Libro de oro de Yungay*, ed. Carrión Vergara, 343.

68. Asociación Automotriz del Perú, *El Perú y sus rutas* (Lima: SESATOR, 1963).

69. J. A. Broggi, Letter to Sr. Director de Aguas e Irrigación (Lima, 26 August 1942), File I-GEOL-003 in UGRH, 3; J. A. Broggi, Letter to Luís Chavez Badani, Director de Aguas e Irrigación (Lima, 21 July 1942), File I-GEOL-001 in UGRH.

70. Comisión de Control de Lagunas de la Cordillera Blanca, "Informes mensuales de los años 1951–1952–1953–1954" (1951–1954), File I-MEMORIAS-004 in UGRH.

71. Grupo Andinista Cordillera Blanca, "Estatutos y Reglamentos del Grupo Andinista "Cordillera Blanca" Aprobados en Asamblea de 9 Octubre [1952]" (Huaraz, 9 October 1952), Ministerio del Interior, Prefectura, File 590, Folio 14, in AGN.

72. "La próxima expedición andinista," *El Departamento*, 1 June 1953, 3.

73. "Benedición del 'Glaciar Miró Quesada,'" *El Departamento*, 5 June 1953, 2; Alejandro Miró Quesada, "El Director de 'El Comercio' agradece al Grupo Andinista," *El Departamento*, 13 June 1953, 2.

74. Trask, "El problema de los aluviones," 41.

75. Kinzl and Schneider, *Cordillera Blanca*, 26.

76. "Visita del Sr. Prefecto del departamento a la laguna de Tullparraju," *El Departamento*, 10 August 1962, 2.

77. G. C. Humberto Ampuero Pérez, "Laguna 'Tullparaju,'" *El Departamento*, 14 August 1962, 2.

78. "Peligrosidad de la laguna Tullparraju desaparecera en Diciembre," *El Departamento*, 14 August 1962, 3.

79. Neumann, *Imposing Wilderness*; Spence, *Dispossessing the Wilderness*.

80. The reference to tourism as an industry without smokestacks comes from Morales Arnao, *Las Cordilleras del Perú*.

81. Oscar Alers, "Population and Development in a Peruvian Community," *Journal of Inter-American Studies* 7, no. 4 (October 1965): 446. For labor practices in Vicos during the 1950s, see Cornell University Library, Ithaca, NY, Special Collections, Vicos Project Archive, Box 5, Folder 1.

82. Comisión de Control de Lagunas de la Cordillera Blanca, "Informes mensuales de los años 1951–1952–1953–1954"; Jaime Fernández Concha, "Informe sobre la investigación efectuada en las obras y contabilidad de las lagunas Cochca y Yanahuanca" (Lima, 24 June 1953), File I-GEOL-012 in UGRH, appendix.

83. Massa G. and Fernández Concha, "Informe sobre los trabajos efectuados," 2.

84. Massa G., Fernández Concha, and Sotillo P., "Informe sobre las actividades de la Comisión."

85. See the October–November 1953 and April 1954 reports in Comisión de Control de Lagunas de la Cordillera Blanca, "Informes mensuales de los años 1951–1952–1953–1954."

86. Carrillo Ramírez, *Ensayo monográfico*, 39.

87. Comisión de Control de Lagunas de la Cordillera Blanca, "Informes mensuales de los años 1951–1952–1953–1954."

88. José Ayllón Lozano, "Of. Circ. No. 37" (Huaraz, 30 November 1954), File I-MEMORIAS-004 in UGRH.

89. See the July 1953 report in Comisión de Control de Lagunas de la Cordillera Blanca, "Informes mensuales de los años 1951–1952–1953–1954."

90. Massa G., Fernández Concha, and Sotillo P., "Informe sobre las actividades de la Comisión," 6.

91. José Ayllón Lozano, Letter to Sr. Ingeniero Jaime Fernández Concha, Miembro Ejecutivo de la Comisión de Control de Lagunas de la Cordillera Blanca (Huaraz, 16 December 1953), File I-GEOL-016 in UGRH.

92. Interviews by author, Ancash, 2003–2004. On links between disaster relief and welfare, see Landis, "Fate, Responsibility, and 'Natural' Disaster Relief."

CHAPTER 5

1. McDowell and Fletcher, "Avalanche!" 856.

2. Anthropologists Anthony Oliver-Smith and Barbara Bode have analyzed the 1970s period of disaster recovery in their pioneering studies of Yungay and Huaraz, respectively. In addition to their numerous articles, see Bode, *No Bells to Toll*; Oliver-Smith, *The Martyred City*. Also see Doughty, "Plan and Pattern in Reaction to Earthquake."

3. Wisner et al., *At Risk*; Alexander, *Confronting Catastrophe*; Hewitt, *Regions of Risk*; Maskrey, ed., *Los desastres no son naturales*; Varley, ed., *Disasters, Development, and Environment*; Eakin, *Weathering Risk in Rural Mexico*.

4. Mitchell's *Rule of Experts* has been influential here. For these nation-building processes in Latin America, see Mallon, *Peasant and Nation*; Craib, *Cartographic Mexico*; Drake and Eric Hershberg, eds., *State and Society in Conflict*.

5. Humberto Silva Varillas, "Un muerto y sepultado habla: Anécdota del aluvión de Ranrahirca," *Forjando Ancash* 4, no. 13 (1962): 31; McDowell and Fletcher, "Avalanche!" 857.

6. Leoncio Guzman Flores and Rigoberto Guzman Flores, "Distrito de Ranrahirca," *Forjando Ancash* 4, no. 13 (1962): 6; Silva Varillas, "El fenómeno geológico," 28–29; Alberto Carrión Vergara, "El aluvión de Ranrahirca," *Forjando Ancash* 4, no. 13 (1962): 22–24; Alicia Torres et al., "Lo que fue antes," *Forjando Ancash* 4, no. 13 (1962): 2–21.

7. On highland-coast migrations see Walton, "Human Spatial Organization."

8. Guillermina Figueroa, "Huarascucho," *Forjando Ancash* 4, no. 13 (1962): 17–18; Comité Coordinadora de Rehabilitación de la Provincia de Yungay, "Plan de rehabilitación de los pueblos afectados," *Forjando Ancash* 4, no. 13 (1962): 42–45.

9. McDowell and Fletcher, "Avalanche!" 872.

10. Eleuterio Angeles, "El Huérfano del Aluvión," *Forjando Ancash* 4, no. 13 (1962): 36.

11. Alberto Romero Leguia, "Ranrahirca Renacera," *Forjando Ancash* 4, no. 13 (1962): 50.

12. Leoncio Guzman Flores and Rigoberto Guzman Flores, "Distrito de Ranrahirca," *Forjando Ancash* 4, no. 13 (1962): 5; Klimes, Vilímek, and Omelka. "Implications of Geomorphological Research."

13. Morales A., "Observaciones sobre el aluvión," 25–27.

14. J. Fernández Concha, Letter to Señor Ingeniero don Pablo Boner, Presidente de la Comisión de Control de Lagunas de la Cordillera Blanca (Huaraz: 8 August 1951), File I-GEOL-009 in UGRH.

15. Ministerio de Fomento, "Comunicado del Ministerio de Fomento sobre obras de defensa hechas en Ancash," *El Comercio*, 15 December 1959, 1, 18.

16. McPhee, *The Control of Nature*; Fleming, "The Pathological History of Weather"; Harper, "Climate Control"; Doel and Harper, "Prometheus Unleashed."

17. See, for example, "En torno a las lagunas de la Cordillera Blanca," *El Departamento*, 24 November 1945, 2; "Exposición del Director de Aguas en Huaraz," *El Comercio*, 2 February 1945, 15; "Se van a desaguar las lagunas," *El Comercio*, 9 February 1945, 4.

18. For example, "Las obras de defensa en la Cordillera Blanca," *El Comercio*, 13 March 1950, reprinted in *El Departamento*, 14 March 1950.

19. La reconstrucción de Huaraz," *El Departamento*, 7 June 1945, 2; "La reconstrucción de la zona del aluvión," *El Departamento*, 21 July 1945, 2; "Obras públicas que requiere Huaraz," *El Departamento*, 2 August 1956, 3; "Asociación de Propietarios de la Zona Aluviónica," *El Departamento*, 12 April 1956, 2.

20. "Edificaciones en El Aluvión," *El Departamento*, 11 August 1951, 2.

21. Oliver-Smith, "Peru's Five-Hundred-Year Earthquake"; Oliver-Smith, "Traditional Agriculture, Central Places"; also Doughty, "Plan and Pattern in Reaction to Earthquake," 245.

22. "Recuperación de sus tierras por los propietarios de la antigua Avenida Raymondi," *El Departamento*, 21 June 1945, 3; "Urbanisación de la zona del aluvión," *El Departamento*, 7 January 1956, 2; "Ansiosa Espectativa Urbanistica," *El Departamento*, 23 August 1951, 2; "Asociación de Propietarios de la Zona Aluviónica," *El Departamento*, 12 April 1956, 2; "Edificaciones en El Aluvión," *El Departamento*, 11 August 1951, 2; "Obras públicas que requiere Huaraz," *El Departamento*, 2 August 1956, 3; Irving, "Lo que el pueblo de Huaraz debe conocer en torno al plano regulador," *El Departamento*, 10 November 1952, 3.

23. "Asociación de Propietarios de la Zona Aluviónica," *El Departamento*, 12 April 1956, 2.

24. Bode, "Disaster, Social Structure, and Myth"; Carey, "Disasters, Development"; Carey, "The Politics of Place."

25. See Ley No. 13998, "Creación del Consejo Interministerial de Defensa y Rehabilitación de las Poblaciones del Callejón de Huaylas," 9 February 1962.

26. Comité Coordinadora de Rehabilitación de la Provincia de Yungay, "Plan de rehabilitación de los pueblos afectados," *Forjando Ancash* 4, no. 13 (1962): 44–45; Artemio Angeles Figueroa, "Apreciaciones de orden jurídico en la caso de Ranrahirca," *Forjando Ancash* 4, no. 13 (1962): 45.

27. "Infundada alarma en Huaraz," *El Departamento*, 7 February 1962, 2.

28. Miguel Elías Pizarro "Carta al Dr. Augusto Soriano Infante, Alcalde del Concejo Provincial de Huaraz, 16 February 1962," reprinted in *El Departamento* 17 February 1962, 3.

29. "Comité Permanente Ancashino de Rehabilitación y Defensa," *El Departamento*, Huaraz, 20 January 1962, 2.

30. "Construcción de viviendas en las márgenes de los ríos," *El Departamento*, 6 February 1962, 2.

31. "La expansión urbanística de las ciudades," *El Departamento* 11 January 1962, 2.

32. For example, "En previsión de otras catástrofes," *El Departamento*, Huaraz, 16 January 1962, 2;" Infundada alarma en Huaraz," *El Departamento*, 7 February 1962, 2.

33. Augusto Soriano Infante, "Telegrama tramitido por el alcalde de Huaraz al Presidente de la República, dando cumplimiento a lo acordado en al Cabildo Abierto," reprinted in *El Departamento*, Huaraz, 15 February 1962, 3.

34. Morales A., "El día más largo."

35. Hugo Córdova Milla, "El Barrio Obrero de Huallanca desapareció en un minuto," in *Vida, muerte y resurrección*, ed. Pajuelo Prieto, 37.

36. For accounts of the May 31, 1970, disaster, see Pajuelo Prieto, *Vida, muerte y resurrección*; Figueroa, *Las horas muertas*; Cabel Moscoso, *Literatura del sismo*; Vergara Collazos, *La tragedia*; Yauri Montero, *Tiempo de rosas*.

37. United States Geological Survey, "Most Destructive Known Earthquakes on Record in the World: Earthquakes with 50,000 or More Deaths," online at http://neic.usgs.gov/neis/eqlists/eqsmosde.html (accessed 14 January 2005).

38. Ericksen, Plafker, and Fernández Concha, "Preliminary Report on the Geological Events," 8–9.

39. Pelayo Aldave Tarazona, "Me salvé en paños menores en el cementerio de Yungay," in *Vida, muerte y resurrección*, ed. Pajuelo Prieto, 127; Vergara Collazos, *La tragedia*, 21; Mateo Casaverde Rio, "El terremoto de Ancash y el alud del Nevado Huascarán," unpublished manuscript in author's possession (Lima, no date).

40. For overviews of Velasco's military dictatorship and his successors' that lasted from 1968 to 1980, see Jaquette and Lowenthal, "The Peruvian Experiment"; Klarén, *Peru*, chap. 11; Contreras and Cueto, *Historia del Perú contemporáneo*, chap. 9.

41. Juan Velasco Alvarado, *Mensaje a la Nación del Señor General de División, Presidente de la República, con motive del 149° aniversario de la independencia* (Lima: Oficina nacional de Información, 1970), quoted in Bode, *No Bells to Toll*, 174.

42. Jaquette and Lowenthal, "The Peruvian Experiment," 285.

43. Decreto Ley No. 18603, "Crean Comisión de Reconstrucción y Rehabilitación de la zona afectada por el terremoto del día 31 de Mayo," 9 June 1970; Oficina Nacional de Información, *¡Cataclismo en el Perú!* (Lima: Oficina Nacional de Información, 1970); Ramírez Gamarra, *Ancash*, 131–132.

44. CRYRZA, *CRYRZA en su etapa de realizaciones* (Huaraz: CRYRZA, 1972), quoted in Bode, *No Bells to Toll*, 178.

45. Oliver-Smith, *The Martyred City*, 106 (ellipsis in original); Bode, *No Bells to Toll*.

46. Personal communication with Morales, January 2002; Bode, *No Bells to Toll*, 17; "Venció el Grupo Andinista el Nevado Hualcán," *El Departamento*, Huaraz, 8 July 1953, 2.

47. Hugo Gálvez Paredes, "Breve información sobre lagunas de la Cordillera Blanca," (Huaraz, April 1970), File 701 27.725 in Biblioteca de Electroperú, Lima.

48. Lliboutry, "Informe preliminar sobre los fenómenos glaciológicos," 21.

49. Corporación Peruana del Santa División de Glaciología y Seguridad de Lagunas, "Estudios Glaciológicos, Bienio 1971–1972" (Huaraz, 1972), File I-GLACIO-015 in UGRH; Electroperú, "Información básica de la labor realizada por la Unidad de Glaciología y Seguridad de Lagunas entre los años 1973 y 1984" (Huaraz, August 1984), File I-MEM-002 in UGRH; Electroperú, "Memoría bienal del Programa de Glaciología y Seguridad de Lagunas" (Huaraz, February 1975), File I-MEMORIAS-008 in UGRH; Electroperú, "Memoría de la labor realizada por el Departamento de Estudios Básicos de Lagunas, Año 1973" (Huaraz, March 1974), File I-MEMORIAS-010 in UGRH; Electroperú (Glaciología y Seguridad de Lagunas), "Plan de Trabajo 1975–1980" (Huaraz, 1980), File I-MEMORIAS-028 in UGRH; Lliboutry et al., "Glaciological Problems...I."

50. Marino Zamora Cobos, "Informe sobre la ascención [sic] al pico norte del Nevado 'Huascarán,'" (Huaraz: October 1973), File I-GLACIO-010 in UGRH, 14; Benjamín Morales A., "Comentarios sobre el memorandum del Dr. Leonidas Castro B. en el Caso Huascarán" (Lima, 20 December 1972), File I-GLACIO-005 in UGRH.

51. Morales A., "El día más largo," 71.

52. Lliboutry et al., *Evaluación de los riesgos*, 65. Also see Luis Oberti I., "Estudio glaciológico del Cono Aluvionico de Huaraz" (Huaraz, March 1975), File I-GLACIO-014 in UGRH, 6.

53. CRYRZA, "La reubicación de las ciudades del Callejón de Huaylas," *Revista Peruana de Andinismo y Glaciología* 19, no. 9 (1970): 28–29; Lliboutry et al., *Evaluación de los riesgos*, 69–70.

54. Lliboutry et al., *Evaluación de los riesgos*, 70.

55. "Yungay, Carhuaz, Mancos y Ranrahirca tendrán otra ubicación, señala CRYRZA," *El Comercio*, 12 November 1970, 1.

56. Ibid.

57. Lliboutry et al., *Evaluación de los riesgos*, 18–22, 30, 45–46; Bode, *No Bells to Toll*.

58. Lliboutry et al., *Evaluación de los riesgos*, 59 (emphasis in original). Also see "El Hualcán presenta fisura de 500 metros con gran masa de hielo: Peligro de desprendimiento sobre la laguna Cochca," *El Comercio*, 19 July 1967; Luis Oberti I., "Informe Hualcán" (Huaraz, April 1973), File I-GLACIO-009 in UGRH, 2–3.

59. "Yungay, Carhuaz, Mancos y Ranrahirca tendrán otra ubicación, señala CRYRZA," *El Comercio*, 12 November 1970, 1.

60. Yauri Montero, *Ancash o la biografía de la inmortalidad*, 135.

61. Interviews by author, Huaraz, 2003–2004.

62. Morales A., "Comentarios sobre el memorandum del Dr. Leonidas Castro B," 2.

63. "Consolidación laguna Palcacocha entrega," *El Diario de Huaraz*, 27 November 1974, 1; Electroperú, "Acta de conclusión de trabajos en la obra 'Consolidación de la laguna Palcacocha'" (Huaraz, 1974), File I-CONSOL-004 in UGRH; Glaciología y Seguridad de Lagunas Electroperú U.C. 16, "Invitación al acto de inauguración de la obra 'Consolidación laguna Shallap'" (Huaraz, 1974), File Caja 050488, No. C in Electroperú-FS, Lima.

64. "Consolidación laguna Palcacocha entrega," *El Diario de Huaraz*, 27 November 1974, 1.

65. INGEMMET (Instituto Geológico Minero y Metalúrgico), *Boletín Informativo, Oficina Regional Huaraz, Programa: Glaciología y Seguridad de Lagunas* (Huaraz: Litho-Offset, 1979); INGEOMIN (Instituto de Geología y Minería), *Boletín informativo de la obra de consolidación "Laguna Llaca"* (Huaraz: Litho-Offset, 1977).

66. "Consolidación laguna Palcacocha entrega," 1.

67. Yauri Montero, *Ancash o la bigrafía de la inmortalidad*, 137.

68. A. Salazar Bondy, "La técnica y la reubicación de Huaraz," *El Diario de Huaraz*, 29 August 1970, 2.

69. "Temen rebalse de la laguna Llanganuco: Señalan urgencia de estudio técnico," *El Comercio*, 21 June 1970, 12.

70. "Nuestro Diario propiciará una Mesa Redonda para tratar sobre las lagunas," *El Diario de Huaraz*, 30 March 1971, 2.

71. Quoted in Bode, *No Bells to Toll*, 143.

72. "3 guias profesionales harán reconocimiento de las lagunas," *El Diario de Huaraz*, 23 July 1970, 4.

73. "Ciudadanos inspeccionan lagunas para controlar seguridad," *El Diario de Huaraz*, 7 January 1971, 3.

74. Yauri Montero, *Ancash o la biografía de la inmortalidad*, 141–143.

75. "Queremos funcionarios capaces," *El Diario de Huaraz*, 20 July 1970, 2.

76. "Un mejor trato piden en Huaraz damnificados. Frecuentes quejas en oficinas de la JAN," *El Comercio*, 17 October 1970, 5.

77. "Nuestro Diario propiciará una Mesa Redonda para tratar sobre las lagunas," *El Diario de Huaraz*, 30 March 1971, 2.

78. Morales A., "Comentarios sobre el memorandum del Dr. Leonidas Castro B."

79. Carlos Vinatea Quevedo, "El gobierno militar tuvo la intención de reubicar a Carhuaz," in *Vida, muerte y resurrección*, ed. Pajuelo Prieto, 68.

80. Yauri Montero, *Ancash o la biografía de la inmortalidad*, 133–137.

81. Oliver-Smith, *The Martyred City*, chap. 4.

82. Pedro Maximo Angeles and Presidente de Centro Unión Yungay, "Acuerdo No. 9: Reubicación y recomendaciones sobre las ciudades y centros poblados en Yungay, 15 de Diciembre," in *Lo mejor de nuestra juventud al servicio de Yungay y de los yungainos por una vida mejor a través del Centro Unión Yungay, institución representativa*

de los hijos de la provincia de Yungay, Ancash, Perú, ed. Centro Unión Yungay y la Junta Directiva (Lima: Centro Unión Yungay, 1970); "Yungaínos acuerdan formar Colonias Hogares en Lima," *El Comercio*, 8 October 1970.

83. Walton, "Human Spatial Organization," 95. On social networks and disaster vulnerability, see Klinenberg, *Heat Wave*.

84. Bode, *No Bells to Toll*, 53.

85. Zavaleta Figueroa, *El Callejón de Huaylas*, 16; Alejandro Flores Vásquez, "Discurso del Prof. Alejandro Flores Vásquez, pronunciado al conmemorarse el Primer Aniversario de la Catástrofe," *Forjando Ancash (Organo del Club Ancash)* 1972, 30–31.

86. Cosme Blas Torres Palomino, "Muchos se fueron de Carhuaz para regresar luego," in *Vida, muerte y resurrección*, ed. Pajuelo Prieto, 61–65.

87. Carlos Vinatea Quevedo, "El gobierno militar tuvo la intención de reubicar a Carhuaz," in *Vida, muerte y resurrección*, ed. Pajuelo Prieto, 68.

88. "Ciudadanos inspeccionan lagunas para controlar seguridad," *El Diario de Huaraz*, 7 January 1971, 3.

89. Bode, *No Bells to Toll*, 139, 202.

90. Miano Pique, *¡¡Basta!! La bomba atómica francesa*, 58–61; Ramírez Gamarra, *Ancash*, 118.

91. Ramírez Gamarra, *Ancash*, 155.

92. Oliver-Smith, "Here There Is Life," 92.

93. Bode, "Disaster, Social Structure, and Myth," 248–250.

94. Quoted in Oliver-Smith, "Disaster Rehabilitation and Social Change," 8.

95. "Piden que el Gobierno profundice estudio sobre reubicación de la ciudad de Yungay," *El Comercio*, 15 November 1970, 10; also see Oliver-Smith, "Traditional Agriculture, Central Places."

96. "Solicitan estudios adecuados para ubicar pueblos de Yungay," *La Prensa*, 29 December 1970; "Surgieron profundizar los estudios de reubicación de pueblos en Prov. Yungay," *El Comercio*, 21 December 1970.

97. Pedro Maximo Angeles and Presidente de Centro Unión Yungay, "Carta al Sr. Director del Diario El Comercio, Lima, 13 de Noviembre," in *Lo mejor de nuestra juventud al servicio de Yungay*; "Piden que el Gobierno profundice estudio sobre reubicación," 10.

98. Leonardo ángeles Asín, "Mientras haya un yungaíno con vida, Yungay no desaparecerá," in *Vida, muerte y resurrección*, ed. Pajuelo Prieto, 191.

99. Pedro Maximo Angeles and Presidente de Centro Unión Yungay, "Carta al Decano del Colegio de Arquitectos del Perú, Lima, 7 de Setiembre," in *Lo mejor de nuestra juventud al servicio de Yungay*.

100. Yauri Montero, *Tiempo de rosas*, 111–112.

101. Olimpio Cotillo Caballero, "Huaraz fue prácticamente un ensayo urbanístico," in *Vida, muerte y resurrección*, ed. Pajuelo Prieto, 110; Yauri Montero, *Ancash o la biografía de la inmortalidad*.

102. Peru Oficina Regional de Dessarrollo del Norte, *Plan de Rehabilitación y Desarrollo de la Zona Afectada por el Terremoto* (Chiclayo: Oficina Regional de

Dessarrollo del Norte, 1971), cited in Walton, "Human Spatial Organization," 202–206.

103. Pantoja Ramos, Ripkens, and Swisshelm, *Cuentos y relatos en el quechua*, 49.

104. Kay, "Achievements and Contradictions," 151; Barker, "National Parks, Conservation," 15; Cabel Moscoso, *Literatura del sismo*, 8.

105. Leonardo Ángeles Asín, "Mientras haya un yungaíno con vida, Yungay no desaparecerá," in *Vida, muerte y resurrección*, ed. Pajuelo Prieto, 189–190.

106. Oliver-Smith, "Here There Is Life," 94.

107. Walter, *La domestication de la nature*, part 1; Oliver-Smith, *The Martyred City*, 161; Bode, *No Bells to Toll*, 50.

108. Ramírez Gamarra, *Ancash*, 153–154.

109. Eakin's *Weathering Risk in Rural Mexico* provides a compelling analysis of local groups' agency in their climatic and economic vulnerability.

CHAPTER 6

1. For Cordillera Blanca-Santa River glacier-water relationships, see Bradley et al., "Threats to Water Supplies in the Tropical Andes"; Coudrain, Francou, and Kundzewicz. "Glacier Shrinkage in the Andes"; Juen, Kaser, and Georges, "Modelling Observed and Future Runoff"; Kaser et al., "The Impact of Glaciers on the Runoff"; Mark, McKenzie, and Gómez, "Hydrochemical Evaluation of Changing Glacier Meltwater"; Mark and Seltzer, "Tropical Glacier Meltwater Contribution to Stream Discharge"; Morales Arnao, "Desglaciación y disminución de recursos hídricos"; Portocarrero, "Retroceso de glaciares en el Perú."

2. Fagan, *The Little Ice Age*, chap. 7; Grove, "Glacier Fluctuations and Hazards"; Ladurie, *Times of Feast, Times of Famine*.

3. Carey, "The History of Ice"; Ben Orlove, Ellen Wiegandt, and Brian H. Luckman, "The Place of Glaciers in Natural and Cultural Landscapes," in *Darkening Peaks*, ed. Orlove, Wiegandt, and Luckman, 3–19.

4. Cronon, "A Place for Stories"; Martinez-Alier, "Ecology and the Poor"; Slater, ed., *In Search of the Rain Forest*; Fairhead and Leach, *Misreading the African Landscape*; Davis, *Resurrecting the Granary of Rome*.

5. Keck, "Social Equality and Environmental Politics"; Sabin, "Searching for Middle Ground."

6. David Bernays, "Tullparaju," *American Alpine Journal* (1963): 344–354.

7. "Jornadas libradas por los montañistas norteamericanos," *El Departamento*, Huaraz, 29 September 1962, 2; Lamberto Guzmán Tapia, "Pudo prevenirse tanta desgracia y muerte," in *Vida, muerte y resurrección*, ed. Pajuelo Prieto, 173–178.

8. Cap. Jefe Político y Militar de la Plaza, "Comunicado al pueblo de Yungay," *El Departamento*, Huaraz, 1 October 1962, 2.

9. Miguel Elías Pizarro, "Comunicado de la Oficina Control de Lagunas Cordillera Blanca," *El Departamento*, Huaraz, 2 October 1962, 3.

10. Interviews by author, Huaraz, 2003–2004.

11. "Informe del montañista Norteamericano Ing. D. Bernays," *El Departamento*, Huaraz, 10 October 1962, 2.

12. David Bernays and Charles Sawyer, "M.I.T. International Expedition Report on Huascarán," *Peruvian Times*, Lima, 12 October 1962, 3 (emphasis in original).

13. Bernays, "Tullparaju."

14. "Piden amplia investigación sobre trabajos ejecutados para la defensa de Huaraz," *El Comercio*, 14 December 1959, 6. Also see "Amenazas Hidrológicas," *La Hora*, 4 July 1955, 2; José Ayllón Lozano, "En torno del control de las lagunas," *La Hora*, 4 March 1955, 3; "En mitin y Cabildo abierto, Huaraz censura negligencia y engaño sobre sus defensas," *El Comercio*, 13 December 1959, 1, 19.

15. "Infundada alarma en Huaraz," *El Departamento*, 7 February 1962, 2; Miguel Elías Pizarro, "Oficina Control Lagunas Cordillera Blanca No. 7," *El Departamento*, 14 February 1962, 3.

16. Miguel Elías Pizarro, "Oficina Control Lagunas, Comunicado No. 6," *El Departamento*, 8 February 1962, 3.

17. Carey, "Living and Dying with Glaciers," 129–130.

18. Miguel Elías Pizarro "Carta al Dr. Augusto Soriano Infante, Alcalde del Concejo Provincial de Huaraz, 16 Febrero 1962," reprinted in *El Departamento*, 17 February 1962, 3.

19. "Corporación del Santa debe controlar lagunas de la Cordillera Blanca," *El Comercio*, Lima, 25 December 1965. For other complaints, see "Memorandum 1: Seguridad de las poblaciones amenazadas por las lagunas y los glaciares," *Forjando Ancash (Vocero del Club Ancash)*, 5, no. 18, Lima, April–December 1963, 34; "Amenaza permanente: las lagunas de la Cordillera Blanca," *El Comercio*, Lima, 11 February 1966; "Previsión de aludes glaciares," *El Comercio*, Lima, 13 January 1967; "Piden fondos para expertos que ven peligro por desbordes de lagunas," *La Cronica*, 7 July 1967.

20. Guzmán Tapia, "Pudo prevenirse tanta desgracia y muerte," in *Vida, muerte y resurrección*, ed. Pajuelo Prieto, 174.

21. Comisión Liquidadora de la Corporación Peruana del Santa, "Memoria general de la Corporación Peruana del Santa, años 1943–1974" (Lima, [1980]), File # Caja 058347, No. 6 in Electroperú-FS, Lima, 22; Electroperú, "Proyectos hidroeléctricos y de regulación de aguas en la cuenca del río Santa," Informe (Huaraz, April 1989), File # I-APROVHID-034 in UGRH, 1–2.

22. In 1981, Electroperú expanded Cañón del Pato production to 150 megawatts.

23. Benjamín Morales A., "Decenio Hidrológico Internacional: Programa de la Comisión Peruana de Glaciología," *Revista Peruana de Andinismo y Glaciología* 19, no. 9, Segunda Parte (1970): 35; Benjamín Morales A., "Estudios glaciológicos-geológicos efectuados en la Cordillera Blanca entre Enero de 1966 a Diciembre de 1967" (Pati, December 1967), File # I-GLACIO-049 in UGRH, 1–4.

24. Morales A., "Estudios glaciológicos-geológicos," 5–6.

25. Benjamín Morales A., "Estudios de ablación en la Cordillera Blanca," *Boletín del Instituto Nacional de Glaciología (Peru)* 1 (1969): 53.

26. Lliboutry, Morales A., and Schneider, "Glaciological Problems...III," 285; Morales A., "Decenio Hidrológico Internacional," 36. For climate-glacier relations in the Cordillera Blanca, see Kaser and Osmaston, *Tropical Glaciers*, 118–121; Kaser, Ames, and Zamora, "Glacier Fluctuations and Climate"; Vuille, Kaser, and Juen, "Glacier Mass Balance Variability."

27. Benjamín Morales A., "Estudio de la evolución de la lengua glaciar del Pucahirca y de la Laguna Safuna," *Boletín del Instituto Nacional de Glaciología (Peru)* 1 (1969): 28; Ames Marquez and Francou, "Cordillera Blanca glaciares en la historia," 46; Ames, "A Documentation of Glacier Tongue Variations," 5–6.

28. Chambers, "Locality and Science"; Cueto, *Excelencia científica en la periféria,* 608–609.

29. Decreto-Ley No. 19242, "A Corporación del Santa encomiendan control de las lagunas de dos cordilleras," 28 December 1971.

30. Racoviteanu, et al., "Decadal Changes in Glacier Parameters"; Georges, "20th-Century Glacier Fluctuations"; Morales, "Estudios de vulnerabilidad."

31. Ames, ed., *Glacier Inventory of Peru,* 1.

32. Benjamín Morales Arnao, preface in ibid.

33. Pulgar Vidal, *Geografía del Perú,* 139.

34. Scott, *Seeing Like a State;* Craib, *Cartographic Mexico.*

35. Nash, "The Changing Experience of Nature."

36. Unidad de Glaciología e Hidrología Hidrandina S.A., "Informe técnico financiero de los proyectos de la Unidad de Glaciología e Hidrología al 30-10-87" (Huaraz, 17 November 1987), File I-MEM-022 in UGRH, 1.

37. Unidad de Glaciología y Recursos Hídricos, "Información básica: Resumen ejecutivo" (Huaraz, February 1996), File I-MEM-033 in UGRH, 1.

38. Unidad de Glaciología e Hidrología, "Información de la Unidad de Glaciología y Seguridad de Lagunas y del Proyecto Parón" (Huaraz, 1987), File I-MEM-020 in UGRH, 3–4; Unidad de Glaciología e Hidrología, "Informe técnico financiero de los proyectos," Appendix 4; Electroperú, "Afianzamiento hídrico río Santa: Proyecto laguna Parón" (Huaraz, 1990), File I-VARIOS-498 in UGRH, 7.

39. Unidad de Glaciología e Hidrología, "Informe de actividades y programas de trabajo de la Unidad de Glaciología e Hidrología de HIDRANDINA S.A." (Huaraz, February 1989), File I-MEM-024 in UGRH.

40. Marino Zamora Cobos, "Plan de emergencia para el control de lagunas y glaciares en las cuencas del río Santa y Pativilca, Deptos. Ancash y Lima" (Huaraz, April 1987), File I-GLACIO-037 in UGRH.

41. "La Cordillera Blanca," *El Comercio,* 10 February 1983; "Hacen llamado para no dejar de controlar peligrosas lagunas de la Cordillera Blanca," *El Comercio,* 7 Febuary 1983; J. Alberto Romero Leguía, "Cuidado con las lagunas de la Cordillera Blanca," *La República,* 23 February 1983, 19.

42. F. Jaramillo M. "Seguridad de Lagunas," *El Departamento,* 14 March 1981.

43. Kattelman, "Glacial Lake Outburst Floods."

44. Local views come from my own interviews and from Stein, *Hualcan,* 295–306.

45. "El Hualcán presenta fisura de 500 metros con gran masa de hielo: Peligro de desprendimiento sobre la laguna Cochca," *El Comercio,* 19 July 1967; Jaime Fernández Concha, "Informe sobre la investigación efectuada en las obras y contabilidad de las lagunas Cochca y Yanahuanca" (Lima, 24 June 1953), File I-GEOL-012 in

UGRH; Jaime Fernández Concha and César Sotillo P., "Informe sobre la inspección de los trabajos en ejecución en las lagunas: Cochca, Lejia y Mullaca" (Lima, 9 April 1953), File I-GEOL-011 in UGRH; Luis Oberti Izquierdo, "Informe Hualcán," *Revista Peruana de Andinismo y Glaciología* 21, no. 10 (1971-1972-1973): 131–138; Subprefecto de Carhuaz Torres Ramos, Telegram to Lorenzo Sousa Iglesia, Prefecto del Departamento (Carhuaz, 30 December 1942), Ministerio del Interior, Prefectura, File 425, Folio 11, in AGN, Lima.

46. Unidad de Glaciología e Hidrología Hidrandina S.A., "Información sobre peligrosidad de los glaciares: Estudio de los glaciares en la cuenca de las lagunas Cullicocha y Rajucocha" (Huaraz, October 1988), File I-GLACIO-040 in UGRH, 2.

47. On Lake 513a, see Unidad de Glaciología e Hidrología, "Informe técnico financiero de los proyectos de la Unidad de Glaciología e Hidrología al 31-12-89" (Huaraz, January 1990), File I-MEM-026 in UGRH; Kaser and Osmaston, *Tropical Glaciers*, prologue; Reynolds, "The Identification and Mitigation of Glacier-Related Hazards"; Reynolds, Dolecki, and Portocarrero, "The Construction of a Drainage Tunnel."

48. E-mail communication with Georg Kaser, November 2008.

49. For the 2003 Truth Commission report describing the two decades of violence, see http://www.cverdad.org.pe.

50. Reynolds, "The Identification and Mitigation of Glacier-Related Hazards," 156.

51. Kaser and Osmaston, *Tropical Glaciers*, 11.

52. Reynolds, Dolecki, and Portocarrero, "The Construction of a Drainage Tunnel."

53. Ames, "A Documentation of Glacier Tongue Variations," 31.

54. Huggel, Haeberli, and Kääb, "Glacial Hazards," 74–76.

55. Unidad de Glaciología e Hidrología, "Informe técnico financiero de los proyectos," 2.

56. Duke Energy Perú, *Cañón del Pato: Hechos, datos y cifras* (Lima: Duke Energy Perú, 2002), 9.

CHAPTER 7

1. Klein, *The Shock Doctrine*; Gunewardena and Schuller, eds., *Capitalizing on Catastrophe*.

2. On neoliberalism and the environment, see Castree, "Neoliberalising Nature"; McCarthy and Prudham, "Neoliberal Nature and the Nature of Neoliberalism." On neoliberalism and nature in Latin America, see the *Singapore Journal of Tropical Geography* 25, no. 3 (November 2004); Liverman and Vilas, "Neoliberalism and the Environment "; Perreault and Martin, "Geographies of Neoliberalism"; Mayer, *The Articulated Peasant*, chap. 10.

3. See, for example, Bury, "Mining Mountains"; Sahley, Torres, and Sanchez, "Neoliberalism Meets Pre-Columbian Tradition"; Bennett, Dávila-Poblete, and Nieves Rico, eds., *Opposing Currents*.

4. On neoliberalism and disaster vulnerability, see Cupples, "Rural Development in El Hatillo"; Eakin, *Weathering Risk in Rural Mexico*; Wisner, "Changes in Capitalism"; Wisner, "Risk and the Neoliberal State."

5. Weyland, "Assessing Latin American Neoliberalism."

6. The 2003 Truth Commission report describes the two decades of violence; see http://www.cverdad.org.pe.

7. On neoliberalism, see Harvey, *A Brief History of Neoliberalism*.

8. Carrión, ed., *The Fujimori Legacy*; Parodi Trece, *Perú 1960–2000*, 252; Klarén, *Peru*, 406–408; Mauceri, "State Reform, Coalitions, and the Neoliberal Autogolpe"; Boloña, "The Viability of Alberto Fujimori's Economic Strategy," 184.

9. Barr, "The Persistence of Neopopulism in Peru?" 1163.

10. Kay, "'Fujipopulism' and the Liberal State," 59–61; Klarén, *Peru*, 424.

11. See Decreto Ley No. 25844, 6 November 1992; Santiváñez, *Electricity Deregulation and Privatization*, 11–16.

12. Resolución Suprema No. 025–96-EM, 25 April 1996; Egenor Duke Energy International, "Modificación Concesión Definitiva Generación C.H. Cañón del Pato" (Lima, 2001), Expediente 11014393, in Ministry of Energy and Mines, Electricity Division, Electric Concessions Directorate, Lima.

13. See www.duke-energy.com; www.duke-energy.com.pe; and Duke Energy Perú, *Cañón del Pato: Hechos, datos y cifras* (Lima: Duke Energy Perú, 2002).

14. Santiváñez, *Electricity Deregulation and Privatization*, 32.

15. See http://www.worldenergy.org/wec-geis/publications/reports/pedc/cases/peru.asp.

16. Boloña, "The Viability of Alberto Fujimori's Economic Strategy," 241, 243.

17. Jesús Ramírez Gutiérrez, letter to Jesús Beoutis (Lima, 6 October 1997), Caja 060902, No. H-10 in Electroperú-FS, Lima.

18. "Alcaldes exigen permanencia e Unidad de Glaciología en Huaraz," Uncited newspaper clipping in Caja 060902, No. H-10, Electroperú-FS, Lima, 23 January 1997.

19. Electroperú, "Situación de la ex-Unidad de Glaciología y Recursos Hídricos" (Lima, June 1997), Caja 061387, No. G.7 in Electroperú-FS, Lima; Fredy Moreno Neglia, Presidente Región Ancash, letter to Jesús Beoutis L., Presidente del Directorio de Electroperú S.A. (Huaraz, 12 March 1997), Caja 06138, No. G.7 in Electroperú-FS, Lima, 2.

20. Electroperú, "Informe: Propuesta para el desarrollo futuro de los programas de glaciología e hidrología" (Lima, 1996), Caja 061387, No. G.7 in Electroperú-FS, Lima; Electroperú, "Situación de la ex-Unidad de Glaciología y Recursos Hídricos"; Jesús Beoutis Ledesma, letter to Luis Dávila Dávila, Vice Ministro de Desarrollo Regional (Lima, 19 September 1997), Caja 060902, No. H-10 in Electroperú-FS, Lima; Homero Nureña León, Jefe del Instituto Nacional de Defensa Civil, letter to Jesús Beoutis Ledesma, Presidente del Directorio de Electroperú S.A. (Lima, 31 March 1997), Caja 061387, No. G.7 in Electroperú-FS, Lima; Hugo Rivera Mantilla, Director Técnico de INGEMMET, letter to Luis Gaviño Vargas, Gerente General, Electroperú S.A. (Lima, 25 March 1997), Caja 061387, No. G.7 in Electroperú-FS, Lima.

21. Ames, "A Documentation of Glacier Tongue Variations," 31.

22. Benjamín Morales A., "Reactivación del Instituto Nacional de Glaciología" (Lima: September 1997), Caja 060902, No. H-10 in Electroperú-FS, Lima; Benjamín Morales A., Presidente del Instituto Andino de Glaciología y Geoambiente, letter to Luis Gavino Vargas, Gerente General, Electroperú (Lima, 8 January 1997), Caja 061387, No. G.7 in Electroperú-FS, Lima; Maximo Villar Lumbreras, Letter to Sr. Primer Ministro y Ministro de Energía y Minas, Ing. Alberto Pandolfi (Lima, 2 October 1997), Caja 060902, No. H-10 in Electroperú-FS, Lima.

23. Decreto Ley No. 26410, 22 December 1994. For CONAM's concern with global warming, see Marticorena, ed., *Perú: Vulnerabilidad frente al cambio climático.*

24. Electroperú, "Contrato de comodato que celebran ELECTROPERU S.A. y el Consejo Nacional del Ambiente" (Lima, 18 September 1997), Caja 060902, No. H-10 in Electroperú-FS, Lima; Patricia Iturregui, Presidente de la Comisión Nacional de Cambio Climático, Letter to Jesús Beoutis Ledesma, Presidente Ejecutivo de Electroperú (Lima, 26 August 1997), Caja 060902, No. H-10 in Electroperú-FS, Lima.

25. Glaciología y Recursos Hídricos Electroperú, "Mapa indice de lagunas de la Cordillera Blanca" (Huaraz, October 1997), File Caja 060902, No. H-10 in Electroperú-FS, Lima; J. Fernández Concha and A. Hoempler, "Indice de lagunas y glaciares de la Cordillera Blanca" (Lima, May 1953), File I-INVEN-011 in UGRH; Marino Zamora Cobos, "Inventario y seguridad de lagunas en la Cordillera Blanca" (Huaraz, November 1983), File I-INVEN-010 in UGRH.

26. IPCC, *Climate Change 2007: The Physical Science Basis*, 356–360; Barry, "The Status of Research on Glaciers"; Dyurgerov and Meier, "Twentieth Century Climate Change"; Oerlemans, "Extracting a Climate Signal."

27. Kattelmann, "Glacial Lake Outburst Floods in the Nepal Himalaya"; Ghimire, "Climate Change and Glacier Lake Outburst Floods."

28. Pradeep Kumar Mool and Samjwal Ratna Bajracharya, *Tista Basin, Sikkim Himalaya: Inventory of Glaciers, Glacial Lakes and the Identification of Potential Glacial Lake Outburst Floods (GLOFs) Affected by Global Warming in the Mountains of Himalayan Region* (Asia-Pacific Network for Global Change Research, ICIMOD, and United Nations Environment Programme, 2003). This consortium also conducted two other inventories: "Pumqu Basin, Tibet Autonomous Region of PR China," and "Astor Basin, Pakistan Himalaya."

29. Huggel, Haeberli, and Kääb, "Glacial Hazards," 74–76; Chiarle et al., "Recent Debris Flow Occurrences."

30. Clague and Evans, "A Review of Catastrophic Drainage of Moraine-Dammed Lakes."

31. Patch, "Life in a Peruvian Indian Community," 2.

32. Marco Zapata Luyo, "Informe de avance sobre tres lagunas peligrosas en la Cordillera Blanca" (Huaraz, 16 October 1997), Caja 060902, No. H-10 in Electroperú-FS, Lima, 1; Marino Zamora Cobos, "Inspección de tres lagunas peligrosas en la Cordillera Blanca, Huaraz, Ancash" (Lima, 23 December 1997), Caja 061387, No. G.7 in Electroperú-FS, Lima, 3.

33. Caviedes, *El Niño in History*; Cushman, "Enclave Vision"; Davis, *Late Victorian*; Glantz, *Currents of Change.*

34. The September 27, 1997, issue of the *Economist* praised Fujimori's initiatives in a story called "Fujimori against El Niño."

35. Glantz, *Currents of Change*, 111–112.

36. For scientific understandings in 1997, see Francou et al., "Balances de glaciares y clima"; Thompson, Mosley-Thompson, and Morales Arnao, "El Niño-Southern Oscillation Events." For a more recent analysis, see Vuille, Kaser, and Juen, "Glacier Mass Balance Variability."

37. Electroperú, "Situación de la ex-Unidad de Glaciología y Recursos Hídricos"; Unidad de Glaciología y Recursos Hídricos, "Ayuda Memoria" (Lima, 15 December 1997), Caja 061387, No. G.7 in Electroperú-FS, Lima; Luis Nicho Díaz, Gerente General Electroperú, letter to Presidente del Directorio, Electroperú S.A. (Lima, 16 July 1997), Caja 060902, No. H-10 in Electroperú-FS, Lima.

38. Glaciología y Recursos Hídricos Electroperú, "Mapa indice de lagunas de la Cordillera Blanca" (Huaraz, October 1997), Caja 060902, No. H-10 in Electroperú-FS, Lima.

39. Instituto Andino de Glaciología y Geoambiente, "Estudio de vulnerabilidad de recursos hídricos de alta montaña: Informe ejecutivo" (Lima, 1998), P10 I464, in Biblioteca de INRENA, Lima. For syntheses of the unpublished INAGGA report, see Morales, "Estudios de vulnerabilidad de recursos hídricos"; Morales, "Desglaciación y disminución de recursos hídricos."

40. Electroperú S.A. (Glaciología y Recursos Hídricos), "Inspección de 31 lagunas de la Cordillera Blanca 1997" (Huaraz, November 1997), File I-CONSOL-064 in UGRH.

41. Jaime Fernández Concha, "Informe sobre el aluvión de Ishinka, proveniente de la laguna Milluacocha" (Lima, 20 November 1952), File I-GEOL-013 in UGRH; Marco Zapata Luyo and César Portocarrero R., "Informe de la inspección efectuada a la quebrada Ishinca con motivo del desborde de las aguas del río Paltay" (Huaraz, 6 September 1982), File I-GEOTEC-045 in UGRH.; Ames Marquez and Francou, "Cordillera Blanca glaciares en la historia," 57–58.

42. Interview by author, Collón, 2004.

43. Interviews by author, Huaraz, 2004.

44. Gustavo Carlos Flores, "Pedido de Congresista Flores Gustavo Carlos: Proyecto de reactivación del Instituto Nacional de Glaciología" (Lima, 18 November 1997), Caja 061387, No. G.7 in Electroperú-FS, Lima.

45. Decreto Supremo No. 031–97-PCM. Presidente de la República, "Decreto de Urgencia" (Lima, 1997), Caja 060902, No. H-10 in Electroperú-FS, Lima.

46. Unidad de Glaciología y Recursos Hídricos, "Ayuda Memoria" (Lima, 15 December 1997), Caja 061387, No. G.7 in Electroperú-FS, Lima, 2–3.

47. Unidad de Glaciología e Hidrología Hidrandina S.A., "Informe técnico financiero de los proyectos de la Unidad de Glaciología e Hidrología al 30-10-87" (Huaraz, 17 November 1987), File I-MEM-022 in UGRH, appendix.

48. Assies, "David versus Goliath in Cochabamba"; Laurie and Marvin, "Globalisation, Neoliberalism, and Negotiated Development"; Scudder, *The Future of Large Dams.*

49. For example, Benjamín Morales A., "Estudios glaciológicos-geológicos efectuados en la Cordillera Blanca entre enero de 1966 a diciembre de 1967" (Pati, December 1967), File I-GLACIO-049 in UGRH; Dirección General de Electricidad Ministerio de Energía y Minas, "Informe geológico de proyectos de reservorios en la cuenca del río Santa" (Lima, September 1972), File I-VARIOS-506 in UGRH; Unidad de Glaciología e Hidrología, "Informe técnico financiero de los proyectos de la Unidad de Glaciología e Hidrología al 30–10–87" (Huaraz, 17 November 1987), File I-MEM-022 in UGRH, Appendix 4; Unidad de Glaciología e Hidrología, "Afianzamiento hídrico del Río Santa, I Etapa" (Huaraz, January 1990), File I-HIDRO-006 in UGRH; "Relación de expedientes de Embalse 1995 solicitados por Electroperú S.A.," in "Proyectos de embalse ubicados dentro del ambito de Parque Nacional Huascarán," Biblioteca del Parque Nacional Huascarán, Huaraz.

50. Egenor Duke Energy International, "Modificación Concesión Definitiva Generación C.H. Cañón del Pato" (Lima, 2001), Expediente 11014393, in Ministry of Energy and Mines, Electricity Division, Electric Concessions Directorate, Lima; Duke Energy Perú, Cañón del Pato, 7.

51. Hilario Gammara O. and Duke Energy International EGENOR, "Informe geológico-geotécnico para la regulación de las lagunas Aguascocha, Auquiscocha y Shallap en el proyecto de afianzamiento del Cañón del Pato" (Lima, 2001), File E P32 G2, in INRENA, Lima, chap. 2; Julio Kuroiwa Zevallos, "Estudio básico de regulación de las lagunas de la cuenca del río Santa," (Lima: Duke Energy International, 2001), File E P10 D9E, in INRENA, Lima.

52. Interviews by author, Huaraz, 2004, 2007.

53. For another case of local frustration with Duke, see, Letter from Comunidad Campesina "Pachacutec" to EGENOR, 26 Dec. 2000 and Letter from Municipalidad Distrital de Mato, Villa Sucre-Huaylas to Duke Energy International, 3 January 2001, in Dirección General de Asuntos Ambientales Energéticos, Expediente EIA-E-3202, No. 1316887, Ministry of Energy and Mines, Electricity Division, Electric Concessions Directorate, Lima.

54. Morales A., "Estudios glaciológicos-geológicos efectuados en la Cordillera Blanca entre enero de 1966 a diciembre de 1967," 5–6; Electroperú, "Proyectos hidroeléctricos y de regulación de aguas en la cuenca del río Santa" (Huaraz, April 1989), File I-APROVHID-034 in UGRH, 6.

55. Interviews by author, Huaraz, 2003–2004.

56. Stein, Hualcan, 305.

57. Glaciología y Seguridad de Lagunas Electroperú U.C. 16, "Invitación al acto de inauguración de la obra 'Consolidación laguna Shallap'" (Huaraz, 1974), Caja 050488, No. C in Electroperú-FS, Lima, 8–9.

58. Morales A., "Estudios glaciológicos-geológicos efectuados en la Cordillera Blanca entre enero de 1966 a diciembre de 1967," 6.

59. Electroperú, "Proyectos hidroeléctricos y de regulación de aguas en la cuenca del río Santa" (Huaraz, April 1989), File I-APROVHID-034 in UGRH, 6; Unidad de Glaciología e Hidrología, "Afianzamiento hídrico del Río Santa, I Etapa" (Huaraz, January 1990), File I-HIDRO-006 in UGRH.

238   NOTES TO PAGES 179–184

60. Egenor Duke Energy International, "Afianzamiento hídrico del río Santa, estudio de regulación de la subcuenca de los ríos Ulta, Tucu y Quilcay: estudios topográficos y batimétricos de las lagunas Auquiscocha, Aguascocha y Shallap" (Lima, 2001), File E P10 D9, in INRENA, Lima; Gammara O. and Duke Energy International EGENOR, "Informe geológico-geotécnico para la regulación de las lagunas Aguascocha, Auquiscocha y Shallap"; Edgar Palma Huerta, "Embalsando el peligro (SOS en los Andes) Shallap," El Eco 2, no. 9 (2003): 4–5; Duke Energy Perú, Cañón del Pato.

61. On the flood, see Unidad de Glaciología y Recursos Hídricos, "Estado situacional de la laguna Palcacocha" (Huaraz, March 2003), in UGRH; Vilímek et al., "Influence of Glacial Retreat on Natural Hazards."

62. David E. Steitz and Alan Buis, "Peril in Peru? NASA Takes a Look at Menacing Glacier," NASA press release, 11 April 2003, on line at http://www.nasa.gov/home/hqnews/2003/apr/HP_News_03138.html (accessed 5 August 2008).

63. For press and scientists' reactions to the NASA press release, see "Consideran alarmista informe de la NASA sobre riesgo de alud en Ancash," El Comercio, 16 April 2003; "Especialistas peruanos califican información de alarmista," Correo, 15 April 2003, http://anteriores.epensa.com.pe/enlinea/ediciones/2003/abr/15/locales/loco2.asp; "Geólogo señala que diez poblados quedarían destruidos," Correo, 15 April 2003, http://anteriores.epensa.com.pe/enlinea/ediciones/2003/abr/15/locales/loco4.asp; Ivette Bendezú, "Hoy sobrevuelan zona de posible desprendimiento de glaciar en Huaraz," Correo, 16 April 2003, http://anteriores.epensa.com.pe/enlinea/ediciones/2003/abr/16/locales/loco1.asp; Ivette Bendezú, "Piden que la NASA confirme lo desmienta caída de glaciar," Correo, 17 April 2003, http://anteriores.epensa.com.pe/enlinea/ediciones/2003/abr/17/locales/loco7.asp.

64. Georg Kaser and Christian Georges, "A Potential Disaster in the Icy Andes: A Regrettable Blunder," technical report, University of Innsbruck, Austria, 26 April 2003, on line at http://geowww.uibk.ac.at/glacio/index.html.

65. Huggel, Haeberli, and Kääb, "Glacial Hazards," 73.

66. "Huaraz: Todavía hay sitio," El Comercio, 16 April 2003.

67. "Solo seis mil visitantes fueron a Huaraz informa Cámara de Turismo," El Comercio, 21 April 2003; Ivette Bendezú, "Hoy sobrevuelan zona de posible desprendimiento de glaciar en Huaraz," Correo, 16 April 2003, http://anteriores.epensa.com.pe/enlinea/ediciones/2003/abr/16/locales/loco1.asp.

68. For example, José Alva S., "Aluvión gigante podría sepultar ciudad de Huaraz," La República, 15 April 2003, http://www3.larepublica.com.pe/2003/ABRIL/pdf15/locales.htm.

69. Vilímek et al., "Influence of Glacial Retreat on Natural Hazards"; UGRH, "Estado situacional de la laguna Palcacocha" (Huaraz, March 2003), in UGRH, 3.

70. "News in Brief: NASA Feels the Heat as Glacier Pictures Cause Unrest in Peru," Nature 422 (24 April 2003): 794.

71. El Surco (Huaraz), 27 March 2003, 7.

72. Sociedad Geológica del Perú, "Evaluación del informe: Regulación de la laguna Shallap, Estudio de Riesgos" (Lima, 6 June 2003), on line at http://www.sgp.org.pe/ (accessed 2004).

73. Interview by author, Lima, 2004.

74. "Dirigentes de Huaraz: Ghilardi debe comenzar a trabajar después de esta manifestación," huarazperu.com, 7 October 2003; "Amenazan con paro si no se entrega estudio definitivo para asfaltado de vía Casma-Huaraz," Coordinadora Nacional de Radio, October 2003, on line at http://www.cnr.org.pe/noticia. php?id=8458 (accessed 4 August 2008).

75. Palma Huerta, "Embalsando el peligro (SOS en los Andes)," 4–5.

76. "¡Movilización histórica!" *El Surco* (Huaraz), 8 October 2003.

77. "Victoria a medias, caso Laguna Shallap," *Impacto: Revista de Actualidad Regional* 6, no. 51 (March 2004): 22–23.

78. The U.S. Bechtel Corporation made a similar discovery in Cochabamba, Bolivia, in 2000 after the privatization of urban water supplies erupted into a violent "water conflict." See Nickson and Vargas, "The Limitations of Water Regulation."

79. I have found little explanation of the 1883 flood, but the event is always listed in secondary sources such as Ames Marquez and Francou, "Cordillera Blanca glaciares en la historia," 56; Benjamín Morales A., "Estudio de las lagunas de Rajucolta y Cashan" (Lima, 8 August 1966), File 701 27.728 in Biblioteca de Electroperú, Lima; Marco Zapata Luyo, "Reconocimiento geológico de la laguna y quebrada Rajucolta" (Huaraz, October 1973), File 1RN 05.448 in Biblioteca de Electroperú, Lima.

80. Electroperú, "Estudio geológico-glaciológico definitivo para fines de seguridad y represamiento de la laguna Rajucolta" (Huaraz, 26 August 1974), File 1RN 05.449 in Biblioteca de Electroperú, Lima.

81. Mark, "Tracing Tropical Andean Glaciers over Space and Time."

CONCLUSION

1. United Nations Environment Program, "Meltdown in the Mountains," press release 16 (March 2008), online at http://www.unep.org/Documents. Multilingual/Default.asp?DocumentID=530&ArticleID=5760&l=en (accessed 26 August 2008).

2. Secretaría General de la Comunidad Andina, *El cambio climático no tiene fronteras: Impacto del cambio climático en la Comunidad Andina* (Lima: Comunidad Andina, 2008), online at http://www.comunidadandina.org/public/libro_cambioclimatico1.pdf (accessed 26 August 2008).

3. For these glacier-water relationships, see Bradley et al., "Threats to Water Supplies in the Tropical Andes"; Coudrain, Francou, and Kundzewicz. "Glacier Shrinkage in the Andes"; Juen, Kaser, and Georges, "Modelling Observed and Future Runoff"; Kaser et al., "The Impact of Glaciers on the Runoff"; Mark, McKenzie, and Gómez, "Hydrochemical Evaluation of Changing Glacier Meltwater"; Mark and Seltzer, "Tropical Glacier Meltwater Contribution to Stream Discharge"; Morales Arnao, "Desglaciación y disminución de recursos hídricos"; Portocarrero, "Retroceso de glaciares en el Perú."

4. Vergara et al., "Economic Impacts of Rapid Glacier Retreat."

5. For the World Bank Andean glacier retreat project, see http://web.worldbank. org/external/projects/main?Projectid=P098248&Type=Overview&theSitePK=40941& pagePK=64283627&menuPK=64282134&piPK=64290415.

6. Reynolds, "The Development of a Combined Regional Strategy."

7. Lagos, "Peru's Approach to Climate Change."

8. McCook, "'Giving Plants a Civil Status'"; Scott, *Seeing Like a State*; Mitchell, *Rule of Experts.*

9. Foucault, *Discipline and Punish*; Scott, *Seeing Like a State*; Mallon, *Peasant and Nation*; Drake and Hershberg, *State and Society in Conflict.*

10. James Painter, "Deglaciation in the Andean Region," occasional paper, Human Development Report Office, United Nations Development Program, 2007, online at http://hdr.undp.org/en/reports/global/hdr2007–2008/papers/painter_ james.pdf (accessed 29 August 2008).

Bibliography

Adger, W. Neil, et al. "Are There Social Limits to Adaptation to Climate Change?" *Climatic Change* 93, nos. 3–4 (2009): 335–354.

Alers, Oscar. "Population and Development in a Peruvian Community." *Journal of Inter-American Studies* 7, no. 4 (October 1965): 423–448.

Alexander, David. *Confronting Catastrophe: New Perspectives on Natural Disasters.* New York: Oxford University Press, 2000.

Alley, Richard. *The Two Mile Time Machine: Ice Cores, Abrupt Climate Change, and Our Future.* Princeton, N.J.: Princeton University Press, 2000.

Alvarez-Brun, Félix. *Ancash: Una historia regional peruana.* Lima: Talleres Gráficos P.L. Villanueva S.A., 1970.

Ames, Alcides. "Chronology of Ice Avalanches and Floods Occurring in the Cordilleras Blanca and Huayhuash since the Beginning of the Eighteenth Century." Unpublished manuscript, Huaraz, 2003.

———. "A Documentation of Glacier Tongue Variations and Lake Development in the Cordillera Blanca, Peru." *Zeitschrift für Gletscherkunde und Glazialgeologie* 34, no. 1 (1998): 1–36.

———, ed. *Glacier Inventory of Peru.* Huaraz: CONCYTEC, 1988.

Ames, Alcides, and Bernard Francou. "Cordillera Blanca glaciares en la historia." *Bulletin de L'Institut Francais d'átudes Andines* 24, no. 1 (1995): 37–64.

Andermann, Jens. *The Optic of the State: Visuality and Power in Argentina and Brazil.* Pittsburgh, Pa.: University of Pittsburgh Press, 2007.

Anderson, Katharine. *Predicting the Weather: Victorians and the Science of Meteorology.* Chicago: University of Chicago Press, 2005.

Angeles Figueroa, Eduardo. *Las horas muertas.* Lima: Fredy's Publicaciones y Servicios, 1999.

Antúnez de Mayolo, Santiago. *Relato de una idea a su realización, ó La Central Hidroeléctrica del Cañón del Pato.* Lima: Editora Médica Peruana, 1957.

Arnold, David. *Colonizing the Body: State Medicine and Epidemic Disease in Nineteenth-Century India.* Berkeley: University of California Press, 1993.

Asdal, Kristin. "The Problematic Nature of Nature: The Post-Constructivist Challenge to Environmental History." *History and Theory* 42 (December 2003): 60–74.

Assies, Willem. "David versus Goliath in Cochabamba: Water Rights, Neoliberalism, and the Revival of Social Protest in Bolivia." *Latin American Perspectives* 30, no. 3 (2003): 14–36.

Atwood, Roger. "Democratic Dictators: Authoritarian Politics in Peru from Leguía to Fujimori." *SAIS Review* 21, no. 2 (2001): 155–176.

Barker, Mary L. "National Parks, Conservation, and Agrarian Reform in Peru." *Geographical Review* 70, no. 1 (1980): 1–18.

Barr, Robert R. "The Persistence of Neopopulism in Peru? From Fujimori to Toledo." *Third World Quarterly* 24, no. 6 (2003): 1161–1178.

Barrionuevo, Leandro. *Ancash Actual (1839–1939).* Huaraz: Editorial Peru Libre, 1937.

Barry, R. G. "The Status of Research on Glaciers and Global Glacier Recession: A Review." *Progress in Physical Geography* 30, no. 3 (2006): 285–306.

Bartle, Jim. *Parque Nacional Huascarán, Ancash, Perú.* Lima: Nuevas Imágenes S.A., 1985.

Bauer, Arnold J. *Goods, Power, History: Latin America's Material Culture.* New York: Cambridge University Press, 2001.

Bennett, Vivienne, Sonia Dávila-Poblete, and Maria Nieves Rico, eds. *Opposing Currents: The Politics of Water and Gender in Latin America.* Pittsburgh, Pa.: University of Pittsburgh Press, 2005.

Berke, Philip R., and Timothy Beatley. *After the Hurricane: Linking Recovery to Sustainable Development in the Caribbean.* Baltimore, Md.: Johns Hopkins University Press, 1997.

Bijker, Wiebe E. *Of Bicycles, Bakelites, and Bulbs: Toward a Theory of Sociotechnical Change.* Cambridge, Mass.: MIT Press, 1995.

Bode, Barbara. "Disaster, Social Structure, and Myth in the Peruvian Andes: The Genesis of an Explanation." *Annals of the New York Academy of Sciences* 293 (1977): 246–274.

———. *No Bells to Toll: Destruction and Creation in the Andes.* New York: Paragon House, 1990.

Boloña, Carlos. "The Viability of Alberto Fujimori's Economic Strategy." In *The Peruvian Economy and Structural Adjustment: Past, Present, and Future,* edited by Efraín Gonzales de Olarte, 183–264. Miami: North-South Center Press, 1996.

Borchers, Philipp, ed. *Die Weisse Kordillere.* Berlin: Verlag Scherl, 1935.

Bowen, Mark. *Thin Ice: Unlocking the Secrets of Climate Change in the World's Highest Mountains.* New York: Henry Holt, 2005.

Bradley, Raymond S., Mathias Vuille, Henry F. Diaz, and Walter Vergara. "Threats to Water Supplies in the Tropical Andes." *Science* 312 (23 June 2006): 1755–1756.

Brannstrom, Christian, ed. *Territories, Commodities and Knowledges: Latin American Environmental Histories in the Nineteenth and Twentieth Centuries.* London: Institute for the Study of the Americas, 2004.

Braun, Bruce. "Producing Vertical Territory: Geology and Governmentality in Late Victorian Canada." *Ecumene* 7, no. 1 (2000): 7–46.

Bravo, Michael T. "Voices from the Sea Ice: The Reception of Climate Impact Narratives." *Journal of Historical Geography* 35, no. 2 (2009): 256–278.

Breien, Hedda, Fabio V. De Blasio, Anders Elverhøi, and Kaare Høeg. "Erosion and Morphology of a Debris Flow Caused by a Glacial Lake Outburst Flood, Western Norway." *Landslides* 5, no. 3 (2008): 271–280.

Broggi, J. A. "La desglaciación andina y sus consecuencias." *Actas de la Academia Nacional de Ciencias Exactas, Físicas y Naturales de Lima,* 6, no. 6 (1943): 12–26.

Burger, Richard L. *Chavín and the Origins of Andean Civilization.* London: Thames and Hudson, 1992.

Burnett, D. Graham. *Masters of All They Surveyed: Exploration, Geography, and a British El Dorado.* Chicago: University of Chicago Press, 2000.

Burt, Jo-Marie. "Contesting the Terrain of Politics: State-Society Relations in Urban Peru, 1950–2000." In *State and Society in Conflict: Comparative Perspectives on Andean Crises,* edited by Paul W. Drake and Eric Hershberg, 220–256. Pittsburgh, Pa.: University of Pittsburgh Press, 2006.

Bury, Jeffrey. "Mining Mountains: Neoliberalism, Land Tenure, Livelihoods, and the New Peruvian Mining Industry in Cajamarca." *Environment and Planning A* 37, no. 2 (2005): 221–239.

Bury, Jeffrey, Adam French, Jeffrey McKenzie, and Bryan G. Mark. "Adapting to Uncertain Futures: A Report on New Glacier Recession and Livelihood Vulnerability Research in the Peruvian Andes." *Mountain Research and Development* 28, nos. 3–4 (2008): 332–333.

Buse, H. *Huarás Chavín.* Lima: Juan Mejía Baca and P. L. Villanueva, 1957.

Byers, Alton C. "An Assessment of Contemporary Glacier Fluctuations in Nepal's Khumbu Himal Using Repeat Photography." *Himalayan Journal of Sciences* 4, no. 6 (2007): 21–26.

———. "Contemporary Landscape Change in the Huascarán National Park and Buffer Zone, Cordillera Blanca, Peru." *Mountain Research and Development* 20, no. 1 (2000): 52–63.

Cabel Moscoso, Domingo Jesús. *Literatura del sismo: Reportaje a Ancash.* Lima: Juan Mejia Baca, 1973.

Camino, Lupe. *Cerros, plantas y lagunas poderosas: La medicina al norte del Perú.* Lima: CIPCA Piura, 1992.

Cañizares-Esguerra, Jorge. *Nature, Empire, and Nation: Explorations of the History of Science in the Iberian World.* Stanford, Calif.: Stanford University Press, 2006.

Carey, Mark. "Beyond Weather: The Culture and Politics of Climate History." In *Oxford Handbook of Environmental History,* edited by Andrew Isenberg. New York: Oxford University Press, forthcoming.

————. "Disasters, Development, and Glacial Lake Control in Twentieth-Century Peru." In *Mountains: Sources of Water, Sources of Knowledge*, edited by Ellen Wiegandt, 181–196. Dordrecht, Netherlands: Springer, 2008.

————. "The History of Ice: How Glaciers Became an Endangered Species." *Environmental History* 12, no. 3 (2007): 497–527.

————. "Latin American Environmental History: Current Trends, Interdisciplinary Insights, and Future Directions." *Environmental History* 14, no. 2 (2009): 221–252.

————. "Living and Dying with Glaciers: People's Historical Vulnerability to Avalanches and Outburst Floods in Peru." *Global and Planetary Change* 47 (2005): 122–134.

————. "The Politics of Place: Inhabiting and Defending Glacier Hazard Zones in Peru's Cordillera Blanca." In *Darkening Peaks: Glacial Retreat, Science, and Society*, edited by Ben Orlove, Ellen Wiegandt and Brian Luckman, 229–240. Berkeley: University of California Press, 2008.

Carranza Calvo, Rubén Darío, et al., eds. *Huandoy y Huascarán: Narraciones orales clásicas de Ancash, Tomo I*. Lima: Editorial San Marcos, 2006.

Carrillo Ramírez, Alberto. *Ensayo monográfico de la Provincia de Bolognesi*. Arequipa, 1953.

Carrión, Julio F., ed. *The Fujimori Legacy: The Rise of Electoral Authoritarianism in Peru*. University Park: Pennsylvania State Press, 2006.

Carrión Vergara, Alberto, ed. *Libro de oro de Yungay*. Lima: Editorial Juridica, S.A., 1962.

Casassa, Gino, et al. "Current Status of Andean Glaciers." *Global and Planetary Change* 59, no. 1–4 (2007): 1–9.

Castree, Noel. "Neoliberalising Nature: The Logics of Deregulation and Reregulation." *Environment and Planning A* 40 (2008): 131–152.

Castro Herrera, Guillermo. "The Environmental Crisis and the Tasks of History in Latin America." *Environment and History* 3, no. 1 (1997): 1–18.

Caviedes, Cesar N. *El Niño in History: Storming Through the Ages*. Gainesville: University Press of Florida, 2001.

Centeno, Miguel Angel, and Patricio Silva, eds. *The Politics of Expertise in Latin America*. New York: St. Martin's Press, 1998.

Chambers, David Wade. "Locality and Science: Myths of Centre and Periphery." In *Mundialización de la ciencia y cultura nacional*, edited by A. Lafuente, A. Elena and M. L. Ortega, 605–618. Madrid: Doce Calles, 1991.

Chiarle, Marta, Sara Iannotti, Giovanni Mortara, and Philip Deline. "Recent Debris Flow Occurrences Associated with Glaciers in the Alps." *Global and Planetary Change* 56, nos. 1–2 (2007): 123–136.

Clague, John J., and Stephen G. Evans. "A Review of Catastrophic Drainage of Moraine-Dammed Lakes in British Columbia." *Quaternary Science Reviews* 19 (2000): 1763–1783.

Clement, Jean-Pierre. "El nacimiento de la higiene urbana en la América Española del Siglo XVIII." *Revista de Indias* 43, no. 171 (1983): 77–95.

Contreras, Carlos, and Marcos Cueto. *Historia del Perú contemporáneo*, 2nd. ed. Lima: Instituto de Estudios Peruanos, 2000.

Contreras, Daniel A. "Reconstructing Landscape at Chavín de Huántar, Perú: A GIS-Based Approach." *Journal of Archaeological Science* 36, no. 4 (2009): 1006–1017.

Coral Miranda, Reynaldo. *El aluvión de Huaraz: Relato de una tragedía*. Lima: Litografia Universo, S.A., 1962.

Coudrain, Anne, Bernard Francou, and Zbigniew W. Kundzewicz. "Glacier Shrinkage in the Andes and Consequences for Water Resources—Editorial." *Hydrological Sciences Journal* 50, no. 6 (2005): 925–932.

Cox, Percy, K. Goudge, T. G. Longstaff, E. Pilditch, and K. S. Sandford. "The Study of Threatening Glaciers: Discussion." *Geographical Journal* 85, no. 1 (1935): 36–41.

Craib, Raymond B. *Cartographic Mexico: A History of State Fixations and Fugitive Landscapes*. Durham, N.C.: Duke University Press, 2004.

Crate, Susan A., and Mark Nuttall, eds. *Anthropology and Climate Change: From Encounters to Actions*. Walnut Creek, Calif.: Left Coast Press, 2009.

Cronon, William. "A Place for Stories: Nature, History, and Narrative." *Journal of American History* 78, no. 4 (March 1992): 1347–1376.

———, ed. *Uncommon Ground: Rethinking the Human Place in Nature*. New York: W. W. Norton, 1996.

Cruikshank, Julie. *Do Glaciers Listen? Local Knowledge, Colonial Encounters, and Social Imagination*. Vancouver: University of British Columbia Press, 2005.

———. "Glaciers and Climate Change: Perspectives from Oral Tradition." *Arctic* 54, no. 4 (2001): 377–393.

Cueto, Marcos. "Andean Biology in Peru: Scientific Styles on the Periphery." *Isis* 80, no. 4 (1989): 640–658.

———. *Excelencia científica en la periferia: Actividades científicas e investigación biomédica en el Perú 1890–1950*. Lima: Grupo de Análisis para el Desarrollo, 1989.

———, ed. *Saberes andinos: Ciencia y tecnología en Bolivia, Ecuador y Perú*. Lima: Instituto de Estudios Peruanos, 1995.

———. "Social Medicine and 'Leprosy' in the Peruvian Amazon." *Americas* 61, no. 1 (2004): 55–80.

Cupples, Julie. "Rural Development in El Hatillo, Nicaragua: Gender, Neoliberalism, and Environmental Risk." *Singapore Journal of Tropical Geography* 25, no. 3 (2004): 343–357.

Cushman, Gregory T. "Enclave Vision: Foreign Networks in Peru and the Internationalization of El Niño Research during the 1920s." *Proceedings of the International Commission on History of Meteorology* 1, no. 1 (2004): 65–74.

———. "'The Most Valuable Birds in the World': International Conservation Science and the Revival of Peru's Guano Industry, 1909–1965." *Environmental History* 10, no. 3 (2005): 477–509.

———. "The Struggle over Airways in the Americas, 1919–1945: Atmospheric Science, Aviation Technology, and Neocolonialism." In *Intimate Universality: Local and Global Themes in the History of Weather and Climate*, edited by James

Rodger Fleming, Vladimir Jankovic, and Deborah R. Coen, 175–222. Sagamore Beach: Science History Publications, 2006.

Daniels, Stephen, and Georgina H. Endfield. "Narratives of Climate Change: Introduction." *Journal of Historical Geography* 35, no. 2 (2009): 215–222.

Davis, Diana K. *Resurrecting the Granary of Rome: Environmental History and French Colonial Expansion in North Africa*. Athens: Ohio University Press, 2007.

Davis, Mike. *Ecology of Fear: Los Angeles and the Imagination of Disaster*. New York: Vintage, 1998.

———. *Late Victorian Holocausts: El Niño Famines and the Making of the Third World*. New York: Verso, 2001.

de la Cadena, Marisol. *Indigenous Mestizos: The Politics of Race and Culture in Cuzco, Peru, 1919–1991*. Durham, NC: Duke University Press, 2000.

———. "Silent Racism and Intellectual Superiority." *Bulletin of Latin American Research* 17, no. 2 (1998): 143–164.

Diamond, Jared. *Collapse: How Societies Choose to Fail or Succeed*. New York: Viking, 2004.

Diaz, Henry F., and David W. Stahle. "Climate and Cultural History in the Americas: An Overview." *Climatic Change* 83, no. 102 (2007): 1–8.

Diez Canseco, Ernesto. *La red nacional de carreteras*. 2nd ed. Lima: Torres Aguirre, 1929.

Doel, Ronald E., and Kristine C. Harper. "Prometheus Unleashed: Science as a Diplomatic Weapon in the Lyndon B. Johnson Administration." *Osiris* 21 (2006): 66–85.

Doughty, Paul L. "Engineers and Energy in the Andes: An Update." In *Technology and Social Change*, edited by H. Bernard and P. Pelto, 111–136, 369–373. Prospect Heights, Ill.: Waveland Press, 1987.

———. *Huaylas: An Andean District in Search of Progress*. Ithaca, N.Y.: Cornell University Press, 1968.

———. "Plan and Pattern in Reaction to Earthquake: Peru, 1970–1998." In *The Angry Earth: Disaster in Anthropological Perspective*, edited by Anthony Oliver-Smith and Susanna M. Hoffman, 234–256. New York: Routledge, 1999.

Drake, Paul W., and Eric Hershberg, eds. *State and Society in Conflict: Comparative Perspectives on Andean Crises*. Pittsburgh, Pa.: University of Pittsburgh Press, 2006.

Drayton, Richard. *Nature's Government: Science, Imperial Britain, and the "Improvement" of the World*. New Haven, Conn.: Yale University Press, 2000.

Dyurgerov, Mark B., and Mark F. Meier. "Twentieth Century Climate Change: Evidence from Small Glaciers." *Proceedings of the National Academy of Sciences of the United States of America* 97, no. 4 (2000): 1406–1411.

Eakin, Hallie. *Weathering Risk in Rural Mexico: Climatic, Institutional, and Economic Change*. Tucson: University of Arizona Press, 2006.

Elías Pizarro, Miguel. "Trabajos de la Comisión Control de Lagunas Cordillera Blanca en Huaraz, Capital del Departamento de Ancash." *Boletín de la Sociedad Geográfica de Lima* 79 (January–April 1962): 55–61.

Ellis, Reuben. *Vertical Margins: Mountaineering and the Landscapes of Neoimperialism* (Madison: University of Wisconsin Press, 2001).

Endfield, Georgina H. *Climate and Society in Colonial Mexico: A Study in Vulnerability.* Oxford, UK: Blackwell Publishing, 2008.

Enock, C. Reginald. "El Huascarán." *Boletín de la Sociedad Geográfica de Lima* 15, no. 2 (1904): 173–178.

Ericksen, George E., George Plafker, and Jaime Fernández Concha. "Preliminary Report on the Geological Events Associated with the May 31, 1970, Peru Earthquake." *United States Geological Survey Circular* 639 (1970): 1–25.

Evans, Sterling. *Bound in Twine: The History and Ecology of the Henequen-Wheat Complex for Mexico and the American and Canadian Plains, 1880–1950.* College Station: Texas A&M University Press, 2007.

Fagan, Brian. *The Little Ice Age: How Climate Made History, 1300–1850.* New York: Basic Books, 2000.

Fairhead, James, and Melissa Leach. *Misreading the African Landscape: Society and Ecology in a Forest-Savanna Mosaic.* New York: Cambridge University Press, 1996.

Fernández, Justo. *Antología de la tradición y la leyenda ancashinas.* Huaraz: Edición Nueva Era, 1946.

———. *13 de Diciembre de 1941: Crónicas completas de la tragedia.* Huaraz: Editorial "Perú Libre," 1942.

Fernández Concha, Jaime. "El problema de las lagunas de la Cordillera Blanca." *Boletín de la Sociedad Geológica del Perú* 32 (1957): 87–95.

Fisher, John, and Natalia Priego. "Ignorance and 'Habitus' Blinkered and Enlightened Approaches toward the History of Science in Latin America." *Bulletin of Latin American Research* 25, no. 4 (2006): 528–540.

Fleming, James Rodger. *The Callendar Effect: The Life and Work of Guy Stewart Callendar (1898–1964), the Scientist Who Established the Carbon Dioxide Theory of Climate Change.* Boston: American Meteorological Society, 2007.

———. *Historical Perspectives on Climate Change.* New York: Oxford University Press, 1998.

———. "The Pathological History of Weather and Climate Modification: Three Cycles of Promise and Hype." *Historical Studies in the Physical and Biological Sciences* 37, no. 1 (2006): 3–25.

Fleming, James Rodger, Vladimir Jankovic, and Deborah R. Coen, eds. *Intimate Universality: Local and Global Themes in the History of Weather and Climate.* Sagamore Beach: Science History Publications, 2006.

Foucault, Michel. *Discipline and Punish: The Birth of the Prison.* 2nd ed. New York: Vintage Books, 1995.

Francou, Bernard, Pierre Ribstein, Hubert Sémiond, César Portocarrero, and Abel Rodríguez. "Balances de glaciares y clima en Bolivia y Perú: Impacto de los eventos ENSO." *Bulletin de L'Institut Francais d'Études Andines* 24, no. 3 (1995): 661–670.

Gade, Daniel W. *Nature and Culture in the Andes.* Madison: University of Wisconsin Press, 1999.

Gamio, Luis M. "Viajando por el Perú: El Departamento de Ancash." *Boletín de la Sociedad Geográfica de Lima* 60, nos. 3–4 (1943): 197–214.

García, María Elena. *Making Indigenous Citizens: Identities, Education, and Multicultural Development in Peru.* Stanford, Calif.: Stanford University Press, 2005.

García Acosta, Virginia, ed. *Historia y desastres en América Latina.* Vols. 1–2. Bogotá: La RED/CIESAS, 1996.

Gelles, Paul H. *Water and Power in Highland Peru: The Cultural Politics of Irrigation and Development.* New Brunswick, N.J.: Rutgers University Press, 2000.

Georges, Christian. "20th-Century Glacier Fluctuations in the Tropical Cordillera Blanca, Peru." *Arctic, Antarctic, and Alpine Research* 36, no. 1 (2004): 100–107.

Ghiglino Antúnez de Mayola, Luis. "Alud de Yungay y Ranrahirca del 31 de Mayo de 1970." *Revista Peruana de Andinismo y Glaciología* 19, no. 9 (1971): 84–88.

Ghimire, Motilal. "Climate Change and Glacier Lake Outburst Floods and the Associated Vulnerability in Nepal and Bhutan." In *Climate Change and Water Resources in South Asia*, edited by M. Monirul Qader Mirza and Q. K. Ahmad, 137–154. London: Taylor and Francis, 2005.

Glantz, Michael H. *Currents of Change: Impacts of El Niño and La Niña on Climate and Society.* 2nd ed. New York: Cambridge, 2001.

Golinski, Jan. *British Weather and the Climate of Enlightenment.* Chicago: University of Chicago Press, 2007.

Gonzales, Francisco. *Huarás: Visión integral.* Huaraz: Eds. Safori, 1992.

Gootenberg, Paul. *Imagining Development: Economic Ideas in Peru's "Fictitious Prosperity" of Guano, 1840–1880.* Berkeley: University of California Press, 1993.

Gordillo, Gastón R. *Landscapes of Devils: Tensions of Place and Memory in the Argentinean Chaco.* Durham, N.C.: Duke University Press, 2004.

Gose, Peter. *Deathly Waters and Hungry Mountains: Agrarian Ritual and Class Formation in an Andean Town.* Toronto: University of Toronto Press, 1994.

———. "Segmentary State Formation and the Ritual Control of Water under the Incas." *Comparative Studies in Society and History* 35, no. 3 (July 1993): 480–514.

Graham, Richard, ed. *The Idea of Race in Latin America, 1870–1940.* Austin: University of Texas Press, 1990.

Gridilla, Alberto. *Huaraz, o apuntes y documentos para la historia de la ciudad.* Huaraz: La Epoca, 1933.

Grötzbach, Erwin. "Tourism in the Cordillera Blanca Region, Peru." *Revista Geográfica (Instituto Panamericano de Geografía e Historia, OEA)* 133 (January–June 2003).

Grove, Jean.M. "Glacier Fluctuations and Hazards." *Geographical Journal* 153, no. 3 (1987): 351–367.

———. *The Little Ice Age.* London: Methuen, 1988.

———. *Little Ice Ages: Ancient and Modern.* New York: Routledge, 2004.

Guerra Martiniére, Margarita. *Manuel Odría.* Lima: Editorial Brasa S.A., 1994.

Guillet, David W. *Covering Ground: Communal Water Management and the State in the Peruvian Highlands.* Ann Arbor: University of Michigan Press, 1992.

Gunewardena, Nandini, and Mark Schuller, eds. *Capitalizing on Catastrophe: Neoliberal Strategies in Disaster Reconstruction.* New York: AltaMira Press, 2008.

Hall, C. Michael, and James Higham, eds. *Tourism, Recreation, and Climate Change.* Buffalo, N.Y.: Channel View Publications, 2005.

Hambrey, Michael, and Jürg Alean. *Glaciers.* 2nd ed. New York: Cambridge University Press, 2004.

Hård, Mikael, and Andrew Jamison. *Hubris and Hybrids: A Cultural History of Technology and Science.* New York: Routledge, 2005.

Harley, J. B. "Deconstructing the Map." *Cartographica* 26, no. 2 (1989): 1–20.

Harper, Kristine C. "Climate Control: United States Weather Modification in the Cold War and Beyond." *Endeavour* 32, no. 1 (2008): 20–26.

Harvey, David. *A Brief History of Neoliberalism.* New York: Oxford University Press, 2005.

Harvey, Penelope. "The Materiality of State-Effects: An Ethnography of a Road in the Peruvian Andes." In *State Formation: Anthropological Perspectives,* edited by Christian Krohn-Hansen and Knut G. Nustad, 123–141. Ann Arbor, Mich.: Pluto Press, 2005.

Headrick, Daniel R. *The Tentacles of Progress: Technology Transfer in the Age of Imperialism, 1850–1940.* New York: Oxford University Press, 1988.

Healey, Mark. "The Fragility of the Moment: Politics and Class in the Aftermath of the 1944 Argentine Earthquake." *International Labor and Working-Class History* 62 (2002): 50–59.

Hegglin, Esther, and Christian Huggel. "An Integrated Assessment of Vulnerability to Glacial Hazards: A Case Study in the Cordillera Blanca, Peru." *Mountain Research and Development* 28, nos. 3–4 (2008): 299–309. Online at http://www.bioone .org/doi/abs/10.1659/mrd.0976

Heim, A. "Observaciones glaciológicas en la Cordillera Blanca." *Boletín de la Sociedad Geológica del Perú* 14–15 (1947): 111–117.

———. *Wunderland Peru. Naturerlebnisse.* Bern: Verlag Hans Huber, 1948.

Hevly, Bruce. "The Heroic Science of Glacier Motion." *Osiris* 11 (1996): 66–86.

Hewitt, Kenneth. *Regions of Risk: A Geographical Introduction to Disaster.* Essex, U.K.: Longman, 1997.

Huertas Vallejos, Lorenzo. *Diluvios andinos: a través de las fuentes documentales.* Lima: Pontificia Universidad Católica del Perú, 2001.

Huggel, Christian, Wilfried Haeberli, and Andreas Kääb. "Glacial Hazards: Perceiving and Responding to Threats in Four World Regions." In *Darkening Peaks: Glacial Retreat, Science, and Society,* edited by Ben Orlove, Ellen Wiegandt and Brian Luckman, 68–80. Berkeley: University of California Press, 2008.

Hulme, Mike, Suraje Dessai, Irene Lorenzoni, and Donald R. Nelson. "Unstable Climates: Exploring the Statistical and Social Constructions of 'Normal' Climate." *Geoforum* 40, no. 2 (2009): 197–206.

Indacochea G., Angel, and Mariano Iberico M. "Aluvionamiento de Chavín de Huantar el 17 de enero de 1945." *Boletín de la Sociedad Geológica del Perú* 20 (1947): 21–28.

Intergovernmental Panel on Climate Change (IPCC). *Climate Change 2007.* 3 vols. New York: Cambridge University Press, 2007.

Isserman, Maurice, and Stewart Weaver. *Fallen Giants: A History of Himalayan Mountaineering from the Age of Empire to the Age of Extremes*. New Haven, Conn.: Yale University Press, 2008.

Jacobsen, Nils. *Mirages of Transition: The Peruvian Altiplano, 1780–1930*. Berkeley: University of California Press, 1993.

Jankovic, Vladimir. *Reading the Skies: A Cultural History of English Weather, 1650–1820*. Chicago: University of Chicago Press, 2001.

Janský, Bohumír, et al. "The Evolution of Petrov Lake and Moraine Dam Rupture Risk (Tien-Shan, Kyrgyzstan)." *Natural Hazards* 50, no. 1 (2009): 83–96.

Jaquette, Jane S., and Abraham F. Lowenthal. "The Peruvian Experiment in Retrospect." *World Politics* 39, no. 2 (January 1987): 280–296.

Jeanneau Gracey, José. "A 200 pies de profundidad en la Cordillera Blanca." *Boletín del Instituto Nacional de Glaciología (Peru)* 1 (1969): 35–39.

Josephson, Paul R. *Industrialized Nature: Brute Force Technology and the Transformation of the Natural World*. Washington, D.C.: Island Press, 2002.

Juen, Irmgard, Georg Kaser, and Christian Georges. "Modelling Observed and Future Runoff from a Glacierized Tropical Catchment (Cordillera Blanca, Perú)." *Global and Planetary Change* 59, nos. 1–4 (2007): 37–48.

Kaser, Georg. "Glacier-Climate Interaction at Low Latitudes." *Journal of Glaciology* 47, no. 157 (2001): 195–204.

Kaser, Georg, Alcides Ames, and Marino Zamora. "Glacier Fluctuations and Climate in the Cordillera Blanca, Peru." *Annals of Glaciology* 14 (1990): 136–140.

Kaser, Georg, and Christian Georges. "Changes of the Equilibrium-Line Altitude in the Tropical Cordillera Blanca, Peru, and Their Spatial Variations." *Annals of Glaciology* 24 (1997): 344–349.

Kaser, Georg, D. R. Hardy, T. Mölg, R. S. Bradley, and T. M. Hyera. "Modern Glacier Retreat on Kilimanjaro as Evidence of Climate Change: Observations and Facts." *International Journal of Climatology* 24 (2004): 329–339.

Kaser, Georg, I. Juen, C. Georges, J. Gomez, and W. Tamayo. "The Impact of Glaciers on the Runoff and the Reconstruction of Mass Balance History from Hydrological Data in the Tropical Cordillera Blanca, Peru." *Journal of Hydrology* 282 (2003): 130–144.

Kaser, Georg, and Henry Osmaston. *Tropical Glaciers*. New York: Cambridge University Press, 2002.

Kattelmann, Richard. "Glacial Lake Outburst Floods in the Nepal Himalaya: A Manageable Hazard?" *Natural Hazards* 28 (2003): 145–154.

Kay, Bruce H. "'Fujipopulism'and the Liberal State in Peru, 1990–1995." *Journal of Interamerican Studies and World Affairs* 38, no. 4 (1996): 55–98.

Kay, Cristóbal. "Achievements and Contradictions of the Peruvian Agrarian Reform." *Journal of Development Studies* 18, no. 2 (January 1982): 141–170.

Keck, Margaret E. "Social Equality and Environmental Politics in Brazil: Lessons from the Rubber Tappers of Acre." *Comparative Politics* 27, no. 4 (1995): 409–424.

Kelman, Ari. *A River and Its City: The Nature of Landscape in New Orleans*. Berkeley: University of California Press, 2003.

Kinzl, Hans. "Alpinismo-Andinismo." *Boletín de la Sociedad Geográfica de Lima* 57, no. 4 (1940): 222–234.

——. "Aufgaben und Reisen des Geographen." In *Die Weisse Kordillere*, edited by Philipp Borchers, 180–203. Berlin: Verlag Scherl, 1935.

——. "Gletscherkundliche Begleitworte zur Karte der Cordillera Blanca." *Zeitschrift für Gletscherkunde* 28 (1942): 1–19.

——. "La ruptura del lago glacial en la quebrada de Ulta en el año 1938." *Boletín del Museo de Historia Natural "Javier Prado"* 4, no. 13 (1940): 153–167.

——. "Las tres expediciones del 'Deutscher Alpenverein'a las cordilleras peruanas." *Boletín del Museo de Historia Natural "Javier Prado"* 4, no. 12 (1940): 3–24.

——. "Los glaciares de la Cordillera Blanca." *Revista de Ciencias (Organo de la Facultad de Ciencias Biológicas, Físicas y Matemáticas de la Universidad Mayor de San Marcos)* 42, no. 432 (1940): 417–440.

Kinzl, Hans, and Erwin Schneider. *Cordillera Blanca (Peru)*. Innsbruck, Germany: Universitats-Verlag Wagner, 1950.

Klarén, Peter Flindell. *Peru: Society and Nationhood in the Andes*. New York: Oxford University Press, 2000.

Klein, Naomi. *The Shock Doctrine: The Rise of Disaster Capitalism*. New York: Metropolitan Books, 2007.

Klimes, Jan, Vít Vilímek, and Marek Omelka. "Implications of Geomorphological Research for Recent and Prehistoric Avalanches and Related Hazards at Huascaran, Peru." *Natural Hazards* 50, no. 1 (2009): 193–209.

Klinenberg, Eric. *Heat Wave: A Social Autopsy of Disaster in Chicago*. Chicago: University of Chicago Press, 2003.

Knight, Peter G. "Glaciers: Art and History, Science and Uncertainty." *Interdisciplinary Science Reviews* 29, no. 4 (2004): 385–393.

Kogan, Georges, and Nicole Leininger. *The Ascent of Alpamayo: An Account of the Franco-Belgian Expedition to the Cordillera Blanca in the High Andes*. London: George G. Harrap, 1954.

Kristal, Efraín. *The Andes Viewed from the City: Literary and Political Discourse on the Indian in Peru 1848–1930*. New York: Peter Lang, 1987.

Lafuente, A., A. Elena, and M. L. Ortega, eds. *Mundialización de la ciencia y cultura nacional: Actas del Congreso Internacional "Ciencia, Descubrimiento y Mundo Colonial."* Madrid: Doce Calles, 1993.

Lagos, Pablo. "Peru's Approach to Climate Change in the Andean Mountain Region: Achieving Multidisciplinary Regional Cooperation for Integrated Assessment of Climate Change." *Mountain Research and Development* 27, no. 1 (2007): 28–31.

Landis, Michele L. "Fate, Responsibility, and 'Natural'Disaster Relief: Narrating the American Welfare State." *Law and Society Review* 33, no. 2 (1999): 257–318.

Langston, Nancy. *Forest Dreams, Forest Nightmares: The Paradox of Old Growth in the Inland West*. Seattle: University of Washington Press, 1995.

——. *Where Land and Water Meet: A Western Landscape Transformed*. Seattle: University of Washington Press, 2003.

Larson, Brooke. *Trials of Nation Making: Liberalism, Race, and Ethnicity in the Andes, 1810–1910.* New York: Cambridge University Press, 2004.

Larson, Erik. *Isaac's Storm: A Man, a Time, and the Deadliest Hurricane in History.* New York: Vintage Books, 2000.

Latour, Bruno. *Reassembling the Social: An Introduction to Actor-Network-Theory.* New York: Oxford University Press, 2005.

Laurie, N., and S. Marvin. "Globalisation, Neoliberalism, and Negotiated Development in the Andes: Water Projects and Regional Identity in Cochabamba, Bolivia." *Environment and Planning A* 31, no. 8 (1999): 1401–1415.

Lefebvre, Thierry. "L'invention occidentale de la haute montagne andine." *Mappemonde* 79, no. 3 (2005). Online at http://mappemonde.mgm.fr/num7/articles/art05307.html (accessed 21 January 2009).

Le Roy Ladurie, Emmanuel. *Times of Feast, Times of Famine: A History of Climate since the Year 1000.* Garden City, N.Y.: Doubleday, 1971.

Linden, Eugene. *The Winds of Change: Climate, Weather, and the Destruction of Civilizations.* New York: Simon and Schuster, 2006.

Liverman, Diana M. "Conventions of Climate Change: Constructions of Danger and the Dispossession of the Atmosphere." *Journal of Historical Geography* 35, no. 2 (2009): 279–296.

Liverman, Diana M., and Silvina Vilas. "Neoliberalism and the Environment in Latin America." *Annual Review of Environment and Resources* 31 (November 2006): 327–363.

Lliboutry, Louis. "Glaciological Problems Set by the Control of Dangerous Lakes in Cordillera Blanca, Peru. II. Movement of a Covered Glacier Embedded within a Rock Glacier." *Journal of Glaciology* 18, no. 79 (1977): 255–273.

———. "Informe preliminar sobre los fenómenos glaciológicos que acompañaron el terremoto y sobre los peligros presentes." *Revista Peruana de Andinismo y Glaciología* 19, no. 9 (1970): 20–26.

Lliboutry, Louis, et al. *Evaluación de los riesgos telúricos en el Callejón de Huaylas, con vista a la reubicación de poblaciones y obras públicas.* Paris: UNESCO, 1970.

Lliboutry, Louis, Benjamín Morales A., André Pautre, and Bernard Schneider. "Glaciological Problems Set by the Control of Dangerous Lakes in Cordillera Blanca, Peru. I. Historical Failures of Morainic Dams, Their Causes and Prevention." *Journal of Glaciology* 18, no. 79 (1977): 239–254.

Lliboutry, Louis, Benjamín Morales A., and Bernard Schneider. "Glaciological Problems Set by the Control of Dangerous Lakes in Cordillera Blanca, Peru. III. Study of Moraines and Mass Balances at Safuna." *Journal of Glaciology* 18, no. 79 (1977): 275–290.

Locke, Adrian Knight. "Catholic Icons and Society in Colonial Spanish America: The Peruvian Earthquake Christs of Lima and Cusco, and Other Comparative Cults (Mexico)." Ph.D. diss., University of Essex, United Kingdom, 2001.

López-Ocón Cabrera, Leoncio. "El nacionalismo y los orígenes de la Sociedad Geográfica de Lima." In *Saberes Andinos: Ciencia y tecnología en Bolivia, Ecuador y*

Perú, edited by Marcos Cueto, 109–125. Lima: Instituto de Estudios Peruanos, 1995.

Lugo Hubp, José, and Moshe Inbar, eds. *Desastres naturales en América Latina.* Mexico City: Fondo de Cultura Económica, 2002.

MacLeod, Roy, ed. "Nature and Empire: Science and the Colonial Enterprise." *Osiris,* 2nd ser., 15 (2001).

Mallon, Florencia. *The Defense of Community in Peru's Central Highlands: Peasant Struggle and Capitalist Transition, 1860–1940.* Princeton, N.J.: Princeton University Press, 1983.

———. *Peasant and Nation: The Making of Postcolonial Mexico and Peru.* Berkeley: University of California Press, 1995.

Mangin, William P. "Estratificación social en el Callejón de Huaylas." *Revista del Museo Nacional (Lima-Perú)* 24 (1955): 174–189.

Mark, Bryan G. "Tracing Andean Glaciers over Space and Time: Some Lessons and Transdisciplinary Implications." *Global and Planetary Change* 60, nos. 1–2 (2008): 101–114.

Mark, Bryan G., Jeffrey M. McKenzie, and Jesús Gómez. "Hydrochemical Evaluation of Changing Glacier Meltwater Contribution to Stream Discharge: Callejon de Huaylas, Peru." *Hydrological Sciences Journal* 50, no. 6 (2005): 975–987.

Mark, Bryan G., and G. O. Seltzer. "Tropical Glacier Meltwater Contribution to Stream Discharge: A Case Study in the Cordillera Blanca, Peru." *Journal of Glaciology* 49, no. 165 (2003): 271–281.

Mark, Bryan G., Geffrey O. Seltzer, Donald T. Rodbell, and Adam Y. Goodman. "Rates of Deglaciation during the Last Glaciation and Holocene in the Cordillera Vilcanota-Quelccaya Ice Cap Region, Southeastern Perú." *Quaternary Research* 57 (2002): 287–298.

Marticorena, Benjamín, ed. *Perú: Vulnerabilidad frente al cambio climático. Aproximaciones a la experiencia con el fenómeno El Niño.* Lima: Consejo Nacional del Ambiente, 1999.

Martinez-Alier, Joan. "Ecology and the Poor: A Neglected Dimension of Latin American History." *Journal of Latin American Studies* 23, no. 3 (1991): 621–639.

Maskrey, Andrew, ed. *Los desastres no son naturales.* Bogotá, Colombia: La Red de Estudios Sociales en Prevención de Desastres en América Latina, 1993.

Mason, Kenneth. "The Study of Threatening Glaciers." *Geographical Journal* 85, no. 1 (1935): 24–35.

Masterson, Daniel M. *Militarism and Politics in Latin America: Peru from Sánchez Cerro to Sendero Luminoso.* New York: Greenwood Press, 1991.

Mauceri, Philip. "State Reform, Coalitions, and the Neoliberal Autogolpe in Peru." *Latin American Research Review* 30, no. 1 (1995): 7–37.

Mayer, Enrique. *The Articulated Peasant: Household Economies in the Andes.* Boulder, Colo.: Westview Press, 2001.

McCarthy, James, and Scott Prudham. "Neoliberal Nature and the Nature of Neoliberalism." *Geoforum* 35, no. 3 (2004): 275–283.

McCook, Stuart. "'Giving Plants a Civil Status': Scientific Representations of Nature and Nation in Costa Rica and Venezuela, 1885–1935." *Americas* 58, no. 4 (2002): 513–536.

———. *States of Nature: Science, Agriculture, and Environment in the Spanish Caribbean, 1760–1940.* Austin: University of Texas Press, 2002.

McDowell, Bart, and John E. Fletcher. "Avalanche! 3,500 Peruvians Perish in Seven Minutes." *National Geographic*, June 1962, 855–880.

McIntosh, Roderick J., Joseph A. Tainter, and Susan Keech McIntosh, eds. *The Way the Wind Blows: Climate, History, and Human Action.* New York: Columbia University Press, 2000.

McNeill, J. R. "Diamond in the Rough: Is There a Genuine Environmental Threat to Security?" *International Security* 30, no. 1 (2005): 178–195.

———. *Something New under the Sun: An Environmental History of the Twentieth-Century World.* New York: W. W. Norton, 2000.

McPhee, John. *The Control of Nature.* New York: Farrar Straus Giroux, 1989.

Méndez Jurado, Pedro, et al., eds. *Monografía de la provincia de Huaylas, "Antena," Edición Extraordinaria, No. VII.* Caraz: Antena, 1945–1946.

Menzies, Charles R., ed. *Traditional Ecological Knowledge and Natural Resource Management.* Lincoln: University of Nebraska Press, 2006.

Miano Pique, Carlos. *¡¡Basta!! La bomba atómica francesa, la contaminación atmosférica y los terremotos.* Lima: Tangrat, 1972.

Miller, Clark A., and Paul N. Edwards, eds. *Changing the Atmosphere: Expert Knowledge and Environmental Governance.* Cambridge, Mass.: MIT Press, 2001.

Mitchell, Timothy. *Rule of Experts: Egypt, Techno-Politics, and Modernity.* Berkeley: University of California Press, 2002.

Mool, Pradeep. "Glacial Lakes and Glacial Lake Outburst Floods." *Mountain Development Profile* 2 (September 2001).

Morales A., Benjamín. "Desglaciación y disminución de recursos hídricos." *Boletín de la Sociedad Geográfica de Lima* 111 (1998): 7–20.

———. "El día más largo en el Hemisferio Sur." *Revista Peruana de Andinismo y Glaciología* 9, no. 9 (1970): 63–71.

———. "Estudios de vulnerabilidad de recursos hídricos de alta montaña en el Perú." In *Perú: Vulnerabilidad frente al cambio climático. Aproximaciones a la experiencia con el fenómeno El Niño*, edited by Benjamín Marticorena, 17–64. Lima: Consejo Nacional de Ambiente, 1999.

———. "Las lagunas y glaciares de la Cordillera Blanca y su control." *Boletín del Instituto Nacional de Glaciología (Peru)* 1 (1969): 14–17.

———. "Observaciones sobre el aluvión de Ranrahirca." *Forjando Ancash* 4, no. 13 (31 March 1962): 25–27.

Morales Arnao, César. *Andinismo en la Cordillera Blanca.* Callao: Imprenta Colegio Militar Leoncio Prado, Le Perla, 1968.

———. *Las Cordilleras del Perú.* Lima: Banco Central de Reserva del Perú, 2001.

Murra, John V. "El 'Archipiélago Vertical' Revisited." In *Andean Ecology and Civilization: An Interdisciplinary Perspective on Andean Ecological Complementarity,* edited by Shozo Masuda, Isumi Shimada, and Craig Morris, 3–14. Tokyo: University of Tokyo Press, 1985.

———. *El mundo andino: Población, medio ambiente y economía.* Lima: Instituto de Estudios Peruanos/Pontificia Universidad Católica del Perú, 2002.

Nash, Linda. "The Changing Experience of Nature: Historical Encounters with a Northwest River." *Journal of American History* 86, no. 4 (March 2000): 1600–1629.

Nathan, Fabien. "Risk Perception, Risk Management and Vulnerability to Landslides in the Hill Slopes in the City of La Paz, Bolivia. A Preliminary Statement." *Disasters* 32, no. 3 (2008): 337–357.

Neate, Jill. *Mountaineering in the Andes: A Sourcebook for Climbers.* 2nd ed. London: Expedition Advisory Centre/Royal Geographical Society, 1994.

Neumann, Roderick P. *Imposing Wilderness: Struggles over Livelihood and Nature Preservation in Africa.* Berkeley: University of California Press, 1998.

Nickson, Andrew, and Claudia Vargas. "The Limitations of Water Regulation: The Failure of the Cochabamba Concession in Bolivia." *Bulletin of Latin American Research* 21, no. 1 (2002): 99–120.

Nugent, David. *Modernity at the Edge of Empire: State, Individual, and Nation in the Northern Peruvian Andes, 1885–1935.* Stanford, Calif.: Stanford University Press, 1997.

Nye, David E. *American Technological Sublime.* Cambridge, Mass.: MIT Press, 1994.

Oels, Angela. "Rendering Climate Change Governable: From Biopower to Advanced Liberal Government?" *Journal of Environmental Policy and Planning* 7, no. 3 (2005): 185–207.

Oerlemans, Johannes. "Extracting a Climate Signal from 169 Glacier Records." *Science* 308, no. 5722 (29 April 2005): 675–677.

———. *Glaciers and Climate Change.* Exton, Penn.: A. A. Balkema Publishers, 2001.

Okereke, Chukwumerije, Harriet Bulkeley, and Heike Schroeder. "Conceptualizing Climate Governance beyond the International Regime." *Global Environmental Politics* 9, no. 1 (2009): 58–78.

Oliver-Smith, Anthony. "Disaster Rehabilitation and Social Change in Yungay, Peru." *Human Organization* 36, no. 1 (1977): 5–13.

———. "Here There Is Life: The Social and Cultural Dynamics of Successful Resistance to Resettlement in Postdisaster Peru." In *Involuntary Migration and Resettlement: The Problems and Responses of Dislocated People,* edited by Art Hansen and Anthony Oliver-Smith, 85–103. Boulder, Colo.: Westview Press, 1982.

———. *The Martyred City: Death and Rebirth in the Andes.* Albuquerque: University of New Mexico Press, 1986.

———. "Peru's Five-Hundred-Year Earthquake: Vulnerability in Historical Context." In *The Angry Earth: Disaster in Anthropological Perspective,* edited by Anthony Oliver-Smith and Susanna M. Hoffman, 74–88. New York: Routledge, 1999.

———. "Traditional Agriculture, Central Places, and Postdisaster Urban Relocation in Peru." *American Ethnologist* 4, no. 1 (1977): 102–116.

Oppenheim, Victor. "Las glaciaciones en el Perú." *Boletín de la Sociedad Geológica del Perú* 18 (1945): 37–43.

———. "Sobre las lagunas de Huaraz." *Boletín de la Sociedad Geológica del Perú* 19 (1946): 68–80.

Oppenheim, Victor, and Hans J. Spann. "Investigaciones glaciologicas en el Perú." *Boletín 5, Instituto Geológico del Perú, Ministerio de Fomento, Dirección de Minas y Petróleo, República del Perú* (1946).

Orlove, Ben. "Down to Earth: Race and Substance in the Andes." *Bulletin of Latin American Research* 17, no. 2 (1998): 207–222.

———. "Glacier Retreat: Reviewing the Limits of Human Adaptation to Climate Change." *Environment*, May–June 2009. Online at http://www.environmentmagazine.org/May-June%202009/Orlove-full.html.

———. "Putting Race in Its Place: Order in Colonial and Postcolonial Peruvian Geography." *Social Research* 60 (Summer 1993): 301–336.

Orlove, Ben, John C. H. Chiang, and Mark A. Cane. "Forecasting Andean Rainfall and Crop Yield from the Influence of El Niño on Pleiades Visibility." *Nature* 403 (6 January 2000): 68–71.

Orlove, Ben, Ellen Wiegandt, and Brian H. Luckman, eds. *Darkening Peaks: Glacial Retreat, Science, and Society.* Berkeley: University of California Press, 2008.

Orsi, Jared. *Hazardous Metropolis: Flooding and Urban Ecology in Los Angeles.* Berkeley: University of California Press, 2004.

Ortner, Sherry B. *Life and Death on Mt. Everest: Sherpas and Himalayan Mountaineering.* Princeton, N.J.: Princeton University Press, 1999.

Pajuelo Prieto, Rómulo. *Vida, muerte y resurrección: Testimonios sobre el Sismo-Alud 1970.* Yungay: Ediciones Elinca, 2002.

Palacios Rodríguez, Raúl. *La Sociedad Geográfica de Lima: Fundación y años iniciales.* Lima: Universidad de Lima, 1988.

Pantoja Ramos, Santiago, José Ripkens, and Germán Swisshelm. *Cuentos y relatos en el quechua de Huaraz.* Huaraz: Publicado por los autores, 1974.

Paredes Arana, Ernesto. "El hombre peruano frente a los desastres naturales." *Boletín de la Sociedad Geográfica de Lima* 112 (1999): 99–104.

Parker, David S. "Civilizing the City of Kings: Hygiene and Housing in Lima." In *Cities of Hope: People, Protests, and Progress in Urbanizing Latin America, 1870–1930*, edited by Ronn F. Pineo and James A. Baer, 153–178. Boulder, Colo.: Westview Press, 1998.

Parodi Trece, Carlos. *Perú 1960–2000: Políticas económicas y sociales en entornos cambiantes.* Lima: Centro de Investigación de la Universidad del Pacífico, 2000.

Patch, Richard W. "Life in a Peruvian Indian Community: A Study of Indian Cultural Homogeneity and Social Isolation." *American Universities Field Staff, West Coast South America Series* 9, no. 1 (1962): 1–29.

Peck, Annie Smith. *A Search for the Apex of America: High Mountain Climbing in Peru and Bolivia.* New York: Dodd Mead, 1911.

Pereyra Chávez, Nelson E. "Los campesinos y la conscripción vial: Aproximaciones al estudio de las relaciones estado-indígenas y las relaciones de mercado en

Ayacucho (1919–1930)." In *Estado y Mercado en la Historia del Perú*, edited by Carlos Contreras and Manuel Glave, 334–350. Lima: Pontificia Universidad Católica del Perú, 2002.

Pérez, Louis A., Jr. *Winds of Change: Hurricanes and the Transformation of Nineteenth-Century Cuba*. Chapel Hill: University of North Carolina Press, 2001.

Perreault, Thomas, and Patricia Martin. "Geographies of Neoliberalism in Latin America." *Environment and Planning A* 37 (2005): 191–201.

Pfister, Christian. "Climatic Extremes, Recurrent Crises and Witch Hunts: Strategies of European Societies in Coping with Exogenous Shocks in the Late Sixteenth and Early Seventeenth Centuries." *Medieval History Journal* 10, nos. 1–2 (2007): 33–73.

Phol, Gustavo A. "El 'Callejón de Huailas.'" *Boletín de la Sociedad Geográfica de Lima* 51, no. 4 (1934): 337–349.

Pielke, Roger, Jr. "Misdefining 'Climate Change' Consequences for Science and Action." *Environmental Science and Policy* 8 (2005): 548–561.

Polia Meconi, Mario. *Las lagunas de los encantos: Medicina tradicional andina del Perú septentrional*. Lima: Grafica Bellido, 1988.

Poniatowska, Elena. *Nothing, Nobody: The Voices of the Mexico City Earthquake*. Philadelphia: Temple University Press, 1995.

Poole, Deborah. "Landscape and the Imperial Subject: U.S. Images of the Andes, 1859–1930." In *Close Encounters of Empire: Writing the Cultural History of U.S.–Latin American Relations*, edited by Gilbert M. Joseph, Catherine C. LeGrand, and Ricardo D. Salvatore, 107–138. Durham, N.C.: Duke University Press, 1998.

———. *Vision, Race, and Modernity: A Visual Economy of the Andean Image World*. Princeton, N.J.: Princeton University Press, 1997.

Porter, Theodore M. *Trust in Numbers: The Pursuit of Objectivity in Science and Public Life*. Princeton, N.J.: Princeton University Press, 1995.

Portocarrero R., César. "Cono Aluvionico de Huaraz." *Boletín del Colegio de Ingenieros del Perú—Filial Zona Sierra de Ancash* 1 (May 1980): 18–20.

———. "Retroceso de glaciares en el Perú: Consecuencias sobre los recursos hídricos y los riesgos geodinámicos." *Bulletin de L'Institut Francais d'átudes Andines* 24, no. 3 (1995): 697–706.

[Prado, Manuel.]*Acción del Presidente Prado en Huaraz*. Lima: Oficina de Informaciones del Perú, 1942.

Prakash, Gyan. *Another Reason: Science and the Imagination of Modern India*. Princeton, N.J.: Princeton University Press, 1999.

Pratt, Mary Louise. *Imperial Eyes: Travel Writing and Transculturation*. New York: Routledge, 1992.

Pulgar Vidal, Javier. *Geografía del Perú: Las ocho regiones naturales*. 10th ed. Lima: Peisa, 1996.

Pyne, Stephen J. *The Ice: A Journey to Antarctica*. Seattle: University of Washington Press, 1998.

Racoviteanu, Adina E., Yves Arnaud, Mark W. Williams, and Julio Ordoñez. "Decadal Changes in Glacier Parameters in the Cordillera Blanca, Peru, Derived from Remote Sensing." *Journal of Glaciology* 54, no. 186 (2008): 499–510.

Radkau, Joachim. *Nature and Power: A Global History of the Environment.* Translated by Thomas Dunlap. New York: German Historical Institute/Cambridge University Press, 2008.

Raffles, Hugh. *In Amazonia: A Natural History.* Princeton, N.J.: Princeton University Press, 2002.

Raimondi, Antonio. *El departamento de Ancachs y sus riquezas minerales.* Lima: Pedro Lira, 1873.

Ramírez Alzamora, Claudio. *Santiago Antúnez de Mayolo.* Lima: Editorial Brasa, 1996.

Ramírez Gamarra, Hugo. *Ancash: Vida y pasión.* Lima: Editorial Universo S.A., 1971.

Ramos Guardia, Victor. "El Callejón de Huaylas: Futuro centro de turismo y de estaciones termales." In *Ancash Actual (1839–1939),* edited by Leandro Barrionuevo, 49–56. Huaraz: Editorial Pero Libre, 1937.

Recharte, Jorge. "La categoría de reserva paisajística como estrategia de conservación en el contexto de los Andes: naturaleza y cultura en la Cordillera de Huayhuash, Perú." In *Paisajes culturales en los Andes: memoria narrativa, casos de estudio, conclusiones y recomendaciones de la reunión de expertos,* edited by Elías Mujica Barreda, 137–148. Lima: UNESCO, 2001.

Reinhard, Johan. "Sacred Landscape: The Prehistoric Cultures of the Andes." In *Extreme Landscape: The Lure of Mountain Spaces,* edited by Bernadette McDonald, 207–225. Washington, D.C.: National Geographic Adventure Press, 2002.

Reuss, Martin. "Seeing Like an Engineer: Water Projects and the Mediation of the Incommensurable." *Technology and Culture* 49, no. 3 (2008): 531–546.

Reynolds, J. M. "The Development of a Combined Regional Strategy for Power Generation and Natural Hazard Risk Assessment in a High-Altitude Glacial Environment: An Example from the Cordillera Blanca, Peru." In *Natural Disasters: Protecting Vulnerable Communities,* edited by P. A. Merriman and C. W. A. Browitt, 38–50. London: Thomas Telford, 1993.

——. "The Identification and Mitigation of Glacier-Related Hazards: Examples from the Cordillera Blanca, Peru." In *Geohazards: Natural and Man-Made,* edited by G. J. H. McCall, D. J. C. Laming and S. C. Scott, 143–157. New York: Chapman and Hall, 1992.

——. "Managing the Risks of Glacial Flooding at Hydro Plants." *Hydro Review Worldwide* 6, no. 2 (1998): 2–6.

Reynolds, J. M., A. Dolecki, and C. Portocarrero. "The Construction of a Drainage Tunnel as Part of Glacial Lake Hazard Mitigation at Hualcán, Cordillera Blanca, Peru." In *Geohazards in Engineering Geology,* edited by J. G. Maund and M. Eddleston, 41–48. London: Geological Society, 1998.

Richardson, Shaun D., and John M. Reynolds. "Degradation of Ice-Cored Moraine Dams: Implications for Hazard Development." In *Debris-Covered Glaciers,* edited by C. F. Raymond M. Nakawo and A. Fountain, 187–198. Oxfordshire, UK: International Association of Hydrological Sciences, 2000.

——. "An Overview of Glacial Hazards in the Himalayas." *Quaternary International* 65–66 (April 2000): 31–47.

Ricker, John F. *Yuraq Janka: Guide to the Peruvian Andes, Part I: Cordilleras Blanca and Rosko.* Seattle: Pacific Press of Seattle, 1977.

Sabin, Paul. "Searching for Middle Ground: Native Communities and Oil Extraction in the Northern and Central Ecuadorian Amazon, 1967–1993." *Environmental History* 3, no. 2 (1998): 144–168.

Sahley, Catherine, Jorge Torres, and Jesús Sanchez. "Neoliberalism Meets Pre-Columbian Tradition: Campesino Communities and Vicuna Management in Andean Peru." *Culture and Agriculture* 26, nos. 1–2 (2004): 60–68.

Saldaña, Juan José, ed. *Historia social de las ciencias en América Latina.* Mexico City: UNAM and M. A. Porrúa, 1996.

Sallnow, Michael J. *Pilgrims of the Andes: Regional Cults in Cusco.* Washington, D.C.: Smithsonian Institution Press, 1987.

Salvatore, Ricardo D. "Local versus Imperial Knowledge: Reflections on Hiram Bingham and the Yale Peruvian Expedition." *Nepantla: Views from the South* 4, no. 1 (2003): 67–80.

Sánchez, Susy. "Clima, hambre y enfermedad en Lima durante la guerra independentista (1817–1826)." In *La Independencia en el Perú: de los borbones a Bolívar,* edited by Scarlett O'Phelan Godoy, 237–263. Lima: Pontificia universidad católica del Perú—Instituto Riva-Agüero, 2001.

Santiago, Myrna I. *The Ecology of Oil: Environment, Labor, and the Mexican Revolution, 1900–1938.* New York: Cambridge University Press, 2006.

Santiváñez, Roberto J. *Electricity Deregulation and Privatization in Peru: A Proposal to Revitalize the Reform.* Lima: Metrocolor S.A., 2001.

Sarewitz, Daniel, Roger Pielke, Jr., and Keykhah Mojdeh. "Vulnerability and Risk: Some Thoughts from a Political and Policy Perspective." *Risk Analysis* 23, no. 4 (2003): 805–810.

Schama, Simon. *Landscape and Memory.* New York: Vintage Books, 1995.

Schiebinger, Londa, and Claudia Swan, eds. *Colonial Botany: Science, Commerce, and Politics in the Early Modern World.* Philadelphia: University of Pennsylvania Press, 2005.

Schrepfer, Susan R. *Nature's Altars: Mountains, Gender, and American Environmentalism.* Lawrence: University Press of Kansas, 2005.

Schuller, Mark. "Deconstructing the Disaster after the Disaster: Conceptualizing Disaster Capitalism." In *Capitalizing on Catastrophe: Neoliberal Strategies in Disaster Reconstruction,* edited by Nandini Gunewardena and Mark Schuller, 17–28. Lanham, Md.: AltaMira Press, 2008.

Schwartz, Stuart B. "The Hurricane of San Ciriaco: Disaster, Politics, and Society in Puerto Rico, 1899–1901." *Hispanic American Historical Review* 72, no. 3 (1992): 303–334.

Scott, James. *Seeing Like a State: How Certain Schemes to Improve the Human Condition Have Failed.* New Haven, Conn.: Yale University Press, 1998.

Scovill, E. T. *In the Department of Ancachs and Other Papers.* Cleveland, Ohio, 1909.

Scudder, Thayer. *The Future Of Large Dams: Dealing with Social, Environmental, Institutional and Political Costs.* London: Earthscan Publications, 2005.

Sedrez, Lise. "Environmental History of Modern Latin America." In *A Companion to Latin American History*, edited by Thomas H. Holloway, 443–460. Malden, Mass.: Blackwell Publishing, 2008.

Seiner Lizárraga, Lizardo. *Estudios de historia medioambiental, Perú, siglos XVI–XX*. Lima: Universidad de Lima, 2002.

Sherbondy, Jeanette E. "Water Ideology in Inca Ethnogenesis." In *Andean Cosmologies through Time: Persistence and Emergence*, edited by Robert V. H. Dover, Katharine E. Seibold, and John H. McDowell, 46–66. Bloomington: Indiana University Press, 1992.

Sikkink, Lynn. "Water and Exchange: The Ritual of 'yaku cambio' as Communal and Competitive Encounter." *American Ethnologist* 24, no. 1 (1997): 170–189.

Silverio, Walter, and Jean-Michel Jaquet. "Glacial Cover Mapping (1987–1996) of the Cordillera Blanca (Peru) Using Satellite Imagery." *Remote Sensing of Environment* 95, no. 3 (2005): 342–350.

Slater, Candace. *Entangled Edens: Visions of the Amazon*. Berkeley: University of California Press, 2002.

———, ed. *In Search of the Rain Forest*. Durham, N.C.: Duke University Press, 2003.

Soluri, John. *Banana Cultures: Agriculture, Consumption, and Environmental Change in Honduras and the United States*. Austin: University of Texas Press, 2005.

Spalding, Karen. *Huarochirí: An Andean Society under Inca and Spanish Rule*. Stanford, Calif.: Stanford University Press, 1984.

Spann, H. J. "Informe sobre el origen de la catástrofe de Chavín de Huantar." *Boletín de la Sociedad Geológica del Perú* 20 (1947): 29–33.

———. "Los nevados Ananea, Salcantay, Umantay, Ausangate y Ampato en el Sur del Perú." *Boletín del Instituto Geológico del Perú, Ministerio de Fomento, Dirección de Minas y Petróleo, República del Perú* 5 (1946): 21–40.

Spence, Mark David. *Dispossessing the Wilderness: Indian Removal and the Making of the National Parks*. New York: Oxford University Press, 2000.

Spufford, Francis. *I May Be Some Time: Ice and the English Imagination*. Boston: Faber and Faber, 1996.

Stein, William W. *Countrymen and Townsmen in the Callejón de Huaylas, Peru: Two Views of Andean Social Structure*. Buffalo: Council on International Studies, State University of New York at Buffalo, 1974.

———. *Deconstructing Development Discourse in Peru: A Meta-Ethnography of the Modernity Project at Vicos*. Revised ed. New York: University Press of America, 2003.

———. *Hualcan: Life in the Highlands of Peru*. Ithaca, N.Y.: Cornell University Press, 1961.

Steinberg, Ted. *Acts of God: The Unnatural History of Natural Disaster in America*. New York: Oxford University Press, 2000.

Stepan, Nancy Leys. *Beginnings of Brazilian Science: Oswaldo Cruz, Medical Research, and Policy, 1890–1920*. New York: Science History Publications, 1981.

———. *Picturing Tropical Nature*. Ithaca, N.Y.: Cornell University Press, 2001.

Stern, Nicholas. *The Global Deal: Climate Change and the Creation of a New Era of Progress and Prosperity.* New York: Public Affairs, 2009.

Stern, Steve J. "Paradigms of Conquest: History, Historiography, and Politics." *Journal of Latin American Studies,* quincentennial supp., 24 (1992): 1–34.

Stonich, Susan. "International Tourism and Disaster Capitalism: The Case of Hurricane Mitch in Honduras." In *Capitalizing on Catastrophe: Neoliberal Strategies in Disaster Reconstruction,* edited by Nandini Gunewardena and Mark Schuller, 47–68. Lanham, Md.: AltaMira Press, 2008.

Stowe, Leland. "El desastre de Huarás." *Selecciones del Reader's Digest,* September 1969, 39–46.

Strauss, Sarah, and Ben Orlove, eds. *Weather, Climate, Culture.* New York: Berg, 2003.

Stroud, Ellen. "Does Nature Always Matter? Following Dirt through History." *History and Theory* 42, no. 4 (2003): 75–81.

Sutter, Paul S. "Nature's Agents or Agents of Empire? Entomological Workers and Environmental Change during the Construction of the Panama Canal." *Isis* 98, no. 4 (2007): 724–754.

Swyngedouw, Erik. *Social Power and the Urbanization of Water: Flows of Power.* New York: Oxford University Press, 2004.

Szepessy Schaurek, Alí de. *Contribución al conocimiento de las lagunas glaciares en la Cordillera Blanca.* Lima: Sociedad Geológica del Perú, Volúmen Jibilar, XXV Aniversario, Parte II, 1949.

Tamayo Herrera, José. *Liberalismo, indigenismo y violencia en los países andinos (1850–1995).* Lima: Fondo de Desarrollo Editorial, Universidad de Lima, 1998.

Taylor, Alan. "'The Hungry Year' 1789 on the Northern Border of Revolutionary America." In *Dreadful Visitations: Confronting Natural Catastrophe in the Age of the Enlightenment,* edited by Alessa Johns, 39–69. New York: Routledge, 1999.

———. "Unnatural Inequalities: Social and Environmental Histories." *Environmental History* 1 (1996): 6–19.

Taype, R. V. "Los desastres naturales como problema de Defensa Civil." *Boletín de la Sociedad Geológica del Perú* 61 (1979): 101–111.

Tello, Julio C. *Chavín.* Lima: Universidad Nacional Mayor de San Marcos, 1960.

Thompson, Lonnie G., Ellen Mosley-Thompson, W. Dansgaard, and P. M. Grootes. "The Little Ice Age as Recorded in the Stratigraphy of the Tropical Quelccaya Ice Cap." *Science* 234, no. 4774 (1986): 361–364.

Thompson, Lonnie G., Ellen Mosley-Thompson, M. E. Davis, P. N. Lin, K. A. Henderson, J. Cole-Dai, J. F. Bolzan, and K. B. Liu. "Late Glacial Stage and Holocene Tropical Ice Core Records from Huascarán, Peru." *Science* 269, no. 5220 (1995): 46–50.

Thompson, Lonnie G., Ellen Mosley-Thompson, and Benjamín Morales Arnao. "El Niño-Southern Oscillation Events Recorded in the Stratigraphy of the Tropical Quelccaya Ice Cap, Peru." *Science* 226, no. 4670 (1984): 50–53.

Thorp, Rosemary, and Geoffrey Bertram. *Peru 1890–1977: Growth and Policy in an Open Economy.* London: Macmillan Press, 1978.

Thurner, Mark. *From Two Republics to One Divided: Contradictions of Postcolonial Nationmaking in Andean Peru*. Durham, N.C.: Duke University Press, 1997.

Trask, Parker D. "El problema de los aluviones de la Cordillera Blanca." *Boletín de la Sociedad Geográfica de Lima* 70 (3rd–4th quarter 1953): 5–75.

Trawick, Paul B. *The Struggle for Water in Peru: Comedy and Tragedy in the Andean Commons*. Stanford, Calif.: Stanford University Press, 2003.

Truett, Samuel. *Fugitive Landscapes: The Forgotten History of the U.S.–Mexico Borderlands*. New Haven, Conn.: Yale University Press, 2006.

Tucker, Richard P. *Insatiable Appetite: The United States and the Ecological Degradation of the Tropical World*. Berkeley: University of California Press, 2000.

Tufnell, Lance. *Glacier Hazards*. London: Longman Group, 1984.

Ueda Tsuboyama, Augusto Martín. *Historia del Cuerpo de Ingenieros de Minas del Perú (1902–1950)*. Lima: Universidad Nacional de Ingeniería, 2002.

Van Buren, Mary. "Rethinking the Vertical Archipelago: Ethnicity, Exchange, and History in the South Central Andes." *American Anthropologist* 98, no. 2 (1996): 338–351.

Varley, Ann, ed. *Disasters, Development and Environment*. New York: John Wiley and Sons, 1994.

Vergara, Walter, et al. "Economic Impacts of Rapid Glacier Retreat in the Andes." *EOS, Transactions, American Geophysical Union* 88, no. 25 (2007): 261–268.

Vergara Collazos, Antonio. *La tragedia*. Peru: Abbacril S.A., 1993.

Vilímek, Vít, Marco Zapata Luyo, Jan Klimeš, Patzelt Zdenek, and Nelson Santillán. "Influence of Glacial Retreat on Natural Hazards of the Palcacocha Lake Area, Peru." *Landslides* 2 (2005): 107–115.

Villón, Pedro C. *Notas Históricas: Huaylas, Carhuaz, Huaraz*. Carhuaz, Peru: Imprenta Ancash, 1942.

Vivanco, Luis A., and Robert J. Gordon, eds. *Tarzan Was an Eco-Tourist—And Other Tales in the Anthropology of Adventure*. New York: Berghahn Books, 2006.

Vuille, Mathias, Bernard Francou, Patrick Wagnon, Irmgard Juen, Georg Kaser, Bryan G. Mark, and Raymond S. Bradley. "Climate Change and Tropical Andean Glaciers: Past, Present and Future." *Earth-Science Reviews* 89, nos. 3–4 (2008): 79–96.

Vuille, Mathias, Georg Kaser, and Irmgard Juen. "Glacier Mass Balance Variability in the Cordillera Blanca, Peru, and Its Relationship with Climate and the Large-Scale Circulation." *Global and Planetary Change* 62, nos. 1–2 (2008): 14–28.

Wakild, Emily. "Naturalizing Modernity: Urban Parks, Public Gardens and Drainage Projects in Porfirian Mexico City." *Mexican Studies/Estudios Mexicanos* 23, no. 1 (2007): 101–123.

Walker, Charles F. *Shaky Colonialism: The 1746 Earthquake-Tsunami in Lima, Peru, and Its Long Aftermath*. Durham, N.C.: Duke University Press, 2008.

———. "The Upper Classes and Their Upper Stories: Architecture and the Aftermath of the Lima Earthquake of 1746." *Hispanic American Historical Review* 83, no. 1 (2003): 53–82.

Walter, Doris. *La domestication de la nature dans les Andes péruviennes: L'alpiniste, le paysay et le Parc National du Huascarán.* Paris: L'Harmattan, 2003.

Walton, Nyle Keith. "Human Spatial Organization in an Andean Valley: The Callejón de Huaylas." Ph.D. diss., University of Georgia, 1974.

Warren, Louis S. *The Hunter's Game: Poachers and Conservationists in Twentieth-Century America.* New Haven, Conn.: Yale University Press, 1997.

Weart, Spencer R. *The Discovery of Global Warming.* Cambridge, Mass.: Harvard University Press, 2003.

———. "Spencer Weart on Depicting Global Warming." *Environmental History* 10, no. 4 (2005): 770–775.

Weber, Max. "Politics as a Vocation." In *From Max Weber: Essays in Sociology*, edited by H. H. Gerth and C. Wright Mills, 77–128. New York: Oxford University Press, 1958.

Weiner, Douglas R. "A Death-Defying Attempt to Articulate a Coherent Definition of Environmental History." *Environmental History* 10, no. 3 (2005): 404–420.

Weyland, Kurt. "Assessing Latin American Neoliberalism: Introduction to a Debate." *Latin American Research Review* 39, no. 3 (2004): 143–149.

White, Richard. *The Organic Machine: The Remaking of the Columbia River.* New York: Hill and Wang, 1995.

Wiegandt, Ellen, and Ralph Lugon. "Challenges of Living with Glaciers in the Swiss Alps, Past and Present." In *Darkening Peaks: Glacial Retreat, Science, and Society*, edited by Ben Orlove, Ellen Wiegandt, and Brian Luckman, 33–48. Berkeley: University of California Press, 2008.

Wilson, Eric G. *The Spiritual History of Ice: Romanticism, Science, and the Imagination.* New York: Palgrave Macmillan, 2003.

Wilson, Fiona. "Indian Citizenship and the Discourse of Hygiene/Disease in Nineteenth-Century Peru." *Bulletin of Latin American Research* 23, no. 2 (2004): 165–180.

Wisner, Ben. "Changes in Capitalism and Global Shifts in the Distribution of Hazard and Vulnerability." In *Natural Disasters and Development in a Globalizing World*, edited by Mark Pelling, 43–56. New York: Routledge, 2003.

———. "Risk and the Neoliberal State: Why Post-Mitch Lessons Didn't Reduce El Salvador's Earthquake Losses." *Disasters* 25, no. 3 (2001): 251–268.

Wisner, Ben, Blaikie Piers, Terry Cannon, and Ian Davis. *At Risk: Natural Hazards, People's Vulnerability and Disasters.* 2nd ed. New York: Routledge, 2004.

Wood, Denis. *The Power of Maps.* New York: Guilford Press, 1992.

Worster, Donald. *Dust Bowl: The Southern Plains in the 1930s.* New York: Oxford University Press, 1979.

———. *Nature's Economy: A History of Ecological Ideas.* 2nd ed. New York: Cambridge University Press, 1994.

———. *The Wealth of Nature: Environmental History and the Ecological Imagination.* New York: Oxford University Press, 1993.

Yauri Montero, Marcos. *Ancash o la biografía de la inmortalidad: Nuevo planteamiento de sus problemas culturales.* Lima: P. L. Villanueva S.A., 1972.

———. *Leyendas ancashinas.* 6th ed. Lima: Lerma Gómez eirl., 2000.

———. *Tiempo de rosas y de sonrisas... Tiempo de dolor y de muerte: Testimonio del cataclismo ocurrido en la zona norte del Perú el 31 de Mayo de 1970.* Lima: ULTRA, S.A., 1971.

Young, Kenneth, and Jennifer Lipton. "Adaptive Governance and Climate Change in the Tropical Highlands of Western South America." *Climatic Change* 78, no. 1 (2006): 63–102.

Zapata Luyo, Marco. "La dinámica glaciar en lagunas de la Cordillera Blanca." *Acta Montana* (Czech Republic) 19, no. 123 (2002): 37–60.

Zapata Velasco, Antonio, and Juan Carlos Sueiro. *Naturaleza y política: el gobierno y el fenómeno del Niño en el Perú, 1997–1998.* Lima: Instituto de Estudios Peruanos, 1999.

Zapatel, César E. *Vialidad y Turismo en el Perú: Touring Club Peruano.* Lima: Empresa "La Editorial" S.A., 1929.

Zavaleta Figueroa, Isaias. *El Callejón de Huaylas antes y después del terremoto del 31 de Mayo de 1970,* Vol 1. Caraz: Ediciones Paron, 1970.

Zimmerer, Karl S. *Changing Fortunes: Biodiversity and Peasant Livelihood in the Peruvian Andes.* Berkeley: University of California Press, 1996.

Zimmerer, Karl S., and Thomas J. Bassett, eds. *Political Ecology: An Integrative Approach to Geography and Environment-Development Studies.* New York: Guilford Press, 2003.

Index

LaVergne, TN USA
24 November 2010
206047LV00003B/1/P